MARK AND Q

BIBLIOTHECA EPHEMERIDUM THEOLOGICARUM LOVANIENSIUM

CXXII

MARK AND Q

A STUDY OF THE OVERLAP TEXTS

HARRY T. FLEDDERMANN

WITH AN ASSESSMENT BY F. NEIRYNCK

LEUVEN
UNIVERSITY PRESS

UITGEVERIJ PEETERS
LEUVEN

1995

CIP KONINKLIJKE BIBLIOTHEEK ALBERT I, BRUSSEL

ISBN 90 6186 710 X (Leuven University Press)
D/1995/1869/51
ISBN 90 6831 712-1 (Uitgeverij Peeters)
D/1995/0602/61

Leuven University Press / Presses Universitaires de Louvain
Universitaire Pers Leuven
Krakenstraat 3, B-3000 Leuven-Louvain (Belgium)

© Uitgeverij Peeters, Bondgenotenlaan 153, B-3000 Leuven (Belgium)

PREFACE

This study has been long in coming. I wrote the first draft during a leave of absence from the College of St. Thomas in the spring semester of 1982, and after many interruptions I completed the revision during a sabbatical leave from Alverno College in the 1992-93 academic year. Both institutions supported the work with summer research stipends. Many people helped me along the way. My two teachers, Piet Ahsmann in Amsterdam and Thomas W. Leahy in Berkeley, provided excellent guidance as I began to find my own way in New Testament exegesis, and for more than ten years I have benefited from discussions with my colleagues in the International Q Project.

I cannot adequately express my debt to Leuven's two great gospel scholars, Jan Lambrecht and Frans Neirynck. The relationship between Mark and Q might easily have dropped out as a topic in gospel studies had not Jan Lambrecht reopened the discussion in the sixties. His careful studies of the overlap texts have helped me at every turn as I pursued my own research. For over thirty years Frans Neirynck has defended the two-source theory with energy and insight from all attacks from whatever quarter they arose. I have drawn constantly on his exegetical studies and the tools he has placed at the service of every student of the gospels. He was also instrumental in seeing that this study was accepted in the BETL series, and he has graciously provided an assessment that is included in this volume. Because I have relied so heavily on these two extraordinary scholars, it is fitting that this book should be published in Leuven.

My wife Margaret has stood by me through these years. Her faith is a constant inspiration to me, and her love has made a long and difficult project possible. I dedicate this book to her as a token of my love.

Milwaukee, June 1995   Harry T. FLEDDERMANN

CONTENTS

ASSESSMENT

by F. NEIRYNCK

I

THE OVERLAP TEXTS

Discussion of the synoptic problem continues unabated. The two chief rivals, the two-source theory and the Griesbach hypothesis, both have vigorous defenders who show no sign they will abandon the fight anytime soon. In addition other theories crowd the field.[1] Confrontation between rival theories, though, does not exhaust the discourse. Among those who accept the two-source theory a serious discussion has been going on for some time about the relationship of the two sources, Mark and Q, to each other.[2]

The two-source theory uses the hypothesis of Marcan priority to explain the triple tradition passages of the synoptic gospels – Matthew and Luke used Mark as their major source in writing their gospels. It then appeals to a hypothetical source called Q to explain the double tradition – Matthew and Luke had access to a second source, mainly sayings

1. A series of conferences in the seventies and eighties facilitated dialogue between advocates of various theories. The papers from the last conference appear in D. L. DUNGAN (ed.), *The Interrelations of the Gospels: A Symposium Led by M.-É. Boismard – W. R. Farmer – F. Neirynck, Jerusalem, 1984* (BETL, 95), Leuven: University Press – Peeters, 1990. The papers include introductions to the two-source theory by F. NEIRYNCK (pp. 3-22), to the two-gospel or Griesbach hypothesis by W. R. FARMER (pp. 125-156), and to the multiple-stage hypothesis by M.-É. BOISMARD (pp. 231-243). For the Griesbach hypothesis see W. R. FARMER, *The Synoptic Problem: A Critical Analysis*, New York: Macmillan, 1964, pp. 199-232. B. ORCHARD provided a translation of Griesbach's *Commentatio qua Marci Evangelium totum e Matthaei et Lucae commentariis decerptum esse monstratur* in "A Demonstration that Mark was Written after Matthew and Luke," in B. ORCHARD & T. R. W. LONGSTAFF (eds.), *J. J. Griesbach: Synoptic and Text-Critical Studies 1776-1976* (SNTS MS, 34), Cambridge: University Press, 1978, pp. 103-135. For the multiple-stage hypothesis see M.-É. BOISMARD, *Synopse des quatre Évangiles en français: Tome II: Commentaire*, Paris: Cerf, 1972, pp. 15-59.

2. For overviews of the discussion see M. DEVISCH, "La relation entre l'évangile de Marc et le document Q," in M. SABBE (ed.), *L'évangile selon Marc*, 1974, ²1988, pp. 59-91; P. VASSILIADIS, "Prolegomena to a Discussion on the Relationship between Mark and the Q-Document," in *DeltBM* 3 (1975) 31-46; R. LAUFEN, *Die Doppelüberlieferungen der Logienquelle und des Markusevangeliums* (BBB, 54), Bonn: Hanstein, 1980, pp. 59-92; F. NEIRYNCK, "Recent Developments in the Study of Q" (1982), in ID., *Evangelica II*, 1991, pp. 409-464, esp. pp. 421-433, 464; ID., "Literary Criticism, Old and New," in C. FOCANT (ed.), *The Synoptic Gospels*, 1993, pp. 13-38, esp. pp. 30-33; J. SCHÜLING, *Studien zum Verhältnis von Logienquelle und Markusevangelium* (FzB, 65), Würzburg: Echter, 1991, pp. 167-187; C. M. TUCKETT, "Mark and Q," in C. FOCANT (ed.), *The Synoptic Gospels*, 1993, pp. 149-175.

of Jesus, which they also incorporated into their gospels.[3] Proponents of
the two-source theory point to the large number of doublets in Matthew
and, to a lesser extent, in Luke as one of several arguments for the existence of Q. The doublets, though, do not just help establish the existence
of Q. They show further that the two sources – Mark and Q – overlap, and
they raise the question of the relationship of these sources to each other.

1. *The Importance of the Overlap Texts*

How Mark and Q relate to each other might appear to interest only
source critics. Actually the relationship impacts many areas of NT study
from gospel exegesis to the historical Jesus and beyond. Take the Mission Discourse as an example. The synoptic gospels record four discourses of Jesus that give instructions for a mission (Matt 9,37-10,42;
Mark 6,7-13; Luke 9,1-6; 10,2-16). Those who support the two-source
theory maintain that both Mark and Q contained versions of a Mission
Discourse. Luke redacted the Marcan version in Luke 9,1-6, and he
reproduced the Q version in Luke 10,2-16. Matthew conflated the two
discourses he found in Mark and Q. The relationship between Mark and
Q acts like a toggle switch in interpreting these texts. If Mark and Q are
independent, then we can use Mark as a witness to the earlier stages in
the development of the discourse. Risto Uro exploits this position in his
study of the Mission Discourse. He analyzes the literary stages of the Q
discourse, peeling off successive additions until he arrives at a kernel
made up of the Equipment Rule and the House Mission (Q 10,4ab.5-
7ab). Since he maintains that Mark and Q are independent, he uses
Mark's much shorter discourse as a control to confirm his analysis. A
similar structure underlies both the Marcan discourse and the Q kernel
confirming the literary analysis.[4] However, if Mark is dependent on Q,
this procedure won't work, and we have no external control to study the

3. For the two-source theory see J. A. FITZMYER, "The Priority of Mark and the 'Q'
Source in Luke" (1970), in ID., *To Advance the Gospel*, 1981, pp. 3-40; F. NEIRYNCK, "Syn-
optic Problem," in R. E. BROWN, J. A. FITZMYER, R. E. MURPHY (eds.), *The New Jerome
Biblical Commentary*, Englewood Cliffs, NJ: Prentice Hall, 1990, pp. 587-595. On Marcan
priority see H. G. WOOD, "The Priority of Mark," in *ExpT* 65 (1953-54) 17-19; G. M.
STYLER, "The Priority of Mark," in C. F. D. MOULE, *The Birth of the New Testament*, San
Francisco: Harper & Row, ³1982, pp. 285-316. On the Q hypothesis see M. DEVISCH, "Le
document Q, source de Matthieu: Problématique actuelle," in M. DIDIER (ed.), *L'évangile
selon Matthieu*, 1972, pp. 71-97; F. NEIRYNCK, "Recent Developments," pp. 409-464.
4. R. URO, *Sheep Among the Wolves: A Study on the Mission Instructions of Q*
(AASF, Dissertationes Humanarum Litterarum, 47), Helsinki: Suomalainen Tiedeakatemia,
1987, pp. 98-110. Arland Jacobson also maintains that the Marcan and Q forms of the
Mission Discourse are independent and that a common pattern underlies both. See A. D.
JACOBSON, "The Literary Unity of Q: Lc 10,2-16 and Parallels as a Test Case," in J.
DELOBEL (ed.), *Logia*, 1982, pp. 419-423, esp. p. 420.

growth of the discourse.[5] However, we have thrown the toggle. A loss for Q becomes a gain for Mark. If Mark knew Q, we can compare the Q discourse with Mark to uncover Mark's redaction.

The relationship between Mark and Q also has implications for studying the historical Jesus. Scholars use the criterion of multiple attestation as one of the main criteria for attributing material to the historical Jesus. They argue that behind the synoptic gospels lie earlier sources – Mark, Q, Matthew's *Sondergut* (M), and Luke's *Sondergut* (L). If a saying or parable is found in more than one source, then it has a greater probability of going back to the historical Jesus.[6] Burkitt tried to use the overlap texts to get at the core of Jesus' teaching. He argued that the starting point for reconstructing the teaching should be the sayings that are attested in Mark and Q, and he went on to list and discuss thirty-one texts.[7] Dodd uses the criterion of multiple attestation to get at Jesus' original teaching on the kingdom of God. Since Mark and Q both attest a belief in the presence of the kingdom in Jesus, Dodd concludes that the kingdom represents a present reality in the earliest tradition.[8] However, if Mark depends on Q, then Burkitt's and Dodd's procedure is questionable, for Mark could have gotten the material from Q. Instead of two witnesses to the tradition, we are left with only one.

The discussion spills over into New Testament christology. Tödt claimed that the Q community was the first to identify the Son of Man with the historical Jesus.[9] But Lührmann objects that the identification

---

5. D. R. CATCHPOLE, "The Mission Charge in Q," in *Semeia* 55 (1991) 147-174, esp. p. 151.

6. W. O. WALKER, "The Quest for the Historical Jesus: A Discussion of Methodology," in *ATR* 51 (1969) 38-56, esp. pp. 41-42; N. J. MCELENEY, "Authenticating Criteria and Mark 7:1-23," in *CBQ* 34 (1972) 431-460, esp. pp. 433-435; R. LATOURELLE, "Critères d'authenticité historique des Évangiles," in *Greg* 55 (1974) 609-638, esp. pp. 619-621; R. N. LONGENECKER, "Literary Criteria in Life of Jesus Research: An Evaluation and Proposal," in G. F. HAWTHORNE (ed.), *Current Issues in Biblical and Patristic Interpretation*, 1975, pp. 217-229, esp. pp. 219-220; H. K. NIELSEN, "Kriterien zur Bestimmung authentischer Jesusworte," in *SNTU* 4 (1979) 5-26, esp. pp. 15-18; R. H. STEIN, "The 'Criteria' for Authenticity," in R. T. FRANCE & D. WENHAM (eds.), *Gospel Perspectives: Vol. I*, 1980, pp. 225-263, esp. pp. 229-232; M. E. BORING, "Criteria of Authenticity: The Lucan Beatitudes as a Test Case," in *Forum* 1/4 (1985) 3-38, esp. p. 8; ID., "The Historical-Critical Method's 'Criteria of Authenticity': The Beatitudes as a Test Case," in *Semeia* 44 (1988) 9-44, esp. pp. 12-13; D. POLKOW, "Method and Criteria for Historical Jesus Research," *SBL 1987 Seminar Papers*, pp. 336-356, esp. pp. 350-351.

7. F. C. BURKITT, *The Gospel History and its Transmission*, Edinburgh: Clark, ²1907, pp. 147-183.

8. Mark 1,14-15; Q 10,9; 11,20; 16,16. C. H. DODD, *The Parables of the Kingdom*, New York: Charles Scribner's Sons, 1961, pp. 25-35.

9. H. E. TÖDT, *Der Menschensohn in der synoptischen Überlieferung*, Gütersloh: Mohn, ²1963, pp. 230-232, 240-241; ET: *The Son of Man in the Synoptic Tradition*, trans. D. M. Barton, Philadelphia: Westminster, 1965, pp. 252-254, 264-265.

must have taken place in the tradition before Q, for Mark also identifies Jesus and the Son of Man.[10] However, if Mark depends on Q, Lührmann's argument won't work, for Mark could then have derived the concept from Q.[11] In this case, though, the point where the term "Son of Man" entered the tradition would be set.

The search for the historical Jesus extends into the non-canonical gospels, especially the Gospel of Thomas. Does Thomas preserve original sayings of Jesus? The lines in this debate have become very sharply drawn. On one side we have scholars like Stevan Davies who claims, "Today many of those seriously concerned with the historical Jesus, with determining the most original forms of the sayings of Jesus, or with the study of Jesus' parables turn to the *Gospel of Thomas* for information as readily as to the Synoptics."[12] On the other side scholars like C. M. Tuckett point out that Thomas probably agrees with redactional elements in the synoptic gospels, so Thomas must depend on the synoptic writers and does not represent material that goes back to Jesus.[13] The debate involves all the synoptic-type sayings in Thomas, not just the overlap texts. However, the overlap texts can play an important role in resolving the argument, for they leave the most complex tradition-historical trail of all the synoptic sayings. For example, the synoptic writers record five versions of the Cross Saying and Thomas has one.[14] The differences between the versions mean that many redactors have had their hand in interpreting the saying. Since so many versions exist, they provide rich data for resolving the question whether Thomas reflects the redactional text of the synoptics. The overlap texts are by far the most complex texts of the gospels, but they are also potentially the most fruitful for studying the relationship of Thomas and the synoptics.

The doublets only seem to occupy a tiny corner of synoptic studies. In reality they impact extensive areas of research into the gospels and the historical Jesus, and they reward careful study.

---

10. D. LÜHRMANN, "The Gospel of Mark and the Sayings Collection Q," in *JBL* 108 (1989) 51-71, esp. p. 64.

11. C. M. TUCKETT, "Mark and Q," p. 151.

12. S. DAVIES, "The Christology and Protology of the *Gospel of Thomas*," in *JBL* 111 (1992) 663-682, esp. p. 664. Contrast Davies' claim with the more moderate estimate of Fallon and Cameron, "On this issue [relationship to the canonical gospels] scholars remain sharply divided and have not reached a conclusion that would solve the problem to everyone's satisfaction." See F. T. FALLON and R. CAMERON, "The Gospel of Thomas: A *Forschungsbericht* and Analysis," in *ANRW* 2. 25. 6 (1988) 4195-4251, esp. p. 4213.

13. C. M. TUCKETT, "Thomas and the Synoptics," in *NT* 30 (1988) 132-157. See also B. DEHANDSCHUTTER, "Recent Research on the Gospel of Thomas," in *The Four Gospels 1992: Festschrift Frans Neirynck*, 1992, 3. 2257-2262.

14. Matt 10,38; 16,24; Mark 8,34b; Luke 9,23; 14,27; Th 55.

2. *The Doublets*

We can define a doublet as the repetition in one gospel of the same or closely similar sections at least a verse in length.[15] Doublets, of course, need not point to the use of separate sources. Writers can, and frequently do, repeat themselves, and the gospel writers do not refrain from the practice. Matthew, for example, uses the sayings on scandal twice (Matt 5,29-30; 18,8-9). Although some scholars want to attribute the first instance to Q and the second to Mark,[16] Luke has no parallel to either so a better explanation sees Matthew repeating the Marcan sayings in the Sermon on the Mount.[17] We need to distinguish these editorial repetitions or "redactional doublets" from other doublets, the "source doublets," that point to the use of sources.[18] The clearest examples appear twice in both Matthew and Luke, once in the triple tradition and once in the double tradition. For instance, both Matthew and Luke record two forms of the Cross Saying.

Matt 16,24	Mark 8,34	Luke 9,23
εἴ τις θέλει	εἴ τις θέλει	εἴ τις θέλει
ὀπίσω μου ἐλθεῖν,	ὀπίσω μου ἀκολουθεῖν,	ὀπίσω μου ἔρχεσθαι,
ἀπαρνησάσθω ἑαυτὸν	ἀπαρνησάσθω ἑαυτὸν	ἀρνησάσθω ἑαυτὸν
καὶ ἀράτω	καὶ ἀράτω	καὶ ἀράτω
τὸν σταυρὸν αὐτοῦ	τὸν σταυρὸν αὐτοῦ	τὸν σταυρὸν αὐτοῦ
καὶ	καὶ	καθ᾽ ἡμέραν καὶ
ἀκολουθείτω μοι.	ἀκολουθείτω μοι.	ἀκολουθείτω μοι.

Matt 10,38	Luke 14,27
καὶ ὃς οὐ λαμβάνει	ὅστις οὐ βαστάζει
τὸν σταυρὸν αὐτοῦ	τὸν σταυρὸν ἑαυτοῦ
καὶ ἀκολουθεῖ	καὶ ἔρχεται
ὀπίσω μου,	ὀπίσω μου,
οὐκ ἔστιν	οὐ δύναται εἶναί
μου ἄξιος.	μου μαθητής.

15. J. C. HAWKINS, *Horae Synopticae: Contributions to the Study of the Synoptic Problem*, Oxford: Clarendon, ²1909, p. 80; F. NEIRYNCK, "The Two-Source Hypothesis: Introduction," in D. L. DUNGAN (ed.), *The Interrelations of the Gospels*, 1990, pp. 3-22, esp. p. 12.

16. See, for example, P. WERNLE, *Die synoptische Frage*, Freiburg i. B.: Mohr – Siebeck, 1899, p. 112; J. C. HAWKINS, *Horae Synopticae*, pp. 82-83; T. SOIRON, *Die Logia Jesu: Eine literarkritische und literargeschichtliche Untersuchung zum synoptischen Problem* (NeutAbh, 6/4), Münster: Aschendorff, 1916, pp. 113-114.

17. T. STEPHENSON, "The Classification of Doublets in the Synoptic Gospels," in *JTS* 20 (1918-19) 1-8, esp. p. 2.

18. On the distinction between redactional doublets and source doublets see T. STEPHENSON, "Classification of Doublets," pp. 1-8; L. VAGANAY, *Le problème synoptique: Une hypothèse de travail* (Bibliothèque de Théologie, 3/1), Paris/Tournai: Desclée,

Matthew and Luke take over the saying in editing Mark's Caesarea Philippi pericope (Matt 16,24; Luke 9,23), and these sayings closely reflect Mark's formulation. The other version (Matt 10,38; Luke 14,27) begins with a negative relative clause instead of Mark's positive conditional, contains no clause on self-denial, and ends in a negative main clause. Furthermore, this second saying occurs in a Q context in both Matthew and Luke, in each case following the Q sayings on Hating One's Relatives (Matt 10,37 par. Luke 14,26). The doublet points to two forms of the saying, one in Mark and one in Q, and it shows clearly that Matthew and Luke drew the sayings from two sources. Doublets like the Cross Saying that appear twice in Matthew and Luke are called "double doublets," and they are not common.[19] More often the doublet appears in only one of the two, Matthew or Luke. For example, the saying on revealing what is hidden appears twice in Luke but only once in Matthew.

Mark 4,22	Luke 8,17
οὐ γάρ ἐστιν κρυπτὸν	οὐ γάρ ἐστιν κρυπτὸν
ἐὰν μὴ ἵνα	ὃ οὐ
φανερωθῇ,	φανερὸν γενήσεται,
οὐδὲ ἐγένετο ἀπόκρυφον	οὐδὲ ἀπόκρυφον
ἀλλ' ἵνα	ὃ οὐ μὴ γνωσθῇ καὶ
ἔλθῃ εἰς φανερόν.	εἰς φανερὸν ἔλθῃ.

Matt 10,26	Luke 12,2
οὐδὲν γὰρ	οὐδὲν δὲ
ἐστιν κεκαλυμμένον	συγκεκαλυμμένον ἐστὶν
ὃ οὐκ ἀποκαλυφθήσεται	ὃ οὐκ ἀποκαλυφθήσεται
καὶ κρυπτὸν	καὶ κρυπτὸν
ὃ οὐ γνωσθήσεται.	ὃ οὐ γνωσθήσεται.

1954, p. 117; A. VAN DULMEN, *De doubletten in het evangelie van Lucas*, unpublished Licentiate dissertation, Leuven: Katholieke Universiteit, 1966, pp. 36-40; F. NEIRYNCK, "Hawkins's Additional Notes to his 'Horae Synopticae,'" in *ETL* 46 (1970) 78-111, esp. p. 91.

19. In an appendix to his dissertation A. Van Dulmen lists several other double doublets. See A. VAN DULMEN, *Doubletten*, pp. xvi-xvii. Some examples:
1. To One Who Has Will be Given: Mark 4,25 (par. Matt 13,12; Luke 8,18)
   Matt 25,29 par. Luke 19,26
2. Losing One's Life: Mark 8,35 (par. Matt 16,25; Luke 9,24)
   Matt 10,39 par. Luke 17,33
3. Jesus and the Son of Man: Mark 8,38 (par. Matt 16,27; Luke 9,26)
   Matt 10,32-33 par. Luke 12,8-9
4. On Accepting: Mark 9,37 (par. Matt 18,5; Luke 9,48)
   Matt 10,40 par. Luke 10,16
5. Family Division: Mark 13,12 (par. Matt 10,21; Luke 21,16)
   Matt 10,34-36 par. Luke 12,51-53.

Matthew passed over the Marcan saying in redacting the Parable Discourse, but he reproduces the Q saying in the Mission Discourse. Luke, on the other hand, records both the Marcan and the Q sayings. Other examples include the Lamp Saying, a doublet in Luke (Luke 8,16; 11,33), and the Divorce Saying, a doublet in Matthew (Matt 5,32; 19,9). These doublets are called "single doublets" because they appear as a doublet in only one gospel.

In still other cases each gospel writer has only one version of the saying, but a comparison of the texts shows that behind the Matthean and Lucan sayings lies a Q text. In the Salt Saying, for example, each writer has only a single saying. However, Matthew and Luke agree so closely that the saying had to appear in Q as well as in Mark.

Mark 9,50

καλὸν τὸ ἅλας·
ἐὰν δὲ τὸ ἅλας
ἄναλον γένηται,
ἐν τίνι αὐτὸ ἀρτύσετε;

Matt 5,13

ὑμεῖς ἐστε τὸ ἅλας
τῆς γῆς·
ἐὰν δὲ τὸ ἅλας
μωρανθῇ,
ἐν τίνι ἁλισθήσεται;
εἰς οὐδὲν
ἰσχύει
ἔτι εἰ μὴ βληθὲν ἔξω
καταπατεῖσθαι
ὑπὸ τῶν ἀνθρώπων.

Luke 14,34-35

καλὸν οὖν τὸ ἅλας·

ἐὰν δὲ καὶ τὸ ἅλας
μωρανθῇ,
ἐν τίνι ἀρτυθήσεται;
οὔτε εἰς γῆν οὔτε εἰς κοπρίαν
εὔθετόν ἐστιν,
ἔξω βάλλουσιν αὐτό.

Doublets like the Salt Saying are called "condensed doublets" because often the Marcan and Q forms are combined in either Matthew or Luke. For instance, Matthew's version of the Mustard Seed (Matt 13,31-32) conflates the Marcan version (Mark 4,30-32) and the Q version found in Luke (Luke 13,18-19).

All of the examples we have considered so far involve single sentences. A few of the doublets, though, are quite extensive. The four longest are the Beelzebul Controversy, the Mustard Seed, the Mission Discourse, and the Demand for a Sign.

The presence of doublets in Matthew and Luke shows that the two evangelists are using two sources, and the doublets quickly evolved into

a classic argument for the existence of Q.[20] The doublets, though, do
more than prove the existence of Q; they also raise the question of the
relationship of Mark and Q to each other. Three answers have been
given to this question in the discussion: Q depends on Mark; Mark
depends on Q; Mark and Q are independent.

3. *Q Depends on Mark*

Julius Wellhausen believed that Q depends on Mark. He could not
conceive that the two works were independent,[21] and he believed that
Mark reflects an earlier stage in the tradition than Q. According to Wellhausen most of Mark reflects the Jewish ministry of Jesus and shows no
Christianizing tendencies, but in the Discipleship Section (Mark 8,27-
10,52) Mark preaches the gospel to the community of his own day with
a developed christology and ecclesiology. Matthew and Luke carry this
Christianizing tendency throughout their gospels, partly under the influence of Q, for Q everywhere shows secondary Christian features.[22]
For example, the Q temptation story (Q 4,2-13) makes explicit messianic
claims whereas Mark's temptation story (Mark 1,12-13) remains in the
Jewish framework of Jesus' ministry. The explicit messianic temptation
in Mark occurs after Peter's confession where Peter expects that Jesus
will go to Jerusalem not as the suffering and dying one but as the Jewish
messiah. The messianic temptation falls in the Christian center of Mark,
but it is dispersed in Q.[23] Since this Christian theologizing permeates all
of Q but is confined to one central section in Mark, Q must come later
than Mark; and, assuming that they cannot be independent, then Q must
depend on Mark.

Wellhausen bolstered his tradition-historical argument with three
additional arguments. The first appeals to the difference in form between
Mark and Q. Mark presents sayings embedded in narratives or loosely

---

20. Besides the doublets two other classic arguments prove the existence of Q: (1) The
close verbal agreement between Matthew and Luke in many double tradition passages,
and (2) the agreement between Matthew and Luke in the order of the double tradition
pericopes. For a brief description of the classic arguments see V. TAYLOR, *The Gospels:
A Short Introduction*, London: Epworth, [7]1952, pp. 20-22. In two important essays Taylor has clarified and strengthened the argument from order. See V. TAYLOR, "The Order
of Q" (1953), in ID., *New Testament Essays*, Grand Rapids, MI: Eerdmans, 1972, pp. 90-94;
ID., "The Original Order of Q" (1959), in ID., *New Testament Essays*, Grand Rapids, MI:
Eerdmans, 1972, pp. 95-118.

21. J. WELLHAUSEN, *Einleitung in die drei ersten Evangelien*, Berlin: Reimer, 1905,
p. 73.

22. *Ibid.*, pp. 79-84.

23. *Ibid.*, p. 74.

strung together as, for example, in Mark 4,21-25 and Mark 9,33-50. Q, on the other hand, offers complete discourses developed around a common theme. The thematic discourses are secondary.[24] Second, Mark strove for completeness. He would not have limited himself to extracts from Q but would have incorporated all of Q in his gospel if Q had been available to him. He did not include certain material like the Sermon on the Mount only because the material did not yet exist.[25] Third, Wellhausen believed that Mark did not show any knowledge of the fall of Jerusalem and must be dated some years after 50 A.D. On the basis of Q 11,49-51 he dates Q after 68 A.D.[26]

Wellhausen did not convince many. Only Eduard Meyer supported his position fully.[27] Jülicher agreed with Wellhausen in dating Q after Mark, but he denied that Q depends on Mark. Jülicher believed that Q was a constantly expanding collection of Jesus' sayings whose beginnings stretched back before Mark. But the form of Q used by Matthew and Luke was later than Mark. Since Q was constantly growing, it was both older and younger than Mark. Jülicher insists, though, that Q is not necessary to understand Mark.[28]

Although Wellhausen's view never commanded a following, his work remains important. He saw clearly that only a careful tradition-historical analysis can determine the relationship between Mark and Q and that form criticism plays a key role in this analysis. He also recognized that Q is not a neutral collection of sayings, but that an advanced theological conception dominates the document. Any treatment of the overlap texts that ignores tradition history or the theology of Q will fail.

4. *Mark Depends on Q*

Although few adopted Wellhausen's position that Q depends on Mark, the opposite view that Mark depends on Q has always had supporters. Before Wellhausen articulated his position, Bernhard Weiss defended the opposite view that Mark knew and used Q.[29] Weiss,

---

24. *Ibid.*, pp. 84-85.
25. *Ibid.*, p. 86.
26. *Ibid.*, pp. 87-88.
27. E. MEYER, *Ursprung und Anfänge des Christentums: I. Die Evangelien*, Stuttgart: Cotta, 1921, 1962 (reprint of 4th and 5th editions, 1924), pp. 234-236.
28. A. JÜLICHER with E. FASCHER, *Einleitung in das Neue Testament*, Tübingen: Mohr – Siebeck, [7]1931, pp. 344-349.
29. B. WEISS, *Lehrbuch der Einleitung in das Neue Testament*, Berlin: Hertz, 1886, pp. 506-507; ET: *A Manual of Introduction to the New Testament*, trans. A. J. K. Davidson, 2 vols., New York: Funk & Wagnalls, 1889, 2. 246-248.

though, reckoned with a vastly expanded Q. Using the minor agreements of Matthew and Luke against Mark, he tried to show, for instance, that Q contained narratives like the Cure of the Leper.[30] Following Weiss, Titius also used the minor agreements to expand Q, although he confined his attention to the sayings material and not the narratives.[31] Johannes Weiss also argued that Mark had at his disposal an expanded collection of sayings.[32] In general, though, the attempt to expand Q won only scattered support.[33]

Streeter addressed the problem of the overlap texts in one of his contributions to *Oxford Studies*.[34] Unlike Bernhard Weiss, he made no attempt to trace the minor agreements back to Q. He confined his attention, instead, to the major agreements of Matthew and Luke against Mark and to the places where Q overlapped Mark. Studying such texts as John's Preaching and the Beelzebul Controversy, he was struck by the fact that Mark's text was shorter, more cryptic, less intelligible than the Q parallel. The Q text did not appear to be an expansion of the Marcan text, but Mark seemed to present a mutilated excerpt of Q. Streeter thus appealed to tradition history to place Mark downstream from Q. Streeter observed further that Mark combined the Beelzebul Controversy and the Unforgivable Sin which were separated in Q. He found the same phenomenon in the cluster of sayings in Mark 4,21-25 where Mark combined five sayings that Q presented separately in more original contexts. Streeter concluded that Mark knew and used Q, but the great differences between Mark and Q in the overlap texts bothered him. In his *Oxford Studies* essay he explained the differences by claiming that Mark quoted Q from memory.[35] By the time he wrote *The Four Gospels* Streeter had decided that the differences were too great to be explained in this way,

30. B. WEISS, *Die Quellen des Lukasevangeliums*, Stuttgart/Berlin: Cotta, 1907, pp. 159-162.

31. A. TITIUS, "Das Verhältnis der Herrnworte im Markusevangelium zu den Logia des Matthäus," in *Theologische Studien: Professor D. Bernhard Weiss zu seinem 70. Geburtstage dargebracht*, Göttingen: Vandenhoeck & Ruprecht, 1897, pp. 284-331.

32. J. WEISS, *Das älteste Evangelium*, Göttingen: Vandenhoeck und Ruprecht, 1903, pp. 370-380.

33. See, for example, F. NICOLARDOT, *Les procédés de rédaction des trois premiers évangélistes*, Paris: Fischbacher, 1908, pp. 215-216, 297-298; W. LARFELD, *Die neutestamentliche Evangelien nach ihrer Eigenart und Abhängigkeit untersucht*, Gütersloh: Bertelsmann, 1925, pp. 251-257.

34. B. H. STREETER, "St. Mark's Knowledge and Use of Q," in W. SANDAY (ed.), *Studies in the Synoptic Problem*, 1911, pp. 165-183.

35. *Ibid.*, pp. 166, 172. See further W. SANDAY, "Introductory," in ID. (ed.), *Studies in the Synoptic Problem*, 1911, pp. vii-xxvii, esp. pp. xvi-xvii.

and he concluded that Mark and Q were independent.[36] Although Streeter's *Oxford Studies* essay does not represent his final opinion, it remains important for several reasons. First, in the study he clearly separated the problem of the overlap texts from the problem of the minor agreements. Second, he did not rely on general arguments, but he confronted each Marcan text with its Q overlap and compared the wording and context of each. Third, like Wellhausen he used tradition history to determine which text was original. In his article Streeter laid the foundation for an adequate methodology appropriate to the study of the overlap texts.

Several scholars attempt to explain the overlap texts by proposing intermediaries either between Mark and Q or between Mark and the later evangelists. Some, for instance, have Mark depend on an edition of Q or a revision of Q. Rawlinson, for example, claimed that Mark had access to the edition of Q current in Rome (Q^R), and he incorporated excerpts from it into his gospel.[37] Honey adopted Rawlinson's Roman Q; and, like Rawlinson, he used it to explain the verbal differences between Mark's overlap texts and the corresponding Q texts.[38] J. P. Brown observed that in the overlap texts Matthew and Mark frequently agree against Luke in the order of the sayings and in secondary features like small additions to the texts. He concluded that Luke remains closest to the original form of Q and that Matthew and Mark derived their Q material from a revision of Q (Q^{rev}).[39]

Instead of using editions of Q to explain the overlap texts Wolfgang Schenk has recourse to an edition of Mark. According to Schenk at times Q shows the more original text of the overlap passages, but at other times Mark has the earlier form. Schenk uses the term priority-discrepancy (*Prioritäten-Diskrepanz*) to describe this phenomenon. He explains the phenomenon by postulating a pre-Marcan tradition (*Prae-Markus*) that is earlier than Q and a Marcan redactor who knew and used Q. Instead of a two-stage Q, Schenk substitutes a two-stage Mark.[40] Wendling had earlier postulated a later Marcan redactor who used Q.[41]

36. B. H. STREETER, *The Four Gospels: A Study of Origins*, London: Macmillan, 1924, pp. 153-154, 186-191.

37. A. E. J. RAWLINSON, *St. Mark: With Introduction, Commentary and Additional Notes* (Westminster Commentaries), London: Methuen, 1925, pp. xxxviii-xl.

38. T. E. F. HONEY, "Did Mark Use Q?," in *JBL* 62 (1943) 319-331.

39. J. P. BROWN, "Mark as Witness to an Edited Form of Q," in *JBL* 80 (1961) 29-44; ID., "The Form of 'Q' Known to Matthew," in *NTS* 8 (1961-62) 27-42.

40. W. SCHENK, "Der Einfluss der Logienquelle auf das Markusevangelium," in *ZNW* 70 (1979) 141-165.

41. E. WENDLING, *Die Entstehung des Marcus-Evangeliums: Philologische Untersuchungen*, Tübingen: Mohr – Siebeck, 1908, pp. 24-27, 34-38, 57-58, 77, 102-106, 109-112, 126; ID., "Neuere Schriften zu den synoptischen Evangelien und zur Apostelgeschichte," in *ZNW* (1909) 135-168, esp. pp. 150-151. See F. NEIRYNCK, "Recent Developments," p. 422 n. 55.

Walter Schmithals proposes an even more complex solution. According to Schmithals the earliest edition of Q contained no christology. Mark took over sayings from this early Q and infused them with christology. Then the Q redactor, under the influence of Mark, introduced christological material into a revision of Q.[42]

Albert Fuchs and his student Franz Kogler appeal to a second edition of Mark to explain the overlap texts. They accept one pillar of the two-source theory – Marcan priority – but they take issue with proponents of the two-source theory about how to explain the double tradition. In the classic two-source theory Matthew and Luke independently of one another combined Mark and Q. According to Fuchs and Kogler a later redactor (*Deuteromarkus*) expanded Mark with the double tradition material, and Matthew and Luke used this expanded Mark rather than canonical Mark in writing their gospels. Besides introducing the double tradition passages, the later redactor also improved the text of Mark. Fuchs and Kogler thus appeal to Deutero-Markus to explain both the double tradition and the minor agreements.[43]

None of the proposals for an edition of Q or of Mark have won wide support. They suffer from two serious flaws. First, they propose complex stages in the development of the tradition for which we have little evidence apart from the overlap texts. Second, they all underestimate the redactional work of the synoptic writers, and they trace to earlier editions changes that the synoptic writers themselves, not their sources, introduced into the texts. Because of these problems most scholars who maintain that Mark used Q claim that Mark had access to final Q, the form of Q that Matthew and Luke incorporated into their gospels.[44] B. W. Bacon and F.

---

42. W. SCHMITHALS, "Die Worte vom leidenden Menschensohn: Ein Schlüssel zur Lösung des Menschensohn-Problems," in C. ANDRESEN & G. KLEIN (eds.), *Theologia Crucis – Signum Crucis: Festschrift für Erich Dinkler zum 70. Geburtstag*, Tübingen: Mohr – Siebeck, 1979, pp. 417-445.

43. A. FUCHS, *Die Entwicklung der Beelzebulkontroverse bei den Synoptikern: Traditionsgeschichtliche und redaktionsgeschichtliche Untersuchung von Mk 3,22-27 und Parallelen, verbunden mit der Rückfrage nach Jesus* (SNTU, B5), Linz: SNTU, 1980; F. KOGLER, *Das Doppelgleichnis vom Senfkorn und vom Sauerteig in seiner traditionsgeschichtlichen Entwicklung: Zur Reich-Gottes-Vorstellung Jesu und ihren Aktualisierungen in der Urkirche* (FzB, 59), Würzburg: Echter, 1988.

44. W. BOUSSET, "Wellhausens Evangelienkritik," in *TR* 9 (1906) 1-14, 43-51; A. LOISY, *Les évangiles synoptiques*, 2 vols., Ceffonds: Privately published, 1907, 1908, 1. 85; W. SANDAY, "The Conditions under which the Gospels were written, in their bearing upon some Difficulties of the Synoptic Problem," in ID. (ed.), *Studies in the Synoptic Problem*, 1911, pp. 1-26; F. BARTH, *Einleitung in das Neue Testament*, Gütersloh: Bertelsmann, [5]1921, p. 236; M. GOGUEL, *Introduction au Nouveau Testament: Tome I: Les évangiles synoptiques*, Paris: Leroux, 1923, pp. 250-267; C. F. BURNEY, *The Poetry of Our Lord: An Examination of the Formal Elements of Hebrew Poetry in the Discourses of Jesus Christ*, Oxford: Clarendon, 1925, p. 8.

C. Grant defended this position, even after Streeter abandoned it.[45] More recent studies also argue that Mark knew final Q.[46]

Throughout his career Jan Lambrecht has advocated the position that Mark knew and used Q. Initially he adopted Brown's view that Mark depended on a revision of Q,[47] but he soon dropped this position and maintained that Mark depended directly on final Q.[48] In discussing an overlap text Lambrecht always begins by reconstructing the original wording of the Q material, and then he compares the Marcan text with Q. Although Streeter made very careful comparisons between Q and Mark, he did not reconstruct the original wording of Q. As a result his comparisons lack the precision that can only come from comparing a Q text freed from Matthean and Lucan alterations with the text of Mark. In his studies Lambrecht also gives a detailed account of the Marcan redaction, showing how one can move from the Q text to Mark's text using Marcan redactional techniques. Lambrecht's procedure marks a real advance over Streeter.

5. *Mark and Q are Independent*

Most scholars who support the two-source theory hold that Mark and Q are independent of each other.[49] New Testament introductions and manuals

45. B. W. BACON, "The Prologue of Mark: A Study of Sources and Structure," in *JBL* 26 (1907) 84-106; ID., *The Beginnings of the Gospel Story*, New Haven: Yale, 1909, pp. xx-xxii; ID., *The Making of the New Testament*, New York: Holt, 1912, pp. 141-145; ID., "The Nature and Design of Q, the Second Synoptic Source," in *HibbJourn* 22 (1923-24) 674-688; ID., *The Gospel of Mark: Its Composition and Date*, New Haven: Yale, 1925, p. 152; F. C. GRANT, "The Mission of the Disciples: Mt. 9:35-11:1 and Parallels," in *JBL* 35 (1916) 293-314; ID., *The Growth of the Gospels*, New York: Abingdon, 1933, pp. 129-131; ID., *The Earliest Gospel*, New York: Abingdon – Cokesbury, 1943, pp. 63, 71; ID., *The Gospels: Their Origin and their Growth*, New York: Harper & Brothers, 1957, pp. 108-109.

46. H. FLEDDERMANN, "The Discipleship Discourse (Mark 9:33-50)," in *CBQ* 43 (1981) 57-75; ID., "A Warning about the Scribes (Mark 12:37b-40)," in *CBQ* 44 (1982) 52-67; ID., "John and the Coming One (Matt 3:11-12 // Luke 3:16-17)," *SBL 1984 Seminar Papers*, pp. 377-384; ID., "The Cross and Discipleship in Q," *SBL 1988 Seminar Papers*, pp. 472-482; ID., "The Mustard Seed and the Leaven in Q, the Synoptics, and Thomas," *SBL 1989 Seminar Papers*, pp. 216-236; D. R. CATCHPOLE, "Mission Charge," pp. 147-174; ID., "The Beginning of Q: A Proposal," in *NTS* 38 (1992) 205-221; ID., *The Quest for Q*, Edinburgh: Clark, 1993, pp. 60-78; 151-188; B. MACK, "Q and the Gospel of Mark: Revising Christian Origins," in *Semeia* 55 (1992) 15-39.

47. J. LAMBRECHT, "Die Logia-Quellen von Markus 13," in *Bib* 47 (1966) 321-360.

48. J. LAMBRECHT, *Die Redaktion der Markus-Apokalypse: Literarische Analyse und Strukturuntersuchung* (AnBib, 28), Rome: Pontifical Biblical Institute, 1967; ID., *Marcus Interpretator: Stijl en boodschap in Mc. 3,20-4,34*, Brugge/Utrecht: Desclée de Brouwer, 1969; ID., "Redaction and Theology in Mk., IV," in M. SABBE (ed.), *L'évangile selon Marc*, 1974, ²1988, pp. 269-308; ID., "Q-Influence on Mark 8,34-9,1," in J. DELOBEL (ed.), *Logia*, 1982, pp. 277-304; ID., "John the Baptist and Jesus in Mark 1.1-15: Markan Redaction of Q?," in *NTS* 38 (1992) 357-384.

49. P. WERNLE, *Synoptische Frage*, pp. 208-215; A. HARNACK, *Sprüche und Reden Jesu: Die zweite Quelle des Matthäus und Lukas* (Beiträge zur Einleitung in das Neue

commonly adopt this position.[50] The two book-length treatments of the
overlap texts that have appeared both conclude that Mark and Q are
independent of one another.[51] We saw earlier that Streeter changed his
mind on the relationship of Mark and Q. In his *Oxford Studies* essay he

Testament, 2), Leipzig: Hinrichs, 1907, pp. 136-157; ET: *The Sayings of Jesus: The
Second Source of St. Matthew and St. Luke*, trans. J. R. Wilkinson, London: Williams &
Norgate/New York: G. P. Putnam's Sons, 1908, pp. 193-227; V. H. STANTON, *The
Gospels as Historical Documents: Part II: The Synoptic Gospels*, Cambridge: University
Press, 1909, pp. 109-112; G. D. CASTOR, "The Relationship of Mark to the Source Q,"
in *JBL* 31 (1912) 82-91; C. S. PATTON, "Did Mark Use Q? Or Did Q Use Mark?," in
American Journal of Theology 16 (1912) 634-642; T. STEPHENSON, "The Overlapping of
Sources in Matthew and Luke," in *JTS* 21 (1919-20) 127-145, esp. p. 132; J. M. C.
CRUM, "Mark and 'Q'," in *Theology* 12 (1926) 275-282; ID., *The Original Jerusalem
Gospel: Being Essays on the Document Q*, New York: Macmillan, 1927, pp. 167-190;
W. BUSSMANN, *Synoptische Studien: 2. Zur Redenquelle*, Halle: Waisenhaus, 1929, pp.
157-203; A. T. CADOUX, *The Sources of the Second Gospel*, London: Clarke, 1935, pp.
13-14; B. H. THROCKMORTON, "Did Mark Know Q?," in *JBL* 67 (1948) 319-329; G. R.
BEASLEY-MURRAY, *Jesus and the Future*, London: Macmillan, 1954, p. 230; H. A. GUY,
The Synoptic Gospels, London: Macmillan, 1960, pp. 89-90; V. TAYLOR, *The Gospel
according to St. Mark*, London: Macmillan, ²1966, p. 87; W. GRUNDMANN, *Das Evan-
gelium nach Markus* (Theologischer Handkommentar zum Neuen Testament, 2), Berlin:
Evangelische Verlagsanstalt, ³1965, p. 9; D. LÜHRMANN, *Die Redaktion der Logienquelle*
(WMANT, 33), Neukirchen-Vluyn: Neukirchener Verlag, 1969, pp. 20-21; M. DEVISCH,
"La relation entre l'évangile de Marc et le document Q," pp. 59-91; R. PESCH, *Das
Markusevangelium* (HTKNT, 2), 2 vols., Freiburg/Basel/Vienna: Herder, 1976, 1977, 1.
30; E. GÜTTGEMANNS, *Candid Questions Concerning Gospel Form Criticism* (Pittsburgh
Theological Monograph Series, 26), Pittsburgh: Pickwick, 1979, p. 337; F. NEIRYNCK,
"Recent Developments," pp. 421-433, 464; C. M. TUCKETT, "Mark and Q," p. 175.

50. J. MOFFATT, *An Introduction to the Literature of the New Testament*, New York:
Charles Scribner's Sons, 1911, pp. 204-206; P. FEINE, *Einleitung in das Neue Testament*,
Leipzig; Quelle & Meyer, ³1923, p. 35; P. FEINE and J. BEHM, *Einleitung in das Neue
Testament*, Leipzig: Quelle & Meyer, ⁸1936, p. 28; E. J. GOODSPEED, *An Introduction to
the New Testament*, Chicago: University of Chicago, 1937, p. 148; R. KNOPF, H. LIETZ-
MANN, and R. WEINEL, *Einführung in das Neue Testament*, Berlin: Töpelmann, ⁵1949, p.
120; A. H. MCNEILE with C. S. C. WILLIAMS, *An Introduction to the Study of the New
Testament*, Oxford: Clarendon, ²1953, pp. 83-84; A. WIKENHAUSER, *Einleitung in das
Neue Testament*, Freiburg/Basel/Vienna: Herder, ⁴1961, pp. 181-182; W. G. KÜMMEL,
Einleitung in das Neue Testament, Heidelberg: Quelle & Meyer, ¹⁷1973, pp. 43-44; ET:
Introduction to the New Testament, trans. H. C. Kee, Nashville: Abingdon, 1975, p. 70;
P. VIELHAUER, *Geschichte der urchristlichen Literatur: Einleitung in das Neue Testament,
die Apokryphen und die Apostolischen Väter*, Berlin/New York: de Gruyter, 1975, pp.
275-276; H. CONZELMANN and A. LINDEMANN, *Arbeitsbuch zum Neuen Testament*, Tübin-
gen: Mohr – Siebeck, ³1977, p. 67; ET: *Interpreting the New Testament: An Introduction
to the Principles and Methods of N. T. Exegesis*, trans. S. S. Schatzmann, Peabody, MA:
Hendrickson, 1988, p. 59; D. GUTHRIE, *New Testament Introduction*, Leicester: Apollos /
Downers Grove, IL: Intervarsity, ⁴1990, pp. 161-162.

51. R. LAUFEN, *Doppelüberlieferungen*, pp. 75, 385; J. SCHÜLING, *Studien*, pp. 180,
215. The same year his book appeared Laufen published separately his study of the Mustard Seed. See R. LAUFEN, "ΒΑΣΙΛΕΙΑ und ΕΚΚΛΗΣΙΑ: Eine traditions- und redaktionsgeschichtliche Untersuchung des Gleichnisses vom Senfkorn," in J. ZMIJEWSKI & E.
NELLESEN (eds.), *Begegnung mit dem Wort: FS Heinrich Zimmermann*, 1980, pp. 105-
140; = *Doppelüberlieferungen*, pp. 174-200.

held that Mark depended on Q, but in *The Four Gospels* he maintained that they were independent.[52]

Those who claim that Mark and Q are independent of one another use a double argumentation. On the one hand they try to show that it is unlikely that Mark depends on Q. A typical argument centers on the extent of the Mark-Q overlap. If Mark depends on Q, why does he take over so little of Q?[53] This argument is at times applied to an individual pericope. For example, if Mark depends on Q for the Mission Discourse, why has he taken over so little of the Q discourse? Another typical argument zeros in on the differences between Mark and Q in the overlap texts. The two texts appear too divergent for one to depend on the other.[54] These differences played a decisive role in Streeter's change of heart.[55]

Besides trying to refute the arguments of those who advocate Marcan dependence, proponents of independence bring forward two positive arguments for independence. First, they point to the fact that at times Mark seems to be more original in the overlap material, at times Q does. Second, they point to the absence of Q redactional elements in Mark.

The first argument centers on what Schenk calls the priority-discrepancy (*Prioritäten-Diskrepanz*).[56] According to this argument, Mark at times preserves the more original form of the overlap texts, at times Q does, so the two must be independent. Laufen, for example, examines nine overlap texts in detail and comes to the conclusion that Q preserves the original form four times, Mark has the prior text twice, and three times both Q and Mark show original elements in the same overlap text.[57]

---

52. After surveying the overlap texts Streeter states in his earlier work, "The *cumulative* effect of these instances is irresistible, and must establish beyond reasonable doubt that Mark was familiar with Q" ("St. Mark's Knowledge and Use of Q," p. 176). Thirteen years later he writes, "On the whole, then, the evidence is decidedly against the view that Mark used Q" (*The Four Gospels*, p. 191). Streeter is not the only one to alter his position. C. A. Briggs confessed that he changed his mind several times on the issue of Mark and Q. See C. A. BRIGGS, "The Use of the Logia of Matthew in the Gospel of Mark," in *JBL* 23 (1904) 191-210, esp. p. 191.

53. See, for example, J. MOFFATT, *Introduction*, p. 205; C. S. PATTON, "Did Mark Use Q? Or Did Q Use Mark?," p. 641; A. T. CADOUX, *Sources*, pp. 13-14; B. H. THROCKMORTON, "Did Mark Know Q?," p. 327.

54. W. G. KÜMMEL, *Einleitung*, pp. 43-44; ET: *Introduction*, p. 70.

55. For example, Streeter writes of the Mission Discourse, "Assuming then, that Luke x. 1-12 (not being conflate with Mark) represents Q, the differences between Mark and Luke are so great and the resemblances so few that they favour the view that Mark's version is independent, not derived from Q" (*The Four Gospels*, p. 190).

56. W. SCHENK, "Einfluss der Logienquelle," p. 145.

57. Q is prior in the saying on Revealing What is Hidden (Mark 4,22 par. Q 12,2), the Mission Discourse (Mark 6,7-13 par. Q 10,1-12), the saying on Losing One's Life (Mark 8,35 par. Q 17,33), the saying on False Messiahs (Mark 13,21 par. Q 17,23). Mark is prior in the saying on John's Prophecy (Mark 1,7-8 par. Q 3,16) and the Cross Saying (Mark

Although Laufen only treats nine texts in detail, in a note he shows how he would extend his conclusions over all of the overlap texts.[58]

The second positive argument concerns Q redactional elements. The presence of redactional elements of one text in a second text shows that the second depends on the first. If Mark depends on Q, then Q redactional elements in the text of Mark would indicate this. In the absence of such redactional elements, the possibility remains open that Mark received the material from the oral tradition and not from Q even if Mark can be shown to reflect a later stage in the development of the tradition.[59]

6. *Design of the Present Study*

We can draw some conclusions from the review of the discussion that will help in the design of the present study. First, as in all source-critical work, general arguments have only limited usefulness. For example, opponents of Mark's dependence on Q often argue that it remains inexplicable why Mark omitted so much of Q. But this general argument too easily calls forth the counter assertion that Mark's community had Q readily available so Mark felt no compulsion to reproduce all of Q.[60] Instead of general arguments progress comes from analyzing the texts. In this book I will study all of the overlap texts. Even a work like Laufen's fails in this respect for he only treats nine texts.[61] More restrictive yet, Schüling only deals with four.[62]

Second, we need to work at separating the overlap texts and the minor agreements. Theoretically we can make a sharp distinction, for the two problems are really quite different. The minor agreements are a phenomenon of the triple tradition and a problem for the priority of Mark.[63] Matthew and Luke constantly correct Mark's rough style. These corrections crop up over and over again in Matthew's and Luke's redaction of Mark, and

---

8,34 par. Q 14,27). Both Q and Mark have original elements in the Beelzebul Controversy (Mark 3,22-26 par. Q 11,15-18), the Parable of the Mustard Seed (Mark 4,30-32 par. Q 13,18-19), and the Divorce Saying (Mark 10,11-12 par. Q 16,18). See R. LAUFEN, *Doppelüberlieferungen*, pp. 385-386.

58. R. LAUFEN, *Doppelüberlieferungen*, p. 398 n. 141.

59. F. NEIRYNCK, "Recent Developments," pp. 425-426; ID., "Literary Criticism," pp. 32-33; J. SCHÜLING, *Studien*, pp. 182-183.

60. W. BOUSSET, "Wellhausens Evangelienkritik," p. 44.

61. Laufen treats Mark 1,7-8; 3,22-26; 4,22.30-32; 6,7-13; 8,34.35; 10,11-12; 13,21.

62. Schüling discusses in detail four double traditions: John the Baptist (Mark 1,7-8 par. Q 3,16); the Beelzebul Controversy (Mark 3,22-26 par. Q 11,14-20); the Mission Discourse (Mark 6,7-13 par. Q 10,2-16); the Cross Saying (Mark 8,38 par. Q 14,27). Schüling treats other texts like Mark 1,2; 8,35.36, but he does not confront these Marcan passages with a reconstructed Q text. Sée J. SCHÜLING, *Studien*, p. 12.

63. We can, of course, conceive of the possibility that Matthew and Luke might agree in altering a Q text. However, in practice Matthean and Lucan agreements in Q material are invariably traced to Q.

at times the later evangelists agree in making the same correction.[64] The overlap texts are a completely different phenomenon. The doublets show that at certain points the triple tradition – the Marcan material – overlapped with the double tradition – the material Matthew and Luke share that they did not derive from Mark. In these overlap texts Matthew and Luke had access to two forms of a saying, a parable, or a discourse – one from Mark and one from Q. The agreements between Matthew and Luke in these texts are substantial, so substantial that we can only conclude that they are drawing on two sources.

Although the two problems are distinct, in practice it has often been difficult to distinguish them because both the minor agreements and the overlap texts show Matthean and Lucan agreement against Mark. Instead of keeping the minor agreements and the overlap texts separate, scholars have at times joined the two problems. First, as we have seen, some scholars like Bernhard Weiss tried to exploit the minor agreements to find additional Q material. Weiss used the minor agreements to expand the double tradition at the expense of the triple tradition. In the present work I will not use the minor agreements to expand the overlap texts.[65] As we will see, Mark and Q overlap extensively without resorting to the minor agreements. Second, a scholar like Albert Fuchs seeks to solve both the problem of the minor agreements and the problem of the overlap texts with a *Deuteromarkus*. According to Fuchs Matthew and Luke used an edition of Mark that had already corrected much of Mark's rough style and in addition had joined the double tradition material to Mark.[66] Fuchs has not been able to demonstrate, though, that a second edition of Mark is necessary to explain Matthew's and Luke's combination of the double tradition and Mark.[67] Matthew and Luke combine them in

---

64. On the minor agreements see especially F. NEIRYNCK, *The Minor Agreements of Matthew and Luke against Mark: With a Cumulative List* (BETL, 37), Leuven: University Press, 1974, pp. 11-48; ID., "The Minor Agreements and the Two-Source Theory," in *Evangelica II: 1982-1991: Collected Essays* (BETL, 99), Leuven: University Press – Peeters, 1991, pp. 3-42; ID., *The Minor Agreements in a Horizontal-Line Synopsis* (Studiorum Novi Testamenti Auxilia, 15), Leuven: University Press – Peeters, 1991.

65. The problem of the overlap texts is clearly separated from the minor agreements by Stephenson and Streeter. See T. STEPHENSON, "Overlapping of Sources," pp. 127-128; B. H. STREETER, *The Four Gospels*, pp. 305-306. See further R. T. SIMPSON, "The Major Agreements of Matthew and Luke against Mark," in *NTS* 12 (1965-66) 273-284, esp. pp. 273-274; F. NEIRYNCK, *The Minor Agreements of Matthew and Luke against Mark*, p. 25 n. 68; ID., "Minor Agreements and the Two-Source Theory," p. 29; M. E. BORING, "The Synoptic Problem, 'Minor' Agreements, and the Beelzebul Pericope," in *The Four Gospels 1992: Festschrift Frans Neirynck*, 1992, 1. 587-619, esp. pp. 591-592.

66. See A. FUCHS, *Entwicklung der Beelzebulkontroverse*, pp. 249-252.

67. See F. NEIRYNCK, "Deuteromarcus et les accords Matthieu-Luc" (1980), in ID., *Evangelica*, 1982, pp. 769-780; M. E. BORING, "Synoptic Problem," pp. 616-618.

such different ways that independent use of Q explains the data better than *Deuteromarkus*.

No consensus exists on the number of overlap texts. Nor will one emerge as long as the extent of Q itself remains uncertain.[68] The various lists of overlap texts, though, do converge around a group of certain texts that are always included.[69] Laufen counts twenty-five overlap texts.[70] However, he splits the Beelzebul Controversy into two texts, separating the Parable of the Strong Man (Mark 3,27) from the first part of Mark's pericope (Mark 3,22-26), so his list really contains twenty-four Marcan texts. The list that I propose contains all twenty-four texts in Laufen's list, but it adds five other Marcan texts for a total of twenty-nine overlap texts. In the Table of Contents (pp. IX-XI) the texts appear in the Marcan order with the Q overlap in parentheses after the Marcan reference.

The five texts not included in Laufen's list are § 16 (Mark 9,40), § 17 (Mark 9,42), § 17a (Mark 14,21), § 20 (Mark 10,31), and § 27 (Mark 13,31). Laufen rejects Mark 9,40 because many scholars do not think that the Marcan saying and the Q saying are variations of a single saying. Even if they are, he does not think we can establish which is the prior form. He rejects Mark 9,42 because he doubts that a Q text lies behind Luke 17,2, and he does not even consider the related text § 17a (Mark 14,21). He rejects Mark 10,31 because the saying could be a *Wanderlogion* that came to Matthew and Luke from the oral tradition. Finally, he rejects Mark 13,31 because he is not sure that Mark and Q present two versions of one logion. They could be two entirely separate sayings.[71] In the detailed discussion that follows I will argue that these disputed texts are true overlap texts, that behind them lies a real Q parallel and a related Marcan saying.

The overlap texts demand a complex methodology that unfolds in three major phases. First, I will reconstruct the Q text from Matthew and Luke (Phase 1). Next I will compare the reconstructed Q text and the Marcan overlap to determine which if either of the texts is prior (Phase 2). Finally, if one of them should prove to be prior, I will explore whether the later text can be derived from the earlier one (Phase 3).

---

68. I attribute to Q the following texts: Q 3,7-9.16-17; 4,2b-13; 6,20-23.27-33.35c. 36.37a.38c.39-49; 7,1b-2.6b-10; 7,18-19.22-28.31-35; 9,57-60; 10,2-16.21-24; 11,2-4.9-13. 14-26.29-32.33-35.39-44.46-52; 12,2-12.22b-31.33-34.39-40.42b-46.51-53.58-59; 13,18-21. 24-30.34-35; 14,5.11 (18,14).16-24.26-27.34-35; 15,4-7; 16,13.16-18; 17,1-2.3-4.6.23-24. 26-30.33-35.37; 19,12-27; 22,28.30.

69. See the list compiled by F. Neirynck in "Recent Developments," p. 433.

70. Mark 1,2.7-8; 3,22-26.27.28-29; 4,21.22.24.25.30-32; 6,7-13; 8,11-12; 8,34.35.38; 9,37.50; 10,11-12; 11,22-23.24; 12,38-39; 13,11.12.21.35. See R. LAUFEN, *Doppelüber-lieferungen*, pp. 91-92.

71. R. LAUFEN, *Doppelüberlieferungen*, pp. 83-91.

First, I will reconstruct the Q form of each overlap text. Reconstructing Q is an arduous task, but it is absolutely essential. Without this first step we cannot compare Mark and Q in detail. In his studies of the overlap texts Lambrecht always carefully reconstructs the Q parallel. Laufen also devotes considerable energy to the Q reconstruction. Schüling, on the other hand, does not adequately reconstruct Q. For the most part he relies on Polag's reconstruction.[72] Although Polag prints a Greek text of Q, he does not give the arguments that led to the reconstruction. Instead he provides an apparatus that collates the opinions of Q researchers, but the apparatus can never replace an argued reconstruction.[73]

Second, I will compare the reconstructed Q text and Mark and use tradition history to determine if either of the texts is earlier than the other.[74] E. P. Sanders disputes the validity of the kinds of arguments that scholars use to show that one text is earlier or later than another. Sanders investigates three typical tendencies of the tradition – increasing length, increasing detail, and diminishing Semitism.[75] He concludes that the tradition developed in opposite directions.[76] Leslie Keylock came to the same conclusion after investigating increasing detail in the synoptic gospels.[77] Although Sanders and Keylock easily challenge the notion that rigid "laws" govern the development of the tradition, we really have no choice but to use internal arguments to determine the relative age of documents like Mark and Q. Neither Mark nor the author of Q tells us when they wrote or what sources they used, and no contemporary reports about the documents have survived if any ever existed. Since the documents share some common material, the question naturally arises whether a literary relationship between them exists, and internal arguments provide the only means we have to answer this question. Internal arguments are not objective criteria that we can rigidly apply to texts. They require judgment, and they only work when they arise out of a detailed analysis

---

72. A. POLAG, *Fragmenta Q: Textheft zur Logienquelle*, Neukirchen-Vluyn: Neukirchener Verlag, ²1982.

73. F. NEIRYNCK, "L'édition du texte de Q" (1979), in ID., *Evangelica*, 1982, pp. 925-933, esp. p. 933.

74. On tradition history, see D. R. CATCHPOLE, "Tradition History," in I. H. MARSHALL (ed.), *New Testament Interpretation*, 1977, pp. 165-180.

75. E. P. SANDERS, *The Tendencies of the Synoptic Tradition* (SNTS MS, 9), Cambridge: University Press, 1969, pp. 46-255.

76. Sanders (*Tendencies*, p. 272) concludes: "On all counts the tradition developed in opposite directions. It became both longer and shorter, both more and less detailed, and both more and less Semitic."

77. L. R. KEYLOCK, "Bultmann's Law of Increasing Distinctness," in G. F. HAWTHORNE (ed.), *Current Issues in Biblical and Patristic Interpretation: FS Merrill C. Tenney*, 1975, pp. 193-210.

of the texts.[78] The tradition-historical arguments I will use will come from a comparison of the Marcan and Q texts, and in general I will try to bring forward more than one argument in each case. The reader will have to judge whether my arguments suffice to establish my conclusions.

Werner Kelber also challenges arguments based on tradition history, but he comes at the problem from a different angle. According to Kelber we must forego any notion of an original form in discussing the synoptic material because the synoptic gospels go back to oral tradition and "each oral performance is an irreducibly unique creation."[79] However, by the time we come to the overlap texts we have long since left the realm of oral tradition. Like Mark, Q is a written text. The close verbal agreements and the common order of the double tradition material in Matthew and Luke prove that Q was a written document. Since we are dealing with two written texts that share common material, we can and should ask how they might relate to each other. In other words we are thrown back on tradition history and the kinds of arguments that tradition history uses. In comparing Mark and Q in the overlap texts we can legitimately raise the question of the original form.[80]

Neither Laufen nor Schüling consistently constructs an adequate tradition history for each saying. For instance, in discussing the saying on John and the Coming One, Laufen does not compare Mark and Q in detail. He assumes, instead, that they both go back to a common ancestor which he tries to reconstruct.[81] But when Mark and Q are compared, Mark is closer to Q than either Q or Mark is to Laufen's hypothetical ancestor.[82] Of course, if neither text should prove to be earlier than the other, then recourse to a hypothetical ancestor becomes necessary. Schüling also does not give an adequate tradition history for each overlap text he discusses. He relies too easily on single arguments without pursuing a detailed comparison of the texts. For instance, in discussing the Beelzebul Controversy Schüling questions whether Mark ever would have omitted the saying on the coming of the kingdom (Q 11,20).[83] He gives no further tradition-historical arguments. Surely there is more to be said about the complex Beelzebul Controversy.

---

78. See the excellent discussion in G. M. STYLER, "Priority of Mark," pp. 289-293.

79. W. H. KELBER, *The Oral and the Written Gospel: The Hermeneutics of Speaking and Writing in the Synoptic Tradition, Mark, Paul, and Q*, Philadelphia: Fortress, 1983, p. 30.

80. For a wider critique of Kelber see J. HALVERSON, "Oral and Written Gospel: A Critique of Werner Kelber," in *NTS* 40 (1994) 180-195.

81. R. LAUFEN, *Doppelüberlieferungen*, pp. 97-116.

82. H. FLEDDERMANN, "John and the Coming One," pp. 382-383.

83. J. SCHÜLING, *Studien*, p. 111.

Third, if one text should prove to be later than the other, I will use redaction criticism to determine if the later text can be derived from the earlier one. Lambrecht's work provides a model. As we have seen, Lambrecht maintains that Mark is dependent on Q, and in his studies he gives a comprehensive account of the Marcan redaction. His methodology, though, is sound. If Q should prove to be dependent on Mark, it should be possible to account for the Q redaction of the prior text.

With each text I will discuss briefly any parallels in Paul, John, or the Gospel of Thomas. Thomas furnishes by far the largest number of parallels. Fourteen overlap texts, roughly half of the total, have at least one, and at times two, parallels in Thomas.

THE OVERLAP TEXTS AND THE GOSPEL OF THOMAS

§ 3. The Beelzebul Controversy	Th 35
§ 4. The Unforgivable Sin	Th 44
§ 5. The Lamp	Th 33
§ 6. What is Hidden Will be Revealed	Th 5 [*P. Oxy.* 654.27-31], 6b
§ 8. To One Who Has Will be Given	Th 41
§ 9. The Mustard Seed	Th 20
§ 10. The Mission Discourse	Th 14, 73
§ 12. The Cross Saying	Th 55
§ 20. The First and the Last	Th 4 [*P. Oxy.* 654.21-27]
§ 21. On Faith	Th 48, 106
§ 22. On Asking and Receiving	Th 2 [*P. Oxy.* 654.5-9], 94
§ 25. Family Division	Th 16
§ 26. Rumors of the Coming	Th 113
§ 27. Jesus' Words	Th 11

The eighteen Thomas parallels will help us clarify the relationship between Thomas and the synoptics.

A key question dominates the present discussion of Thomas and the synoptics. Does the Gospel of Thomas reflect the redactional text of the synoptic gospels? Answers to the question frequently hinge on identifying what constitutes a redactional trait of the evangelists. John Sieber, for example, admits as editorial only the ordering of sayings, the special style or vocabulary of an evangelist, or an evangelist's theological concerns. He tends, though, to take an extremely restricted view of what constitutes admissible evidence. For example, he does not accept "kingdom of heaven" as a Matthean trait because of its Jewish origin. He only admits a term like "righteousness" as Matthean because it discloses Matthew's thought.[84] Scholars working on the synoptic problem have traditionally considered redactional all changes that one writer introduces into the text of a source. Even minor changes are important, and they have been admitted as evidence in proposed solutions. For example, proponents of the two-source theory compare the texts of Matthew and Luke with Mark and observe that Matthew and Luke frequently have a smoother style in the triple tradition passages. These subtle differences indicate that Matthew and Luke come later. When we extend the investigation to the Gospel of Thomas, we likewise need to consider all the changes one writer introduces into the text of another. If Matthew, for example, changes a Marcan or Q saying and the change shows up in Thomas, it indicates that Thomas depends on Matthew's gospel because the change did not enter the tradition of that saying until Matthew introduced it.[85]

I will treat the overlap texts in the order in which they appear in Mark's gospel with one exception. Mark has two texts that overlap the Q Scandal Saying (Q 17,1b-2). I will treat the second text (Mark 14,21) immediately after the first one (Mark 9,42). All other overlap texts will be treated in the Marcan order. I have grouped the overlap texts into eight chapters. Most of the groupings are natural. Chapter II treats the two texts that center on Jesus and John; Chapter III deals with the Beelzebul Controversy and the Unforgivable Sin that form a unit in Mark; and Chapter IV discusses the five overlap texts in the Parable Discourse. Chapter V treats the Mission Discourse and the Demand for a Sign. Although these two texts appear widely separated in Q and in Mark, I have drawn them together because they are the only other overlap texts in the first half of Mark. Chapter VI treats the three overlap texts in the Caesarea Philippi pericope and Chapter VII the four overlap texts in the Discipleship Discourse plus the related saying in Mark 14,21. Chapter VIII gathers together the five sayings that appear in Mark 10-12, and Chapter IX deals with the five sayings in the Eschatological Discourse. The final chapter of the book summarizes the results of the investigation and draws some implications for gospel studies.

---

84. J. H. SIEBER, *A Redactional Analysis of the Synoptic Gospels with Regard to the Question of the Sources of the Gospel according to Thomas* (unpublished doctoral dissertation), Claremont, CA: Claremont Graduate School, 1966, pp. 17-18, 260-263; ID., "The Gospel of Thomas and the New Testament," in *Gospel Origins and Christian Beginnings: FS James M. Robinson*, 1990, pp. 64-73, esp. p. 69.

85. See further B. DEHANDSCHUTTER, "Recent Research," pp. 2261-2262.

One final point. The discussion of the overlap texts began as a topic in source criticism. How are the two sources of the two-source theory related to one another? This question remains important, but we can now formulate it in different terms. In recent years Q studies have vigorously pursued the question of Q's genre, and increasingly scholars have identified Q as a gospel.[86] If Q should ultimately prove to be a gospel as I think it will, then the question how Mark and Q relate to each other shifts. Now instead of asking just about the relationship of sources, we ask how the first two Christian gospels relate to one another. The answer to this question will illuminate the development of the gospel genre as well as shed light on early Christian thinking about Jesus.[87]

86. On the genre of Q see J. M. ROBINSON, "LOGOI SOPHON: On the Gattung of Q," in J. M. ROBINSON and H. KOESTER, *Trajectories through Early Christianity*, Philadelphia: Fortress, 1971, pp. 71-113; ID., "The Sayings Gospel Q," in *The Four Gospels 1992: Festschrift Frans Neirynck*, 1992, 1. 361-388, esp. pp. 370-371; J. S. KLOPPENBORG, *The Formation of Q: Trajectories in Ancient Wisdom Collections* (Studies in Antiquity & Christianity), Philadelphia: Fortress, 1987, pp. 263-316; R. HORSLEY, "Logoi Propheton?: Reflections on the Genre of Q," in *The Future of Early Christianity: FS Helmut Koester*, Minneapolis: Fortress, 1991, pp. 195-209; A. D. JACOBSON, *The First Gospel: An Introduction to Q* (Foundations & Facets), Sonoma, CA: Polebridge, 1992, pp. 19-32.

87. In this study Q passages are referred to by their Lucan chapter and verse numbers. Thus Q 10,21-22 refers to the Q text that lies behind Matt 11,25-27 par. Luke 10,21-22.

Statistics for words and expressions that appear in the synoptic gospels and Acts are given by four figures. The four figures refer to the number of times the word or expression occurs in Matthew, Mark, Luke, and Acts–always in that order. Occasionally the figures are based on the author's own count, but the vast majority come from three sources: J. C. HAWKINS, *Horae Synopticae: Contributions to the Study of the Synoptic Problem*, Oxford: Clarendon, [2]1909; K. ALAND, *Vollständige Konkordanz zum griechischen Neuen Testament: Band II: Spezialübersichten*, Berlin/New York: de Gruyter, 1978; F. NEIRYNCK and F. VAN SEGBROECK with H. LECLERCQ, *New Testament Vocabulary: A Companion Volume to the Concordance* (BETL, 65), Leuven: University Press – Peeters, 1984.

II

JOHN AND JESUS

Mark and Q overlap right from the start. The opening verses of Mark introduce John and Jesus and spell out their relationship. Q also treats the relationship of John and Jesus extensively, and in two places Mark and Q overlap, Mark 1,2 (Q 7,27) and Mark 1,7-8 (Q 3,16-17).

§ 1. THE MESSENGER

Mark 1,2 (Matt 11,10 par. Luke 7,27)

After John sends his disciples to question Jesus in Q (Q 7,18-23), Jesus questions the crowd about John and then gives his own testimony to John (Q 7,24-28). Jesus' comment includes a double scripture quotation, the combination of Exod 23,20 and Mal 3,1.

Matt 11,10	Luke 7,27
οὗτός ἐστιν περὶ οὗ γέγραπται·	οὗτός ἐστιν περὶ οὗ γέγραπται·
ἰδοὺ ἐγὼ ἀποστέλλω τὸν ἄγγελόν μου	ἰδοὺ ἀποστέλλω τὸν ἄγγελόν μου
πρὸ προσώπου σου,	πρὸ προσώπου σου,
ὃς κατασκευάσει τὴν ὁδόν σου	ὃς κατασκευάσει τὴν ὁδόν σου
ἔμπροσθέν σου.	ἔμπροσθέν σου.

Matthew and Luke only differ in one word – Matthew expresses the subject ἐγώ and Luke does not. Matthew often introduces a redactional ἐγώ[1] whereas Luke at times omits expressed personal pronouns,[2] so at first glance it appears equally probable that Matthew added the pronoun or that Luke omitted it. However, Matthean and Lucan usage with ἀποστέλλω decides the issue. Matthew always expresses the subject ἐγώ with ἀποστέλλω (Matt 10,16; 11,10; 23,34). Luke at times omits

---

1. See Matt 5,22.28.32.34.39.44; 10,32 (diff. Luke 12,8).33 (diff. Luke 12,9); 16,18; 21,24 bis (diff. Mark 11,29); 23,34 (diff. Luke 11,49); 26,15 (diff. Mark 14,10); 28,20. See P. HOFFMANN, Studien zur Theologie der Logienquelle (NeutAbh, 8), Münster: Aschendorff, ³1982, p. 264 n. 102.
2. See Luke 6,36 (diff. Matt 5,48); 12,7 (diff. Matt 10,31); 20,37 (diff. Mark 12,26); 22,34 (diff. Mark 14,30). See H. J. CADBURY, The Style and Literary Method of Luke, Cambridge: Harvard University, 1920, pp. 191-192.

the pronoun with ἀποστέλλω (Luke 7,27; 10,3; compare also Luke 11,49; 22,35; Acts 7,34), but at other times he expresses it (Acts 26,17; compare also Acts 10,20; 22,21). Since Luke shows flexibility and Matthew does not, Luke probably reproduces his source Q accurately. Matthew added the pronoun to bring the quotation into line with his own usage and with the Septuagint.[3] We can now compare the Q text and Mark.

Q 7,27	Mark 1,2
οὗτός ἐστιν περὶ οὗ γέγραπται·	καθὼς γέγραπται
	ἐν τῷ Ἠσαΐα τῷ προφήτῃ·
ἰδοὺ ἀποστέλλω τὸν ἄγγελόν μου	ἰδοὺ ἀποστέλλω τὸν ἄγγελόν μου
πρὸ προσώπου σου	πρὸ προσώπου σου,
ὃς κατασκευάσει τὴν ὁδόν σου	ὃς κατασκευάσει τὴν ὁδόν σου· ...
ἔμπροσθέν σου.	

Laufen does not think that this passage has anything to contribute to the question of the relationship of Mark and Q because it is a scripture quotation.[4] However, as we shall see, nothing could be further from the truth. Precisely because it is a scripture quotation, the passage gives us an insight into the Q redaction and enables us to compare Mark and the redactional text of Q. The quotation combines two OT passages, and it is the only scripture quotation in Q which might reflect the Massoretic Text.[5] The first part of the quotation follows the first half of Exod 23,20 LXX exactly except that Q drops two words, καί and ἐγώ: καὶ ἰδοὺ ἐγὼ ἀποστέλλω τὸν ἄγγελόν μου πρὸ προσώπου σου, ἵνα φυλάξῃ σε ἐν τῇ ὁδῷ (Exod 23,20 LXX). The second part of the quotation adapts the second half of Mal 3,1 in a form that differs significantly from the Septuagint: ἰδοὺ ἐγὼ ἐξαποστέλλω τὸν ἄγγελόν μου, καὶ ἐπιβλέψεται ὁδὸν πρὸ προσώπου μου (Mal 3,1 LXX).[6] The second half of the Q quotation begins with the relative ὅς instead of the conjunction καί; it has the article and the personal pronoun σου with ὁδόν, κατασκευάσει for ἐπιβλέψεται, and ἔμπροσθέν σου for πρὸ προσώπου μου. Most of these changes assimilate the Malachi text to Exodus and adapt it to the context in Q. The relative improves the syntax following the Greek tendency to subordinate in more elegant prose.[7] The

---

3. The ἐγώ is expressed in Exod 23,20 LXX. See further S. SCHULZ, *Q*, p. 229.

4. R. LAUFEN, *Doppelüberlieferungen*, p. 83.

5. See the discussion in D. S. NEW, *Old Testament Quotations in the Synoptic Gospels, and the Two-Document Hypothesis* (SBL Septuagint and Cognate Studies Series, 37), Atlanta: Scholars Press, 1993, pp. 59-64.

6. Mal 4,5-6 (3,22-23 LXX) interprets the messenger in Mal 3,1 as Elijah.

7. BDF, § 458; C. F. D. MOULE, *An Idiom-Book of New Testament Greek*, Cambridge: University Press, ²1959, pp. 172-173.

article with ὁδόν and the substitution of ἔμπροσθεν for πρὸ προσώπου are stylistic variations demanded by the combination of the two texts. The redactor uses τὴν ὁδόν σου to balance τὸν ἄγγελόν μου and ἔμπροσθέν σου to avoid repeating πρὸ προσώπου σου.[8] The redactor switches verbs because the Septuagintal verb would not work in the context of John's Question. In Mal 3,1 the Septuagint translates the Massoretic Text's "and he will prepare the way before me" with καὶ ἐπιβλέψεται ὁδὸν πρὸ προσώπου μου ("and he will look attentatively upon the way before me"). The verb κατασκευάσει would appear to be closer to the Hebrew, but it is not an altogether obvious choice. Besides its occurrence in this overlap text, the verb occurs another eight times in the NT and thirty times in the Septuagint, but nowhere else with ὁδός or any similar word.[9] We should probably, though, not look to the Massoretic Text for the explanation of the unusual verb. Nowhere else does Q reflect the Hebrew text of the OT. All the other scripture quotations in Q depend on the Greek OT,[10] and in the present quotation the possible contact with the Hebrew text is confined to a single word, the verb κατασκευάσει. Rather than invoke the Hebrew text to account for a single word, we can better explain the verb as a free adaptation of the Greek text of the OT.[11]

The most important change in the quotation is the double use of the second person singular pronoun σοῦ. In the Exodus text God addresses Moses, so the σοῦ is natural, and in the Q context the pronoun just as naturally refers to Jesus. The Malachi text poses a problem because in it God speaks in the first person, referring to "my messenger" and "before me." The redactor can not take over the phrase "before me," but switches

---

8. Besides the present verse the word ἔμπροσθεν occurs another five times in Q (Q 10,21; 12,8*bis*.9*bis*).

9. J. C. HAWKINS, *Horae Synopticae*, p. 58. The use of κατασκευάζω in the sense of preparing a road is found in a fourth century B.C. Greek inscription. See J. H. MOULTON and G. MILLIGAN, *The Vocabulary of the Greek Testament Illustrated from the Papyri and Other Non-Literary Sources*, Grand Rapids, MI: Eerdmans, 1982, p. 332.

10. To see Q's reliance on the Greek OT compare Deut 8,3b LXX with Q 4,4; Psa 90,11-12 LXX with Q 4,10-11; Deut 6,16 LXX with Q 4,12; Deut 6,13a LXX with Q 4,8; Isa 61,1 LXX with Q 7,22; Isa 14,13-15 LXX with Q 10,15; Mic 7,6 LXX with Q 12,52-53; Dan 4,21 Theodotion with Q 13,19; Psa 6,9 LXX with Q 13,27; Psa 106,3 LXX with Q 13,29; Jer 22,5 LXX and Psa 117,26 LXX with Q 13,35; Gen 7,7.13 LXX with Q 17,27. See P. WERNLE, *Synoptische Frage*, pp. 115-116; S. E. JOHNSON, "The Biblical Quotations in Matthew," in *HTR* 36 (1943) 135-153, esp. pp. 144-148; A. W. ARGYLE, "The Accounts of the Temptations of Jesus in Relation to the Q Hypothesis," in *ExpT* 64 (1952-53) 382; ID., "Scriptural Quotations in Q Material," in *ExpT* 65 (1953-54) 285-286; K. STENDAHL, *The School of St. Matthew*, Lund: Gleerup, ²1968, pp. 88-94; S. SCHULZ, *Q*, pp. 27-28.

11. P. WERNLE, *Synoptische Frage*, pp. 115-116.

instead to "before you" to bring the Malachi quotation into line with the Exodus passage. The redactor adds a second σοῦ to modify τὴν ὁδόν so that τὴν ὁδόν σου balances τὸν ἄγγελόν μου.

Who combined these two texts? Could Q have derived the combined quotation from a collection of proof texts? We have no evidence that Q drew on a collection of proof texts, and the combined quotation fits perfectly into Q's understanding of John. Initially Q's view of John seems blurred, for two opposing views compete for attention. On the one hand Q praises John and sets him squarely on Jesus' side opposed to "this genera-tion."[12] On the other hand Q appears to have reservations about John, and Q clearly subordinates John to Jesus.[13] The double quotation in Q 7,27 both secures John's greatness and subordinates him to Jesus by assigning him a precise role – as Elijah he prepares the way for Jesus. The Q redactor com-bined the two texts to draw the two views of John together.

When we compare Mark and Q we note that they differ in the intro-ductory phrase, but with the exception of the final prepositional phrase they agree word for word in the double quotation itself. Mark's text continues with an additional quotation that differs only slightly from Isa 40,3 LXX.

Mark 1,3

φωνὴ βοῶντος ἐν τῇ ἐρήμῳ·
ἑτοιμάσατε τὴν ὁδὸν κυρίου,
εὐθείας ποιεῖτε τὰς τρίβους αὐτοῦ.

The only difference between Mark 1,3 and the Septuagint comes at the end of the quotation. For the Septuagint's τοῦ θεοῦ ἡμῶν Mark substi-tutes the pronoun αὐτοῦ to apply the quotation to Jesus.[14] In his introduc-tory verse (v. 2a) Mark erroneously ascribes the entire quotation to Isaiah.

When we compare Mark and Q in the double quotation they share, we notice striking agreement. The very close verbal agreement, including the use of κατασκευάσει, means that there must be some relationship between Mark and Q. Mark and Q could not have independently com-bined the two OT passages, one quotation following the Septuagint closely and the other introducing an expression unusual in the Greek Bible.[15] Although the two OT texts have obvious affinities that invite comparison, no Jewish precedent exists for the interpenetration of the

---

12. Q 3,7-9.16-17; 7,24-26.28a.31-35.

13. Q 7,23.28b; 16,16.

14. R. PESCH, *Markusevangelium*, 1. 77.

15. Mark and Q agree so closely in such an unusual quotation that a connection between them seems certain. See B. W. BACON, "Prologue of Mark," p. 94; ID., "Nature and Design of Q," p. 684; D. R. CATCHPOLE, "Beginning of Q," p. 214. Goulder tries to

two texts.[16] Either Mark derives from Q, or Q from Mark, or they both go back to a common ancestor. We should postulate a common ancestor only if we can find no other way to account for the differences between the texts. First we must determine whether one text is prior to the other.

Four considerations show that Mark is secondary to Q. First, the Q introductory clause, "This is the one of whom it is written," is more original than Mark's "As it is written in the prophet Isaiah." The Q clause is an identification formula, and it fits the context of the Q pericope where the question of John's identity has already been raised (Q 7,24-26). Mark's introductory clause, on the other hand, does not work as well, for it contains a factual error – the following quotation does not come exclusively from Isaiah. Second, Q's parallelism is probably original. The two objects – τὸν ἄγγελόν μου and τὴν ὁδόν σου – balance each other as do the two prepositional phrases – πρὸ προσώπου σου and ἔμπροσθέν σου. In comparison Mark's text appears truncated since it has only one prepositional phrase. Third, Q combines two quotations, but Mark's text links three OT passages. It is more probable that Mark expanded the quotation than that Q contracted it. Fourth, the Q context is more original than the Marcan context. We can see this most clearly in the pronoun σοῦ. As we have seen, in Exod 23,20 "you" refers to Moses. The Malachi quotation originally referred to Yahweh, but when the two quotations were combined, the redactor conformed the Malachi text to Exodus, replacing μοῦ with σοῦ in the prepositional phrase and adding another σοῦ to modify ὁδόν. The resulting text fits smoothly in Q. On Jesus' lips it is as if God were speaking to Jesus about John.[17] In Mark the pronoun σοῦ is not clear. Mark does not introduce a speaker at the beginning of the gospel, and the natural way to read v. 2 is to understand that the narrator is addressing the reader. However, this reading does not make sense since the text goes on to describe the work of John preparing the way for Jesus, so the reader can only understand the σοῦ as referring to Jesus, again as if God were talking to Jesus about John. In other words the reader is forced to read Mark 1,2 in the context the quotation appears in in Q. These four considerations show that Mark is secondary to Q.

get around Q by claiming that Matthew redacted Mark, and Luke copied Matthew, but Tuckett has shown that his arguments fail to establish his conclusion. See M. D. GOULDER, "On Putting Q to the Test," in *NTS* 24 (1977-78) 218-234, esp. pp. 224-225; C. M. TUCKETT, "On the Relationship between Matthew and Luke," in *NTS* 30 (1984) 130-142, esp. pp. 134-135.

16. D. R. CATCHPOLE, "Beginning of Q," p. 210.

17. J. P. BROWN, "Mark as Witness to an Edited Form of Q," pp. 42-43. See also P. HOFFMANN, *Studien*, pp. 218-219; J. SCHÜLING, *Studien*, pp. 70-71.

We can go further. Since the pronoun "you" is a redactional alteration
of the Malachi text to fit the context of Q, Mark's use of the quotation
with the altered pronoun proves that Mark knew redactional Q. Not only
is Mark secondary to Q, Mark depends on Q. The erroneous ascription
of the whole quotation to Isaiah confirms this conclusion. As we have
seen the combination of Exod 23,20 and Mal 3,1 is skillfully done. Mark
could not have combined the texts and been ignorant of their sources.
Attributing the quotation to Isaiah makes sense, though, if Mark found
the quotation in Q which identified it as scripture but did not specify the
exact place where it could be found.

Once we see that Mark derived the quotation from Q, Mark's redaction
makes sense. Mark introduces the quotation with "As it is written in the
prophet Isaiah."[18] Since we have seen that Mark is using Q, we can explain how the error in the introduction occurred. Q identified the quotation
as scripture, but did not specify where the quotation came from. Mark
took over the Q quotation, joined the additional quotation from Isaiah to
it, and then erroneously attributed the whole to Isaiah because he only
knew the origin of the last part of the combined quotation.[19] Furthermore,
the differences between Mark and Q stem from Marcan redaction. Mark
built his introduction out of his own καθώς,[20] Q's γέγραπται, and the
prepositional phrase referring to Isaiah.[21] He broke off the ending of the
Q quotation to make room for his additional quotation from Isa 40,3
LXX which links up with τὴν ὁδόν σου.[22]

18. The full form occurs only here in Mark, although a shorter form, "as is written,"
appears in Mark 9,13 and 14,21 (compare also Mark 7,6-7). For parallels to the longer
form see Luke 2,23; Acts 7,42; 13,33; 1 Cor 9,9; 14,21 (compare 4QFlor 1:15, 16). See
J. A. FITZMYER, "The Use of Explicit Old Testament Quotations in Qumran Literature
and in the New Testament" (1960-61), in ID., Essays on the Semitic Background, 1974,
pp. 3-58, esp. pp. 9-10.

19. For other examples of double quotations in Mark, see the quotation of Isa 56,7 and
Jer 7,11 in Mark 11,17 and the quotation of Psa 110,1 and Dan 7,13 in Mark 14,62. See
H. C. KEE, "The Function of Scriptural Quotations and Allusions in Mark 11-16," in
Jesus und Paulus: FS Werner Georg Kümmel, 1975, pp. 165-188, esp. pp. 175-179.

20. 3 8 17 11. Of Mark's eight cases, three have καθώς εἶπεν (Mark 11,6; 14,16;
16,7) and three καθώς γέγραπται (Mark 1,2; 9,13; 14,21). See J. LAMBRECHT, "Redaction and Theology," p. 275 n. 26; D. B. PEABODY, Mark as Composer (New Gospel Studies, 1) Macon, GA: Mercer University Press, 1987, p. 35.

21. Compare Mark's other reference to Isaiah: καλῶς ἐπροφήτευσεν Ἡσαΐας περὶ
ὑμῶν τῶν ὑποκριτῶν, ὡς γέγραπται (Mark 7,6).

22. In the double quotation Mark introduces a term "the way" that will play a key
role in his portrayal of discipleship (Mark 6,8; 8,27; 9,33.34; 10,17.32.46.52; 12,14). See
E. BEST, "Discipleship in Mark: Mark 8:22-10:52" (1970), in ID., Disciples and Discipleship: Studies in the Gospel according to Mark, Edinburgh: Clark, 1986, pp. 1-16, esp.
pp. 4-6.

Laufen seriously misjudged the importance of this first overlap text. It actually carries us very far since it shows that Mark knew redactional Q. The second overlap text extends the conclusions we have come to on the basis of the first.

§ 2. JOHN AND THE COMING ONE

Mark 1,7-8 (Matt 3,11-12 par. Luke 3,16-17)

Q and Mark also overlap in the saying on John and the Coming One. Can we expand the overlap even further? Jan Lambrecht argues from the minor agreements between Matt 3,1-6 and Luke 3,1-6 that Q contained a description of John like the one we find in Mark 1,2-6.[23] Michel Devisch has shown, however, that independent editing of Mark can explain the minor agreements without recourse to Q.[24] The investigation should center on the true overlap, the saying on John and the Coming One.

In John and the Coming One Q forges a complex statement about baptism, the Coming One, and judgment.[25]

23. Matthew and Luke agree against Mark in four ways. First, both set John's appearance in the desert before the Isaiah quotation. Second, both omit the Malachi quotation. Third, both follow John's coming immediately with his preaching (Matt 3,7-10; Luke 3,7-9). Fourth, they agree in writing πᾶσα ἡ περίχωρος τοῦ Ἰορδάνου (Matt 3,5; Luke 3,3). According to Lambrecht these four agreements taken together indicate that Matthew and Luke drew on a Q version of John's appearance in the desert. See J. LAMBRECHT, "John the Baptist and Jesus," p. 363. See also J. S. KLOPPENBORG, "City and Wasteland: Narrative World and the Beginning of the Sayings Gospel (Q)," in *Semeia* 52 (1990) 145-160, esp. pp. 149-151; D. R. CATCHPOLE, "Beginning of Q," pp. 216-218.

24. First, Matthew and Luke reverse Mark's order and place the quotation after John's appearance because they both have infancy narratives and they cannot introduce the quotation without a transition. Second, they both omit the Malachi quotation because they record it later (Matt 11,10 par. Luke 7,27) and they recognize that it doesn't fit the reference to Isaiah in Mark 1,2. Third, they both follow John's coming with his preaching because they independently found the most appropriate place in their Marcan source to introduce the Q material. Fourth, πᾶσα ἡ περίχωρος τοῦ Ἰορδάνου is a Septuagintal expression, and both Matthew and Luke elsewhere replace a Marcan χώρα with περίχωρος. For πᾶσα ἡ περίχωρος τοῦ Ἰορδάνου see Gen 13,10.11; 2 Chr 4,17. Matthew changes χώρα to περίχωρος in Matt 14,35 (diff. Mark 6,55). Luke alternates between χώρα and περίχωρος in the Gerasene Demoniac pericope (compare Luke 8,26 and Luke 8,37 with Mark 5,17). See M. DEVISCH, *De geschiedenis van de Quellehypothese: I. Inleiding; II. Van J. G. Eichhorn tot B. H. Streeter; III. De recente exegese* (unpublished doctoral dissertation), 3 vols.; Leuven: Katholieke Universiteit, 1975, 3. 402-421. See further F. NEIRYNCK, "The International Q Project," in *ETL* 69 (1993) 221-225, esp. p. 223.

25. A parallel appears in John 1,26-27. Other forms of the saying occur in John 1,15.30.31.33 and Acts 1,5; 11,16; 13,25; 19,4.

Matt 3,11-12	Luke 3,16-17
11 ἐγὼ μὲν ὑμᾶς βαπτίζω	16 ἐγὼ μὲν ὕδατι βαπτίζω
ἐν ὕδατι εἰς μετάνοιαν,	ὑμᾶς·
ὁ δὲ ὀπίσω μου ἐρχόμενος	ἔρχεται δὲ ὁ
ἰσχυρότερός μού ἐστιν,	ἰσχυρότερός μου,
οὗ οὐκ εἰμὶ ἱκανὸς	οὗ οὐκ εἰμὶ ἱκανὸς
τὰ ὑποδήματα βαστάσαι·	λῦσαι τὸν ἱμάντα
	τῶν ὑποδημάτων αὐτοῦ·
αὐτὸς ὑμᾶς βαπτίσει	αὐτὸς ὑμᾶς βαπτίσει
ἐν πνεύματι ἁγίῳ καὶ πυρί·	ἐν πνεύματι ἁγίῳ καὶ πυρί·
12 οὗ τὸ πτύον ἐν τῇ χειρὶ αὐτοῦ	17 οὗ τὸ πτύον ἐν τῇ χειρὶ αὐτοῦ
καὶ διακαθαριεῖ τὴν ἅλωνα αὐτοῦ	διακαθᾶραι τὴν ἅλωνα αὐτοῦ
καὶ συνάξει τὸν σῖτον	καὶ συναγαγεῖν τὸν σῖτον
αὐτοῦ εἰς τὴν ἀποθήκην,	εἰς τὴν ἀποθήκην αὐτοῦ,
τὸ δὲ ἄχυρον κατακαύσει	τὸ δὲ ἄχυρον κατακαύσει
πυρὶ ἀσβέστῳ.	πυρὶ ἀσβέστῳ.

In the first clause Matthew preserves the original position of ὑμᾶς as we can confirm by comparing its position in the αὐτός-clause where Matthew and Luke agree. The αὐτός-clause also shows that Q originally had the preposition ἐν before ὕδατι. Luke moved the object after the verb,[26] and he omitted the preposition ἐν.[27] Matthew added the phrase εἰς μετάνοιαν to Q. The phrase breaks the parallelism with the αὐτός-clause; Luke does not have the expression; and repentance reflects a Matthean theme. Matthew highlights the theme in summaries of John's and Jesus' preaching (Matt 3,2 and 4,17). Since Q also mentions the theme (Q 3,8), Matthew's addition brings together his own concern and the emphasis of Q.[28] He also draws John's baptism into line with his preaching.[29]

Matthew preserves the Q text of the following clause: ὁ δὲ ὀπίσω μου ἐρχόμενος ἰσχυρότερός μού ἐστιν. Q refers to the Coming One in two other key texts (Q 7,19; 13,35),[30] and the sentence structure of Matthew's clause reflects that of another Q passage: ὁ δὲ μικρότερος

26. See Luke 5,14 (diff. Mark 1,44); Luke 9,40 (diff. Mark 9,18); Luke 19,36 (diff. Mark 11,8); Luke 20,9 (diff. Mark 12,1); Luke 20,19 (diff. Mark 12,12); Luke 20,25 (diff. Mark 12,17); Luke 22,61 (diff. Mark 14,72); Luke 22,71 (diff. Mark 14,63). See H. J. CADBURY, Style and Literary Method, pp. 152-153.

27. Luke avoids ἐν in awkward expressions. See Luke 4,33 (diff. Mark 1,23); Luke 8,4 (diff. Mark 4,2); Luke 8,27 (diff. Mark 5,2); Luke 20,9 (diff. Mark 12,1). See H. J. CADBURY, Style and Literary Method, pp. 204-205. Luke always avoids ἐν with ὕδατι (compare especially Acts 11,16). See further C. F. D. MOULE, Idiom-Book, p. 77.

28. H. FLEDDERMANN, "John and the Coming One," p. 378.

29. P. HOFFMANN, Studien, p. 22.

30. The Coming One links widely separated blocks of Q material (Q 3,16-17; 7,19; 13,35). It is one of the overarching terms that unifies the entire document. See J. M. ROBINSON, "Sayings Gospel," pp. 362-366.

ἐν τῇ βασιλείᾳ τοῦ θεοῦ μείζων αὐτοῦ ἐστιν (Q 7,28).[31] Luke assimilates the Q text to Mark (ἔρχεται δὲ ὁ ἰσχυρότερός μου) because the Marcan form better suits his redactional purpose. In his introductory question Luke has the people wonder whether John is the Christ (Luke 3,15). Mark's text which states that the stronger one is coming better suits Luke's intention than the Q text which emphasizes the superiority of the coming one.[32] Luke undoubtedly knew the Matthean form as Acts 19,4 shows: εἰς τὸν ἐρχόμενον μετ' αὐτόν. Luke omitted the phrase ὀπίσω μου because he does not want to give the impression that Jesus is a disciple of John. Although the phrase designates a temporal succession in Q as it does in several Septuagintal passages, it suggested to Luke the spatial following that symbolized discipleship.[33]

Matthew and Luke agree in the beginning of the first οὗ-clause (οὗ οὐκ εἰμὶ ἱκανός), but they differ in the infinitive phrase. Several scholars prefer Matthew,[34] but Schürmann points out that Matthew simplifies the diction.[35] Instead of simplifying the diction, we can more accurately describe Matthew's procedure as simplifying the imagery. The same tendency surfaces in other passages as well. In the Salt Saying Luke probably preserves the complex Q image that describes the fate of the salt: οὔτε εἰς γῆν οὔτε εἰς κοπρίαν εὔθετόν ἐστιν, ἔξω βάλλουσιν αὐτό (Luke 14,35). Matthew simplifies the imagery with a less graphic expression: εἰς οὐδὲν ἰσχύει ἔτι εἰ μὴ βληθὲν ἔξω καταπατεῖσθαι ὑπὸ τῶν ἀνθρώπων (Matt 5,13).[36] In the Mission Discourse Matthew's ἀσπάσασθε αὐτήν (Matt 10,12) simplifies Q's πρῶτον λέγετε· εἰρήνη τῷ οἴκῳ τούτῳ (Q 10,5). We observe the same simplification in the Faith Saying. Matthew's μετάβα ἔνθεν ἐκεῖ (Matt 17,20) simplifies

---

31. John Kloppenborg ("City and Wasteland," p. 148) uses only part of Matthew's clause (ὁ δὲ ὀπίσω μου ἐρχόμενος) in his reconstruction. He claims that ἰσχυρότερός μου is Marcan redaction and cites John 1,27 as confirmation. But nothing in ἰσχυρότερός μου suggests Marcan redaction, and ἰσχυρότερός μού ἐστιν had to drop out when John added the clause μέσος ὑμῶν ἕστηκεν ὃν ὑμεῖς οὐκ οἴδατε. Furthermore, the stylistic and thematic parallel in Q 7,28 confirms Matthew's whole clause, not just the first half.

32. R. LAUFEN, *Doppelüberlieferungen*, pp. 94-95.

33. See 3 Kgdms 1,6.24; 2 Esdr 3,16.17; Eccl 10,14 and Dan 2,39; 7,6 (Theodotion). See V. TAYLOR, *Mark*, pp. 156-157; R. LAUFEN, *Doppelüberlieferungen*, pp. 113-114. For ὀπίσω in a spatial sense indicating discipleship, see Luke 9,23 and 14,27. In Acts 13,25 and 19,4 Luke substitutes μετά for ὀπίσω to avoid any suggestion that Jesus might be a disciple of John. See further H. FLEDDERMANN, "John and the Coming One," pp. 378-379.

34. P. HOFFMANN, *Studien*, p. 23; S. SCHULZ, *Q*, p. 368; R. LAUFEN, *Doppelüberlieferungen*, p. 95; U. LUZ, "Q 3-4," *SBL 1984 Seminar Papers*, pp. 375-376.

35. H. SCHÜRMANN, *Das Lukasevangelium: Erster Teil: Kommentar zu Kap. 1,1-9,50* (HTKNT, 3), Freiburg/Basel/Vienna: Herder, 1969, p. 173 n. 79.

36. S. SCHULZ, *Q*, p. 471; H. FLEDDERMANN, "Discipleship Discourse," p. 72 n. 75.

either Luke's ἐκριζώθητι καὶ φυτεύθητι ἐν τῇ θαλάσσῃ (Luke 17,6) or Mark's ἄρθητι καὶ βλήθητι εἰς τὴν θάλασσαν (Mark 11,23). Some stylistic features also show that Luke is original. The singular of the noun ἱμάς occurs only in this overlap text in the NT.[37] Luke's redundant αὐτοῦ reflects Semitic syntax.[38] The position of the αὐτοῦ at the end of the clause mirrors the αὐτοῦ at the end of the first three clauses in Q 3,17, indicating that Luke preserves the original Q text.

Matthew and Luke agree word for word in the αὐτός-clause.

In the second οὖ-clause Luke twice substitutes infinitives for Q's finite verbs, but Luke agrees with Matthew in the final future κατακαύσει. Matthew's verb διακαθαρίζω appears nowhere else in Greek literature.[39] It is original. Matthew shifts the final αὐτοῦ forward, because he allegorizes the wheat. In the parable of the Weeds among the Wheat (Matt 13,24-30.36-43) the wheat symbolizes the elect. Luke had no reason to delay the pronoun, so his position reflects the original Q position.[40]

We can now compare the Q text with Mark.

Q 3,16-17	Mark 1,7-8

16 ἐγὼ μὲν ὑμᾶς βαπτίζω
    ἐν ὕδατι,
    ὁ δὲ ὀπίσω μου ἐρχόμενος
    ἰσχυρότερός μού ἐστιν,
    οὗ οὐκ εἰμὶ ἱκανὸς
    λῦσαι τὸν ἱμάντα
    τῶν ὑποδημάτων αὐτοῦ·
	7 ἔρχεται ὁ ἰσχυρότερός μου
	    ὀπίσω μου,
	    οὗ οὐκ εἰμὶ ἱκανὸς
	    κύψας λῦσαι τὸν ἱμάντα
	    τῶν ὑποδημάτων αὐτοῦ.
	8 ἐγὼ ἐβάπτισα ὑμᾶς
	    ὕδατι,

αὐτὸς ὑμᾶς βαπτίσει
    ἐν πνεύματι ἁγίῳ καὶ πυρί·
17 οὗ τὸ πτύον ἐν τῇ χειρὶ αὐτοῦ
    καὶ διακαθαριεῖ τὴν ἅλωνα
    αὐτοῦ καὶ συνάξει τὸν σῖτον
    εἰς τὴν ἀποθήκην αὐτοῦ,
    τὸ δὲ ἄχυρον κατακαύσει
    πυρὶ ἀσβέστῳ.
	αὐτὸς δὲ βαπτίσει ὑμᾶς
	    πνεύματι ἁγίῳ.

Some scholars claim that πνεῦμα originally meant "wind" in the Q saying.[41] However, any attempt to follow this line of interpretation falters on gospel word usage and the adjective "holy." The synoptic writers use

---

37. For the plural, see Acts 22,25.
38. BDF, § 297.
39. W. D. Davies and D. C. Allison, *Matthew*, vol. 1, 1988, p. 318.
40. H. Fleddermann, "John and the Coming One," p. 380.
41. See, for example, E. Best, "Spirit-Baptism," in *NT* 4 (1960) 236-243; A. D. Jacobson, *First Gospel*, p. 84.

πνεῦμα almost one hundred and fifty times, and nowhere else does it mean "wind."[42] The three synoptic writers and Q consistently use ἄνεμος for "wind."[43] Furthermore, understanding πνεῦμα as "wind" means that the adjective "holy" must be a later addition.[44] The Q saying never referred to "wind." The saying does, though, show some signs of redactional reworking. The words πνεύματι ἁγίῳ καί appear to be an addition to the original form of the saying. The ἐγώ-clause has a simple ἐν ὕδατι, and since parallelism plays such a strong role in the saying, the αὐτός-clause probably originally contained just a contrasting ἐν πυρί. The second οὗ-clause confirms this conclusion for it develops the fire imagery, but not the reference to the Holy Spirit. We cannot determine with certainty when the additional words were added. They could have been added in the pre-Q tradition, or the Q redactor could be responsible. Two other Q texts refer to the Holy Spirit (Q 12,10) or the Spirit of God (Q 11,20). The first of these two texts (Q 12,10) is probably redactional,[45] so the Q redactor could have been responsible for interpolating πνεύματι ἁγίῳ καί between ἐν and πυρί.[46]

Both Laufen and Schüling treat the saying on John and the Coming One. Laufen does not compare Mark and Q in detail. Instead he discusses briefly whether the baptism saying and the saying about the stronger one were originally intertwined as in Q or separate as in Mark. He decides that they were originally separate. Then he tries to reconstruct a hypothetical ancestor of Mark and Q, an original form of the sayings that gave rise to the forms in Mark and Q. If the sayings are separate, then the αὐτός in the baptism saying won't work as a subject since it would have no antecedent. Laufen posits ὁ ἐρχόμενος as the original subject. He assumes further that there was no direct address, so the ὑμᾶς drops out. Finally, he assumes that "fire" was not part of the original saying. In the saying on the stronger one he prefers ἔρχεται as the original form. When the sayings were combined in the Q form the editor shifted ὁ ἐρχόμενος from the baptism saying to the saying about the stronger one.[47] The hypothetical ancestor of Q and Mark would look like this:

1. ἔρχεται (ὁ) ἰσχυρότερός (μου ὀπίσω μου), οὗ οὐκ εἰμὶ ἱκανὸς λῦσαι τὸν ἱμάντα τῶν ὑποδημάτων αὐτοῦ (or: ὑποδήματα βαστάσαι).

2. ἐγὼ βαπτίζω ἐν ὕδατι, ὁ δὲ ἐρχόμενος βαπτίσει ἐν πνεύματι (ἁγίῳ).[48]

42. Statistics on πνεῦμα: 19 23 36 70.
43. For Q's use of ἄνεμος, see Q 6,48.49; 7,24.
44. See P. HOFFMANN, *Studien*, p. 30.
45. See Chapter III below.
46. H. FLEDDERMANN, "John and the Coming One," p. 381.
47. R. LAUFEN, *Doppelüberlieferungen*, pp. 97-115.
48. *Ibid.*, p. 116.

Laufen, though, constructs a house of cards by piling hypothesis on top of hypothesis. When we compare Mark and Q to each other, Mark is really closer to Q than either Mark or Q is to Laufen's hypothetical ancestor. The only element of Mark not in Q is the participle κύψας.

Schüling's discussion leaves even more questions. Schüling also does not compare Mark and Q in detail. To establish the independence of Mark and Q he simply states that Mark would never have left out so much Q material if he had taken over the sayings in Mark 1,2 and Mark 1,7-8 from Q.[49] Since Mark does not record a parallel to Q 3,17, Schüling maintains that Q 3,16 was originally independent. The independent saying initially contained no reference to a baptism with fire which was only added when the saying was joined to Q 3,7-9.17. Besides eliminating "fire" as a later addition, Schüling also drops the saying on the stronger one as a later Christian interpretation. He ends up with an original, "I baptize you with water, you will be baptized with the Holy Spirit." Schüling finds confirmation for his original form in Acts 1,5; 11,16.[50] We cannot use Mark, though, as a control to Q without first establishing the independence of Mark with stronger arguments than the general one that Mark would never have left out so much material if he had access to Q. A more detailed comparison of the two texts yields different results.

When we compare Mark and Q, several features show that Mark is secondary to Q. First, Mark's finite verb ἔρχεται anticipates Jesus' coming in Mark 1,9, and the aorist ἐβάπτισα looks back on the work of John in Mark 1,4-5. Both expressions are secondary adaptations of the saying to the historicizing gospel genre. Q's participle ἐρχόμενος and present verb βαπτίζω are more original. Second, the Q text refers to baptism in the Holy Spirit and in fire, but Mark's text only mentions baptism in the Holy Spirit. Mark thus emphasizes Christian spirit baptism more strongly than Q because the reference to the baptism in fire drops out. This Christian emphasis shows that Mark is secondary to the Q saying. Third, the Q saying emphasizes the coming judgment as well as the contrast between John and Jesus. Mark does not mention the judgment, and his separate sentences concentrate the sayings more emphatically on Jesus. The christological concentration is a further sign that Mark is secondary.[51] Fourth, Q reflects Semitic idiom with the preposition ἐν.

---

49. J. SCHÜLING, *Studien*, p. 58.

50. *Ibid.*, pp. 59-65.

51. M. GOGUEL, *Introduction*, pp. 257-259; R. PESCH, "Anfang des Evangeliums Jesu Christi: Eine Studie zum Prolog des Markusevangeliums (Mk 1,1-15)," in *Die Zeit Jesu: FS Heinrich Schlier*, 1970, pp. 108-144, esp. p. 121.

Mark's instrumental datives show a more refined Greek. Fifth, the reference to the Holy Spirit is a redactional addition to the original saying. It disturbs the parallelism between ἐν ὕδατι and ἐν πυρί, and the fire symbolism alone is developed in the second οὗ-clause. We can mark three stages in the development of the saying. Originally the saying did not mention the Spirit; it contrasted baptism in water with baptism in fire. In a second stage, reflected in Q, the reference to the Holy Spirit was added to make the saying more explicitly Christian. In the third stage, reflected in Mark, the spirit baptism has crowded out the fire baptism which now appeared superfluous. Mark reflects the latest stage in the development of the saying. These arguments prove that Mark is secondary to Q.[52]

Mark may show knowledge of redactional Q. It is probable, but not certain, that the Q redactor added the reference to the Holy Spirit. The other references to the Spirit in Q also relate the Spirit closely to the inbreaking of the kingdom and the life of the Christian (Q 11,20; 12,10). In other words, Q presents a coherent picture of the Spirit. If the reference to the Holy Spirit stems from the Q redactor, then Mark shows knowledge of the Q redaction.

If we start with the Q text, we can explain Mark's text. Mark resolves Q's carefully intertwined sentences into two separate sentences. He wants to begin immediately with Jesus' story so he reduced John to a forerunner. John has no independent message and no independent mission in Mark. In keeping with this view of John, Mark wants John's first words to be not about his own baptism but about the coming of Jesus. Mark draws the middle sentence forward, turning Q's participle into a finite verb ἔρχεται that announces the coming of Jesus. In the process Mark takes over the first οὗ-clause from Q, but he adds a participle κύψας to heighten the slave imagery.[53] Mark then draws the two halves of the baptism sentence together in a way that strongly contrasts John and Jesus. Mark changes Q's present βαπτίζω to an aorist ἐβάπτισα because this verse (Mark 1,8) signals a turning point. The baptist belongs to the past. From this point on he only functions as the one who baptized Jesus (Mark 1,9-11). After the baptism Mark always refers to him in the past (Mark 6,14-29; 9,11-13; 11,27-33). Mark moves both objects after

52. H. FLEDDERMANN, "John and the Coming One," pp. 382-383.
53. Such redundant participles are common in Mark. See Mark 1,35; 2,14; 4,39; 7,24; 8,28; 9,5; 10,1.24.51; 11,14; 12,26.35; 14,48; 15,12. The closest parallel is Mark's redundant use of ἀναστάς (Mark 1,35; 2,14; 7,24; 10,1). See V. TAYLOR, *Mark*, p. 63; E. J. PRYKE, *Redactional Style in the Marcan Gospel: A Study of Syntax and Vocabulary as Guides to Redaction in Mark* (SNTS MS, 33), Cambridge: University Press, 1978, pp. 99-103.

the verb and he twice turns Q's prepositional phrases into instrumental datives for stylistic reasons. The fire baptism and the second οὗ-clause drop out because Mark intends to define Jesus and his mission in three short scenes that describe his baptism (Mark 1,9-11), his temptation (Mark 1,12-13), and his preaching (Mark 1,14-15).[54] So not only is Mark secondary to Q; Mark's text makes perfect sense as a redaction of the Q saying.[55]

John also has a parallel to the saying in John 1,26-27:

26   ἐγὼ βαπτίζω ἐν ὕδατι·
     μέσος ὑμῶν ἔστηκεν ὃν ὑμεῖς οὐκ οἴδατε,
27   ὁ ὀπίσω μου ἐρχόμενος,
     οὗ οὐκ εἰμὶ ἄξιος ἵνα λύσω αὐτοῦ τὸν ἱμάντα τοῦ ὑποδήματος.

According to some scholars John preserves an independent version of the saying.[56] However, when we allow for John's redaction, John's saying reflects the synoptic saying.[57] John does not refer to the "stronger" one because he has inserted a new clause after the initial baptism statement – "among you stands one you do not know." The expressions μέσος ὑμῶν ἔστηκεν, ὃν ὑμεῖς οὐκ οἴδατε, and ἵνα all carry Johannine credentials.[58] By dropping ἰσχυρότερός μού ἐστιν John sets ὁ ὀπίσω μου ἐρχόμενος in apposition to the subject of the inserted clause. John has nothing corresponding to the judgment clause (Matt 3,12 par. Luke 3,17). Instead of referring to Jesus as judge, John twice has the Baptist state that the one coming after him was "before him" (John 1,15.30). For John Jesus is not the coming judge but the preexistent one.[59] John's saying resembles the reconstructed Q form more closely than any other. In the ἐγώ-clause John agrees with Matthew and Q against Mark and Luke in using ἐν. In v. 27

54. In eliminating the fire baptism and the second οὗ-clause Mark alters the threatening tone that dominates the Q saying. See J. S. KLOPPENBORG, *Formation of Q*, pp. 106-107.

55. H. FLEDDERMANN, "John and the Coming One," pp. 383-384.

56. P. GARDNER-SMITH, *Saint John and the Synoptic Gospels*, Cambridge: University Press, 1938, pp. 3-4, 10; R. E. BROWN, *The Gospel according to John* (AB, 29), vol. 1, 1966, p. 52.

57. On the relationship of John and the synoptics see F. NEIRYNCK, "John and the Synoptics" (1977), in ID., *Evangelica*, 1982, pp. 365-400; ID., "John and the Synoptics: 1975-1990," in A. DENAUX (ed.), *John and the Synoptics*, 1992, pp. 3-62.

58. For μέσος ὑμῶν ἔστηκεν compare ἔστη εἰς τὸ μέσον in John 20,19.26; for ὃν ὑμεῖς οὐκ οἴδατε see John 7,28 (compare also John 4,32). John uses ἵνα 145 times. The clause ὃν ὑμεῖς οὐκ οἴδατε occurs in the list of Johannine expressions in F. NEIRYNCK with J. DELOBEL, T. SNOY, G. VAN BELLE, F. VAN SEGBROECK, *Jean et les Synoptiques: Examen critique de l'exégèse de M.-É. Boismard* (BETL, 49), Leuven: University Press, 1979, p. 59 (no. 276).

59. R. SCHNACKENBURG, "Tradition und Interpretation im Spruchgut des Johannesevangeliums," in *Begegnung mit dem Wort: FS Heinrich Zimmermann*, 1980, pp. 141-159, esp. pp. 143-144.

John again agrees with Matthew and Q against Mark and Luke in using the participle ἐρχόμενος instead of the finite verb. John parts company with Matthew just where Matthew abandons Q, in the phrase about loosening the sandal strap. John agrees with Acts 13,25 in substituting ἄξιος for ἱκανός and in using the singular "sandal." Dependence on the synoptics could explain John's saying, but his saying makes most sense if he also had access to Q.

With the two texts on John and Jesus, we have just begun to investigate the overlap texts, but the study has already produced significant findings. In both texts multiple arguments demonstrated that Mark lies downstream from Q in the development of the tradition. Furthermore, in the first text Mark certainly shows knowledge of redactional Q. The pronoun "you" that appears in Mark entered the tradition when the Q redactor assimilated the Malachi quotation to Exodus to fit the context of John's Question. Mark probably reflects redactional Q in the second text as well although the evidence is not as clear as in the first saying. In both overlap texts the differences between Mark and Q result from Marcan redaction. We do not need a third factor like the oral tradition to account for them. The evidence shows that Mark knew and used Q.

also common;[8] and Matthew combines the two expressions four times.[9] The noun ἄνθρωπος is part of Matthew's characteristic vocabulary.[10] The adjective κωφός provides the only exact contact with Luke 11,14.[11]

Matt 12,22 is also mainly redactional.[12] Again we find προσφέρω and δαιμονίζομαι. Matthew uses τότε very frequently,[13] and τυφλός[14] and θεραπεύω[15] are both Matthean. Mark 3,20 possibly suggested the construction using ὥστε with the infinitive, although the conjunction is common in Matthew.[16] Matthew needs the infinitive βλέπειν after his redactional τυφλός, and its position in second place also shows that Matthew added it. The adjective κωφός and the verb λαλέω come from Q (compare Luke 11,14).

When we turn to Luke 11,14 we also find signs of redactional activity, but Matt 9,33 agrees closely with Luke 11,14 and we can recover the Q exorcism account with relative ease from Luke's text.[17] Luke's paratactic καί is probably original but not the periphrastic construction. If the Q pericope began with καί, then we can explain both the δέ in Matt 9,32 and the τότε in Matt 12,22, for Matthew makes both substitutions frequently.[18] The periphrastic with the imperfect of εἰμί is very common in Luke.[19]

---

8. 7 4 1 0. It is redactional at Matt 4,24; 8,28.33; 9,32; 12,22; 15,22. See R. Laufen, *Doppelüberlieferungen*, pp. 127, 428 n. 19; W. D. Davies and D. C. Allison, *Matthew*, 1. 418.

9. Matt 4,24; 8,16; 9,32; 12,22. See A. Fuchs, *Entwicklung der Beelzebulkontroverse*, pp. 123-124.

10. 115 56 95 46. U. Luz, *Das Evangelium nach Matthäus: 1. Teilband: Mt 1-7* (EKK NT, 1), Zürich/Einsiedeln/Cologne: Benziger – Neukirchen-Vluyn: Neukirchener Verlag, 1985, p. 36; ET: *Matthew 1-7: A Commentary*, trans. W. C. Linss, Minneapolis: Augsburg, 1989, pp. 54-55.

11. Compare also δαιμονιζόμενον (Matt 9,32) with δαιμόνιον (Luke 11,14).

12. The verse resembles in some ways the summary in Matt 15,30-31. See W. D. Davies and D. C. Allison, *Matthew*, 2. 334.

13. 90 6 15 21.

14. 17 5 8 1. U. Luz, *Evangelium nach Matthäus*, p. 52; ET: *Matthew 1-7*, p. 69.

15. 16 5 14 5. The verb is redactional at Matt 4,23.24; 8,7; 9,35; 10,1; 12,22; 14,14; 15,30; 17,16.18; 19,2; 21,14. See R. Laufen, *Doppelüberlieferungen*, pp. 127, 428 n. 18.

16. Statistics on ὥστε: 15 13 4 8. Matthew introduces ὥστε in Matt 8,28; 10,1; 12,12; 13,54; 15,31.33; 24,24; 27,1.

17. The longer reading in Luke 11,14 καὶ αὐτὸ ἦν (A^c C K W X Δ Θ Π Ψ f^13 *et al.*) should be rejected. The shorter reading is much more strongly attested (P^45 P^75 ℵ A* B L f^1 *et al.*). See I. H. Marshall, *The Gospel of Luke: A Commentary on the Greek Text* (New International Greek Testament Commentary), Exeter: Paternoster / Grand Rapids, MI: Eerdmans, 1978, p. 472.

18. For Matthew's substitution of δέ and τότε for καί, see A. H. McNeile, "Τότε in St. Matthew," in *ExpT* 12 (1910-11) 127-128; F. Neirynck, *Minor Agreements of Matthew and Luke*, pp. 203-207.

19. Luke uses the periphrastic with the imperfect in Luke 1,7.10.21.22; 2,26.33.51; 3,23; 4,16.17.20.31.38.44; 5,1.16.17ter.18.29; 6,12; 8,2.32.40; 9,32.45.53; 11,14; 13,10. 11; 14,1; 15,1.24; 18,34; 19,47; 21,37; 23,8.19.51.53.55; 24,13.32; Acts 1,10.13.14.17;

Since the rest of the verse unfolds in the aorist, we can reasonably re-construct the beginning with the aorist as well, so the Q pericope began with καὶ ἐξέβαλεν δαιμόνιον κωφόν. In the second half of the verse Luke introduced ἐγένετο δέ,[20] but the rest agrees closely with Matt 9,33. After a genitive absolute construction Matthew and Luke agree word for word: ἐλάλησεν ὁ κωφὸς καὶ ἐθαύμασαν οἱ ὄχλοι. Matthew preserves the Q genitive absolute καὶ ἐκβληθέντος τοῦ δαιμονίου. Luke sacrificed καί to his ἐγένετο δέ. He also switched the order of the noun and participle, moving the noun forward for emphasis. At first glance, it might appear that Matthew introduced ἐκβάλλω because he has just used ἐξέρχομαι for the crowds in Matt 9,32. Furthermore, Q uses ἐξέρχομαι twice for the departed spirit in Q 11,24-26. However, Luke frequently uses ἐξέρχομαι in accounts of exorcisms;[21] and Q uses ἐκβάλλω in formulating the charge that Jesus casts out demons by Beelzebul (Q 11,15), so Matthew's ἐκβληθέντος is original. After the genitive absolute, Q simply stated that the crowds were amazed. Matthew furnished two expressions of amazement: "Never has anything like this appeared in Israel" (Matt 9,33) and "Isn't this the Son of David?" (Matt 12,23). Both are redactional since Luke records nothing similar and the expressions reflect Matthean theology.[22]

2,2.5.42; 4,31; 8,1.13.16.28; 9,9.28.33; 10,24.30; 11,5; 12,5.6.12.20; 13,48; 14,7.26; 16, 9.12; 18,7.25; 19,32; 20,8.13; 21,3.29; 22,19.20.29. See A. FUCHS, *Entwicklung der Beelze-bulkontroverse*, pp. 126-127. On the periphrastic construction see J. C. HAWKINS, *Horae Syn-opticae*, p. 24; J. SCHMID, *Matthäus und Lukas: Eine Untersuchung des Verhältnisses ihrer Evangelien* (Biblische Studien, 23/2-4), Freiburg: Herder, 1930, pp. 40-41; J. LAMBRECHT, *Marcus Interpretator*, p. 36 n. 67; E. HAENCHEN, *Die Apostelgeschichte* (Kritisch-exege-tischer Kommentar über das Neue Testament, 3), Göttingen: Vandenhoeck & Ruprecht, [15]1968, pp. 116-117 n. 7; ET: *The Acts of the Apostles: A Commentary*, trans. R. McL. Wil-son, Philadelphia: Westminster, 1971, p. 149 n. 7; J. A. FITZMYER, *The Gospel according to Luke* (AB 28, 28A), 2 vols., Garden City, NY: Doubleday, 1981, 1985, 1. 122-123.

20. For ἐγένετο δέ see Luke 1,8; 2,1.6; 3,21; 5,1; 6,1.6.12; 8,22; 9,28.37.51; 11,14.27; 16,22; 18,35; 22,24; 23,12; Acts 4,5; 5,7; 8,1.8; 9,19.32.37.43; 10,10; 11,26; 14,1; 15,39; 16,16; 19,1.23; 22,6.17; 23,9; 28,8.17. See J. JEREMIAS, *Die Sprache des Lukasevangeliums: Redaktion und Tradition im Nicht-Markusstoff des dritten Evange-liums* (Kritisch-exegetischer Kommentar über das Neue Testament), Göttingen: Vanden-hoeck & Ruprecht, 1980, p. 199; J. A. FITZMYER, *Luke*, 1. 119; F. NEIRYNCK, "Le texte des Actes des Apôtres et les caractéristiques stylistiques lucaniennes" (1985), in ID., *Evangelica II*, 1991, pp. 243-278, esp. p. 258.

21. See Luke 4,36; 8,35.38 where he introduces ἐξέρχομαι into Mark. In Luke 4,41 he substitutes an expression with ἐξέρχομαι for one with ἐκβάλλω (compare Mark 1,34). Compare also Acts 8,7; 16,18. See further, J. LAMBRECHT, *Marcus Interpretator*, pp. 33-34 n. 47; F. NEIRYNCK, "Texte des Actes," p. 260.

22. Matthew uses the clause "Never has anything like this appeared in Israel" (Matt 9,33) to conclude the miracle section (Matt 8,1-9,34). The title "Son of David" appears throughout Matthew's gospel (Matt 1,1; 9,27; 12,23; 15,22; 20,30.31; 21,9.15; compare also Matt 22,42.43.45). See A. FUCHS, *Entwicklung der Beelzebulkontroverse*, pp. 132-143, 152-157; R. LAUFEN, *Doppelüberlieferungen*, pp. 126, 427-428 n. 10.

Luke 11,15 substantially preserves the Q version of the charge against Jesus. Luke only added the phrase ἐξ αὐτῶν;[23] τινές, though, comes from Q. In v. 16 Luke uses ἕτεροι to designate those who demand a sign. The pair τινὲς ... ἕτεροι is the plural form of the coordinated pair εἷς ... ἕτερος that crops up from time to time in Q.[24] Except for ἐξ αὐτῶν every detail of Luke 11,15 is confirmed either by Matt 9,34 or Matt 12,24, although both verses show signs of Matthean reworking. Matthew twice redactionally identifies the adversaries as Pharisees (Matt 9,34; 12,24).[25] Matt 12,24 recasts the charge in a sentence that uses a οὗτος οὐκ ... εἰ μή ... construction. This construction picks up the οὗτος from Matt 12,23 (μήτι οὗτός ἐστιν ὁ υἱὸς Δαυίδ;) and uses an οὐκ ... εἰ μή construction that appears elsewhere in Matthew.[26] Matt 9,34 formulates the charge in a way that is similar to Luke 11,15 except that it does not name the prince of demons. However, Matt 12,24 agrees with Luke 11,15 in identifying the figure as Beelzebul. Matthew only differs in the position of the article. In Q 11,19 Matthew and Luke agree in using the name without the article. When Matthew changed the construction in Matt 12,24, he moved the article forward to produce a more compact prepositional phrase. In Q the article before ἄρχοντι served to identify Beelzebul to an audience who might not know who he was.

Neither Matthew nor Luke show any Marcan influence in the introductory exorcism or in the charge against Jesus.[27] Both edit Q.

Q 11,14-15

14 καὶ ἐξέβαλεν δαιμόνιον κωφόν·
  καὶ ἐκβληθέντος τοῦ δαιμονίου ἐλάλησεν ὁ κωφὸς
  καὶ ἐθαύμασαν οἱ ὄχλοι.
15 τινὲς δὲ εἶπον·
  ἐν Βεελζεβοὺλ τῷ ἄρχοντι τῶν δαιμονίων ἐκβάλλει τὰ δαιμόνια.

---

23. Compare Luke 11,5.11; 12,6; 14,28; 15,4a.4b; 17,7; 22,23.50; 24,13.22; Acts 6,3; 11,20.28; 15,2.22.24; 17,4.12; 23,21. See J. DUPONT, "Renoncer à tous ses biens (Lc 14,33)" (1971), in ID., *Études sur les Évangiles synoptiques*, 1985, 2. 1076-1097, esp. p. 1084 n. 29; I. H. MARSHALL, *Luke*, p. 472.

24. Q 9,57-60; 16,13; compare also Q 17,34-35. See H. T. FLEDDERMANN, "The Demands of Discipleship: Matt 8,19-22 par. Luke 9,57-62," in *The Four Gospels 1992: Festschrift Frans Neirynck*, 1992, 1. 541-561, esp. p. 543.

25. Compare Matt 3,7; 22,34 where Matthew introduces the Pharisees into his sources. See A. FUCHS, *Entwicklung der Beelzebulkontroverse*, pp. 158-159.

26. See Matt 5,13 (diff. Luke 14,35); Matt 14,17 (diff. Mark 6,38). See J. LAMBRECHT, *Marcus Interpretator*, p. 34.

27. The only possible exception is Matthew's ὥστε with the infinitive in Matt 12,22 (compare Mark 3,20).

In Q Jesus answers the charge with a logical refutation that unfolds in three parts.[28] The first part deals with the inner contradiction in Beelzebul being divided against himself.

<table>
<tr><td align="center">Matt 12,25-26</td><td align="center">Luke 11,17-18</td></tr>
<tr><td>

25 εἰδὼς δὲ
    τὰς ἐνθυμήσεις αὐτῶν
    εἶπεν αὐτοῖς·
    πᾶσα βασιλεία μερισθεῖσα
    καθ᾽ ἑαυτῆς
    ἐρημοῦται καὶ πᾶσα
    πόλις ἢ οἰκία μερισθεῖσα
    καθ᾽ ἑαυτῆς οὐ σταθήσεται.
26 καὶ εἰ ὁ σατανᾶς
    τὸν σατανᾶν ἐκβάλλει,
    ἐφ᾽ ἑαυτὸν ἐμερίσθη·
    πῶς οὖν σταθήσεται
    ἡ βασιλεία αὐτοῦ;

</td><td>

17 αὐτὸς δὲ εἰδὼς
    αὐτῶν τὰ διανοήματα
    εἶπεν αὐτοῖς·
    πᾶσα βασιλεία ἐφ᾽ ἑαυτὴν
    διαμερισθεῖσα
    ἐρημοῦται
    καὶ οἶκος ἐπὶ οἶκον πίπτει.

18 εἰ δὲ καὶ ὁ σατανᾶς

    ἐφ᾽ ἑαυτὸν διεμερίσθη,
    πῶς σταθήσεται
    ἡ βασιλεία αὐτοῦ;
    ὅτι λέγετε ἐν Βεελζεβοὺλ
    ἐκβάλλειν με τὰ δαιμόνια.

</td></tr>
</table>

Matthew and Luke agree closely in the transitional phrase, "But knowing their thoughts, he said to them…" (Matt 12,25a par. Luke 11,17a). Matthew has seven Greek words and Luke eight, and they have five words in common. Furthermore, the differences between them seem fairly easy to resolve. For example, Luke's αὐτός is redactional.[29] Luke's διανοήματα, a NT *hapax legomenon*, appears more original than Matthew's ἐνθυμήσεις. Matthew introduces τὰς ἐνθυμήσεις in Matt 9,4 in his redaction of Mark 2,8, and he also uses the verb ἐνθυμέομαι twice (Matt 1,20; 9,4). Luke uses the noun in Acts 17,29 so he had no reason to change it.[30] An underlying Q text seems inevitable, and its reconstruction presents little problem.[31] Despite the very close agreement between Matthew and Luke, Frans Neirynck questions whether the transitional verse stood in Q. Matthew and Luke could have produced the agreement through independent editing of Mark 3,23a: καὶ προσκαλεσάμενος

---

28. J. Lambrecht (*Marcus Interpretator*, p. 50) calls Q 11,17-20 the "Logical Refutation." The title appropriately describes this section of the discourse.

29. The combination αὐτὸς δέ is Lucan. See J. LAMBRECHT, *Marcus Interpretator*, p. 39 n. 78; H. J. CADBURY, *Style and Literary Method*, pp. 150, 193. Luke needed αὐτός after inserting v. 16. See S. SCHULZ, *Q*, p. 205.

30. See J. LAMBRECHT, *Marcus Interpretator*, p. 39 n. 80; R. LAUFEN, *Doppelüberlieferungen*, p. 128.

31. The most difficult decision concerns the position of αὐτῶν. Does Matthew move it to the post-position or does Luke anticipate it? See the discussion below.

αὐτοὺς ἐν παραβολαῖς ἔλεγεν αὐτοῖς.³² According to Neirynck Mark's expression fits awkwardly in the context of a controversy so Matthew replaced it with an expression which he used earlier (Matt 9,4) that better suits the controversy form.³³ For Neirynck a different line of thought led Luke to make almost the same change as Matthew. Luke inserted v. 16 (ἕτεροι δὲ πειράζοντες σημεῖον ἐξ οὐρανοῦ ἐζήτουν παρ᾽ αὐτοῦ) in the Beelzebul Controversy in order to create a complex introduction for Luke 11,14-36. The use of πειράζοντες suggested the theme of "knowing their thoughts" from Mark 12,15 (ὁ δὲ εἰδὼς αὐτῶν τὴν ὑπόκρισιν εἶπεν αὐτοῖς· τί με πειράζετε;) so Luke introduced the theme in v. 17a.³⁴

According to the scenario sketched by Neirynck, Matthew and Luke must make connections between far-flung Marcan texts in order to eliminate an expression, προσκαλεσάμενος, that they don't want to take over from Mark. That one might do it is possible; that both would go through different lines of reasoning and end up at almost the same result seems less likely. Furthermore, Neirynck's position means that Matthew and Luke have independently of one another substituted the participle εἰδώς for Mark's προσκαλεσάμενος. How plausible is this substitution? In the Beelzebul Controversy εἰδώς is awkward because there isn't any reference to the adversaries' commenting "in their hearts."³⁵ Mark's participle προσκαλεσάμενος actually would work better. Only some of the crowd (τινές) voiced the charge against Jesus, and προσκαλεσάμενος would work well to summon Jesus' accusers to hear his defense. Why would Matthew and Luke both eliminate an adequate expression and replace it with a difficult one? Elsewhere they use the aorist participle of προσκαλέομαι freely.³⁶

Rather than editing Mark, Matthew and Luke depend on a Q transitional verse that included εἰδώς, δέ, a plural object, αὐτῶν, and εἶπεν αὐτοῖς. We saw above that Luke added αὐτός, but he preserved the Q object διανοήματα. We need only resolve the position of αὐτῶν. Most probably Luke moved αὐτῶν to the pre-position as he does elsewhere.³⁷

32. F. NEIRYNCK, "Mt 12,25a / Lc 11,17a et la rédaction des évangiles" (1986), in ID., *Evangelica II*, 1991, pp. 481-492.
33. *Ibid.*, pp. 486-487.
34. *Ibid.*, pp. 487-490.
35. Contrast Mark 2,6.8.
36. Matt 10,1; 15,10.32; 18,2.32; 20,25; Luke 7,18; 15,26; 16,5; Acts 5,40; 6,2; 13,7; 23,17.18.23.
37. Compare Luke 19,35 diff. Mark 11,7 (αὐτῶν τὰ ἱμάτια) and Luke 24,31 (αὐτῶν δὲ διηνοίχθησαν οἱ ὀφθαλμοί), and Luke 24,45 (αὐτῶν τὸν νοῦν). See F. NEIRYNCK, "Mt 12,25a / Lc 11,17a," pp. 490-492.

In Q 11,17bc Matthew's simple verb μερίζω is to be preferred to Luke's compound.[38] Luke's ἐφ᾽ ἑαυτήν is primary. Matthew has a preference for κατά, but even he uses ἐπί in Matt 12,26, thus confirming it as the Q preposition in this passage.[39] Although Luke has the original wording of the prepositional phrase, Matthew preserves the original position. Luke moved it forward for emphasis.[40] It is difficult to choose between Matthew's "and every city or house divided against itself will not stand" and Luke's "and house falls against house." Most likely Luke reflects Q and Matthew has taken up Mark 3,25 and expanded it with the addition of "city" thus creating an anticlimax – "kingdom," "city," "house."[41] Three facts support Lucan originality. First, in the application only the term "kingdom" is taken up by both Matthew (Matt 12,26) and Luke (Luke 11,18). Second, in the Beelzebul Controversy Matthew and Mark use "house" with two different meanings – "building" and "family." Luke uses it only in the sense of "building," first literally in v. 17, then figuratively in v. 24.[42] In v. 17 Luke presents a consistent picture of a civil war, culminating in the collapse of house against house. If Luke had found a section in Q on the divided house or "family," he would not have omitted it as he frequently uses "house" in the sense of "family."[43] Third, Luke's imagery and vocabulary reflect Q. Q uses the image of a collapsing house in Q 6,49, and οἶκος, πίπτω, and ἐπί are all Q words.[44]

Luke 11,18a is substantially Q. Luke introduced only minor changes. He substituted εἰ δὲ καί for Q's καὶ εἰ (Matt 12,26a),[45] and he again changed a simple verb into a compound. Matthew's ὁ σατανᾶς τὸν

---

38. Matthew uses the compound διαμερίζω in Matt 27,35, taking it over from Mark 15,24 (compare Psa 21,19 LXX). See S. SCHULZ, *Q*, p. 205.

39. Compare Matt 27,1 where Matthew also introduces κατά into his source (Mark 15,1).

40. Compare Luke 23,28: πλὴν ἐφ᾽ ἑαυτὰς κλαίετε καὶ ἐπὶ τὰ τέκνα ὑμῶν.

41. Compare the anticlimax "gold," "silver," "copper" in Matt 10,9. Matthew added "city" in Matt 8,34 (diff. Mark 5,15); 9,1 (diff. Mark 2,1); 9,35 (diff. Mark 6,6); 10,11 (diff. Mark 6,10); 21,10 (diff. Mark 11,11); 21,17 (diff. Mark 11,11); 21,18 (diff. Mark 11,12). See J. SCHMID, *Matthäus und Lukas*, p. 292 n. 1; J. LAMBRECHT, *Marcus Interpretator*, p. 38 n. 74.

42. J. LAMBRECHT, *Marcus Interpretator*, p. 38 n. 73.

43. Luke 1,27.33.69; 2,4; 19,9; Acts 2,36; 7,42; 10,2; 11,14; 16,15.31; 18,8. See J. C. HAWKINS, *Horae Synopticae*, pp. 20, 44.

44. For οἶκος, see Q 10,5; 11,24; 13,35; 14,23. For πίπτω, see Q 6,49; 12,6. The preposition ἐπί serves as a catchword in the Beelzebul pericope (Q 11,17.18.20) and it appears frequently in the rest of Q (Q 4,4.9.11; 6,35 *bis*.48 *ter*.49; 10,6; 12,3.25.42.44; 15,7; 22,30).

45. Luke likes δὲ καί. See J. C. HAWKINS, *Horae Synopticae*, pp. 17, 37; H. J. CADBURY, *Style and Literary Method*, p. 146.

σατανᾶν ἐκβάλλει is an insertion from Mark 3,23. Matthew also introduced οὖν.[46] Luke 11,18b is redactional. This awkward repetition of the charge is necessary because Luke intertwined the Beelzebul Controversy with the Demand for a Sign. After the interruption of v. 16, he needed to inform his readers that the present discussion answers the charge that Jesus drives out demons by Beelzebul, not the demand for a sign. Luke 11,18b probably anticipates Mark 3,30 (ὅτι ἔλεγον· πνεῦμα ἀκάθαρτον ἔχει).[47]

We can now display the first part of the refutation, the divided kingdom. In this section Matthew conflates Mark and Q. In v. 25 he takes over the divided house from Mark 3,25 and expands it by adding "city," and in v. 26 he takes the clause "Satan casts out Satan" from Mark 3,23. Luke basically rewrites Q. He does anticipate Mark's concluding verse (Mark 3,30) in an addition to the end of v. 18, but within vv. 17-18a he edits Q. He even passes over the Marcan divided house in favor of the original Q image of a civil war.

Q 11,17-18

17 εἰδὼς δὲ τὰ διανοήματα αὐτῶν εἶπεν αὐτοῖς·
   πᾶσα βασιλεία μερισθεῖσα ἐφ᾽ ἑαυτὴν ἐρημοῦται
   καὶ οἶκος ἐπὶ οἶκον πίπτει.
18 καὶ εἰ ὁ σατανᾶς ἐφ᾽ ἑαυτὸν ἐμερίσθη,
   πῶς σταθήσεται ἡ βασιλεία αὐτοῦ;

The logical refutation continues with two further arguments – a comparison between Jesus and Jewish exorcists and an indication of the true source of Jesus' power.

Matt 12,27-28	Luke 11,19-20
27 καὶ εἰ ἐγὼ ἐν Βεελζεβοὺλ	19 εἰ δὲ ἐγὼ ἐν Βεελζεβοὺλ
ἐκβάλλω τὰ δαιμόνια,	ἐκβάλλω τὰ δαιμόνια,
οἱ υἱοὶ ὑμῶν ἐν τίνι ἐκβάλλουσιν;	οἱ υἱοὶ ὑμῶν ἐν τίνι ἐκβάλλουσιν;
διὰ τοῦτο	διὰ τοῦτο
αὐτοὶ κριταὶ ἔσονται ὑμῶν.	αὐτοὶ ὑμῶν κριταὶ ἔσονται.
28 εἰ δὲ ἐν πνεύματι θεοῦ	20 εἰ δὲ ἐν δακτύλῳ θεοῦ
ἐγὼ ἐκβάλλω τὰ δαιμόνια,	ἐγὼ ἐκβάλλω τὰ δαιμόνια,
ἄρα ἔφθασεν ἐφ᾽ ὑμᾶς	ἄρα ἔφθασεν ἐφ᾽ ὑμᾶς
ἡ βασιλεία τοῦ θεοῦ.	ἡ βασιλεία τοῦ θεοῦ.

In the second part of the logical refutation Jesus compares himself to "your sons" (Q 11,19).[48] Matthew preserves the Q conjunction "and" in

46. J. Schmid, *Matthäus und Lukas*, p. 292.
47. F. Neirynck, "Mt 12,25a / Lc 11,17a," p. 488.
48. Robert Shirock claims that "your sons" refers not to Jewish exorcists but to Jesus' disciples. In Shirock's interpretation, though, the argument would not work, for the

Matt 12,27. Luke switched to "but" as he did in v. 18. According to Jeremias Luke preserves the original position of the second ὑμῶν.[49] However, more probably Luke moved the pronoun forward for emphasis as he does in Luke 12,30 (diff. Matt 6,32). In Luke 12,30 Luke shifts ὑμῶν to set up a strong contrast between the gentiles and the disciples.[50] He proceeds similarly in v. 19. He wants to set up a strong contrast between Jesus' opponents and their "sons," so he moves ὑμῶν forward to juxtapose it to αὐτοί.

The third part of the logical refutation describes the true source of Jesus' power (Q 11,20). First, a textual problem. It is difficult to decide whether we should read ἐγώ as part of Luke's text.[51] The pronoun is read by P[75] ℵ[1] B C L R f[13] 33 892 et al. It is omitted by P[45] ℵ* A W Θ Ψ f[1] et al. We probably should read it, but even if we do not read it in Luke's text we should restore it to Q with Matthew. Both Matthew and Luke have ἐγώ in Q 11,19, and the emphasis on Jesus continues in Q 11,20. The major difference between Matthew and Luke lies in the prepositional phrase that describes the true source of Jesus' power. Matthew has "by the spirit of God" and Luke "by the finger of God."[52] At first glance it appears that Luke preserves the Q text. Luke refers to the spirit seventeen times in the Gospel and fifty-five times in Acts, so it might seem unlikely that he would eliminate a reference to the spirit from his source. Matthew would have switched to "spirit" to avoid the anthropomorphism and to prepare for the further references to the spirit in the passage that follows in his gospel (Matt 12,31-32).[53] However, Luke's interest in the spirit is not overriding. Mark refers to the spirit six times (Mark 1,8.10.12; 3,29; 12,36; 13,11). Luke drops two of Mark's references. In Luke 20,42 he replaces Mark's "David himself said in the Holy Spirit" (Mark 12,36) with "David himself says in the Psalms," and

opponents would also trace the disciples' exorcisms to Beelzebul. See R. SHIROCK, "Whose Exorcists are They? The Referents of οἱ υἱοὶ ὑμῶν at Matthew 12.27/Luke 11.19," in *JSNT* 46 (1992) 41-51.

49. J. JEREMIAS, *Sprache*, p. 201.

50. See P. HOFFMANN, "Der Q-Text der Sprüche vom Sorgen: Mt 6,25-33 / Lk 12,22-31: Eine Rekonstruktionsversuch," in *Studien zum Matthäusevangelium: FS Wilhelm Pesch*, 1988, pp. 127-155, esp. p. 149; F. NEIRYNCK, "Mt 12,25a / Lc 11,17a," p. 491.

51. See R. LAUFEN, *Doppelüberlieferungen*, pp. 129, 431 n. 46.

52. Both Matthew's and Luke's sayings have the same content – through Jesus' power God's power reveals itself. See T. LORENZMEIER, "Zum Logion Mt 12,28; Lk 11,20," in *Neues Testament und christliche Existenz: FS Herbert Braun*, 1973, pp. 289-304, esp. p. 291.

53. T. W. MANSON, *The Teaching of Jesus: Studies in its Form and Content*, Cambridge: University Press, ²1935, pp. 82-83; ID., *The Sayings of Jesus*, London: SCM, 1949, p. 86.

in Luke 21,15 he replaces Mark's "but whatever is given to you in that hour, say this; for it is not you who are speaking, but the Holy Spirit" (Mark 13,11) with "for I will give you a mouth and wisdom which all your adversaries will not be able to withstand or contradict." So Luke does eliminate references to the spirit from his sources.[54] Furthermore, "the finger of God" does not stand alone as an isolated expression in Luke's writings. Luke refers to God's "hand" (Luke 1,66; Acts 4,28.30; 7,50; 11,21; 13,11) and God's "arm" (Luke 1,51; Acts 13,17).[55] Luke made the change from "spirit of God" to "finger of God" to allude to Exod 8,15 LXX: "Then the magicians said to Pharoah: 'This is the finger of God!'"[56] Matthew's "spirit" fits the context. Beelzebul and the demons are unclean spirits (Q 11,24-26); Jesus opposes these unclean spirits with the spirit of God.[57] This verse is the only Q text in which Matthew preserves the Q expression "the kingdom of God" instead of substituting his usual "the kingdom of heaven."[58] The phrase provides additional proof that Matthew here follows his source Q exactly.[59] The evidence shows that Matthew's "spirit of God" stood in Q.

We can now print the second and third parts of the logical refutation. We should note that the reconstructed text agrees exactly with Matthew. Although Matthew conflated Mark and Q in the section on the divided kingdom (Matt 12,25-26), he takes over the sayings on "your sons" and the arrival of the kingdom unchanged. He did not even alter "the king-dom of God" to his customary "the kingdom of heaven."

Q 11,19-20

19 καὶ εἰ ἐγὼ ἐν Βεελζεβοὺλ ἐκβάλλω τὰ δαιμόνια,
οἱ υἱοὶ ὑμῶν ἐν τίνι ἐκβάλλουσιν;
διὰ τοῦτο αὐτοὶ κριταὶ ἔσονται ὑμῶν.
20 εἰ δὲ ἐν πνεύματι θεοῦ ἐγὼ ἐκβάλλω τὰ δαιμόνια,
ἄρα ἔφθασεν ἐφ᾽ ὑμᾶς ἡ βασιλεία τοῦ θεοῦ.

54. C. S. RODD, "Spirit or Finger," in *ExpT* 72 (1960-61) 157-158; R. G. HAMERTON-KELLY, "A Note on Matthew xii.28 par. Luke xi.20," in *NTS* 11 (1964-65) 167-169; J. E. YATES, "Luke's Pneumatology and Lk. 11,20," in *Studia Evangelica II*, 1964, pp. 295-299; A. GEORGE, "Note sur quelques traits lucaniens de l'expression 'Par le doigt de Dieu' (Luc XI,20)," in *ScEccl* 18 (1966) 461-466.

55. A. GEORGE, "Note," p. 462; J.-M. VAN CANGH, "'Par l'esprit de Dieu – par le doigt de Dieu' Mt 12,28 par. Lc 11,20," in J. DELOBEL (ed.), *Logia*, 1982, pp. 337-342, esp. p. 341.

56. A. GEORGE, "Note," pp. 461-462.

57. J. LAMBRECHT, *Marcus Interpretator*, p. 39.

58. Q uses "the kingdom of God" ten times (Q 6,20; 7,28; 10,9; 11,20.52; 13,18.20.29; 16,16; 22,30). Matthew substitutes "the kingdom of heaven" in Matt 5,3; 8,11; 10,7; 11.11.12; 13,31.33; 23,13 and "regeneration" in Matt 19,28. Compare also Q 11,2; 12,31; 13,28.

59. C. S. RODD, "Spirit or Finger," p. 158; J. E. YATES, "Luke's Pneumatology," p. 299.

After the logical refutation Q continues with the parable of the Strong Man followed by a minatory saying.

Matt 12,29-30	Luke 11,21-23
29 ἢ πῶς δύναταί τις εἰσελθεῖν εἰς τὴν οἰκίαν τοῦ ἰσχυροῦ καὶ τὰ σκεύη αὐτοῦ ἁρπάσαι, ἐὰν μὴ πρῶτον δήσῃ τὸν ἰσχυρόν; καὶ τότε τὴν οἰκίαν αὐτοῦ διαρπάσει.	21 ὅταν ὁ ἰσχυρὸς καθωπλισμένος φυλάσσῃ τὴν ἑαυτοῦ αὐλήν, ἐν εἰρήνῃ ἐστὶν τὰ 22 ὑπάρχοντα αὐτοῦ· ἐπὰν δὲ ἰσχυρότερος αὐτοῦ ἐπελθὼν νικήσῃ αὐτόν, τὴν πανοπλίαν αὐτοῦ αἴρει ἐφ᾽ ᾗ ἐπεποίθει καὶ τὰ σκῦλα αὐτοῦ διαδίδωσιν.
30 ὁ μὴ ὢν μετ᾽ ἐμοῦ κατ᾽ ἐμοῦ ἐστιν, καὶ ὁ μὴ συνάγων μετ᾽ ἐμοῦ σκορπίζει.	23 ὁ μὴ ὢν μετ᾽ ἐμοῦ κατ᾽ ἐμοῦ ἐστιν, καὶ ὁ μὴ συνάγων μετ᾽ ἐμοῦ σκορπίζει.

Reconstruction of the final saying (Q 11,23) presents no problems since Matthew and Luke agree word for word. They diverge sharply in the parable of the Strong Man, however, and the Q reconstruction faces many difficult questions. We begin with Luke's redaction.

Luke radically redacted the Q text of the Strong Man.[60] Luke's strong man carries full armor, he presides over a palace, and he must first be conquered before he can be stripped of his armor and the spoils divided. We can best approach the Lucan redaction through the phrase ἐφ᾽ ᾗ ἐπεποίθει "(the armor) on which he relied" (Luke 11,22). This phrase articulates the familiar Lucan theme of the rich relying on their riches. The closest parallel is the parable of the Rich Man (Luke 12,16-21) which brands the rich man a fool for relying on his possessions.[61] So we can expect that all the trappings of the fully armed prince go back to Luke. Indeed, much of the vocabulary is Lucan. The words καθωπλισμένος, ἐπέρχομαι, νικάω, πανοπλία, σκῦλα, διαδίδωμι are found only in Luke among the synoptic writers.[62] Furthermore, the words φυλάσσω,[63] ἑαυτοῦ,[64]

---

60. S. LÉGASSE, "L''homme fort' de Luc xi 21-22," in *NT* 5 (1962) 5-9.

61. Compare also Luke 12,13-15.33-34.

62. The words καθωπλισμένος and σκῦλα are *hapax legomena* in the NT; πανοπλία is found only here and in Eph 6,11.13 in the NT; Luke is the only synoptic writer to use ἐπέρχομαι (0 0 3 4), νικάω (0 0 1 0), and διαδίδωμι (0 0 2 1). On ἐπέρχομαι see J. C. HAWKINS, *Horae Synopticae*, p. 29. On διαδίδωμι see Luke 18,22 diff. Mark 10,21 (compare also Acts 4,35).

63. 1 1 6 8. J. C. HAWKINS, *Horae Synopticae*, p. 23.

64. 32 24 57 21. H. FLEDDERMANN, "Mustard Seed and the Leaven," p. 222 n. 29.

εἰρήνη,[65] and ὑπάρχω[66] are all Lucan characteristic expressions, and ἐπάν and αὐλή, although not characteristically Lucan, surface elsewhere in Luke.[67] The theme and the vocabulary are Luke's own.

Since Luke has thoroughly reworked the Q text, initially it appears he can provide little control for the reconstruction of Q. However, Luke and Matthew have solid points of contact in ὁ ἰσχυρός, the conditional clause (ἐὰν μή – ἐπὰν δέ), and a compound of ἔρχομαι (εἰσελθεῖν – ἐπελθών). In addition, both texts also contain two different clauses on despoiling the strong man, an initial clause (καὶ τὰ σκεύη αὐτοῦ ἁρπάσαι – τὴν πανοπλίαν αὐτοῦ αἴρει ἐφ᾽ ᾗ ἐπεποίθει) and a concluding clause (καὶ τότε τὴν οἰκίαν αὐτοῦ διαρπάσει – καὶ τὰ σκῦλα αὐτοῦ διαδίδωσιν).

Despite the great disparity between Matthew and Luke, we can recover the Q text because there are several indications that Matthew has taken over the Q text unchanged. The argument has three parts. First, I will show that we can derive Luke's version from Matthew's if we pay careful attention to the structure of the section. Second, I will point out some features of Matthew's text that make sense as parts of a Q text. Third, I will draw attention to the way Matthew treats the material immediately before and after the Strong Man.

To show that Luke derives from the Q text preserved in Matthew we can best begin with Luke's v. 22. In Matthew, the conditional clause separates the two clauses on despoiling. Luke draws the two despoiling clauses together by transposing the conditional clause from between them to before both of them. He also edits both despoiling clauses to contrast two attitudes toward riches, relying on riches which he condemns and distributing riches which he advocates. In the place of Matthew's first clause (καὶ τὰ σκεύη αὐτοῦ ἁρπάσει) Luke writes τὴν πανοπλίαν αὐτοῦ αἴρει ἐφ᾽ ᾗ ἐπεποίθει. With the final phrase "on which he relied" Luke shows the futility of relying on one's riches. The two concluding clauses are extremely close. Luke replaces the Q expression διαρπάσει with another διά-compound διαδίδωσιν because διαδίδωμι expresses Luke's positive teaching on riches, that they should be distributed not hoarded. Two passages – one in the gospel, one in Acts – especially highlight this theme. Later in Luke's gospel Jesus advises the Ruler, "Sell all that you own and distribute (διάδος) it to the poor" (Luke 18,22). In Acts those who owned land or houses sold them,

---

65. 4 1 14 7. J. C. HAWKINS, *Horae Synopticae*, p. 17.
66. 3 0 15 25. J. C. HAWKINS, *Horae Synopticae*, p. 23.
67. For ἐπάν see Luke 11,34; for αὐλή see Luke 22,55.

brought the proceeds to the apostles, and "it was distributed (διεδίδετο) to each as any had need" (Acts 4,34-35). Once Luke introduced "distribute" he had to change the object, so he substituted τὰ σκῦλα αὐτοῦ for τὴν οἰκίαν αὐτοῦ which would not make sense with the new verb. Luke dropped τότε because it no longer fits once the two despoiling clauses follow one another without interruption. Matthew's conditional clause states the need to first bind the strong man. Luke envisions an armed combat with a "stronger one." He draws the entering motif from the beginning of the Q section (εἰσελθεῖν εἰς τὴν οἰκίαν τοῦ ἰσχυροῦ) but he reduces it to participle (ἐπελθών). Instead of binding the strong man, Luke has the stronger one conquer him.

Once we understand how Luke has constructed v. 22 from Q, we can see how he proceeds with v. 21. Since Luke wants to show the futility of relying on riches, he needs a strong contrast so he creates v. 21 to portray the strong man at peace before the stronger one enters. The following section in Q, the Return of the Unclean Spirit (Q 11,24-26), begins with a ὅταν-clause, so Luke borrows the construction to begin v. 21. He picks up ὁ ἰσχυρός from Q. The rest of the vocabulary is Lucan except for the *hapax legomenon* καθωπλισμένος which Luke needs for his theme. So we can understand Luke's text as a redaction of the Q text reflected in Matthew.

Furthermore, Matthew's text has a Q flavor. The initial construction, a question introduced by ἢ πῶς δύναται followed by an infinitive, has a Q parallel in the Sermon (Q 6,42). Luke 6,42 begins with πῶς δύνασαι λέγειν τῷ ἀδελφῷ σου, while the Matthean parallel has ἢ πῶς ἐρεῖς τῷ ἀδελφῷ σου (Matt 7,4). Matthew's ἢ πῶς is probably original, because Q has another rhetorical question in the preceding verse (Q 6,41) and Q elsewhere uses the particle ἤ to join two rhetorical questions.[68] Matthew's future ἐρεῖς is redactional since Matthew introduces similar futures in Matt 17,20 (diff. Luke 17,6) and 21,3 (diff. Mark 11,3).[69] So Q 6,42a probably began with ἢ πῶς δύνασαι λέγειν τῷ ἀδελφῷ σου, closely parallelling Matt 12,29 ἢ πῶς δύναταί τις εἰσελθεῖν. The ἢ πῶς in Q 11,21 picks up the πῶς in Q 11,18.[70] Q 6,42 also provides a parallel to the use of πρῶτον ... καὶ τότε. Furthermore, we encounter the adjective πρῶτος and the adverb τότε further down in the Beelzebul Controversy.[71]

---

68. Q joins rhetorical questions with ἤ in Q 6,44 and 11,11-12. Elsewhere Q uses ἤ in Q 10,12.14; 12,11 (πῶς ἢ τί).29 *bis*; 15,7; 16,13 *bis*.

69. U. Luz, *Evangelium nach Matthäus*, p. 44; ET: *Matthew 1-7*, p. 62.

70. For πῶς see also Q 12,27, and for δύναται see Q 12,25.

71. For πρῶτος see Q 11,26 (compare also πρῶτον in Q 9,59; 10,5; 12,31); for τότε see Q 11,24.26.

The verb ἁρπάζω is attested in Q 16,16, and the cognate noun ἁρπαγή appears in Q 11,39.[72] So Matthew's text has several Q features that indicate that he preserves the Q text of the Strong Man.

We can confirm this conclusion by examining Matthew's treatment of the Q material immediately before and after the parable. As we have seen, Matthew took over the two preceding verses unchanged (Matt 12,27-28). Since Matthew and Luke agree word for word in the saying on opposition to Jesus (Q 11,23), Matthew also took over the following saying unchanged. Matthew copies Q word for word immediately before and after the Strong Man, increasing the probability that he also copies the Strong Man exactly. He does not intervene at all in four verses (Matt 12,27-30). Such a procedure might appear improbable, but other instances exist. In Matt 3,7b-10 Matthew takes over the first part of John's Preaching without introducing any changes.[73] In the Demands of Discipleship Matthew alters the narrative frame, but he takes over the dialogue unchanged.[74] Matthew also takes over the Mammon Saying unchanged in Matt 6,24.[75] Although Matthew reverses the order of the sayings on the Queen of the South and the Ninevites (Q 11,31-32), he does not alter the wording of either saying.[76] In the Beelzebul Controversy Matthew conflates Mark and Q at the beginning of Jesus' response (Matt 12,25-26), and he will conflate Mark and Q's sayings on the Unforgivable Sin (Matt 12,31-32), but between these two passages he not only follows Q exclusively, he reproduces Q exactly.

Q 11,21-23

21 ἢ πῶς δύναταί τις εἰσελθεῖν εἰς τὴν οἰκίαν τοῦ ἰσχυροῦ
   καὶ τὰ σκεύη αὐτοῦ ἁρπάσαι,
22 ἐὰν μὴ πρῶτον δήσῃ τὸν ἰσχυρόν;
   καὶ τότε τὴν οἰκίαν αὐτοῦ διαρπάσει.
23 ὁ μὴ ὢν μετ' ἐμοῦ κατ' ἐμοῦ ἐστιν,
   καὶ ὁ μὴ συνάγων μετ' ἐμοῦ σκορπίζει.

The Q pericope concludes with a section on the Return of the Unclean Spirit. Matthew delays the section, but Luke preserves the Q position immediately following the parable of the Strong Man and the saying about being against Jesus.[77]

72. Luke recast the Q saying on the kingdom suffering violence (Q 16,16), but Matthew's καὶ βιασταὶ ἁρπάζουσιν αὐτήν is original. See S. SCHULZ, Q, p. 262.
73. H. FLEDDERMANN, "The Beginning of Q," SBL 1985 Seminar Papers, pp. 153-159.
74. H. T. FLEDDERMANN, "Demands of Discipleship," pp. 542-552, 555-556.
75. S. SCHULZ, Q, p. 459.
76. See Chapter V below.
77. See W. BUSSMANN, Synoptische Studien, p. 69; V. TAYLOR, "Original Order of Q," p. 115; S. SCHULZ, Q, p. 476 n. 562; P. VASSILIADIS, "The Original Order of Q: Some Residual Cases," in J. DELOBEL (ed.), Logia, 1982, pp. 379-387, esp. p. 384.

Matt 12,43-45	Luke 11,24-26

43 ὅταν δὲ τὸ ἀκάθαρτον πνεῦμα
  ἐξέλθῃ ἀπὸ τοῦ ἀνθρώπου,
  διέρχεται δι᾽ ἀνύδρων τόπων
  ζητοῦν ἀνάπαυσιν
  καὶ οὐχ εὑρίσκει.
44 τότε λέγει·
  εἰς τὸν οἶκόν μου ἐπιστρέψω
  ὅθεν ἐξῆλθον·
  καὶ ἐλθὸν εὑρίσκει σχολάζοντα
  σεσαρωμένον καὶ κεκοσμημένον.
45 τότε πορεύεται
  καὶ παραλαμβάνει μεθ᾽ ἑαυτοῦ
  ἑπτὰ ἕτερα πνεύματα
  πονηρότερα ἑαυτοῦ
  καὶ εἰσελθόντα κατοικεῖ ἐκεῖ·
  καὶ γίνεται τὰ ἔσχατα
  τοῦ ἀνθρώπου ἐκείνου
  χείρονα τῶν πρώτων.
  οὕτως ἔσται καὶ τῇ γενεᾷ
  ταύτῃ τῇ πονηρᾷ.

24 ὅταν τὸ ἀκάθαρτον πνεῦμα
  ἐξέλθῃ ἀπὸ τοῦ ἀνθρώπου,
  διέρχεται δι᾽ ἀνύδρων τόπων
  ζητοῦν ἀνάπαυσιν
  καὶ μὴ εὑρίσκον·
  τότε λέγει·
  ὑποστρέψω εἰς τὸν οἶκόν μου
  ὅθεν ἐξῆλθον·
25 καὶ ἐλθὸν εὑρίσκει
  σεσαρωμένον καὶ κεκοσμημένον.
26 τότε πορεύεται
  καὶ παραλαμβάνει
  ἕτερα πνεύματα
  πονηρότερα ἑαυτοῦ ἑπτὰ
  καὶ εἰσελθόντα κατοικεῖ ἐκεῖ·
  καὶ γίνεται τὰ ἔσχατα
  τοῦ ἀνθρώπου ἐκείνου
  χείρονα τῶν πρώτων.

Matthew and Luke are strikingly similar in the Return of the Unclean Spirit. Matthew joined the section to the preceding with a redactional δέ; Luke, reflecting Q, does not have δέ. Matthew preserves an original εὑρίσκει, whereas Luke subordinates.[78] Luke changed ἐπιστρέψω to ὑποστρέψω.[79] He also improved the word order by moving the verb before the prepositional phrase. In this way he brings εἰς τὸν οἶκόν μου right before the ὅθεν-clause which modifies it. Matthew added σκολάζοντα. It appears without a connecting καί like the two participles that Matthew and Luke share which shows that Matthew added it. Matthew also added μεθ᾽ ἑαυτοῦ.[80] Luke changed the position of the numeral "seven" for emphasis.[81] Matthew added the final clause οὕτως ἔσται καὶ τῇ γενεᾷ ταύτῃ πονηρᾷ. He has just written γενεὰ πονηρά in Matt 12,39 and οὕτως ἔσται in Matt 12,40. With this closing sentence he refers to the demand for a sign (Matt 12,38) and comments that such

78. J. Schmid, *Matthäus und Lukas*, p. 295.
79. Luke favors ὑποστρέφω (0 0 21 11); compare ἐπιστρέφω (4 4 7 11). See especially the redactional use of ὑποστρέφω in Luke 4,14 (diff. Mark 1,14); 8,37 (diff. Mark 5,18); 8,39 (diff. Mark 5,19); 8,40 (diff. Mark 5,21); 9,10 (diff. Mark 6,30). Furthermore, ἐπιστρέφω is attested in Q (see Q 10,6).
80. Compare Matt 17,3 (diff. Mark 9,4); 17,17 (diff. Mark 9,19); 26,29 (diff. Mark 14,25); 26,36 (diff. Mark 14,32); 26,38 (diff. Mark 14,34); 26,40 (diff. Mark 14,37); 27,54 (diff. Mark 15,39). See J. Schmid, *Matthäus und Lukas*, p. 295.
81. See Luke 8,2; 9,17.33; Acts 6,3.

a demand means falling back into the power of the unclean spirit.[82] The
Return of the Unclean Spirit completes the Q Beelzebul Controversy.

Q 11,24-26

24 ὅταν τὸ ἀκάθαρτον πνεῦμα ἐξέλθῃ ἀπὸ τοῦ ἀνθρώπου,
   διέρχεται δι᾽ ἀνύδρων τόπων ζητοῦν ἀνάπαυσιν
   καὶ οὐχ εὑρίσκει. τότε λέγει·
   εἰς τὸν οἶκόν μου ἐπιστρέψω ὅθεν ἐξῆλθον.
25 καὶ ἐλθὸν εὑρίσκει σεσαρωμένον καὶ κεκοσμημένον.
26 τότε πορεύεται καὶ παραλαμβάνει
   ἑπτὰ ἕτερα πνεύματα πονηρότερα ἑαυτοῦ
   καὶ εἰσελθόντα κατοικεῖ ἐκεῖ·
   καὶ γίνεται τὰ ἔσχατα τοῦ ἀνθρώπου ἐκείνου
   χείρονα τῶν πρώτων.

We can now compare the reconstructed Q text and Mark.

Q 11,14-15.17-26	Mark 3,22-27
14 καὶ ἐξέβαλεν δαιμόνιον κωφόν· καὶ ἐκβληθέντος τοῦ δαιμονίου ἐλάλησεν ὁ κωφὸς καὶ ἐθαύμασαν οἱ ὄχλοι.	
15 τινὲς δὲ εἶπον·	22 καὶ οἱ γραμματεῖς οἱ ἀπὸ Ἱεροσολύμων καταβάντες ἔλεγον ὅτι
ἐν Βεελζεβοὺλ τῷ ἄρχοντι τῶν δαιμονίων ἐκβάλλει τὰ δαιμόνια.	Βεελζεβοὺλ ἔχει καὶ ὅτι ἐν τῷ ἄρχοντι τῶν δαιμονίων ἐκβάλλει τὰ δαιμόνια.
17 εἰδὼς δὲ τὰ διανοήματα αὐτῶν	23 καὶ προσκαλεσάμενος αὐτοὺς ἐν παραβολαῖς
εἶπεν αὐτοῖς·	ἔλεγεν αὐτοῖς· πῶς δύναται σατανᾶς σατανᾶν ἐκβάλλειν;
πᾶσα βασιλεία μερισθεῖσα ἐφ᾽ ἑαυτὴν ἐρημοῦται	24 καὶ ἐὰν βασιλεία ἐφ᾽ ἑαυτὴν μερισθῇ, οὐ δύναται σταθῆναι ἡ βασιλεία ἐκείνη·
καὶ οἶκος ἐπὶ οἶκον πίπτει.	25 καὶ ἐὰν οἰκία ἐφ᾽ ἑαυτὴν μερισθῇ, οὐ δυνήσεται ἡ οἰκία ἐκείνη σταθῆναι.
18 καὶ εἰ ὁ σατανᾶς ἐφ᾽ ἑαυτὸν ἐμερίσθη, πῶς σταθήσεται ἡ βασιλεία αὐτοῦ;	26 καὶ εἰ ὁ σατανᾶς ἀνέστη ἐφ᾽ ἑαυτὸν καὶ ἐμερίσθη, οὐ δύναται στῆναι ἀλλὰ τέλος ἔχει.

82. J. LAMBRECHT, Marcus Interpretator, pp. 44-45.

19 καὶ εἰ ἐγὼ ἐν Βεελζεβοὺλ
  ἐκβάλλω τὰ δαιμόνια,
  οἱ υἱοὶ ὑμῶν ἐν τίνι ἐκβάλλουσιν;
  διὰ τοῦτο αὐτοὶ κριταὶ
  ἔσονται ὑμῶν.
20 εἰ δὲ ἐν πνεύματι θεοῦ
  ἐγὼ ἐκβάλλω τὰ δαιμόνια,
  ἄρα ἔφθασεν ἐφ᾽ ὑμᾶς
  ἡ βασιλεία τοῦ θεοῦ.
21 ἢ πῶς δύναταί τις εἰσελθεῖν   27 ἀλλ᾽ οὐ δύναται οὐδεὶς
  εἰς τὴν οἰκίαν τοῦ   εἰς τὴν οἰκίαν τοῦ
  ἰσχυροῦ   ἰσχυροῦ εἰσελθὼν
  καὶ τὰ σκεύη αὐτοῦ ἁρπάσαι,   τὰ σκεύη αὐτοῦ διαρπάσαι,
22 ἐὰν μὴ πρῶτον δήσῃ   ἐὰν μὴ πρῶτον
  τὸν ἰσχυρόν;   τὸν ἰσχυρὸν δήσῃ,
  καὶ τότε τὴν οἰκίαν αὐτοῦ   καὶ τότε τὴν οἰκίαν αὐτοῦ
  διαρπάσει.   διαρπάσει.
23 ὁ μὴ ὢν μετ᾽ ἐμοῦ κατ᾽ ἐμοῦ
  ἐστιν, καὶ ὁ μὴ συνάγων μετ᾽
  ἐμοῦ σκορπίζει.
24 ὅταν τὸ ἀκάθαρτον πνεῦμα
  ἐξέλθῃ ἀπὸ τοῦ ἀνθρώπου,
  διέρχεται δι᾽ ἀνύδρων τόπων
  ζητοῦν ἀνάπαυσιν
  καὶ οὐχ εὑρίσκει. τότε λέγει·
  εἰς τὸν οἶκόν μου ἐπιστρέψω
  ὅθεν ἐξῆλθον.
25 καὶ ἐλθὸν εὑρίσκει
  σεσαρωμένον καὶ κεκοσμημένον.
26 τότε πορεύεται καὶ παραλαμβάνει
  ἑπτὰ ἕτερα πνεύματα
  πονηρότερα ἑαυτοῦ
  καὶ εἰσελθόντα κατοικεῖ ἐκεῖ·
  καὶ γίνεται τὰ ἔσχατα
  τοῦ ἀνθρώπου ἐκείνου
  χείρονα τῶν πρώτων.

The two texts differ dramatically in length. Mark's version covers only six verses, whereas the Q pericope stretches over twelve verses. Numerous differences in detail separate the two accounts, but the disparity in length comes from large blocks of material in Q that have nothing comparable in Mark. Q contains five sections without any parallel in Mark: (1) The exorcism of the demoniac (Q 11,14), (2) The saying about "your sons" (Q 11,19), (3) The saying about the arrival of the kingdom of God (Q 11,20), (4) The saying about opposition to Jesus (Q 11,23), (5) The return of the unclean spirit (Q 11,24-26).

Despite Q's greater overall length, in three places Mark presents a more expansive text than Q. First, Q has a single charge against Jesus, that he casts out demons by Beelzebul the prince of demons (Q 11,15). Mark has a double charge, that Jesus is possessed by Beelzebul and that he drives out demons by the prince of demons (Mark 3,22). Second, Mark begins Jesus' defense with a rhetorical question, "How can Satan cast out Satan?" (Mark 3,23). Q has nothing corresponding to Mark's question at the beginning of Jesus' defense. Third, Q begins Jesus' refutation with a single parable – the divided kingdom (Q 11,17-18). Mark begins with two parables – the divided kingdom and the divided house (Mark 3,24-26).

How do we evaluate the differences between these two texts? Views differ sharply. In his early work Streeter claimed that "...the abbreviated version of Mk iii. 22-6 has such close verbal resemblances in what it has in common with Q, and loses so much force by what it omits from Q, that we can only regard it as a mutilated excerpt from that source."[83] Taking an opposite tack Schüling maintains that Mark cannot possibly depend on Q because we cannot explain why Mark would omit so much material, particularly Jesus' pronouncement on the arrival of the kingdom (Q 11,20).[84] Whether Streeter's early view, Schüling's position, or some other explanation prevails depends on an examination of the differences between the two texts.

Two Q sections that Mark lacks show clearly that Mark is secondary to Q. First, the saying on "your sons" concedes too much because it implies that Jesus operates on the same level as his opponents. The church's developing christology could not admit such equality. Furthermore, Mark's own views on exorcism clash with the saying. According to Mark any exorcist is automatically on Jesus' side (Mark 9,38-40). To cast out demons is a work of the kingdom. In Mark's view Jesus' enemies, the hostile scribes, could never succeed in casting out a demon so the saying had to drop out. Second, the Return of the Unclean Spirit also shows that Mark is secondary. Here, too, dogmatic considerations intrude. The Q passage appears to suggest that Jesus' power to exorcise can be undone, that the evil can return. The tendency of the tradition would be to drop any limitation on Jesus' power. We can see this clearly in Matthew's and Luke's editing of Mark.[85] These two Q sections that

83. B. H. STREETER, "St. Mark's Knowledge and Use of Q," p. 171.

84. J. SCHÜLING, *Studien*, p. 111.

85. For example, Luke drops and Matthew alters Mark's statement that Jesus could not work any wonder in his native place (Mark 6,5). Matthew and Luke both omit the Cure of the Deaf Man (Mark 7,31-37) and the Cure of the Blind Man (Mark 8,22-26) because Jesus appears to have difficulty healing the two men.

Mark lacks are particularly telling. Given Q we can easily explain why Mark would have omitted the sections. Given Mark it is difficult to explain Q as the sections Q would have added are the weakest.[86]

Although these two sections show clearly that Mark is secondary, the other three sections lacking in Mark also point in the same direction. First, Q's initial exorcism makes a natural introduction to the dispute. Mark's combination of the dispute with the section about Jesus' family is more artificial. Q's introduction has a more original ring. Second, the saying about opposition to Jesus appeared too harsh to Mark. He replaced it with his account of the strange exorcist (Mark 9,38-40) which shows a more tolerant attitude toward outsiders. Third, the saying on the true source of Jesus' power forms a fitting climax to Jesus' defense. It is clearly original. In the logical refutation Jesus first gives two reasons why his exorcisms can't be the result of an alliance with Beelzebul, the parable of the divided kingdom and the saying about "your sons" (Q 11,17-19). At the end of this negative refutation, Jesus gives the true source of his power. It might appear strange that Mark omitted the saying on the true source of Jesus' power, but he has already said as much in his introductory summary of Jesus' teaching (Mark 1,14-15). Mark 1,14-15 identifies Jesus' entire ministry with the coming of the kingdom, not just the exorcisms.

The five sections that Mark lacks all show that Mark is secondary to Q. The same appears true for two of the places where Mark is more expansive than Q. First, the initial charge is heightened in Mark. In Q Jesus is accused of casting out demons through the power of Beelzebul (Q 11,15). In Mark a further charge is added – Jesus is possessed (Mark 3,22). This heightening of the charge reflects a heightening of the op-position to Jesus. The adversaries have become even more hostile. The heightening of both the charge and the opposition shows Mark's text is secondary. Furthermore, the rest of the pericope takes no note of the charge that Jesus is possessed; it surfaces again only in v. 30. The rest of the Beelzebul Controversy reacts only to the charge that Jesus expels demons through Beelzebul. Mark's further charge is clearly a later development.[87] Second, Q begins Jesus' refutation with the single parable of the divided kingdom (Q 11,17-18). A detail of this parable – one house falling against another – graphically portrays the devastation of a civil war. Mark has two parables – the divided kingdom and the divided

86. On the differences between Mark and Q in the Beelzebul Controversy, see further R. A. PIPER, *Wisdom in the Q-Tradition: The Aphoristic Teaching of Jesus* (SNTS MS, 61), Cambridge: University Press, 1989, p. 157.

87. J. SCHÜLING, *Studien*, p. 113.

house (Mark 3,24-26). It is more probable that Mark expanded a detail of the Q parable into a separate parable than that Q collapsed a second parable into a detail of the first.[88]

Granted that Mark is secondary to Q, does Mark depend on Q? Could Mark have derived the Beelzebul Controversy from the oral tradition? Several considerations show that Mark depends on Q. For example, the phenomenon of order makes most sense if Mark took the Beelzebul Controversy from Q. The Q pericope is made up of various sections. Although Mark's text is considerably shorter than Q's, the sections Mark shares with Q appear in the same order they have in Q. That Mark has them in the same order as Q indicates that he took them over from a written document and not from the oral tradition. Furthermore, the three places where Mark expands the Beelzebul Controversy all have roots in Q. First, the additional charge in Mark 3,22 that Jesus "has Beelzebul" (Βεελζεβοὺλ ἔχει) comes from Q 7,33 where John's opponents claim that he "has a demon" (δαιμόνιον ἔχει). Second, Mark's rhetorical question, "How can Satan cast out Satan?,", picks up πῶς δύναται from Q 11,21, σατανᾶς from Q 11,18, and ἐκβάλλω from Q 11,15 (par. Mark 3,22). Third, the parable of the divided house (Mark 3,25) develops the Q image of house falling against house (Q 11,17). In addition, Mark saves one of the sections he eliminated from Q – the saying on opposition (Q 11,23) – to use later in the Discipleship Discourse (Mark 9,40). Mark also joins another Q passage, the Unforgivable Sin logion (Q 12,10), to the Beelzebul Controversy, using it to comment further on opposition to Jesus (Mark 3,28-30). Mark did not derive the Beelzebul Controversy from the oral tradition. He had the written Q before him. After eliminating some sections of the Q Beelzebul Controversy, he reached out to different sections of Q to expand and supplement the parts of the controversy he took over.

When we turn to an examination of Mark's redaction, the evidence that Mark depends on Q increases because we find that the overall structural principles of Mark's text and even small details have roots in Q.

Mark omits Q's introductory exorcism because he intertwines the Beelzebul Controversy with the pericope of Jesus' True Family (Mark 3,20-21.31-35).[89] Mark frequently frames one pericope with the parts of

---

88. T. W. MANSON, *Sayings of Jesus*, p. 86.

89. On the intertwining of the two pericopes see E. BEST, "Mark III. 20, 21, 31-35" (1975-76), in ID., *Disciples and Discipleship: Studies in the Gospel according to Mark*, Edinburgh: Clark, 1986, pp. 49-63, esp. pp. 55-56.

another, so the setting has solid Marcan credentials.⁹⁰ Mark begins with his usual καί-parataxis.⁹¹ Q left the adversaries general, but Mark designates them as scribes from Jerusalem. The scribes are the chief adversaries of Jesus in Mark,⁹² and Jerusalem, in contrast with Galilee, is the place of opposition to Jesus.⁹³ Mark has two charges to Q's single charge. The reason lies in the new context Mark created for the Beelzebul Controversy. To intertwine the Beelzebul Controversy with Jesus' True Family Mark relates the charge of the scribes to the reaction of Jesus' relatives using a double ἔλεγον and three ὅτι-clauses (Mark 3,21b-22).⁹⁴ Mark preserves the Q charge in his third ὅτι-clause: "he drives out demons by the prince of demons." He takes the name Beelzebul and creates a new charge that Jesus "has Beelzebul" by borrowing an expression he read elsewhere in Q, δαιμόνιον ἔχει (Q 7,33). This additional charge forms a bridge between the charge of Jesus' family that he is crazy (Mark 3,21b) and the Q charge that Jesus drives out demons by Beelzebul.⁹⁵ The differences between Mark and Q come entirely from Mark's redaction of the Q text.

After the charge Q introduces Jesus' response with the verse εἰδὼς δὲ τὰ διανοήματα αὐτῶν εἶπεν αὐτοῖς (Q 11,17a). Mark writes instead καὶ προσκαλεσάμενος αὐτοὺς ἐν παραβολαῖς ἔλεγεν αὐτοῖς (Mark 3,23a). The two verses share a double third person plural pronoun and a verb of saying. The differences result from Marcan redaction. Again we find Mark's familiar parataxis. The phrase προσκαλεσάμενος αὐτούς reappears often in Marcan passages.⁹⁶ "In parables" expresses Mark's own understanding of the parables because Mark often brings the parables

---

90. See Mark 5,21-43; 6,7-30; 11,12-25; 14,1-11.53-72. See further F. NEIRYNCK, *Duality in Mark: Contributions to the Study of the Markan Redaction* (BETL, 31), Leuven: University Press, 1972; Leuven: University Press – Peeters, ²1988, p. 133.

91. J. C. HAWKINS, *Horae Synopticae*, pp. 150-152; F. NEIRYNCK, *Minor Agreements of Matthew and Luke*, pp. 203-211.

92. J. D. CROSSAN, "Mark and the Relatives of Jesus," in *NT* 15 (1973) 81-113, esp. pp. 88-89; H. FLEDDERMANN, "Warning about the Scribes," p. 53 n. 4.

93. The way of Jesus runs through Galilee to Jerusalem (Mark 9,30; 10,32-34). During the final period of his life Jesus leaves the city of Jerusalem at night for Bethany or the Mount of Olives (Mark 11,11; 13,1-2; 14,3.26). Only on the night of the passion does he stay in the city (Mark 14,53). Because the city is the symbol of opposition to Jesus, Jesus' opponents are characterized at times as coming from Jerusalem (Mark 3,22; 7,1).

94. The redactional nature of this double ἔλεγον followed by ὅτι can be seen by comparing the pericope of the Death of John the Baptist: καὶ ἔλεγον ὅτι Ἰωάννης... ἄλλοι δὲ ἔλεγον ὅτι Ἠλίας... ἄλλοι δὲ ἔλεγον ὅτι προφήτης... (Mark 6,14-15). See J. LAMBRECHT, *Marcus Interpretator*, p. 57.

95. J. D. CROSSAN, "Mark and the Relatives of Jesus," p. 89.

96. Compare Mark 7,14; 8,1.34; 10,42; 12,43; 15,44.

into connection with misunderstanding and hostility.[97] Finally, Mark uses the imperfect very frequently.[98]

Mark begins Jesus' defense with a rhetorical question. He draws the form of the question, πῶς δύναται with the infinitive, from Q (Q 11,21).[99] Q also provided the name "Satan" (Q 11,18) and the infinitive "to cast out" (Q 11,15). With the rhetorical question Mark increases the liveliness of the scene,[100] and he also announces a major theme – Jesus' power. The rest of Jesus' defense constantly picks up the δύναται that Mark sets programmatically at the beginning of Jesus' response.

23 How can (πῶς δύναται) Satan cast out Satan?
24 And if a kingdom is divided against itself, that kingdom cannot (οὐ δύναται) stand;
25 and if a house is divided against itself, that house will not be able (οὐ δυνήσεται) to stand.
26 And if Satan has risen up against himself and is divided, he cannot (οὐ δύναται) stand, but his end has come.
27 But no one entering the house of a strong man can (οὐ δύναται) despoil him of his possessions, unless he first bind the strong man, and then he will despoil his house.

Mark regularly uses δύναμις and δύναμαι to describe the power of God at work in Jesus.[101] The repeated use of the verb climaxes in v. 27 which underscores Jesus' power over Satan. The Q text handed Mark his theme as well as the vocabulary to express it.

Mark follows the initial rhetorical question with three symmetrically constructed sentences each of which begins with a conditional clause followed by a main clause that draws the conclusion. Even here Mark probably took his cue from Q. Q 11,18 has a conditional clause. Mark uses the construction along with δύναμαι to create a stylistic unit in vv. 24-26. To avoid monotony he shifts from ἐάν to εἰ in v. 26, from a present main verb to the future in v. 25, and from σταθῆναι to στῆναι in v. 26. The first sentence is a Marcan reworking of the Q image of the divided kingdom (Q 11,17). Mark substituted a conditional clause for the Q participial phrase to begin his series of three parallel sentences. In the

---

97. Mark 4,2.11.34; 12,1. See J. LAMBRECHT, *Marcus Interpretator*, pp. 55-56.

98. Hawkins provides the following statistics: 94 228 259 329. See J. C. HAWKINS, *Horae Synopticae*, pp. 51-52.

99. Compare also πῶς σταθήσεται ἡ βασιλεία αὐτοῦ; (Q 11,18).

100. J. LAMBRECHT, *Marcus Interpretator*, p. 68.

101. For δύναμις see Mark 5,30; 6,2.5.14; 9,1.39; 12,24; 13,26; 14,62. For δύναμαι see Mark 1,40; 2,7; 3,27; 5,3; 6,5; 8,4; 9,3.22.23.28.29.39; 15,31. Compare also the adjective δυνατός in Mark 9,23; 10,27; 14,36. See V. K. ROBBINS, "*Dynameis* and *Semeia* in Mark," in *BR* 18 (1973) 5-20, esp. pp. 8-15; M. E. BORING, "Synoptic Problem," p. 616.

main clause he substituted οὐ δύναται σταθῆναι ἡ βασιλεία ἐκείνη for Q's ἐρημοῦται. As we have seen, the negative expression οὐ δύναται picks up δύναται from the rhetorical question. Mark draws the infinitive "stand" and the demonstrative "that" from further down in the Q discourse (Q 11,18.26). Mark follows the divided kingdom with a closely paralleled sentence on the divided house (Mark 3,25). In Q house means a "building," and the detail simply illustrates the complete destruction of the kingdom. In Mark house means "family," and Mark builds it into an independent image. Mark paralleled the kingdom image with the family image to further intertwine the Beelzebul Controversy with the framing story of Jesus' True Family. The framing pericope provides a concrete example of a family divided. In the final logion (v. 26) Mark edits Q 11,18. He takes over and expands the Q conditional clause and substitutes a main clause that uses οὐ δύναται to parallel vv. 24 and 25. In both clauses he introduces typically Marcan duality: ἀνέστη ἐφ᾽ ἑαυτὸν καὶ ἐμερίσθη and οὐ δύναται στῆναι ἀλλὰ τέλος ἔχει.[102] Mark's dualistic expansions add more weight to the final logion in the series.

Mark only slightly changed the parable of the Strong Man. Since he used the question form in v. 23, he switches to a typical double negative ἀλλ᾽ οὐ δύναται οὐδείς.[103] He turns the first Q infinitive into a participle, uses the compound verb instead of Q's simple verb, and changes the word order. Mark uses the participle to subordinate the first infinitive to the second and to compress the sentence slightly. Q uses both the simple verb ἁρπάζω and the compound διαρπάζω. For stylistic reasons Mark twice uses the compound. The change in word order is also stylistic. By moving τὸν ἰσχυρόν before the verb, Mark assimilates the word order of the conditional clause to that of the main clause.

Mark completes his redaction of the Beelzebul Controversy by appending the Unforgivable Sin logion (Mark 3,28-30). Again Mark drew the logion from Q (Q 12,10). At the end of the Unforgivable Sin Mark comments "because they said, 'He has an unclean spirit'" (Mark 3,30). This comment forms an *inclusio* with the initial charge, "He has Beelzebul" (Mark 3,22).

We can now evaluate other treatments of the Beelzebul Controversy. Streeter's claim that Mark is a "mutilated excerpt" of Q is too harsh.[104]

---

102. Mark likes constructions with οὐκ ... ἀλλά, and he uses synonymous expressions frequently. See F. NEIRYNCK, *Duality in Mark*, pp. 90-94, 101-106.

103. Οὐδείς (19 26 33 25); with a second negative (1 15 6 2). See J. LAMBRECHT, *Marcus Interpretator*, p. 70 n. 227.

104. B. H. STREETER, "St. Mark's Knowledge and Use of Q," p. 171.

Mark does have a much shorter discourse, but he edits Q carefully. He highlights Jesus' power by exploiting the Q verb δύναμαι. Mark skillfully links the Beelzebul Controversy to Jesus' Family by adding a second charge that Jesus is possessed, by developing the Divided House (Mark 3,25), and by creating the framing *inclusio* (Mark 3,22.30). Laufen tries to uncover an original version (*Urfassung*) of the controversy that lies behind Mark and Q.[105] The tradition-historical investigation showed, however, that Mark is secondary to Q, and the redaction-critical investigation showed that we can derive Mark from Q. The two versions do not go back to an *Urfassung*; Mark goes back to Q. Schüling also assumes too easily that Mark could not depend on Q. He advances only one detailed argument, that Mark would not have omitted the saying on the arrival of the kingdom (Q 11,20).[106] As we have seen, the kingdom arrives with Jesus for Mark as well as for Q, but for Mark the saying plays such an important role that he uses a version of it to preface the entire ministry of Jesus (Mark 1,14-15). Fuchs claims that a later editor (*Deuteromarkus*) combined the Marcan and Q versions of the controversy in a new edition of Mark that Matthew and Luke then used instead of canonical Mark.[107] However, Luke does not show Marcan expansions like Satan casting out Satan (Mark 3,23) or the divided house (Mark 3,25). Matthew first conflated Mark and Q, not Fuchs' *Deuteromarkus*.[108] Years ago Lambrecht got it right – Mark depends on Q in the Beelzebul Controversy.[109]

We are also now in a position to evaluate the parallel to the Strong Man in the Gospel of Thomas (Th 35).

> Jesus said, "It is impossible for anyone to enter the house of the strong man and take him by violence, unless (εἰ μήτι) he bind his hands; then (τότε) he will plunder his house."

Two details of Thomas' saying have nothing corresponding in the synoptics. In Thomas the intruder takes the strong man "by violence" and binds "his hands." Both details are secondary embellishments; neither is an original feature of the saying.[110] We can see the secondary nature of the additions most easily with "hand" which crops up often in

---

105. R. LAUFEN, *Doppelüberlieferungen*, pp. 132-136.
106. J. SCHÜLING, *Studien*, p. 111.
107. A. FUCHS, *Entwicklung der Beelzebulkontroverse*, pp. 35-121.
108. See further M. E. BORING, "Synoptic Problem," pp. 616-618.
109. J. LAMBRECHT, *Marcus Interpretator*, pp. 72-74.
110. M. FIEGER, *Das Thomasevangelium: Einleitung, Kommentar und Systematik* (NeutAbh, 22), Münster: Aschendorff, 1991, p. 126.

Thomas and seems to be a favorite term of the author.[111] The Thomas version is closest to Mark. In particular, it begins with a negative statement rather than a positive question as in Matthew.[112] We have seen that Matthew's version of the parable preserves the original Q form, and that Mark changed the question to a negative statement to bring the parable into line with the other negative δύναμαι-statements in his Beelzebul Controversy (Mark 3,24.25.26). Since Thomas reflects the redactional text of Mark, Thomas drew the Strong Man from the synoptic gospels, not an independent tradition.

Mark uses the Unforgivable Sin logion (Mark 3,28-30) as a final comment on the Beelzebul Controversy. It's time to move on.

§ 4. The Unforgivable Sin

Mark 3,28-30 (Matt 12,32 par. Luke 12,10)

Luke preserves the original position of the saying in the Q section on Fearless Preaching (Q 12,2-12). Matthew moved the Q saying to Mark's position and conflated it with the Marcan saying.[113]

Matt 12,32	Luke 12,10
καὶ ὃς ἐὰν εἴπῃ λόγον	καὶ πᾶς ὃς ἐρεῖ λόγον
κατὰ τοῦ υἱοῦ τοῦ ἀνθρώπου,	εἰς τὸν υἱὸν τοῦ ἀνθρώπου,
ἀφεθήσεται αὐτῷ·	ἀφεθήσεται αὐτῷ·
ὃς δ᾽ ἂν εἴπῃ κατὰ	τῷ δὲ εἰς τὸ ἅγιον πνεῦμα
τοῦ πνεύματος τοῦ ἁγίου,	βλασφημήσαντι
οὐκ ἀφεθήσεται αὐτῷ	οὐκ ἀφεθήσεται.
οὔτε ἐν τούτῳ τῷ αἰῶνι	
οὔτε ἐν τῷ μέλλοντι.	

Luke's πᾶς is original. Although πᾶς is a favorite word of Luke,[114] its use with the relative is attested in Q.[115] The preceding saying in Q, the saying on Confessing and Denying (Q 12,8-9), begins with πᾶς ὅς,[116] so Luke's καὶ πᾶς ὅς probably preserves the Q beginning of the Unforgivable Sin.[117]

111. Th 17, 21, 22, 35, 41, 98.
112. F. Neirynck, "The Apocryphal Gospels and the Gospel of Mark" (1989), in Id., *Evangelica II*, 1991, pp. 715-772, esp. p. 726.
113. R. Holst, "Reexamining Mk 3:28f. and Its Parallels," in *ZNW* 63 (1972) 122-124.
114. 129 66 158 172.
115. Q 6,47; 12,8.
116. For the reconstruction, see H. Fleddermann, "The Q Saying on Confessing and Denying," *SBL 1987 Seminar Papers*, pp. 606-616.
117. M. E. Boring eliminates the πᾶς from his reconstruction because it is so common in Luke. He does not investigate the Q context where πᾶς appears in both Matthew's and

Luke's future in the relative clause also reflects Q. In conditional relative clauses the future indicative has the same meaning as the subjunctive.[118] The subjunctive, however, is much more common in these clauses. In the synoptics there are eighty-five conditional relative clauses with the subjunctive,[119] but only nine with the future indicative.[120] As a result we would expect a strong tendency to shift from the future indicative to the subjunctive. Mark has only one future indicative in a conditional relative clause (Mark 8,35) and both Matthew and Luke switch to the subjunctive in their editing of this verse (Matt 16,25; Luke 9,24).[121] So Luke's future indicative reflects Q. The preceding Q saying confirms this conclusion, for in the saying on Confessing and Denying (Q 12,8-9), the future indicative also appeared in a conditional relative clause.[122] The choice between κατά and εἰς is difficult, and some scholars follow Matthew.[123] However, Matthew uses κατά with the genitive often.[124] He made a similar substitution of κατά for ἐπί in the Beelzebul Controversy,[125] and he will make the same substitution in the pericope on Family Divisions (compare Matt 10,34-36 with Luke 12,51-53). So Luke's εἰς with the accusative is the Q expression. In the second half of the sentence Luke

Luke's version of the saying on Confessing and Denying (Matt 10,32 par. Luke 12,8). See M. E. BORING, "The Unforgivable Sin Logion Mark iii 28-29 / Matt xii 31-32 / Luke xii 10: Formal Analysis and History of the Tradition," in *NT* 18 (1976) 258-279, esp. p. 266.

118. N. TURNER in J. H. MOULTON, W. F. HOWARD, *A Grammar of New Testament Greek*, vol. 3, Edinburgh: Clark, 1963, pp. 106-110; H. P. V. NUNN, *A Short Syntax of New Testament Greek*, Cambridge: University Press, ⁵1938, p. 121; M. ZERWICK, *Graecitas Biblica Exemplis Illustratur*, Rome: Biblical Institute, ³1955, pp. 96-97; ET: *Biblical Greek Illustrated by Examples*, trans. J. Smith, Rome: Biblical Institute, 1963, pp. 113-116; BDF, § 380.

119. Matt 5,19*bis*.21.22*bis*.31.32; 7,12; 10,11.14.33.42; 11,6.27; 12,32*bis*.50; 14,7; 15,5*bis*; 16,19*bis*25*bis*; 18,5.6.18*bis*.19; 19,9; 20,4.26.27; 21,22.24.44; 22,9; 23,3.16*bis*. 18*bis*; 26,48; Mark 3,28.29.35; 6,11.22.23; 7,11; 8,35.38; 9,37*bis*.41.42; 10,11.15.35. 43.44; 11,23; 13,11; 14,44; Luke 4,6; 7,23; 8,18*bis*; 9,4.5.24*bis*.26.48*bis*; 10,5.8.10. 22.35; 12,8; 17,33*bis*; 18,17; 20,18. See H. FLEDDERMANN, "Q Saying on Confessing and Denying," p. 609 n. 25.

120. Matt 5,41; 10,32; 12,36; 18,4; 23,12*bis*; Mark 8,35; Luke 12,10; 17,31. See H. FLEDDERMANN, "Q Saying on Confessing and Denying," p. 609 n. 26.

121. Compare also Luke 8,18 with Mark 4,25.

122. Boring ("Unforgivable Sin," pp. 266-267) opts for Matthew's subjunctive. However, the Q context (Q 12,8-9), Matthew's and Luke's editing of Mark 8,35, and statistics on the subjunctive and future indicative in conditional relative clauses prove that Q had the future indicative. For the reconstruction of Q 12,8-9, see Chapter VI below.

123. Harnack and Boring choose Matthew's κατά for their reconstructions. See A. HARNACK, *Sprüche und Reden*, p. 97; ET: *Sayings of Jesus*, p. 140; M. E. BORING, "Unforgivable Sin," pp. 266-267.

124. 16 7 6 16.

125. Contrast Matt 12,25 with Luke 11,17 where Matthew makes the substitution, and compare Matt 12,26 with Luke 11,18 where they agree in using ἐπί.

substitutes a participle for the Q relative clause. In editing Mark Luke uses a participle forty times to eliminate parataxis,[126] four times to replace a relative clause,[127] and nine times to replace a variety of other constructions.[128] In other Q texts Matthew has a relative clause and Luke a participle.[129] Given Luke's preference for participles, most of the participles must be traced to his redactional activity. In the present verse the parallelism demands a relative clause in the second half of the sentence. Luke borrowed the verb "blaspheme" from Mark. In his editing of the overlap texts Luke at times switches words between his Marcan source and Q.[130] Matthew preserves the Q verb, but the verb would be in the future indicative. Matthew eliminated the object, but the parallelism of the verse indicates that it stood in Q. Matthew again changed the preposition to κατά with the genitive. Mowery argues that Luke preserved the original Q expression τὸ ἅγιον πνεῦμα in the prepositional phrase. He traces to Q the word order article-adjective-noun found in both Luke 12,10 and Luke 12,12.[131] However, the Q text behind Luke 12,12 probably did not refer to the Holy Spirit.[132] More probably Luke changed the position of the adjective and dropped an article as he does in several other places.[133] So the Q phrase was εἰς τὸ πνεῦμα τὸ ἅγιον. Luke eliminated a superfluous αὐτῷ as he frequently does.[134] Matthew's "neither in this age nor in the age to come" is an expansion of Mark's εἰς τὸν αἰῶνα (Mark 3,29).

We can now compare Q and Mark.

---

126. Luke 4,42; 5,13.24.25; 8,6.7.15.24.25.39.41.47.51: 9,1.10.11.22.28; 18,16.28.33. 38; 19,30*bis*.32.35.46; 20,10.11.15.27.29; 22,13.19.20.41.42.45.64; 23,52. See H. J. CADBURY, *Style and Literary Method*, pp. 134-135; J. JEREMIAS, *Sprache*, p. 116.

127. Luke 8,8 (diff. Mark 4,9); 8,21 (diff. Mark 3,35); 20,27 (diff. Mark 12,18); 23,49 (diff. Mark 15,41). See further H. J. CADBURY, *Style and Literary Method*, pp. 135-136; J. JEREMIAS, *Sprache*, p. 116 n. 3.

128. Luke 5,14; 8,38.45; 9,25.33.48; 18,18; 20,2; 22,3. See H. J. CADBURY, *Style and Literary Method*, p. 136; J. JEREMIAS, *Sprache*, p. 116 n. 4.

129. See, for example, Q 6,47-49; 12,8-9.

130. For instance, Luke introduces elements from the Q Mission Discourse into this redaction of Mark's Mission Discourse. In Luke 9,2 (diff. Mark 6,7) he introduces a reference to preaching the kingdom of God (compare Luke 10,9) and in Luke 9,3 (diff. Mark 6,8) he introduces "silver" into the list of forbidden items (compare Matt 10,9).

131. R. L. MOWERY, "The Articular References to the Holy Spirit in the Synoptic Gospels and Acts," in *BR* 31 (1986) 26-45, esp. pp. 34-35.

132. See the discussion of Mark 13,11 par. Q 12,11-12 in Chapter IX.

133. Luke omits a second article in 4,36 (diff. Mark 1,27), 8,15 (diff. Mark 4,20); 9,26 (diff. Mark 8,38); 12,12 (diff. Mark 13,11); 19,30 (diff. Mark 11,2); and 21,26 (diff. Mark 13,25). See also Acts 1,8; 2,38; 4,31; 9,31; 10,45; 13,4; 16,6. See H. J. CADBURY, *Style and Literary Method*, pp. 197-198.

134. Luke eliminates datives in Luke 5,12.13; 8,30.38.54: 9,18.20.41.49; 18,21; 20,24; 22,51. See H. J. CADBURY, *Style and Literary Method*, pp. 191-192.

Q 12,10	Mark 3,28-30
	28 ἀμὴν λέγω ὑμῖν ὅτι
καὶ πᾶς ὃς ἐρεῖ λόγον	πάντα ἀφεθήσεται τοῖς υἱοῖς
εἰς τὸν υἱὸν τοῦ ἀνθρώπου,	τῶν ἀνθρώπων τὰ ἁμαρτήματα
ἀφεθήσεται αὐτῷ·	καὶ αἱ βλασφημίαι
	ὅσα ἐὰν βλασφημήσωσιν·
ὃς δὲ ἐρεῖ λόγον	29 ὃς δ᾽ ἂν βλασφημήσῃ
εἰς τὸ πνεῦμα τὸ ἅγιον,	εἰς τὸ πνεῦμα τὸ ἅγιον,
οὐκ ἀφεθήσεται αὐτῷ.	οὐκ ἔχει ἄφεσιν εἰς τὸν αἰῶνα
	ἀλλὰ ἔνοχός ἐστιν
	αἰωνίου ἁμαρτήματος.
	30 ὅτι ἔλεγον·
	πνεῦμα ἀκάθαρτον ἔχει.

There are three indications that Mark is secondary. First, the Q text shows a tight parallelism in four clauses. The Marcan text is redundant and expansive with repetitions especially at the end of v. 28 and v. 29.[135] The expansions make the saying more explicit, a sign that Mark is secondary. Second, the Q form refers to the Son of Man. Mark makes no mention of the Son of Man, but he has the unusual double plural τοῖς υἱοῖς τῶν ἀνθρώπων.[136] Here again Mark is secondary. The Son of Man is a powerful figure in the gospels. If the Son of Man has authority that approaches that of God (Mark 2,1-12) and is Lord even of the sabbath (Mark 2,28), then opposition to him is not something that can be forgiven.[137] The Q saying is a difficult saying. Mark eliminates the difficulty by altering the reference to the Son of Man. The more difficult saying is original.[138] Third, Mark's verb "blaspheme" is more technical and theological than the Q expression "speak against," again a sign that Mark is secondary.[139]

Granted that Mark is secondary to Q, does Mark mirror redactional Q as well? The Q saying may not be an independent saying that could have come to Mark from the oral tradition. In the Q context of the section on Fearless Preaching (Q 12,2-12) it comments on and corrects the saying on Confessing and Denying (Q 12,8-9). The Q saying on Confessing and Denying itself probably stems from the Q redactor

135. J. LAMBRECHT, Marcus Interpretator, p. 66.
136. Compare Eph 3,5; 1 Clem. 61,2; T. Reu. 4,7; T. Levi 3,10; 4,1.
137. H. E. TÖDT, Menschensohn, p. 111; ET: Son of Man, p. 120.
138. O. J. F. SEITZ, "The Rejection of the Son of Man: Mark Compared with Q," Studia Evangelica VII, 1982, pp. 451-465, esp. p. 460.
139. H. E. TÖDT, Menschensohn, pp. 284-287; ET: Son of Man, pp. 315-317; K. BERGER, Die Amen-Worte Jesu: Eine Untersuchung zum Problem der Legitimation in apokalyptischer Rede (BZNW, 39), Berlin: Walter de Gruyter, 1970, p. 36.

because it articulates clearly the Son of Man christology of the final document.[140] If the saying on Confessing and Denying comes from the Q redactor, the commenting saying on the Unforgivable Sin does also. In treating the Q saying on John and the Coming One (Q 3,16-17), we saw that the reference to the Holy Spirit was a later insertion in the saying that probably goes back to the Q redactor.[141] Q contains only two references to the Holy Spirit. The first one is a later insertion into a saying, and the second one comes in a saying that comments on the previous saying and corrects it. Both are later additions, and both probably come from the same pen, that of the Q redactor.

Mark joins the saying to the pericope of the Beelzebul Controversy by the solemn "Amen I say to you." Mark adds this expression elsewhere in the overlap texts.[142] In order to avoid saying that a sin against the Son of Man can be forgiven, Mark generalizes the Q saying to include forgiveness of all sins and blasphemies except blasphemy against the Holy Spirit. He omits Q's first relative clause and makes "all sins and blasphemies" subject of the Q main verb ἀφεθήσεται. All this will be forgiven "the sons of men." Mark then adds a redundant relative clause "as much as they blaspheme." Synonymous expressions like the redundant clause are characteristic of Mark.[143] In the second half Mark makes the Q verb "to speak against" more precise by substituting "to blaspheme." He has already anticipated the change in the first half with the words "blasphemy" and "to blaspheme." Both the noun and the verb are Marcan.[144] Mark also makes the saying more explicit by twice adding an eternal note to the statement that the sin will never be forgiven. The οὐκ ... ἀλλά construction he uses is typically Marcan.[145] The repetitions at the end of v. 28 and v. 29 clearly come from Mark.[146]

Besides linking the saying to the Beelzebul Controversy with "Amen I say to you," Mark adds an explicit reference to the charge that Jesus is possessed at the end of the saying: "because they said, 'He has an unclean spirit'" (Mark 3,30).[147] This addition forms an *inclusio* with

---

140. See H. FLEDDERMANN, "Q Saying on Confessing and Denying," pp. 606-616.

141. See Chapter II above.

142. Compare Mark 8,12 with Q 11,29; Mark 11,23 with Q 17,6. See J. LAMBRECHT, *Marcus Interpretator*, p. 66 n. 212.

143. F. NEIRYNCK, *Duality in Mark*, pp. 101-106.

144. For the noun see Mark 7,22; 14,64; for the verb see Mark 2,7; 15,29. See further J. LAMBRECHT, *Marcus Interpretator*, p. 52 n. 137.

145. F. NEIRYNCK, *Duality in Mark*, pp. 90-94.

146. J. LAMBRECHT, *Marcus Interpretator*, p. 67.

147. The adjective ἀκάθαρτος is Marcan (2 11 6 5). See J. C. HAWKINS, *Horae Synopticae*, p. 12.

Mark's redactional addition, "He has Beelzebul" (Mark 3,22), at the beginning of the Beelzebul pericope. Mark picked up the Unforgivable Sin logion from Q; he carefully edited the Q saying; and he used it as a final judgment on the opposition of both Jesus' family and the scribes.

The Gospel of Thomas has a parallel to the logion in Th 44.

> Jesus said, "Whoever blasphemes against the Father will be forgiven, and whoever blasphemes against the Son will be forgiven, but (δέ) whoever blasphemes against the Holy Spirit (πνεῦμα) will not be forgiven, either (οὔτε) on earth or (οὔτε) in heaven."

The Thomas saying consists of three similarly formulated statements about blaspheming against the Father, the Son, and the Holy Spirit. Each statement begins with a relative clause. The first two statements have a postive main verb, but the third concludes with a negative main verb and an additional phrase "either on earth or in heaven." Instead of "the Son of Man" Thomas has "the Son." The omission of the genitive τοῦ ἀνθρώπου does not come from any aversion to the Son of Man title, as Thomas preserves the title in Th 86. The trinitarian expansion of the saying meant that Thomas had to drop the genitive.[148] Th 44 uses the verb "blaspheme." We have seen that the original saying used "speak against" as in Matthew and the first half of Luke's saying. Mark introduced "blaspheme" redactionally into the saying, and Luke picked up the verb from Mark and introduced it into the second half of his saying. Thomas' "blaspheme" thus reflects either redactional Mark or redactional Luke. Thomas also reflects redactional Matthew in the final phrase. Thomas shifted from the temporal terms of Matthew ("this age" / "the coming age") to spatial terms ("earth" / "heaven"), but the double οὔτε ... οὔτε shows that Thomas here follows Matthew.[149] Thomas thus depends on two of the synoptic writers, Matthew and either Mark or Luke.[150] This saying shows how the author of Thomas compared different

---

148. W. Schrage, *Das Verhältnis des Thomas-Evangeliums zur synoptischen Tradition und zu den koptischen Evangelienübersetzungen: Zugleich ein Beitrag zur gnostischen Synoptikerdeutung* (BZNW, 29), Berlin: Töpelmann, 1964, p. 99.

149. J.-É. Ménard, *L'évangile selon Thomas* (Nag Hammadi Studies, 5), Leiden: Brill, 1975, p. 144.

150. Helmut Koester considers the elaboration of the Thomas saying as an independent development. However, the presence of redactional elements of the synoptics in Thomas shows that Thomas depends on the canonical gospels. See H. Koester, *Ancient Christian Gospels: Their History and Development*, London: SCM / Philadelphia: Trinity Press International, 1990, pp. 92-93. For a critique of Koester see C. M. Tuckett, "Q and Thomas: Evidence of a Primitive 'Wisdom Gospel'? A Response to H. Koester," in *ETL* 67 (1991) 346-360, esp. p. 355.

versions of the synoptic sayings and drew terms from more than one
gospel in editing the sayings.

Mark proved to be secondary to Q in the two overlap texts we studied in
the previous chapter. We also found evidence that Mark knew redactional
Q, especially the pronoun "you" which fit the Q context of John's Question
(Q 7,27) but was awkward in Mark's prologue (Mark 1,2). Mark is clearly
secondary to Q in both overlap texts we studied in this chapter. Does
Mark also show signs of the Q redaction? I think so, but the evidence is
more complex. To grasp the evidence we must consider not only the
Beelzebul Controversy and the Unforgivable Sin (Mark 3,22-30) but
also the framing pericope – Jesus' True Family (Mark 3,20-21.31-35).

Jesus has already encountered controversy in Mark (Mark 2,1-3,6),
but the controversy came from his adversaries. Now Mark adds another
dimension. He portrays opposition from those close to Jesus – his own
family – and he relates Jesus' family to his adversaries and to the disciples.
Mark contrasts Jesus' family and the disciples in the pericope of Jesus'
True Family (Mark 3,20-21.31-35). Jesus' family claims he is crazy
(Mark 3,21) while Jesus declares that "those about him" who do God's
will make up his true family (Mark 3,34). In the middle of this pericope
Mark inserts a new section that relates his adversaries to his family. To
formulate the new section Mark reaches out to various parts of the Q
document. For the core of the passage he drastically shortens the Beelzebul
Controversy by omitting several sections of the Q pericope. He then
expands the shortened controversy in four ways, all with links to Q. He
adds a second charge against Jesus by reaching back to the Q charge
leveled against John that John is possessed (Q 7,33). To introduce Jesus'
answer he formulates a rhetorical question which draws on two rhetorical
questions in the Q controversy (Q 11,18.21). He adds the parable of the
divided house, developing a new parable out of a detail of Q's divided
kingdom (Q 11,17). Finally, he reaches forward to the Q section on
Fearless Preaching (Q 12,2-12) to use the saying on the Unforgivable
Sin (Q 12,10) as a final comment on the Beelzebul charge. In other
words, in Mark 3,22-30 we have a complex composition every part
of which goes back to Q. The root passages are dispersed in Q
in more original settings, and Mark draws them together into a new
composition.

Must we trace the section back to Mark? Could not Mark have drawn
the material from a pre-Marcan composition? And if Mark seems
responsible, does he have to draw on Q? Could he not gather the material for his composition from the oral tradition?

Mark clearly composed the section. The framing technique betrays Mark's hand, for Mark uses this literary technique throughout his gospel.[151] Mark carefully relates the Beelzebul Controversy to Jesus' True Family at the beginning, middle, and end of the inserted section. At the beginning he creates a new charge that Jesus "has Beelzebul" (Mark 3,22) to connect the charge that Jesus is crazy to the Q charge that he casts out demons by Beelzebul. In the middle he expands the parable of the divided kingdom by adding a section on the divided house to refer to Jesus' split with his family (Mark 3,25). At the end Mark repeats the charge that Jesus "has an unclean spirit" (Mark 3,30). The theme of the section, Jesus' power, is also Marcan. Mark uses δύναμαι and its cognate noun and adjective repeatedly to highlight God's power at work in Jesus.[152] So both the literary form and the theme carry Mark's finger-prints.

But couldn't Mark simply draw the material from the oral tradition? If Mark were drawing the material from the oral tradition, we would expect to find some non-Q material mixed in, but every aspect of these verses goes back to a Q passage. Even an insignificant detail, like the repetition of the demonstrative "that" (Mark 3,24.25), has roots in Q (Q 11,26).

The conclusion seems inevitable. Mark had the Q document in front of him, and he drew on various parts to compose his version of the Beelzebul Controversy. Mark knew redactional Q.

---

151. Mark 3,20-21.22-30.31-35; Mark 5,21-24.25-34.35-43; Mark 6,7-13.14-29.30; Mark 11,12-14.15-19.20-25; Mark 14,1-2.3-9.10-11; Mark 14,53.54.55-65.66-72.
152. Mark 1,40; 2,7; 3,27; 5,3.30; 6,2.5.14; 8,4; 9,1.3.22.23.28.29.39; 10,27; 12,24; 13,26; 14,36.62; 15,31.

IV

THE PARABLE DISCOURSE

The overlap texts often come in clusters. The Unforgivable Sin logion follows the Beelzebul Controversy immediately and comments on the charges of both the scribes and Jesus' family. We encounter the next five overlap texts crowded together in Mark's Parable Discourse. Four of them appear in a cluster that follows the interpretation of the Sower (Mark 4,21-25), and a fifth, the Mustard Seed (Mark 4,30-32), rounds out the discourse's seed parables.

§ 5. The Lamp

Mark 4,21 (Matt 5,15 par. Luke 11,33)

Luke has a parallel to Mark 4,21 in Luke 8,16 as part of his redaction of Mark's Parable Discourse. He also has another form of the saying which derives from Q (Luke 11,33). Matthew records only the Q saying (Matt 5,15).

Matt 5,15	Luke 11,33
οὐδὲ καίουσιν λύχνον	οὐδεὶς λύχνον ἅψας
καὶ τιθέασιν αὐτὸν	εἰς κρύπτην τίθησιν
ὑπὸ τὸν μόδιον	
ἀλλ᾽ ἐπὶ τὴν λυχνίαν,	ἀλλ᾽ ἐπὶ τὴν λυχνίαν,
καὶ λάμπει	ἵνα οἱ εἰσπορευόμενοι
πᾶσιν τοῖς ἐν τῇ οἰκίᾳ.	τὸ φῶς βλέπωσιν.

According to Gerhard Schneider Matthew's syntax reflects Semitic features that Luke removes and replaces with better Greek. Matthew uses the impersonal third person plural with passive meaning (καίουσιν), and joins the first two verbs with "and." In Schneider's view Luke replaces the Semitic impersonal construction with an indefinite expression, and instead of Matthew's parataxis Luke subordinates.[1] Schneider's

---

1. G. Schneider, "Das Bildwort von der Lampe: Zur Traditionsgeschichte eines Jesus-Wortes" (1970), in Id., *Jesusüberlieferung und Christologie*, 1992, pp. 116-142, esp. pp. 117-118. For other examples of Luke's subordination see Luke 14,28.31; 15,4.8. See S. Schulz, *Q*, p. 474 n. 553. When he subordinated, Luke moved the object before

argumentation needs only a slight correction. Matthew's parataxis is original, but his impersonal plurals are not. Matthew links the saying to the preceding one by οὐδέ. He uses the same redactional procedure in Matt 9,16-17, changing an οὐδείς-saying in his source (Mark 2,22) to an impersonal plural linked to the preceding saying by οὐδέ.[2] So Luke's οὐδείς is original.[3] Luke's verb ἅπτω, though, is redactional. Luke alone among NT writers uses the verb with λύχνος and πυρά.[4] Matthew uses καίω only here in his gospel; it reflects Q.[5] So the first clause in Q probably read: οὐδεὶς καίει λύχνον. Matthew offers "under the bushel basket" as the place where the lamp is concealed. Most manuscripts have a double place of concealment in Luke 11,33 ("in a cellar" ..."under the bushel basket"), but "under the bushel basket" is not read by some very important witnesses and it should be rejected as a harmonizing addition.[6] Matthew's "under the bushel basket" preserves the Q wording; Luke substituted "in a cellar" for the Q phrase. The word "cellar" is a *hapax legomenon* in the NT and is quite rare outside the NT.[7] Despite its rarity there are several indications that it is redactional. First, it mirrors conditions outside Palestine as ordinary Palestinian houses lacked cellars. Luke elsewhere changes his sources to reflect conditions outside Palestine. For instance, he shifts to "tiles" in Luke 5,19 because his readers would not readily understand Mark's text.[8] Second, κρύπτην does not have the article. If original we would expect εἰς τὴν κρύπτην corresponding to ἐπὶ τὴν λυχνίαν. Third, Luke substitutes σκεύει for ὑπὸ τὸν μόδιον in his redaction of Mark 4,21 in Luke 8,16

---

the participle. Dupont follows Schneider's reconstruction. See J. DUPONT, "La transmission des paroles de Jésus sur la lampe et la mesure dans Marc 4,21-25 et dans la tradition Q" (1982), in ID., *Études sur les Évangiles synoptiques*, 1985, 1. 259-294, esp. pp. 268-270.

2. Matthew changes Mark's καὶ οὐδεὶς βάλλει (Mark 2,22) to οὐδὲ βάλλουσιν (Matt 9,17).

3. F. HAHN, "Die Bildworte vom neuen Flicken und vom jungen Wein (Mk. 2,21 f parr)," in *EvT* 31 (1971) 357-375, esp. p. 360; ID., "Die Worte vom Licht Lk 11,33-36," in *Orientierung an Jesus: Zur Theologie der Synoptiker: FS Josef Schmid*, 1973, pp. 107-138, esp. p. 111 n. 11.

4. Luke 8,16; 11,33; 15,8; Acts 28,2. Compare also Luke 12,49 (ἀνήφθη) and Luke 22,55 (περιαψάντων). Luke does not avoid καίω (see Luke 12,35; 24,32).

5. G. SCHNEIDER, "Bildwort von der Lampe," p. 118.

6. "Under the bushel basket" is not read by P[45] P[75] L Ξ 0124 f[1] 700 1241 syr[s] cop[sa] arm geo. See B. M. METZGER, *A Textual Commentary on the Greek New Testament*, London/ New York: United Bible Societies, 1971, p. 159; J. DUPONT, "La lampe sur le lampadaire dans l'évangile de saint Luc (Lc 8,16; 11,33)" (1969), in ID., *Études sur les Évangiles synoptiques*, 1985, 2. 1032-1048, esp. pp. 1034-1035; G. SCHNEIDER, "Bildwort von der Lampe," p. 138.

7. G. SCHNEIDER, "Bildwort von der Lampe," p. 118.

8. J. A. FITZMYER, *Luke*, 1. 582.

following his general tendency to omit or translate foreign words.[9] So we should reject εἰς κρύπτην as Lucan. Luke also dropped a superfluous αὐτόν. Thus Matthew basically reproduces the second Q clause except that the verb would be in the singular instead of Matthew's impersonal plural.

The reconstruction of the last clause is difficult. Steinhauser basically follows Luke although he makes two adjustments. He eliminates Luke's participle εἰσπορευόμενοι, and he recasts Luke's purpose clause into a present indicative linked paratactically to the preceding: καὶ οἱ ἐν τῇ οἰκίᾳ τὸ φῶς βλέπωσιν.[10] Schneider, though, correctly sees that Matthew's last clause preserves Q.[11] Luke picks up the purpose clause from Mark 4,21, but he fills it with the content of the last Q clause preserved in Matt 5,15. He shifts the accent, though, from the lamp to those who enter and see the light. Luke's clause contains a Lucan expression οἱ εἰσπορευόμενοι. The participle εἰσπορευόμενος is found seven times in Luke-Acts,[12] and five of these passages have the plural οἱ εἰσπορευόμενοι.[13] Not only is the diction of the ἵνα-clause Lucan, the thought is as well. Luke consistently equates light with God and salvation throughout Luke-Acts.[14] Luke adds an almost identical clause in his redaction of Mark 4,21 in Luke 8,16.[15] We can now compare the Q saying with Mark.

Q 11,33	Mark 4,21
	καὶ ἔλεγεν αὐτοῖς·
οὐδεὶς καίει λύχνον	μήτι ἔρχεται ὁ λύχνος
καὶ τίθησιν αὐτὸν	
ὑπὸ τὸν μόδιον	ἵνα ὑπὸ τὸν μόδιον τεθῇ
	ἢ ὑπὸ τὴν κλίνην;
ἀλλ' ἐπὶ τὴν λυχνίαν,	οὐχ ἵνα ἐπὶ τὴν λυχνίαν τεθῇ·
καὶ λάμπει	
πᾶσιν τοῖς ἐν τῇ οἰκίᾳ.	

9. Compare, for example, Luke 6,14 (diff. Mark 3,17); Luke 6,15 (diff. Mark 3,18); Luke 8,12 (diff. Mark 4,15); Luke 8,54 (diff. Mark 5,41); Luke 9,3 (diff. Mark 6,8); Luke 18,35 (diff. Mark 10,46); Luke 19,38 (diff. Mark 11,9-10); Luke 21,2 (diff. Mark 12,42). See further H. J. CADBURY, *Style and Literary Method*, pp. 156-157.

10. M. G. STEINHAUSER, "The Sayings of Jesus in Mark 4:21-22, 24b-25," in *Forum* 6/3-4 (1990) 197-217, esp. pp. 200-201.

11. G. SCHNEIDER, "Bildwort von der Lampe," pp. 118-119.

12. Luke 8,16; 11,33; 19,30; Acts 3,2; 8,3; 9,28; 28,30.

13. Luke 8,16; 11,33; 19,30; Acts 3,2; 28,30.

14. See Luke 1,76-79; 9,29; Acts 9,3; 12,7; 22,6.9; 26,13.18. See S. R. GARRETT, "'Lest the Light in You be Darkness': Luke 11:33-36 and the Question of Commitment," in *JBL* 110 (1991) 93-105, esp. pp. 95-96.

15. If φῶς is read in Luke 11,33 the clauses differ only in word order. According to Schneider ("Bildwort von der Lampe," p. 117 n. 3) the much rarer φέγγος should be read as the more difficult reading with P⁴⁵ A K L W *et al.* But the reading φῶς has much stronger attestation (P⁷⁵ ℵ B C D θ f¹ f¹³ 33 892 *et al.*) and should be read.

When we compare the two sayings, we find strikingly different formulations. The Q form of the saying presents a straightforward image about the proper placement of a lamp. The Marcan form allegorizes and personifies the lamp. The lamp now has the article, and the human agent disappears. Instead of someone lighting and placing the lamp, in Mark the lamp itself comes. The lamp has become a symbol of the Word. The evolution of image into symbol shows that Mark is secondary to Q. Furthermore, the Q saying, like many aphorisms, simply lays out a statement and refrains from any explicit interpretation. Mark's form is more explicitly didactic. The two rhetorical questions engage the reader directly, and the twin purpose clauses raise the question of meaning more explicitly than the Q understatement. The didactic nature of Mark's text shows that Mark is secondary. Finally, Mark has a double place of concealment, "under the bushel basket" and "under the bed," whereas Q mentions only one. The double place heightens the contrast between the proper and improper placement of the lamp. Since the contrast plays a central role in the saying, it is more likely that Mark heightened it than that Q toned it down.

We can trace the differences between the two sayings to Marcan redaction. The expression καὶ ἔλεγεν αὐτοῖς is typically Marcan.[16] The double καὶ ἔλεγεν αὐτοῖς in v. 21 and v. 24 neatly divides the cluster of four sayings in Mark 4,21-25 into two parts.[17] Mark transferred the οὐκ ... ἀλλά construction of the Q saying to v. 22.[18] The two rhetorical questions are Marcan. Mark frequently uses rhetorical questions[19] and double questions.[20] He also commonly lets the same speaker follow a question with a statement.[21] For Mark the lamp is the Word.[22] The article

---

16. Mark 2,27; 4,2.11.21.24; 6,4.10; 7,9; 8,21; 9,1.31; 11,17. See P. DSCHULNIGG, *Sprache, Redaktion und Intention des Markus-Evangeliums: Eigentümlichkeiten der Sprache des Markus-Evangeliums und ihre Bedeutung für die Redaktionskritik* (SBB, 11), Stuttgart: Katholisches Bibelwerk, 1984, pp. 86-87.

17. J. DUPONT, "Transmission des paroles de Jésus," pp. 259-260.

18. J. LAMBRECHT, "Redaction and Theology," pp. 288-289.

19. Mark 1,24*bis*.27; 2,7*bis*.8.9; 3,4*bis*.33; 4,13*bis*.21*bis*.30*bis*.40*bis*; 5,35.39; 6,2*bis*.3*bis*; 8,12.17*ter*.18.21.36.37; 9,19*bis*; 12,24.26; 14,37*bis*.63.

20. Mark 1,24; 2,7.8-9; 3,4; 4,13.21.30.40; 6,2.3; 7,18-19; 8,17-20.36-37; 9,19; 11,28; 12,14; 13,4; 14,37.63-64. See F. NEIRYNCK, *Duality in Mark*, pp. 125-126.

21. Mark 1,24.27; 2,7.9-10; 4,13-14.21-22; 8,12.36-38; 9,19; 12,15; 14,37-38.63-64. See G. SCHNEIDER, "Bildwort von der Lampe," p. 130 n. 61; F. NEIRYNCK, *Duality in Mark*, p. 61.

22. For J. P. Heil the lamp symbolizes both Jesus' identity and his teaching. See J. P. HEIL, "Reader-Response and the Narrative Context of the Parables about Growing Seed in Mark 4:1-34," in *CBQ* 54 (1992) 271-286, esp. p. 281 n. 25.

with "lamp" serves Mark's purpose. Since the lamp is the Word, Mark emphasizes it by making it the subject and by adding the article. Mark suppresses the human agent; the lamp itself "comes." The use of ἔρχε-ται with a non-personal subject is found in Greek in the sense of the beginning of an event,[23] and this usage surfaces elsewhere in Mark. Mark uses ἔρχομαι for the coming of days (Mark 2,20), the coming of the hour (Mark 14,41), the coming of the kingdom (Mark 9,1; 11,10), as well as the coming of Jesus and the Son of Man.[24] The verb "come" portrays the proclamation of the Word as an event. Mark has a corresponding "come" in the ἔλθῃ of the following verse (v. 22). Just as the lamp comes to be placed on the lampstand, so what becomes hidden is hidden only "to come to light." The two ἵνα-clauses have a parallel formulation with the same main verb (τεθῇ). The verb comes from Q, but the passive comes from Mark's redactional decision to personify the lamp and eliminate the human agent. The two ἵνα-clauses also parallel the two ἵνα-clauses in v. 22 which express Mark's view that the word is hidden to be revealed.[25] Mark's addition "under the bed" is a typically Marcan synonymous expression.[26] The doubling of the place of concealment could be an attempt to imitate the rather full treatment given to the negative fate much of the seed suffers in the Sower (Mark 4,3-9.13-20) or it could warn against an esoteric understanding of the Word.[27] Mark had to omit the last Q clause "and it gives light to all in the house" once he recast the saying into the double rhetorical question with the two final clauses.

The Lamp Saying corrects the parable theory (Mark 4,10-12). The parable theory plays an important role in the central theme of Mark, the messianic secret.[28] Jesus may conceal the Word in parables so that the outsiders may not see or understand, but it belongs in the public forum just as the lamp is meant for the lampstand. The lamp comes to be placed on the lampstand; just so the Word comes for full disclosure. Mark will also emphasize full revelation in the following saying (Mark 4,22).

23. Compare the coming of scandals in Q 17,1-2. See J. SCHNEIDER, "ἔρχομαι," *TDNT* 2 (1964) 666-684, esp. p. 667.

24. Jesus "comes" in Mark 1,7.9.14.24.39; 2,17; 6,1.48; 7,31; 8,10; 10,1; 11,9. The Son of Man "comes" in Mark 8,38; 10,45; 13,26; 14,62.

25. Lambrecht correctly insists that the four ἵνα-clauses must be interpreted together and that all four are redactional. See J. LAMBRECHT, "Redaction and Theology," pp. 288-289.

26. For a list of synonymous expressions in Mark, see F. NEIRYNCK, *Duality in Mark*, pp. 101-106.

27. G. SCHNEIDER, "Bildwort von der Lampe," p. 132; J. LAMBRECHT, "Redaction and Theology," p. 288.

28. On the parable theory see W. WREDE, *Das Messiasgeheimnis in den Evangelien: Zugleich ein Beitrag zum Verständnis des Markusevangeliums*, Göttingen: Vandenhoeck & Ruprecht, ³1965, pp. 54-65; ET: *The Messianic Secret*, trans. J. C. G. Grieg, Greenwood, SC: Attic, 1971, pp. 56-66.

The Gospel of Thomas has a version of the Lamp Saying in Th 33.

> Jesus said, "What you will hear in your ear proclaim in the other ear upon your housetops. For (γάρ) no one lights a lamp (and) puts it under a bushel, nor (οὐδέ) does he put it in a hidden place, but (ἀλλά) he puts it upon the lampstand (λυχνία), so that all who go in and come out will see its light."

The first half of the Thomas saying develops the second saying of the pericope on Fearless Preaching (Matt 10,27 par. Luke 12,3); the second half parallels the Lamp Saying. Thomas appears closest to the two Lucan sayings (Luke 8,16; 11,33). For example, Thomas presupposes Luke's οὐδείς at the beginning of the saying. We have seen that οὐδείς belongs to the original Q saying. Thomas does reflect, though, three redactional changes that Luke introduced into the saying. First, Thomas' "in a hidden place" picks up Luke's εἰς κρύπτην (Luke 11,33). Second, Thomas' "who go in" reflects Luke's οἱ εἰσπορευόμενοι (Luke 8,16; 11,33).[29] Third, Thomas' "see its light" echoes Luke's τὸ φῶς βλέπωσιν (Luke 8,16; 11,33). Since Thomas reflects the redactional text of Luke, the Thomas saying is secondary.[30] Thomas also reflects redactional Matthew, not in the wording of the saying but in its position. Immediately before the Lamp Saying (Matt 5,15) Matthew has the logion on the city built on a mountain (Matt 5,14b). Thomas also places the logion on the city (Th 32) immediately before the lamp saying (Th 33). Matt 5,13-16, though, consists of originally separate sayings that Matthew has secondarily drawn together,[31] so in these two sayings (Th 32, 33) Thomas reflects the redactional order of Matthew (Matt 5,14b. 15).[32] Th 33 again demonstrates how the author of Thomas compared various forms of the synoptic sayings and drew elements from several of them to compose his new versions of the sayings. In doing so Thomas often picks up redactional features of the synoptics, thus showing that he depends on the synoptic gospels in their final form.

---

29. John Kloppenborg (*Formation of Q*, p. 135 n. 144) disputes the redactional nature of οἱ εἰσπορευόμενοι, pointing to the presence of the phrase in Q 11,52. However, Q 11,52 uses οἱ εἰσερχόμενοι, not the Lucan οἱ εἰσπορευόμενοι (Luke 8,16; 11,33; 19,30; Acts 3,2; 28,30).

30. G. SCHNEIDER, "Bildwort von der Lampe," pp. 139-140; W. D. DAVIES and D. C. ALLISON, *Matthew*, 1. 478 n. 18.

31. W. D. DAVIES and D. C. ALLISON, *Matthew*, 1. 470-471.

32. F. HAHN, "Worte vom Licht," pp. 113-114; S. J. PATTERSON, "Introduction," in *Q-Thomas Reader*, 1990, pp. 77-123, esp. pp. 86, 122 n. 12.

§ 6. What is Hidden Will be Revealed

Mark 4,22 (Matt 10,26 par. Luke 12,2)

The Q saying begins a section on Fearless Confession (Q 12,2-12). Luke has both the Q saying (Luke 12,2) and a redaction of Mark 4,22 in Luke 8,17, but Matthew passes over Mark 4,22 and only records the Q saying (Matt 10,26). Matthew and Luke interpret the saying differently. Matthew uses it to encourage the disciples to confess publicly (Matt 10,27) whereas Luke uses it to warn against hypocrisy (compare Luke 12,1.3). Despite the different applications, Matthew and Luke agree closely in the wording of the saying which makes the Q reconstruction relatively easy.

Matt 10,26	Luke 12,2
μὴ οὖν φοβηθῆτε αὐτούς·	
οὐδὲν γάρ ἐστιν κεκαλυμμένον	οὐδὲν δὲ συγκεκαλυμμένον ἐστὶν
ὃ οὐκ ἀποκαλυφθήσεται	ὃ οὐκ ἀποκαλυφθήσεται
καὶ κρυπτὸν	καὶ κρυπτὸν
ὃ οὐ γνωσθήσεται.	ὃ οὐ γνωσθήσεται.

Matthew's introduction "therefore do not fear them" is redactional. It both concludes his passage on persecution (Matt 10,17-25) and anticipates a major theme of the Q section (Q 12,4.7).[33] It is also somewhat awkward in that it does not fit the thought of the Q saying very well.[34] Matthew's γάρ links the saying to his introductory summons not to fear, and Luke's δέ extends the thought of his redactional introduction Luke 12,1. Both conjunctions are redactional since they bind the saying to the immediate context of each gospel.[35] Luke's compound verb is secondary. In general Luke likes compound verbs, and he is especially fond of compounds with σύν.[36] Matthew preserves the Q word order in the first clause. Luke places a participle in the pre-position fairly frequently.[37] In Luke 20,6 Luke introduces a participle in the pre-position into his redaction of Mark (compare Mark 11,32). Matthew also occasionally has a participle in the pre-position (Matt 3,15; 10,30; 12,4), even in redactional texts (Matt 3,15; 12,4). Matthew did not feel a need to change a participle from the pre-position in Matt 10,30, so it is unlikely he would shift one

33. S. Schulz, Q, p. 461; R. Laufen, Doppelüberlieferungen, p. 156.
34. S. Schulz, Q, p. 461.
35. S. Schulz, Q, p. 461; J. Dupont, "Transmission des paroles de Jésus," p. 272.
36. H. J. Cadbury, Style and Literary Method, pp. 166-168; J. Schmid, Matthäus und Lukas, p. 49; J. Jeremias, Sprache, pp. 86-87.
37. Luke 1,7; 20,6; 24,32.38; Acts 1,10.17; 2,13; 14,7; 20,13; 25,10.

a few verses earlier in the same passage. In other words, we can explain Luke's but not Matthew's hypothetical change. We can now compare Q and Mark.

Q 12,2	Mark 4,22
οὐδέν ἐστιν κεκαλυμμένον	οὐ γάρ ἐστιν κρυπτὸν
ὃ οὐκ ἀποκαλυφθήσεται	ἐὰν μὴ ἵνα φανερωθῇ,
καὶ κρυπτὸν	οὐδὲ ἐγένετο ἀπόκρυφον
ὃ οὐ γνωσθήσεται.	ἀλλ᾽ ἵνα ἔλθῃ εἰς φανερόν.

There are two indications that the Q saying is more original than the Marcan saying. First, the Q saying is a wisdom saying that expresses the general truth that what is hidden inevitably comes to light. Compared to the Q saying, the Marcan saying seems contrived. Mark's saying has the form of a general wisdom aphorism, but it does not describe a general occurrence. It rather presents a paradox – that something would be concealed in order to be revealed. The artificial nature of Mark's saying shows that it is secondary.[38] Second, the paradox is such logical nonsense that it makes sense only in the context of Mark's Parable Discourse, referring specifically to the parable theory (Mark 4,10-12).[39] We can see the harshness of Mark's saying at a glance by comparing Luke's redaction of it where he eliminates the two purpose clauses (Luke 8,17).[40] Since Mark's saying could only exist in the context of Mark's gospel, the Q saying is original.

Synonymous parallelism dominates both the Marcan and the Q saying. The differences between the sayings can be explained as Marcan redaction. Mark replaced Q's οὐδέν with οὐ γάρ because the saying gives the theological principle behind the Lamp Saying.[41] In both halves of the

---

38. J. DUPONT, "Transmission des paroles de Jésus," p. 274.

39. J. Jeremias and H. Zimmermann claim that the logion pairs in vv. 21-22 and 24cd-25 were joined in the pre-Marcan tradition. However, since v. 22 clearly refers to Mark's parable theory, it blocks any attempt to see a pre-Marcan cluster in vv. 21-22. See J. JEREMIAS, *Die Gleichnisse Jesu*, Göttingen: Vandenhoeck & Ruprecht, ⁸1970, pp. 90-91; ET: *The Parables of Jesus*, trans. S. H. Hooke, New York: Charles Scribner's Sons, ²1963, p. 91, H. ZIMMERMANN, *Neutestamentliche Methodenlehre: Darstellung der historisch-kritischen Methode*, Stuttgart: Katholisches Bibelwerk, ³1970, pp. 187-188. See further E. BEST, "Mark's Preservation of the Tradition" (1974), in ID., *Disciples and Discipleship: Studies in the Gospel according to Mark*, Edinburgh: Clark, 1986, pp. 31-48, esp. pp. 43-45.

40. J. C. HAWKINS, *Horae Synopticae*, pp. 100-101.

41. Compare a similar use of γάρ in v. 25. Mark uses γάρ to link sayings in clusters. See, for example, Mark 8,35.36.37.38 and Mark 9,39.40.41.49. Explanatory γάρ-clauses are quite common in Mark. See, for example, Mark 1,16.22; 2,15; 3,10.21; 5,8.28.42; 6,14.18.31.52; 9,6*bis*.31.34; 10,22; 11,18*bis*; 12,12; 14,2.40; 15,10; 16,4.8*bis*. See T. SNOY, "La rédaction marcienne de la marche sur les eaux (Mc., VI,45-52)," in *ETL* 44 (1968) 205-241, 433-481, esp. p. 448 n. 218.

saying Mark substituted purpose clauses for Q's relative clauses. The two purpose clauses correspond closely to the two purpose clauses in v. 21.[42] Just as the lamp comes to be placed on the lampstand, not under the bushel basket or the bed, so what is hidden is hidden only to be revealed. Mark drew the adjective "hidden" from the second half of the Q saying and moved it forward to set up the contrast "hidden" – "made known" which he expresses in both halves of the saying. Instead of Q's ἀποκαλύπτω Mark substituted φανερόω to express the revelation. Although the verb appears only here in Mark, Mark uses the adjective φανερός in the second purpose clause, and the adjective plays a role in Mark's messianic secret.[43] In the second half of the saying Mark used another adjective "concealed" to balance "hidden," and he switched from ἐστίν to ἐγένετο to move from static to dynamic terms leading to the second purpose clause ἵνα ἔλθῃ εἰς φανερόν. The ἔλθῃ in the last clause corresponds to ἔρχεται in the Lamp Saying. Just as the lamp comes (ἔρχεται) not to be put under the bushel basket or the bed but on the lampstand, so what becomes concealed becomes concealed only in order to come (ἔλθῃ) to light. Mark also shifted the οὐκ ... ἀλλά construction from the Q Lamp Saying to the second half of v. 22.[44]

With vv. 21-22 Mark looks back on the parable theory (Mark 4,10-12) and the explanation of the Sower (Mark 4,13-20) and forward to the two parables of the Seed Growing Secretly (Mark 4,26-29) and the Mustard Seed (Mark 4,30-32). The adjectives "hidden" and "concealed" are related to the "mystery" in Mark 4,11, and the verbs in v. 22 stress the stages in God's plan and thus give Mark's view of salvation history. This concept of salvation history adds an historical dimension to the secrecy motif of the parable theory (Mark 4,10-12). The hidden must and will be revealed.[45] Mark here expresses his view that the gospel, the mystery of the kingdom of God, the secret of Jesus' person, was concealed only to be revealed. The revelation will ultimately unfold in the worldwide proclamation of the gospel (Mark 13,10; 14,9). The privilege of the disciples carries within it the mission to announce the Word.[46] The

42. Mark frequently uses ἵνα-clauses (39 64 46 15). For multiple ἵνα-clauses see Mark 3,9.14; 5,23. On ἀλλ' ἵνα, see Mark 14,49. On the four ἵνα-clauses in vv. 21-22, see J. LAMBRECHT, "Redaction and Theology," p. 289 n. 86.

43. Compare Mark 3,12; 6,14.

44. F. Neirynck (*Duality in Mark*, pp. 90-94) lists eighty-six examples of οὐκ...ἀλλά and related constructions in Mark.

45. G. SCHNEIDER, "Bildwort von der Lampe," p. 129; R. LAUFEN, *Doppelüberlieferungen*, pp. 165-166.

46. J. LAMBRECHT, *Once More Astonished: The Parables of Jesus*, New York: Crossroad, 1983, p. 96.

sayings in vv. 21-22 also generalize and extend the parable explanation given in vv. 14-20. The hidden speaking in parables has an inner dynamic that drives toward revelation.[47] Finally they also point forward to the twin parables of the Seed Growing Secretly and the Mustard Seed. The hidden and apparently insignificant beginning stage of sowing a tiny seed drives toward a magnificent result which everyone can see – the harvest and the mature mustard plant.[48]

Thomas has a parallel to the saying in Th 5.

> Jesus said, "Know what is before your face, and that which is hidden from you will be revealed to you. For (γάρ) there is nothing hidden which will not be revealed."

The second sentence in Th 5 agrees closely with Luke 8,17, the Lucan parallel to Mark 4,22.[49] In editing Mark 4,22 Luke replaced Mark's conditional clause (ἐὰν μὴ ἵνα φανερωθῇ) with a relative (ὃ οὐ φανερὸν γενήσεται). The Thomas saying has the relative clause, so it depends on the redactional text of Luke. The original Greek form is preserved in *P. Oxy*. 654.27-31.[50]

> λέγει Ἰη(σοῦ)ς· γ[νῶθι τὸ ὃν ἔμπροσ]θεν τῆς ὄψεως σου, καὶ [τὸ κεκαλυμμένον] ἀπό σου ἀποκαλυφ(θ)ήσετ[αί σοι· οὐ γάρ ἐσ]τιν κρυπτὸν ὃ οὐ φανε[ρὸν γενήσεται] καὶ θεθαμμένον ὃ ο[ὐκ ἐγερθή-σεται].

The Greek version contains an additional clause not present in the Coptic, but the rest of the Greek saying corresponds closely to the Coptic. Although the papyrus is damaged, the critical relative is preserved, so not only does the Coptic saying depend on redactional Luke, the underlying Greek saying does as well.[51] We can trace Thomas' dependence on the synoptics as far back as we can trace Thomas.

---

47. H. Zimmermann, *Methodenlehre*, p. 187.
48. G. Schneider, "Bildwort von der Lampe," p. 129.
49. The sentence "For there is nothing hidden which will not be revealed" is repeated exactly in Th 6b.
50. For the reconstruction, see J. A. Fitzmyer, "The Oxyrhynchus Logoi of Jesus and the Coptic Gospel according to Thomas" (1959), in Id., *Essays on the Semitic Background*, 1974, pp. 355-433, esp. pp. 381-384.
51. C. Tuckett, "Thomas and the Synoptics," pp. 145-146.

§ 7. THE MEASURE

Mark 4,24cd (Matt 7,2b par. Luke 6,38c; Matt 6,33b par. Luke 12,31b)

Mark 4,24cd parallels two Q texts. Mark 4,24c is similar to Q 6,38c and Mark 4,24d to Q 12,31b.

Matt 7,2b	Luke 6,38c
καὶ ἐν ᾧ μέτρῳ μετρεῖτε	ᾧ γὰρ μέτρῳ μετρεῖτε
μετρηθήσεται ὑμῖν.	ἀντιμετρηθήσεται ὑμῖν.

Matt 6,33	Luke 12,31
ζητεῖτε δὲ πρῶτον	πλὴν ζητεῖτε
τὴν βασιλείαν	τὴν βασιλείαν αὐτοῦ,
καὶ τὴν δικαιοσύνην αὐτοῦ,	
καὶ ταῦτα πάντα	καὶ ταῦτα
προστεθήσεται ὑμῖν.	προστεθήσεται ὑμῖν.

Matthew and Luke agree fairly closely in the first passage. Luke probably preserved the Q conjunction γάρ. To decide between the two conjunctions we need to evaluate the contexts the saying appears in. We can claim neither Matt 7,2a[52] nor Luke 6,37bc-38ab[53] for Q. Probably both are redactional which means that originally Matt 7,2b par. Luke 6,38c followed Matt 7,1 par. Luke 6,37a.[54] Luke's γάρ fits perfectly, and Matthew, in fact, uses γάρ in Matt 7,2a. Luke dropped the preposition ἐν for stylistic reasons.[55] Matthew reflects the Q verb in the main clause as Luke loves to introduce compounds, and he especially likes to lengthen the already long forms of the future passive.[56]

In the second Q text Luke substituted πλήν for an original δέ preserved by Matthew. Luke uses πλήν frequently.[57] It is not impossible that the word appeared here for it is attested elsewhere in Q,[58] but Matthew and Luke both use the word redactionally,[59] so Matthew had no

52. "For with the judgment you judge, you will be judged."
53. "Condemn not and you will not be condemned; forgive, and you will be forgiven, give, and it will be given to you; good measure, pressed down, shaken together, running over, will be put into your lap."
54. "Judge not that you be not (Luke: "and you will not be") judged."
55. Luke omitted a similar ἐν in Luke 3,16. See also S. SCHULZ, Q, pp. 146-147.
56. Luke lengthens συναχθήσονται (Matt 24,28) to ἐπισυναχθήσονται (Luke 17,37). Compare also ἐπαναπαήσεται (Luke 10,6), ἀφαιρεθήσεται (Luke 10,42), ἀνταποδοθήσεται (Luke 14,14), συνθλασθήσεται (Luke 20,18). See H. FLEDDERMANN, "Q Saying on Confessing and Denying," p. 612 n. 40.
57. 5 1 15 4.
58. The word is certainly attested in Q 10,14; 17,1.
59. Matt 11,24; 26,39.64; Luke 6,24.35; 10,11.20; 11,41; 13,33; 18,8; 19,27; 22,21.42; 23,28.

reason to avoid it if he had found it in Q.[60] Matthew's πρῶτον reflects Q.[61] Matthew skillfully slips καὶ τὴν δικαιοσύνην between βασιλείαν and the genitive pronoun αὐτοῦ.[62] Matthew's "all" comes from Q (compare Q 12,30).

We can now compare the two Q texts and Mark.

Q 6,38c	Mark 4,24cd
ἐν ᾧ γὰρ μέτρῳ μετρεῖτε	ἐν ᾧ μέτρῳ μετρεῖτε
μετρηθήσεται ὑμῖν.	μετρηθήσεται ὑμῖν

Q 12,31	
ζητεῖτε δὲ πρῶτον τὴν βασιλείαν αὐτοῦ	
καὶ ταῦτα πάντα	καὶ
προστεθήσεται ὑμιν.	προστεθήσεται ὑμῖν.

Two considerations show that Mark's saying is later than the Q saying. First, Mark's saying contains a secondary addition. In the Q Measure Saying the same norm one uses for others will be used by God (theological passive) for oneself. The words καὶ προστεθήσεται ὑμῖν do not fit in this context. They make sense in Q 12,31 where the admonition not to worry about food and clothing culminates in the command to seek the kingdom and "all these things" will be added.[63] The addition of the words in the Measure Saying breaks the mold of the Q aphorism, but it fits perfectly in the context of Mark's Parable Discourse. Mark has just emphasized the superabundant harvest of the Word (Mark 4,20). Mark uses the Measure Saying to urge the disciples to pay close attention to the Word, and he introduces the saying with a double summons to hear in vv. 23-24ab. If the disciples listen they will be rewarded generously, even beyond the measure of their own generosity. Second, Mark's form of the saying shifts the meaning of the word "measure." In Q "measure" refers to the judgment in both parts of the saying. In the measure you measure (the way you judge others), it will be measured to you (you will be judged). In Mark "measure" refers to attentive listening to the Word in the first part of the saying. In the second part of the saying Mark

60. See further H. J. CADBURY, *Style and Literary Method*, p. 147.
61. The adverb is attested three times in Q (Q 6,42; 9,59; 11,22). Compare also Q 11,26.
62. The noun δικαιοσύνη is redactional in Matt 3,15; 5,6.10.20; 6,1.33; 21,32. See S. SCHULZ, *Q*, p. 152 n. 102. After τὴν βασιλείαν many manuscripts read τοῦ θεοῦ. However, the shorter reading has excellent credentials (א B it[1] *al.*), and it explains the longer readings. See B. M. METZGER, *Textual Commentary*, pp. 18-19.
63. J. C. HAWKINS, "Three Limitations to St. Luke's Use of St. Mark's Gospel," in W. SANDAY (ed.), *Studies in the Synoptic Problem*, 1911, pp. 27-94, esp. p. 32.

comes closer to the Q meaning "judge." According to Mark the measure
with which the disciples measure (i.e., the generosity with which they
listen to the Word) will be the measure (norm) by which they are measured
(judged), and even more will be added. This shift in the meaning of
"measure" indicates that the Q saying is original.[64]

In taking over the Measure Saying Mark omits Q's γάρ because he
has created a more elaborate introduction with his standard καὶ ἔλεγεν
αὐτοῖς followed by the command to pay attention βλέπετε τί ἀκούετε.
Otherwise he takes over the Q saying unchanged. He dropped the first
half of the second saying because it did not suit his context. Q's "all these
things" had to drop out when the saying was taken from its Q context.
By adding "and it will be added to you" to the Q Measure Saying Mark
creates a transition to the following saying (Mark 4,25).[65]

Mark conflated two Q texts. He altered the texts only slightly, but the
conflation of the two texts and the new context in the Parable Discourse
shattered the Q Measure Saying. What led to the conflation? Mark uses
the Measure Saying to highlight the rewards that the disciples will enjoy
if they listen to the Word. The rewards come from hearing the Word
which is nothing less than the mystery of the kingdom of God (Mark
4,11). The Q Kingdom Saying centers on the reward that comes from
seeking the kingdom. The thought of the Kingdom Saying lay so close
to Mark's intention that he naturally conflated it with the Measure Saying.
Again we find evidence that Mark had the Q document in front of him,
and he combined Q sayings into new creations.

§ 8. To One Who Has Will Be Given

Mark 4,25 (Matt 25,29 par. Luke 19,26)

The Q parallel concludes the parable of the Talents or Pounds. Both
Matthew and Luke also redacted Mark 4,25 in their versions of the Parable Discourse (Matt 13,12; Luke 8,18).

Matt 25,29	Luke 19,26
	λέγω ὑμῖν ὅτι
τῷ γὰρ ἔχοντι παντὶ δοθήσεται	παντὶ τῷ ἔχοντι δοθήσεται,
καὶ περισσευθήσεται,	
τοῦ δὲ μὴ ἔχοντος	ἀπὸ δὲ τοῦ μὴ ἔχοντος
καὶ ὃ ἔχει ἀρθήσεται ἀπ' αὐτοῦ.	καὶ ὃ ἔχει ἀρθήσεται.

64. J. LAMBRECHT, *Marcus Interpretator*, p. 118 n. 42.
65. H. ZIMMERMANN, *Methodenlehre*, p. 190; R. LAUFEN, *Doppelüberlieferungen*, p. 166.

Luke's λέγω ὑμῖν ὅτι is redactional. Luke introduces a tiny dialogue at the end of the parable of the Pounds. When the master orders the single pound given to the one who has ten, Luke introduces a protest: "And they said to him, 'Lord, he has ten pounds'" (Luke 19,25). Luke's λέγω ὑμῖν ὅτι continues the dialogue with the master's reply.[66] Q connected the saying to the parable by γάρ as in Matthew. Matthew also reflects the original position of παντί. It appears to limp badly, but the τοῦ δέ of the second clause picks up the τῷ γάρ of the initial clause, indicating that the γάρ is original and that it displaced παντί. Matthew added καὶ περισσευθήσεται. He attached the same clause to his redaction of Mark 4,25 (compare Matt 13,12). Luke improves the syntax in the second half of the sentence. Matthew's τοῦ δὲ μὴ ἔχοντος is a *casus pendens*.[67] Luke frequently removes anacolouthon where it occurs in his sources; he also makes sentences more compact.[68] By dropping αὐτοῦ and drawing ἀπό forward Luke eliminates the anacolouthon and creates a more compact sentence. We can compare the reconstructed Q saying with Mark.

Q 19,26	Mark 4,25
τῷ γὰρ ἔχοντι παντὶ δοθήσεται,	ὃς γὰρ ἔχει, δοθήσεται αὐτῷ·
τοῦ δὲ μὴ ἔχοντος	καὶ ὃς οὐκ ἔχει,
καὶ ὃ ἔχει ἀρθήσεται ἀπ᾽ αὐτοῦ.	καὶ ὃ ἔχει ἀρθήσεται ἀπ᾽ αὐτοῦ.

The Q saying and the Marcan saying are close. They express the same idea, but employ different syntax. Where Q has participles, Mark writes relative clauses. The Q syntax appears original. It is easier to see a shift from the *casus pendens* of the second Q participle to Mark's relative clause than to imagine the reverse change.

Mark's redaction is straightforward. He removes the grammatical difficulty by turning the second Q participial phrase into a relative clause. For symmetry he also replaces the first participle with a relative clause. This pattern recurs in the overlap texts. On three other occasions Mark introduces relative clauses where Q has participles.[69] The shift to relative

---

66. F. NEIRYNCK, "Recent Developments," p. 443.

67. A. H. MCNEILE, *The Gospel according to St. Matthew*, London: Macmillan, 1915, p. 367.

68. Compare Luke 6,29 (diff. Matt 5,40); Luke 6,30 (diff. Matt 5,42); Luke 20,46-47 (diff. Mark 12,38-40); Luke 21,4 (diff. Mark 12,44). See H. J. CADBURY, *Style and Literary Method*, pp. 148-149, 151-152.

69. Compare Mark 9,37 (diff. Q 10,16); Mark 9,40 (diff. Q 11,23); Mark 10,11-12 (diff. Q 16,18). Ernest Best notes this pattern of relative clauses in Mark where Q has participles, but he attributes the difference to translation variants. Marcan redaction of Q better accounts for the different forms. See E. BEST, "An Early Sayings Collection" (1976), in ID., *Disciples and Discipleship*, 1986, pp. 64-79.

clauses meant that Mark had to add αὐτῷ to the first main clause. Mark could take over Q's γάρ because he uses the saying to comment on the Measure Saying just as he used v. 22 to comment on the Lamp Saying. Mark eliminated "all" because it does not fit his context. In Mark δοθήσε-ται αὐτῷ points back to ὑμῖν ... δέδοται (Mark 4,11).[70] To one who has the Word, the mystery of the kingdom will be given in ever greater measure, but the outsiders will be stripped of whatever they have.

Where did the sayings in Mark 4,21-25 come from? Who collected them? Did they come from the oral tradition?[71] Does the collection go back to a pre-Marcan redactor? The evidence suggests that Mark himself composed the section out of sayings he drew from Q. If Mark were drawing on the oral tradition we would expect to find non-Q sayings in the collection. Instead five Q sayings lie behind the section indicating that Mark is drawing on Q. We can also rule out a pre-Marcan redactor because the section expresses Mark's theology, developing the parable theory which forms part of the messianic secret.

Mark corrects and extends the parable theory (Mark 4,10-12) and the explanation of the Sower (Mark 4,13-20) with the sayings in vv. 21-25. The parable theory concentrates on the privilege of the disciples. In the two sayings in vv. 21-22 Mark opens up a salvation history perspective. The lamp comes to be set on the lampstand. What is hidden is hidden in order to be revealed. This revelation will eventually open out into the worldwide proclamation of the Word (Mark 13,10; 14,9). However, if the disciples are to preach they must first attend to the Word. The double summons to hear (Mark 4,23-24ab), and the Measure Saying emphasize the responsibility of the disciples. If they respond generously, God will more than generously reward them, for God will give increasingly to those who have, but one who fails to respond will lose even what he has (Mark 4,25). The last two sayings develop the exhortation and warning implied in the explanation of the Sower (Mark 4,13-20). Just as the seed sown on good ground bears abundant fruit while that sown on unproductive soil perishes, so those who have the Word will receive even more (vv. 24d-25a), while those who do not will lose everything (v. 25b).

The Gospel of Thomas has a parallel in Th 41.

> Jesus said, "He who has (something) in his hand, to him will be given (more), and he who has nothing, from him will be taken even the little which he has."

---

70. R. LAUFEN, *Doppelüberlieferungen*, p. 171.
71. See H. A. A. KENNEDY, "The Composition of Mark iv. 21-25: A Study in the Synoptic Problem," in *ExpT* 25 (1913-14) 301-305.

Thomas' two additions to the saying, "in his hand" and "the little," are secondary embellishments rather than original features.[72] Clarifying explanations like the ones in this saying characterize Thomas' handling of proverbs.[73] The author of Thomas especially likes the word "hand" which crops up in several sayings.[74] The Thomas saying agrees with Mark in eliminating "all." Since this is a redactional change of Mark, Thomas depends on the redactional text of Mark.

§ 9. THE MUSTARD SEED

Mark 4,30-32 (Matt 13,31-32 par. Luke 13,18-19)

In Q the Mustard Seed and the Leaven form a parable pair.[75] Mark does not record the Leaven. Although Matthew and Luke agree quite closely in the Leaven, they diverge significantly in the Mustard Seed.

Matt 13,31-32	Luke 13,18-19
31 ἄλλην παραβολὴν παρέθηκεν αὐτοῖς λέγων·	18 ἔλεγεν οὖν·
	τίνι ὁμοία ἐστὶν ἡ βασιλεία τοῦ θεοῦ καὶ τίνι ὁμοιώσω αὐτήν;
ὁμοία ἐστὶν ἡ βασιλεία τῶν οὐρανῶν	19 ὁμοία ἐστὶν
κόκκῳ σινάπεως, ὃν λαβὼν ἄνθρωπος ἔσπειρεν ἐν τῷ ἀγρῷ αὐτοῦ·	κόκκῳ σινάπεως, ὃν λαβὼν ἄνθρωπος ἔβαλεν εἰς κῆπον ἑαυτοῦ,
32 ὃ μικρότερον μέν ἐστιν πάντων τῶν σπερμάτων, ὅταν δὲ αὐξηθῇ,	
μεῖζον τῶν λαχάνων ἐστὶν καὶ γίνεται δένδρον,	καὶ ηὔξησεν
ὥστε ἐλθεῖν	καὶ ἐγένετο εἰς δένδρον καὶ
τὰ πετεινὰ τοῦ οὐρανοῦ καὶ κατασκηνοῦν ἐν τοῖς κλάδοις αὐτοῦ.	τὰ πετεινὰ τοῦ οὐρανοῦ κατεσκήνωσεν ἐν τοῖς κλάδοις αὐτοῦ.

72. M. FIEGER, Thomasevangelium, p. 138.
73. W. A. BEARDSLEE, "Proverbs in the Gospel of Thomas," in Studies in New Testament and Early Christian Literature: FS Allen P. Wikgren, 1972, pp. 92-103, esp. p. 102.
74. Th 17, 21, 22, 35, 41, 98. See J.-É. MÉNARD, L'évangile selon Thomas, p. 142.
75. J. DUPONT, "Le couple parabolique du sénevé et du levain: Mt 13,31-33; Lc 13,18-21" (1975), in ID., Études sur les Évangiles synoptiques, 1985, 2. 609-623.

Matthew's introduction ἄλλην παραβολὴν παρέθηκεν αὐτοῖς λέγων is a redactional formulation that repeats Matt 13,24.[76] Luke's ἔλεγεν οὖν is also redactional. Luke is fond of οὖν, and he inserts it several times when editing his sources.[77] Luke uses the particle to bind the Mustard Seed and the Leaven to the Healing of the Crippled Woman (Luke 13,10-17). The healing ends with Jesus confounding his adversaries and astounding the crowd, and Luke uses the Mustard Seed and the Leaven to continue the note of triumph, joining them to the healing with οὖν.[78] Luke also introduced the imperfect ἔλεγεν. Luke often employs the imperfect to begin a long speech.[79] So both Matthew's and Luke's introductions stem from the evangelists. To recover the Q introduction we need to extrapolate from the introduction to the Leaven. To introduce the Leaven Matthew uses a variation of his stereotyped formula – ἄλλην παραβολὴν ἐλάλησεν αὐτοῖς (Matt 13,33a) – but Luke probably preserves the original Q introduction – καὶ πάλιν εἶπεν (Luke 13,20a). Luke usually avoids πάλιν, consistently eliminating it from his sources.[80] If καὶ πάλιν εἶπεν is the introduction to the Leaven, then εἶπεν or καὶ εἶπεν probably introduced the Mustard Seed. Since the Mustard Seed followed the pericope about Agreeing with One's Opponent (Q 12,58-59) which ends with a λέγω σοι saying, καὶ εἶπεν is more probable.

The parable itself begins with a statement in Matthew, but with a double question in Luke. Matthew's ὁμοία ἐστὶν ἡ βασιλεία τῶν οὐρανῶν is a stylized parable introduction in Matthew.[81] Some scholars question whether Luke's double question might come from Mark.[82] But this is not likely.

---

76. Compare also Matt 13,33. See H. ZIMMERMANN, *Methodenlehre*, p. 127; S. SCHULZ, *Q*, pp. 298-299; R. LAUFEN, *Doppelüberlieferungen*, p. 174.

77. Luke uses οὖν 33 times in the gospel and 61 times in Acts. For Luke's editing compare Luke 4,7 (diff. Matt 4,9); 7,31 (diff. Matt 11,16); 8,18 (diff. Mark 4,24); 14,34 (diff. Matt 5,13); 20,15 (diff. Mark 12,9); 20,17 (diff. Mark 12,10); 20,29 (diff. Mark 12,20); 20,33 (diff. Mark 12,23); 20,44 (diff. Mark 12,37); 21,7 (diff. Mark 13,4); 21,14 (diff. Mark 13,11). See H. FLEDDERMANN, "Mustard Seed and the Leaven," p. 218.

78. J. DUPONT, "Les paraboles du sénevé et du levain (Mt 13,31-33; Lc 13,18-21)" (1967), in ID., *Études sur les Évangiles synoptiques*, 1985, 2. 592-608, esp. p. 604.

79. The imperfect is quite common in Luke (94 228 259 329). See J. C. HAWKINS, *Horae Synopticae*, p. 51. Luke begins speeches with ἔλεγεν in Luke 3,7.11; 5,36; 6,20; 9,23; 10,2; 12,54; 13,6.18; 14,7.12; 16,1; 18,1; 21,10. See M. DEVISCH, *Geschiedenis*, 2. 498-500.

80. Mark uses πάλιν 28 times, and Luke has parallels to 13 of these Marcan texts, but he only takes over the adverb once in Luke 23,20. See H. FLEDDERMANN, "Mustard Seed and the Leaven," 218.

81. Matt 13,33.44.45.47. Compare Matt 13,24; 18,23; 22,2; 25,1.

82. H. K. MCARTHUR, "The Parable of the Mustard Seed," in *CBQ* 33 (1971) 198-210, esp. p. 200; F. NEIRYNCK, "Recent Developments," p. 432; T. A. FRIEDRICHSEN, "'Minor' and 'Major' Matthew-Luke Agreements against Mk 4,30-32," in *The Four Gospels 1992: Festschrift Frans Neirynck*, 1992, 1. 649-676, esp. pp. 662-675.

Although Luke uses questions in dialogue, he tends to avoid double questions, questions associated with their answers, and rhetorical questions.[83] Luke frequently eliminates double questions from Mark.[84] Furthermore, Luke's questions do not resemble Mark's very closely, but a very close Q parallel exists in the parable of the Children in the Market Place (Q 7,31-35) where we encounter a similar double question.

Luke 7,31	Luke 13,18
τίνι οὖν ὁμοιώσω	τίνι ὁμοία ἐστὶν
τοὺς ἀνθρώπους τῆς γενεᾶς ταύτης	ἡ βασιλεία τοῦ θεοῦ
καὶ τίνι εἰσὶν ὅμοιοι;	καὶ τίνι ὁμοιώσω αὐτήν;

These two double questions are closer to one another than Luke 13,18 is to Mark 4,30. Friedrichsen claims that they both are influenced by Mark.[85] However, there is no other example of this procedure in Luke. Luke does at times use the wording of Q to influence his editing of the corresponding Marcan overlap text. For example, he imports elements from the Q Mission Discourse into his version of Mark's Mission Discourse.[86] Luke may also use a Marcan term in the corresponding Q overlap text. For

---

83. See, for example, Luke 8,11 (diff. Mark 4,13); 8,21 (diff. Mark 3,33); 8,25 (diff. Mark 4,40); 9,41 (diff. Mark 9,19); 20,22 (diff. Mark 12,14); 22,46 (diff. Mark 14,37); 22,71 (diff. Mark 14,63-64). Luke eliminated rhetorical questions from Q in Luke 6,32 (diff. Matt 5,46); 6,33 (diff. Matt 5,47); 6,44 (diff. Matt 7,16); 12,23 (diff. Matt 6,25); 12,24 (diff. Matt 6,26); 12,28 (diff. Matt 6,30). Q regularly uses rhetorical questions to begin a section. For examples, see Q 3,7; 7,31; 12,42b; 13,18.20. See further A. HARNACK, *Sprüche und Reden*, pp. 9, 23, 51, 62; ET: *Sayings of Jesus*, pp. 6, 26, 69, 86; H. J. CADBURY, *Style and Literary Method*, pp. 81-83; J. SCHMID, *Matthäus und Lukas*, p. 276 n. 2.

84. Luke takes over five double questions from Mark: Luke 4,34 (par. Mark 1,24); 5,21 (par. Mark 2,7); 5,22-23 (par. Mark 2,8-9); 20,2 (par. Mark 11,28); 21,7 (par. Mark 13,4). He drops at least one question nine times: Luke 6,9 (diff. Mark 3,4); 8,16 (diff. Mark 4,21); 8,25 (diff. Mark 4,40); 9,25 (diff. Mark 8,36-37); 9,41 (diff. Mark 9,19); 20,22 (diff. Mark 12,14); 20,34-37 (diff. Mark 12,24-26); 22,46 (diff. Mark 14,37); 22,71 (diff. Mark 14,63-64). Friedrichsen ("'Minor' and 'Major' Matthew-Luke Agreements," p. 665 n. 84) tries to reduce the number of times Luke eliminates at least one double question from Mark. He eliminates Luke 6,9 because Luke's ἐπερωτῶ ὑμᾶς εἰ changes the situation. However, this is precisely the point; Luke turns the two rhetorical questions into a statement with an indirect question. In Luke 8,16 Friedrichsen suggests that Luke follows Q. Again, even if Luke follows Q, he uses Q to eliminate the double questions from Mark 4,21 which he is editing in Luke 8,16. Friedrichsen claims that the single question in Luke 9,41 preserves the content of the two questions in Mark 9,19. Again, though, Luke shows an aversion to double questions. He may take over the content, but he eliminates one of Mark's questions. Finally Friedrichsen questions Luke 20,34-37 and 22,71 because the questions do not follow one another immediately. The fact remains, though, that Luke's source has two questions and they don't survive in Luke's redaction.

85. T. A. FRIEDRICHSEN, "'Major' and 'Minor' Matthew-Luke Agreements," p. 670.

86. Luke inserts a command to preach the kingdom and to heal into the Marcan discourse in Luke 9,2 (compare Q 10,9), and he transfers "silver" from the Q Equipment Rule (Q 10,4) to his redaction of Mark's Equipment Rule (Luke 9,3).

example, he transfers "blaspheme" from Mark's Unforgivable Sin logion which he omits to the Q overlap saying (Luke 12,10). Luke also at times introduces the same expression into both the Q text and its Marcan overlap. For example, he concludes both the Q and Marcan Lamp Sayings with almost identical purpose clauses (Luke 8,16; 11,33). No other example exists, though, of Luke taking elements from a Marcan overlap text and using them to redact a different Q text. Furthermore, the double questions in Luke 7,31 and 13,18 use the same vocabulary and form, and the vocabulary is not Lucan. The expressions τίνι … καὶ τίνι, ὁμοιώσω, and ὅμοιος with the copula are not usual Lucan terms. Luke uses the verb ὁμοιόω and the adjective ὅμοιος almost exclusively in Q contexts, and the combination τίνι … καὶ τίνι occurs nowhere else in Luke-Acts.[87] The questions, though, do have a Q ring to them. Q uses rhetorical questions extensively, including double rhetorical questions.[88] Besides the Children in the Market Place, the Mustard Seed, and the Leaven, Q uses rhetorical questions to begin a section on five other occasions – John's Preaching (Q 3,7-9.16-17), the Servant Left in Charge (Q 12,42b-46), Family Division (Q 12,51-53), Falling into a Pit (Q 14,5), and the Lost Sheep (Q 15,4-7). The Servant Left in Charge and the Lost Sheep are also parables, so Q precedents exist for seeing the rhetorical questions at the beginning of the Children in the Market Place (Q 7,31), the Mustard Seed (Q 13,18) and the Leaven (Q 13,20) as coming from Q. Five parables in Q begin with rhetorical questions. Luke preserves the original Q beginning of the parable.

After the double question Q continued as in Luke ὁμοία ἐστὶν κόκκῳ σινάπεως. Because Matthew eliminated the double question, he had to add a reference to the kingdom.[89] Luke basically reflects the Q relative clause. Matthew drew the verb σπείρω from Mark and his own

---

87. The verb ὁμοιόω occurs only three times in Luke's gospel in three Q texts (Luke 7,31; 13,18.20). Luke uses the adjective ὅμοιος eight times in Q contexts (Luke 6,47.48.49; 7,31.32; 13,18.19.21) and only once elsewhere (Luke 12,36).

88. Q uses rhetorical questions thirty-nine times: Q 3,7b; 6,32a.32b.33a.33b.39a.39b. 41.42a.44b.46; 7,24b.24c.25a.25b.26a.26b.31a.31b; 10,15; 11,11.12.18.19.21-22; 12,6a. 23.24.25.26.28.42b.51; 13,18a.18b.20; 14,5.34; 15,4. Double rhetorical questions occur eight times in Q 6,39a.39b; Q 6,41.42a; Q 7,26a.26b; Q 7,31a.31b; Q 11,11.12; Q 11,18.19; Q 12,25.26; Q 13,18a.18b. Q even has two sets of four rhetorical questions: Q 6,32a.32b.33a.33b and Q 7,24b.24c.25a.25b.

89. The Q expression was "the kingdom of God" as in Luke and not "the kingdom of heaven" as in Matthew. Matthew alone uses "the kingdom of heaven" and he frequently substitutes it for "the kingdom of God." See Matt 4,17 (diff. Mark 1,15); 13,11 (diff. Mark 4,11); 19,14 (diff. Mark 10,14); 19,23 (diff. Mark 10,23). See H. FLEDDERMANN, "Mustard Seed and the Leaven," p. 221 n. 25.

parable of the Weeds among the Wheat.[90] The prepositional phrase "in the field" also assimilates the parable to the Weeds among the Wheat and the Hidden Treasure.[91] Luke's ἔβαλεν εἰς κῆπον comes from Q. McArthur disputes this. He claims that the mustard plant was excluded from gardens in Palestine, and so Luke's text reflects a Hellenistic milieu.[92] But the end of the parable quotes from the Greek OT, so the parable had already undergone Hellenistic influence before it reached Q. Luke changed an original αὐτοῦ to ἑαυτοῦ.[93]

At this point Matthew switches to the present. He borrows μικρότερον, πάντων τῶν σπερμάτων, μεῖζον τῶν λαχάνων, and the conjunction ὅταν from Mark. He wraps the Marcan terms around Q's αὐξάνω. He improves the syntax by adding the copula twice, by introducing μὲν ... δέ, and by eliminating Mark's duplicate expressions ὅταν σπαρῇ and ἐπὶ τῆς γῆς. Luke's καὶ ηὔξησεν preserves the Q text.

Luke's next clause, καὶ ἐγένετο εἰς δένδρον, is also original. Matthew's καὶ γίνεται δένδρον combines Mark's present verb with Q's "tree." Luke also preserves the original form of the final scripture quotation. Matthew borrows Mark's ὥστε with the infinitive construction, but he substitutes ἐλθεῖν for Mark's δύνασθαι, coordinating it with Mark's second infinitive κατασκηνοῦν.[94] He retains the Q prepositional phrase "in its branches" because he retains Q's tree image. We can now compare Mark and Q.

Q 13,18-19	Mark 4,30-32
18 καὶ εἶπεν·	30 καὶ ἔλεγεν·
τίνι ὁμοία ἐστὶν	πῶς ὁμοιώσωμεν
ἡ βασιλεία τοῦ θεοῦ	τὴν βασιλείαν τοῦ θεοῦ
καὶ τίνι ὁμοιώσω αὐτήν;	ἢ ἐν τίνι αὐτὴν παραβολῇ θῶμεν;
19 ὁμοία ἐστὶν κόκκῳ σινάπεως	31 ὡς κόκκῳ σινάπεως,
ὃν λαβὼν ἄνθρωπος	ὃς ὅταν σπαρῇ
ἔβαλεν εἰς κῆπον αὐτοῦ,	ἐπὶ τῆς γῆς,
	μικρότερον ὃν
	πάντων τῶν σπερμάτων
	τῶν ἐπὶ τῆς γῆς,
	32 καὶ ὅταν σπαρῇ,
καὶ ηὔξησεν	ἀναβαίνει

---

90. See Mark 4,31.32; Matt 13,24.25.27.37.39.

91. Matt 13,24.27.36.38.44. Contrast Mark 4,31. See further H. ZIMMERMANN, *Methodenlehre*, p. 127; R. LAUFEN, *Doppelüberlieferungen*, p. 175.

92. H. K. McARTHUR, "Mustard Seed," p. 201.

93. Luke uses ἑαυτοῦ frequently (32 24 57 21). He substituted ἑαυτοῦ for αὐτοῦ in Luke 13,34 (diff. Matt 23,37); 14,27 (diff. Matt 10,38); 19,36 (diff. Mark 11,8). See J. SCHMID, *Matthäus und Lukas*, p. 277 n. 3.

94. See H. FLEDDERMANN, "Mustard Seed and the Leaven," p. 223.

καὶ ἐγένετο εἰς δένδρον   καὶ γίνεται μεῖζον
                                  πάντων τῶν λαχάνων
                                  καὶ ποιεῖ κλάδους μεγάλους,
                                  ὥστε δύνασθαι
                                  ὑπὸ τὴν σκιὰν αὐτοῦ
καὶ τὰ πετεινὰ τοῦ οὐρανοῦ   τὰ πετεινὰ τοῦ οὐρανοῦ
κατεσκήνωσεν   κατασκηνοῦν.
ἐν τοῖς κλάδοις αὐτοῦ.

Both versions begin with a double question. Q uses the aorist throughout, whereas Mark employs the present. They differ dramatically in the portrayal of the central image. Q describes the mustard as a "tree" while Mark states that it is "greater than all the shrubs." Both versions climax in a quotation or allusion to the OT passages that use a cedar or a tree to describe a powerful kingdom or king. Ezek 17,22-24 describes how God will plant a sprig of cedar on a lofty mountain and the birds will live in its shadow. Ezek 31,1-18 compares mighty Assyria to a cedar that shelters birds and animals. Dan 4,1-37 likens Nebuchadnezzar to a tree in whose branches the birds nest. Dupont has shown that the Q parable alludes to Dan 4,21 Theodotion.[95] He has also shown that Ezek 17,23 LXX is the source of the phrase ὑπὸ τὴν σκιὰν αὐτοῦ in Mark.[96]

After Laufen reconstructs the Q parable, he immediately tries to probe behind Mark and Q for a common ancestor.[97] Friedrichsen claims that the two forms of the parable are different "performances" of the Mustard Seed.[98] Neither analyzes the tradition history of the texts to determine if one might be prior to the other. Kogler does compare the two texts using tradition history. He maintains that the Marcan text is original because it describes conditions in Palestine where the mustard plant could never be mistaken for a tree. He attributes the description of the full grown mustard as a tree to a Deutero-Marcan redactor who was unfamiliar with conditions in Palestine.[99] However, as we shall see, Kogler's argument falters on the OT allusions at the end of the parable.

95. The Daniel text reads: καὶ ἐν τοῖς κλάδοις αὐτοῦ κατεσκήνουν τὰ ὄρνεα τοῦ οὐρανοῦ (Dan 4,21 Theodotion). The author of Q: (1) shifted to the aorist to bring the quotation into line with the rest of the parable; (2) changed the unusual ὄρνεα to the more common πετεινά; and (3) switched the subject and the prepositional phrase to reflect the position of the other prepositional phrases in the parable which all fall at the end of a clause. See J. DUPONT, "Le couple parabolique," pp. 620-621; H. FLEDDERMANN, "Mustard Seed and the Leaven," p. 232.

96. J. DUPONT, "Le couple parabolique," p. 621. Kogler (Doppelgleichnis, pp. 156-157) notes the presence of Mark's prepositional phrase in the Septuagint. However, he believes that Mark alludes to the Hebrew text of Ezek 17,31 (Doppelgleichnis, pp. 158-168).

97. R. LAUFEN, Doppelüberlieferungen, pp. 176-182.

98. T. A. FRIEDRICHSEN, "'Minor' and 'Major' Matthew-Luke Agreements," p. 657.

99. F. KOGLER, Doppelgleichnis, p. 145.

If we compare Mark and Q to try to determine which version of the parable is prior, two main considerations show that Mark is secondary. First, Q characterizes the mustard plant as a "tree." This description is a technically inaccurate exaggeration which Mark corrects by describing the plant as "greater than all the shrubs." The correction is clearly secondary. Kogler's position that originally the parable spoke of a shrub and that the tree was a later shift is not likely, for Mark refers to the classic OT texts that develop the tree symbol. In other words the scripture reference in Mark demonstrates that the mustard had been identified with the tree, and Mark moves to correct the identification. Second, Q only implies a contrast between the mustard seed and the tree. Q simply juxtaposes the tiny seed and the large tree without explicitly drawing attention to the contrast between them. Mark explicitly works out the contrast in clauses exclusively devoted to it: "when it is sown in the earth, it is the smallest of all the seeds on the earth, and when it is sown it increases and becomes greater than all the shrubs and produces large branches" (Mark 4,31-32). This making explicit what is implicit is also a sign that Mark is secondary.[100]

If we now turn to study Mark's redaction, the secondary character of Mark becomes even clearer. Two concerns drive Mark's redaction. First, Mark wants to eliminate the exaggeration of a tree, and in doing this he also makes the contrast explicit. Second, Mark wants to integrate the Mustard Seed into his Parable Discourse, particularly adapting it to the Seed Growing Secretly. Both parables have the same introduction, both are seed parables, both mention the kingdom of God, both have similar connotations, both contain a scriptural quotation or allusion. The structure and the phraseology of the two parables is similar. Both begin with an aorist subjunctive and then switch to the present. The sowing and growth is similarly described.[101]

vv. 26-27	vv. 31-32
as a man	as a mustard seed
casts seed	which when it is sown
on the earth	on the earth
and the seed sprouts	and when it is sown, rises
and grows	and becomes great

Mark's introductory phrase καὶ ἔλεγεν conforms the parable to the Seed Growing Secretly (compare Mark 4,26). Like Q Mark begins with a double question. He draws the Q verb from the second question into

---

100. T. E. F. HONEY, "Did Mark Use Q?," pp. 325-326.
101. J. LAMBRECHT, "Redaction and Theology," pp. 291, 296-297.

the first, and he uses a Marcan term πῶς to introduce the question.[102] Mark reformulates the second question to make it symmetrical with the first. Both questions have first person plural verbs and direct objects. The phrase ἐν τίνι ... παραβολῇ is more explicit than Q's τίνι. This combination of greater symmetry and more explicitness is a sign of redactional reworking. Besides πῶς the phrase ἐν ... παραβολῇ has a Marcan ring to it.[103] Compared with the Q beginning of the parable Mark's ὡς κόκκῳ σινάπεως ὅς is compressed. Since Mark wants to concentrate on the seed as a symbol of the kingdom, he suppresses the human agent. The ὡς reflects the πῶς of the first question and the ὡς which introduces the parable of the Seed Growing Secretly (Mark 4,26). Since Mark eliminates the tree as an exaggeration, he compensates by explicitly emphasizing how small the seed is and how big the mature shrub becomes. Typically Marcan is the repetition of ὅταν σπαρῇ[104] and ἐπὶ τῆς γῆς.[105] Mark replaces Q's ηὔξησεν with a verb he uses in the Sower, ἀναβαίνει.[106] For Q's aorist ἐγένετο he writes the present γίνεται,[107] and he replaces Q's "tree" with "greater than all the shrubs." Once Mark eliminated the tree from the parable, he had to alter the scripture quotation at the end, although he retains all of the Q vocabulary. He can no longer depict the birds as dwelling in the tree's branches, but he creates a new clause to describe the size of the shrub using Q's "branches." Borrowing from Ezek 17,23 LXX he portrays the birds as dwelling in the shadow of the shrub. The construction with ὥστε δύνασθαι appears elsewhere in Mark.[108] All the differences between Q and Mark come from Mark.

The Mustard Seed also appears in the Gospel of Thomas (Th 20).

> The disciples said to Jesus, "Tell us what the kingdom of the heavens is like." He said to them, "It is like a grain of mustard seed, smaller than all the seeds. But when it falls on the earth which has been cultivated, it puts forth a large branch (and) becomes a shelter for birds of the heaven."

Certain features of Thomas do not correspond to any synoptic version of the parable. In the synoptic versions Jesus addresses his audience directly. In Thomas the disciples first say to Jesus, "Tell us what the

---

102. Πῶς is frequent in Mark (14 14 16 9). It is redactional at least in Mark 3,23; 4,13; 9,12; 14,1.11. See J. LAMBRECHT, "Redaction and Theology," p. 294 n. 114.

103. Compare Mark 4,2.11. See J. LAMBRECHT, "Redaction and Theology," p. 294.

104. Compare σπόρον in v. 26 and σπείρω in vv. 3-9.14-20.

105. Compare Mark 4,26.

106. Compare Mark 4,7.8.

107. Compare Mark 2,15.21; 4,11.19; 11,23.

108. Compare Mark 1,45; 3,20.

kingdom of the heavens is like." Jesus replies with the parable. This
aphoristic dialogue form pops up over and over again in Thomas.[109]
Jeremias has shown that it is a later development.[110] After describing the
seed falling on the earth, Thomas adds "which has been cultivated." The
addition allegorizes the earth which bears no special significance in the
synoptic parable. The allegorical detail is also a secondary development.[111]
Thomas also has the singular "branch" instead of the plural "branches"
found in all three synoptic writers. This change undoubtedly comes from
the author of Thomas because we find similar singulars in two other
sayings (Th 57, 86).[112]

Th 20 reflects redactional Mark in using the present tense. Like Mark
Thomas concentrates on the seed and does not mention the sower.
Thomas also has two redactional phrases of Mark, "smaller than all the
seeds" and "large branch." In addition Thomas, like Mark, states that
the seed falls on the "earth" (*kah*) instead of in the "field" (Matthew) or
a "garden" (Luke). Thomas also reflects redactional Matthew in referring
to "the kingdom of the heavens," and in using ὅταν δέ. Thomas normally
refers either to "the kingdom" (Th 3, 22, 27, 46, 49, 107, 109, 113) or
"the kingdom of the Father" (Th 57, 76, 96, 97, 98, 99, 113).[113] Thomas
uses "the kingdom of the heavens" only three times, and in each of the
other two passages Matthean influence appears probable.[114] Thomas'
ὅταν δέ also reflects redactional Matthew. Tuckett claims the phrase is
too common to trace it to Matthew, but Thomas has the expression in
exactly the same place as Matthew, right after the clause that describes
the size of the seed.[115] Again Thomas compared two synoptic versions of
the parable and drew from both. Thomas clearly depends on the synoptics.

---

109. Th 6, 12, 18, 20, 22, 24, 37, 43, 51, 52, 53, 99, 100, 113, 114. See C. L.
BLOMBERG, "Tradition and Redaction in the Parables of the Gospel of Thomas," in D.
WENHAM (ed.), *The Jesus Tradition outside the Gospels*, 1985, pp. 177-205, esp. p. 187.
110. J. JEREMIAS, *Gleichnisse*, p. 97; ET: *Parables*, p. 98.
111. J. A. FITZMYER, *Luke*, 2. 1015-1016; J. JEREMIAS, *Gleichnisse*, pp. 64-88; ET:
Parables, pp. 66-89.
112. In Th 57 Thomas writes "weed" for Matthew's "weeds" (Matt 13,24-30), and in
Th 86 Thomas has "nest" for Q's "nests" (Matt 8,20 par. Luke 9,58).
113. K. KING, "Kingdom in the Gospel of Thomas," in *Forum* 3/1 (1987) 48-97, esp.
p. 82.
114. Th 54 combines Matthew's and Luke's first beatitude, and Th 114 contains the
phrase "to enter the kingdom of the heavens" which occurs only in Matthew (Matt 5,20;
7,21; 18,3; 19,23; compare also Matt 23,13). See J.-É. MÉNARD, *L'évangile selon Thomas*,
p. 109.
115. C. TUCKETT, "Thomas and the Synoptics," p. 153 n. 81.

Mark's Parable Discourse confronts us with the same phenomenon we encountered in the Beelzebul Controversy and the Unforgivable Sin – the clustering of overlap texts in Mark. No less than six Q texts play a role in Mark's discourse. We do not find the texts dispersed throughout the chapter, but concentrated at the end, most strikingly in the collection of sayings in Mark 4,21-25. How can we explain this collection? Four sayings appear tightly organized into a two-part unit. All four sayings have roots in Q, and one of them conflates two Q texts. If these sayings had come to Mark from the oral tradition we would expect to find some non-Q material mixed in. Furthermore, the cluster has been edited to develop the Marcan parable theory which is part of the messianic secret, the central theme of Mark's gospel. Who but Mark could have combined the sayings in this way? These sayings did not come from the oral tradition or from a pre-Marcan cluster. Mark had Q before him and he drew on six Q pericopes to develop his thoughts on the mystery of the kingdom.

V

MISSION AND SIGN

Only two overlap texts – the Mission Discourse and the Demand for a Sign – lie between the Parable Discourse and the Caesarea Philippi pericope. No study of the overlap texts can ignore the Mission Discourse. Like the Beelzebul Controversy the Mission Discourse offers us an extended text with which to explore the relationship of Mark and Q. The Demand for a Sign also yields fruitful insights. Although shorter, it presents special problems that influence any final view of Mark and Q.

§ 10. THE MISSION DISCOURSE

Mark 6,7-13 (Matt 9,37-38; 10,7-16; 11,21-23; 10,40 par. Luke 10,2-16)

Luke has two missions of the disciples and two discourses. Jesus first sends out the Twelve during the Galilean ministry (Luke 9,1-6), and then during the Journey Narrative he sends out a larger group of seventy or seventy-two disciples (Luke 10,2-16). In his first discourse Luke edits Mark, but we shall see that he incorporates some Q elements into his redaction. His second discourse basically reproduces Q. Matthew has a single complex Mission Discourse (Matt 9,36-11,1) that combines Q, Mark, and Matthean *Sondergut*.

Matthew provides a narrative setting for the discourse by anticipating Mark 6,34 (Matt 9,36).[1] Luke also creates a narrative setting for the discourse (Luke 10,1).[2] Both Matthew and Luke begin the sermon itself with a brief introductory clause (Matt 9,37a par. Luke 10,2a) which reflects the beginning of the Q discourse. Matthew and Luke agree closely in the initial Harvest Saying. After the Harvest Saying Matthew incorporates the Call of the Twelve (Matt 10,1-4) from Mark (compare Mark 3,13-19; 6,7), a *Sondergut* passage (Matt 10,5-6), and a commission

1. "Seeing the crowds he had pity on them because they were harrassed and helpless like sheep without a shepherd" (Matt 9,36). Matthew later redacts Mark 6,34 a second time in Matt 14,14.
2. "After these things the Lord appointed another seventy(-two) and sent them out ahead of him two by two into every city and place where he intended to go" (Luke 10,1).

that appears later in Luke (Matt 10,7-8; compare Luke 10,9). Luke, though, follows the initial saying with a commission (Luke 10,3) that Matthew records later in the discourse (Matt 10,16).

Matt 9,37-38; 10,16	Luke 10,2-3
37 τότε λέγει τοῖς μαθηταῖς αὐτοῦ·	2 ἔλεγεν δὲ πρὸς αὐτούς·
ὁ μὲν θερισμὸς πολύς,	ὁ μὲν θερισμὸς πολύς,
οἱ δὲ ἐργάται ὀλίγοι·	οἱ δὲ ἐργάται ὀλίγοι·
38 δεήθητε οὖν	δεήθητε οὖν
τοῦ κυρίου τοῦ θερισμοῦ	τοῦ κυρίου τοῦ θερισμοῦ
ὅπως ἐκβάλῃ ἐργάτας	ὅπως ἐργάτας ἐκβάλῃ
εἰς τὸν θερισμὸν αὐτοῦ.	εἰς τὸν θερισμὸν αὐτοῦ.
16 ἰδοὺ ἐγὼ ἀποστέλλω ὑμᾶς	3 ὑπάγετε· ἰδοὺ ἀποστέλλω ὑμᾶς
ὡς πρόβατα ἐν μέσῳ λύκων.	ὡς ἄρνας ἐν μέσῳ λύκων.

Both evangelists adapted the original Q introduction. Matthew uses a favorite expression τότε to connect the pericope to the preceding.[3] Luke's δέ links Jesus' speech to his redactional introduction (Luke 10,1). In Q the Mission Discourse followed the Demands of Discipleship (Q 9,57-60), so a simple καί would suffice as a connective. Neither Matthew nor Luke preserves the original form of the verb. Matthew uses the historic present λέγει frequently, substituting it often for the aorist εἶπεν.[4] The historic present marks an important highpoint for Matthew, and he uses it here to emphasize Jesus' speech.[5] The combination of τότε and λέγει appears twelve times in Matthew.[6] Luke often introduces an extended speech with the imperfect.[7] Q probably had the aorist εἶπεν. The expression πρὸς αὐτούς is Lucan.[8] Schulz claims that "disciples" is

3. 90 6 15 21. See J. C. HAWKINS, *Horae Synopticae*, p. 8; U. LUZ, *Evangelium nach Matthäus*, 1. 52; ET: *Matthew 1-7*, p. 69.

4. See Matt 4,19 (diff. Mark 1,17); 8,20 (diff. Luke 9,58); 8,22 (diff. Luke 9,60); 8,26 (diff. Mark 4,40); 17,20 (diff. Mark 9,29); 19,8 (diff. Mark 10,5); 20,23 (diff. Mark 10,39); 21,19 (diff. Mark 11,14); 22,21 (diff. Mark 12,17); 26,64 (diff. Mark 14,62). See H. T. FLEDDERMANN, "The Demands of Discipleship: Matt 8,19-22 par. Luke 9,57-62," in *The Four Gospels 1992: Festschrift Frans Neirynck*, 1992, 1. 541-561, esp. pp. 545-546, 548.

5. Compare Matt 4,10.19; 8,4.7.20.22.26; 9,9.28; 13,32; 14,31; 15,34; 16,15; 17,20; 18,22; 19,8; 20,8.23; 21,13.16.31.42; 22,8.12.21.43; 26,31.52.64; 28,10. See W. SCHENK, "Das Präsens Historicum als makrosyntaktisches Gliederungssignal im Matthäusevangelium," in *NTS* 22 (1975-76) 464-475.

6. Matt 4,10; 9,6.37; 12,13.44; 22,8.21; 26,31.38.52; 27,13; 28,10. See W. D. DAVIES and D. C. ALLISON, *Matthew*, 2. 148.

7. The imperfect is very common in Luke (94 228 259 329). See J. C. HAWKINS, *Horae Synopticae*, p. 51. Luke uses it to introduce a speech in Luke 3,7.11; 5,36; 6,20; 9,23; 12,54; 13,6.18; 14,7.12; 16,1; 18,1; 21,10.

8. The preposition πρός used with a verb of speaking occurs over 150 times in Luke-Acts (0 5 99 52). See J. C. HAWKINS, *Horae Synopticae*, pp. 21, 45-46.

Matthean.[9] Matthew does mention the disciples often, but Q also refers to the disciples (Q 6,40; 14,26-27), and Luke's πρὸς αὐτούς confirms that Q designated the audience of the discourse.

Matthew and Luke agree word for word in the opening saying except for the position of ἐργάτας. Matthew mirrors the Q order; Luke draws the object forward for emphasis.[10]

Luke preserves the original position of the Commission Saying (Luke 10,3). Matthew delays the saying to join it with the saying about being wise as serpents and innocent as doves (Matt 10,16b).[11] With these two sayings Matthew introduces a section on persecution (Matt 10,17-25). To fit the new context he drops the imperative ὑπάγετε.[12] Although Luke can use ὑπάγω redactionally,[13] he generally avoids the imperative. Except for the present passage he only uses it in Luke 19,30 where he takes it over from Mark (compare Mark 11,2). Several times he eliminates the imperative from his Marcan source, so it runs counter to his style and almost certainly reflects Q.[14] Matthew adds ἐγώ.[15] According to Hoffmann and Uro Luke substituted a precise or a more literary expression, ἄρνας, for a general and less literary one, πρόβατα.[16] However, πρόβατον appears frequently in Matthew, and it often carries ecclesial connotations.[17] Matthew uses it twice more in the Mission Discourse (Matt 9,36; 10,6), so Matthew simply assimilates v. 16 to the other two Matthean verses. Luke does not change Q's πρόβατον in the Lost Sheep (Luke 15,4.6), so he probably takes over ἄρνας from Q. Luke, then, takes over the Commission Saying unchanged just as Matthew took over the Harvest Saying unchanged.

Q 10,2-3

2 καὶ εἶπεν τοῖς μαθηταῖς αὐτοῦ·
   ὁ μὲν θερισμὸς πολύς, οἱ δὲ ἐργάται ὀλίγοι·
   δεήθητε οὖν τοῦ κυρίου τοῦ θερισμοῦ
   ὅπως ἐκβάλῃ ἐργάτας εἰς τὸν θερισμὸν αὐτοῦ.
3 ὑπάγετε· ἰδοὺ ἀποστέλλω ὑμᾶς ὡς ἄρνας ἐν μέσῳ λύκων.

9. S. SCHULZ, *Q*, pp. 404-405 n. 6.

10. P. HOFFMANN, *Studien*, p. 263; S. SCHULZ, *Q*, p. 405.

11. R. URO, *Sheep Among the Wolves*, p. 47.

12. *Ibid.*, p. 75.

13. Luke 8,42 (diff. Mark 5,24); compare also Luke 17,14.

14. Compare Luke 5,14 (diff. Mark 1,44); 5,24 (diff. Mark 2,11); 8,39 (diff. Mark 5,19); 8,48 (diff. Mark 5,34); 18,22 (diff. Mark 10,21); 18,42 (diff. Mark 10,52); 22,10 (diff. Mark 14,13). See further H. J. CADBURY, *Style and Literary Method*, pp. 173-174.

15. We have seen above in discussing Matt 11,10 (diff. Luke 7,27) that Matthew always uses ἐγώ with ἀποστέλλω.

16. P. HOFFMANN, *Studien*, p. 264; R. URO, *Sheep Among the Wolves*, p. 76.

17. 11 2 2 1. For the ecclesial usage compare Matt 9,36; 10,6; 15,24; 18,12; 25,32.33; 26,31.

After the Commission Saying Luke continues with the Equipment Rule.

Matt 10,9-10	Luke 10,4
9 μὴ κτήσησθε χρυσὸν μηδὲ ἄργυρον μηδὲ χαλκὸν εἰς τὰς ζώνας ὑμῶν,	4 μὴ βαστάζετε βαλλάντιον,
10 μὴ πήραν εἰς ὁδὸν μηδὲ δύο χιτῶνας μηδὲ ὑποδήματα μηδὲ ῥάβδον...	μὴ πήραν, μὴ ὑποδήματα, καὶ μηδένα κατὰ τὴν ὁδὸν ἀσπάσησθε.

The Equipment Rule presents greater problems than the two preceding sayings. Matthew's main verb κτήσησθε expresses a particular Matthean nuance. Although Matthew only uses it here, its basic meaning, "to procure for oneself," "to get," "to gain," fits Matthew's intention. Matthew emphasizes the prohibition against carrying money by building the triad "gold," "silver," "copper." He frames the Equipment Rule with two sayings – "you have received freely, give freely" (Matt 10,8b) and "the laborer is worthy of his food" (Matt 10,10b). As a result he shifts the original charge not to take provisions to the command not to use missionary activity for financial gain.[18] Luke's βαστάζετε is also redactional. Although Luke can take over the verb from his sources,[19] he often uses it redactionally. In the Cross Saying (Luke 14,27) Luke substitutes βαστάζει for Q's λαμβάνει (Matt 10,38).[20] Q probably had λαμβάνετε.[21]

The forbidden objects also pose problems. Of Matthew's triad – "gold," "silver," "copper" – copper comes from Mark (compare Mark 6,8). Although Luke does not specifically mention money in v. 4, he indirectly refers to money by forbidding a purse (βαλλάντιον), and in Luke 9,3 he introduces "silver" into his redaction of Mark. "Silver" headed the Q list of objects and probably in Matthew's form ἄργυρον. Everywhere except in this verse Matthew uses the more common ἀργύριον.[22] Matthew joined Q's "silver" and Mark's "copper" and

---

18. P. HOFFMANN, "Lk 10,5-11 in der Instruktionsrede der Logienquelle," in *Evangelisch-Katholischer Kommentar zum Neuen Testament: Vorarbeiten Heft 3*, Neukirchen-Vluyn: Neukirchener Verlag / Zürich: Benziger, 1971, pp. 37-53, esp. p. 38; ID., *Studien*, pp. 264-265.
19. See Luke 22,10 (par. Mark 14,13).
20. See the discussion of the Cross Saying (Mark 8,34b par. Q 14,27) in Chapter VI.
21. For λαμβάνω in Q see Q 11,10; 13,19.21 as well as Q 14,27.
22. Matt 25,18.27; 26,15; 27,3.5.6.9; 28,12.15. Luke uses ἄργυρος once (Acts 17,29) but elsewhere always ἀργύριον (Luke 9,3; 19,15.23; 22,5; Acts 3,6; 7,16; 8,20; 19,19; 20,33) so a change on his part makes sense.

added "gold" to form his triad.[23] The knapsack (πήραν) appears in Matt 10,10 and in both Luke 9,3 and Luke 10,4. Matthew's "for the road" comes from Mark 6,8. Matthew also forbids taking two coats. Although Luke 10,4 doesn't mention the coats, Luke forbids them in Luke 9,3. Hoffmann and Uro think that Q also forbade two coats.[24] However, the coats come from Mark. Q prohibits certain objects whereas Mark allows the missionaries to take some things with them. Forbiding two coats falls into the Marcan pattern – the missionaries are at least allowed one coat. Matthew and Luke agree against Mark in prohibiting "shoes" (Matt 10,10; Luke 10,4) and a "staff" (Matt 10,10; Luke 9,3), so Q listed four forbidden objects – "silver," "knapsack," "shoes," and "staff."[25] Q joined the objects by a simple μή. Luke ordinarily avoids asyndeton, so he probably took it over from Q. Matthew does not have a full parallel to Luke's final clause "and do not greet anyone along the way." However, he echoes the clause in his imperative ἀσπάσασθε in Matt 10,12, so the clause probably stood in Q.[26] Q's Equipment Rule allowed the missionaries no necessities let alone comforts.

Q 10,4

μὴ λαμβάνετε ἄργυρον, μὴ πήραν, μὴ ὑποδήματα, μὴ ῥάβδον·
καὶ μηδένα κατὰ τὴν ὁδὸν ἀσπάσησθε.

After the Equipment Rule the Q discourse had a section on how the missionaries were to act in a house.

Matt 10,11-13.10c	Luke 10,5-7
11 εἰς ἣν δ' ἂν πόλιν ἢ κώμην εἰσέλθητε, ἐξετάσατε τίς ἐν αὐτῇ ἄξιός ἐστιν· κἀκεῖ μείνατε ἕως ἂν ἐξέλθητε.	
12 εἰσερχόμενοι δὲ εἰς τὴν οἰκίαν ἀσπάσασθε αὐτήν·	5 εἰς ἣν δ' ἂν εἰσέλθητε οἰκίαν, πρῶτον λέγετε· εἰρήνη τῷ οἴκῳ τούτῳ.
13 καὶ ἐὰν μὲν ᾖ ἡ οἰκία ἀξία ἐλθάτω ἡ εἰρήνη ὑμῶν ἐπ' αὐτήν,	6 καὶ ἐὰν ἐκεῖ ᾖ υἱὸς εἰρήνης, ἐπαναπαήσεται ἐπ' αὐτὸν ἡ εἰρήνη ὑμῶν·

---

23. The three terms "gold," "silver," "copper" form an anticlimax. Compare the anticlimax "kingdom," "city," "house" in Matt 12,25.

24. P. Hoffmann, *Studien*, pp. 266-267; R. Uro, *Sheep Among the Wolves*, p. 77.

25. Both Hoffmann and Uro list these four objects as belonging to the original Q text. In addition, they suggest that Q might have prohibited two coats. The coats, though, probably come from Mark. See P. Hoffmann, *Studien*, pp. 264-267; R. Uro, *Sheep Among the Wolves*, pp. 76-77. Dieter Zeller lists just the four objects. See D. Zeller, *Kommentar zur Logienquelle* (Stuttgarter kleiner Kommentar: Neues Testament, 21), Stuttgart: Katholisches Bibelwerk, 1984, p. 46.

26. R. Uro, *Sheep Among the Wolves*, pp. 77-78.

ἐὰν δὲ μὴ ᾖ ἀξία,   εἰ δὲ μή γε,
ἡ εἰρήνη ὑμῶν πρὸς ὑμᾶς   ἐφ' ὑμᾶς
ἐπιστραφήτω.   ἀνακάμψει.
                   7 ἐν αὐτῇ δὲ τῇ οἰκίᾳ
                   μένετε ἐσθίοντες καὶ πίνοντες
                   τὰ παρ' αὐτῶν·
10 ἄξιος γὰρ ὁ ἐργάτης   ἄξιος γὰρ ὁ ἐργάτης
τῆς τροφῆς αὐτοῦ.   τοῦ μισθοῦ αὐτοῦ.
                   μὴ μεταβαίνετε
                   ἐξ οἰκίας εἰς οἰκίαν.

There are several indications that Luke 10,5 stood in Q. Almost every detail of Luke 10,5 is confirmed by echoes in Matt 10,11-13. Matthew took over the relative clause in v. 11 from the Q clause preserved essentially in Luke 10,5, but he substituted πόλιν ἢ κώμην for Q's οἰκίαν to assimilate the verse to his summary of Jesus' activity in Matt 9,35 (περιῆγεν ὁ Ἰησοῦς τὰς πόλεις πάσας καὶ τὰς κώμας). In this way he brings the activity of the disciples into line with that of Jesus. It may also have struck him as strange that the Q discourse recounts the reception of the disciples in a house (Q 10,5) before their reception in a city (Q 10,8). Matthew's ἀσπάσασθε αὐτήν (Matt 10,12) looks like a simplification of the Lucan πρῶτον λέγετε· εἰρήνη τῷ οἴκῳ τούτῳ.[27] His "peace" in v. 13 also presupposes the traditional Jewish greeting. So Matthew really confirms Luke's text. In addition, Luke's direct address runs counter to his ordinary redactional procedure to avoid direct speech.[28] Luke made only a minor change in his source, shifting the word order by placing the verb before the noun in the relative clause.[29]

In v. 11 Matthew makes a programmatic statement that announces a major theme of his discourse. To formulate the statement Matthew draws on both Q and Mark. We saw above that he adapted the relative clause from Q. His first imperative clause (ἐξετάσατε τίς ἐν αὐτῇ ἄξιός ἐστιν) states the theme. In the clause Matthew introduces the word "worthy" which will become a catchword for his Mission Discourse.[30]

27. See Chapter II above on John and the Coming One (Q 3,16-17) where Matthew also simplifies a Q passage.
28. H. J. CADBURY, *Style and Literary Method*, pp. 79-81; J. SCHMID, *Matthäus und Lukas*, pp. 109 n. 5, 263 n. 2.
29. The word order in Matt 10,11a (εἰς ἣν δ' ἂν πόλιν ἢ κώμην εἰσέλθητε) matches the order in Luke 10,8a (καὶ εἰς ἣν ἂν πόλιν εἰσέρχησθε) and Luke 10,10a (εἰς ἣν δ' ἂν πόλιν εἰσέλθητε).
30. The word appears seven times in Matthew's discourse (Matt 10,10.11.13*bis*.37 *bis*.38). Outside of the Mission Discourse Matthew takes over "worthy" once from Q (Matt 3,8) and he uses it once more redactionally in the parable of the Wedding Feast (Matt 22,8). Of the seven occurrences in the Mission Discourse only the first comes from Q (compare Luke 10,7). It is not unusual for Matthew to pick up a word or phrase from

The purpose of the mission is to find those who are "worthy." What Matthew means by "worthy" appears most clearly in the parable of the Wedding Feast. When those initially invited refuse to come, the king says to his servants, "The wedding is ready, but those invited were not worthy (ἄξιοι)" (Matt 22,8). If the parable explicitly applies the term to those initially called, implicitly it also applies ἄξιοι to the Christian community. If those first invited failed to respond and showed themselves unworthy, still the question remains whether those who have taken their place are themselves worthy.[31] The word thus forms part of the complex of motifs Matthew uses to portray the church as a *corpus mixtum* that will be subject to the judgment.[32] To round out the programmatic statement Matthew draws a second imperative clause (κἀκεῖ μείνατε ἕως ἂν ἐξέλθητε) from Mark 6,10.[33]

In v. 12 Matthew condenses Q 10,5. Since he used the relative clause in his previous verse, he replaces it here with a participial phrase, "but entering into the house." "House" appears abruptly in Matthew's text. Matthew created the difficulty when he switched to "city or village" in v. 11. In the main clause Matthew replaces "first say, 'Peace to this house'" with "greet it," drawing the verb "greet" from the final clause of the Equipment Rule (Q 10,4) which he dropped.

Luke 10,6 also substantially reproduces Q, but Luke has edited the verse lightly, especially altering the verbs. Although Matthew edited the Q verse more radically, his v. 13 contains some original elements of Q. Two concerns drive Matthew's redaction. He intends to develop the "worthy" theme he announced in v. 11, and he wants to extend the parallelism of the two halves of the verse. In the first half of the verse Luke substituted ἐπαναπαήσεται for Q's ἐλθάτω.[34] Luke likes compound verbs

one of his sources and construct a theme around it. For example, Matthew picks up "little faith" from Q (Matt 6,30 par. Luke 12,28) and uses it several times to characterize the disciples (Matt 8,26; 14,31; 16,8; compare also Matt 17,20). He takes Q's "there will be weeping and gnashing of teeth" (Matt 8,12 par. Luke 13,28) and repeats it five more times (Matt 13,42.50; 22,13; 24,51; 25,30). See further W. D. DAVIES and D. C. ALLISON, *Matthew*, 2. 144.

31. See W. TRILLING, "Zur Überlieferungsgeschichte des Gleichnisses vom Hochzeitsmahl Mt 22,1-14," in *BZ* 4 (1960) 251-265, esp. p. 258.

32. Besides the Wedding Feast (Matt 22,1-14) see the parables of the Weeds among the Wheat (Matt 13,24-30.36-43) and the Net (Matt 13,47-50) and Matthew's Last Judgment scene (Matt 25,31-46).

33. The crasis form κἀκεῖ occurs also in Matt 5,23; 28,10. Matthew drops Mark's redundant ἐκεῖθεν, and he switches to the aorist imperative to assimilate the second imperative in the verse to the first one (ἐξετάσατε).

34. For the form ἐλθάτω compare Q 11,2.

and Septuagintal verbs.[35] The future is probably a Lucan improvement, for the future reflects a better Greek style.[36] Luke also changed the word order by moving the prepositional phrase forward, placing it immediately after the verb compounded with the same preposition which he introduced into the verse. In the first half of the verse Matthew begins to unfold the parallelism by introducing the particle μέν.[37] For υἱὸς εἰρήνης he substitutes ἡ οἰκία ἀξία to develop his "worthy" theme. This substitution means that ἐκεῖ has to drop out. In the second half of the verse Luke added γε[38] and substituted ἀνακάμψει for ἐπιστραφήτω.[39] To make the second half parallel to the first Matthew repeats the subject in the main clause, and he has a full conditional clause instead of Q's elliptical εἰ δὲ μή. Matthew also substituted πρός for ἐπί. Both Matthew and Luke have ἐπί in the first half of the verse, and Luke uses πρός with ἀνακάμπτω in Acts 18,21 so he had no reason to avoid it.

Luke 10,7 also contains original Q material, but we can recover the Q text only with difficulty. Matthew does not have a parallel to Luke 10,7a and 10,7c, and he has Luke 10,7b in a different form and in a different context in his v. 10. Furthermore, in the verse we encounter the first of a series of repetitions in Luke's text. Within the verse itself the final imperative μὴ μεταβαίνετε ἐξ οἰκίας εἰς οἰκίαν repeats the thought of the initial imperative μένετε. Luke also echoes the participial phrase ἐσθίοντες καὶ πίνοντες τὰ παρ' αὐτῶν in the following verse with ἐσθίετε τὰ παρατιθέμενα ὑμῖν (Luke 10,8). Further down in the discourse Luke twice refers to entering a city (Luke 10,8.10), and he has the missionaries twice announce that the kingdom has drawn near (Luke 10,9.11). As we shall see, each of these repetitions contains an original Q element that Luke doubles.

We begin with Luke 10,7a. Q must have referred in some way to food, because, although Matthew has no parallel to Luke's v. 7a, in v. 10 he states that the laborer is worthy of his food. Luke, though, has redacted the Q saying. The imperative μένετε comes from Mark 6,10.

---

35. For Luke's preference for compound verbs, see H. J. CADBURY, *Style and Literary Method*, pp. 166-168; for Luke's dependence on the Septuagint, see J. C. HAWKINS, *Horae Synopticae*, pp. 198-207.

36. R. LAUFEN, *Doppelüberlieferungen*, pp. 216-217.

37. Matthew introduces the particle redactionally at least in Matt 13,8 (diff. Mark 4,8); 13,23 (diff. Mark 4,20); 13,32 (diff. Mark 4,31); 16,14 (diff. Mark 8,28); 20,23 (diff. Mark 10,39); 21,35 (diff. Mark 12,3); 22,5 (diff. Luke 14,18); 22,8 (diff. Luke 14,21).

38. The expression εἰ δὲ μή γε is Lucan (2 0 5 0). See J. C. HAWKINS, *Horae Synopticae*, pp. 17, 38. Luke changed εἰ δὲ μή to εἰ δὲ μή γε in Luke 5,36 (diff. Mark 2,21); 5,37 (diff. Mark 2,22).

39. Luke again chose a Septuagintal verb. Luke also uses the verb in Acts 18,21.

Uro disputes this, claiming that Luke shows no sign of the Marcan discourse in Luke 10,2-12.[40] But we saw above that Luke introduced a Q term, "silver," in his version of Mark's Equipment Rule (Luke 9,3 diff. Mark 6,8). In his redaction of the Marcan discourse he also introduces a reference to preaching the kingdom of God from Q.[41] If Luke can import Q expressions into Mark, he can carry over Marcan terms into Q. If we strike μένετε as a Marcan intrusion, then the prepositional phrase ἐν αὐτῇ δὲ τῇ οἰκίᾳ should also be eliminated. The prepositional phrase and the imperative simply repeat in different words the thought of Luke's v. 7c, "Do not move from house to house." If we eliminate μένετε, that means that Luke's participle ἐσθίοντες was originally in the imperative – the form we find in Luke 10,8, ἐσθίετε. Luke probably added the word "drinking" to Q. Although Q can join "eating" and "drinking," Luke at times expands "eating" in his sources to "eating" and "drinking."[42] Since Luke 10,8 mentions only "eating," Luke probably added "drinking" in v. 7. Luke is also responsible for the object τὰ παρ᾽ αὐτῶν.[43] The original Q expression was probably the τὰ παρατιθέμενα ὑμῖν of Luke 10,8. Although παρατίθημι appears several times in Luke-Acts,[44] it fits naturally in the context of eating as its frequent use in the feeding miracle stories shows.[45] To summarize, the Q expression behind Luke 10,7a was ἐσθίετε τὰ παρατιθέμενα ὑμῖν. Luke transferred this clause to v. 8, and constructed a new clause to replace it around Mark's μένετε. He added the initial prepositional phrase, expanded "eating" to "eating and drinking," and changed the object.

Luke 10,7b preserves the Q explanatory clause. Matthew shifted the saying about the worker to use it as a conclusion to the prohibitions not to take provisions for the journey in Matt 10,9-10. He is also responsible for the change from "reward" to "food."[46] Both μισθός and τροφή are Matthean.[47]

---

40. R. Uro, *Sheep Among the Wolves*, p. 80.

41. See Luke 9,2 (diff. Mark 6,7) and compare Luke 10,9.11.

42. Q refers to "eating" and "drinking" in Q 7,33.34; 12,45; 17,27. Luke adds "drinking" to "eating" in Luke 5,30 (diff. Mark 2,16). Compare also Luke 5,33 (diff. Mark 2,18); 13,26 (diff. Matt 7,22); 22,30 (diff. Matt 19,28).

43. The expression τό, τά, before prepositions is characteristic of Luke (1 2 8 15). See J. C. Hawkins, *Horae Synopticae*, pp. 22, 47-48.

44. Besides Luke 10,8 Luke takes the verb over once from Mark (Luke 9,16 par. Mark 6,41), introduces it once into Marcan material (Luke 23,46 diff. Mark 15,37), and uses it twice in his special material (Luke 11,6; 12,48). He uses it four times in Acts (Acts 14,23; 16,34; 17,3; 20,32).

45. Mark 6,41; 8,6 *bis*.7; Luke 9,16. Compare also 1 Cor 10,27.

46. P. Hoffmann, "Lk 10,5-11," p. 38.

47. The statistics for μισθός (10 1 3 1) and τροφή (4 0 1 7) show Matthew's preference for the terms. J. C. Hawkins, *Horae Synopticae*, pp. 6, 8.

Three factors influenced Matthew to make the change. First, μισθός is primarily the end-time reward for Matthew.[48] Second, Matthew's theme in this section is that the disciples are not to enrich themselves through the mission, so "reward" would give the wrong impression. Third, Matthew wants to emphasize the necessity of supporting the missionaries, and since he omits the sentence on eating (Luke 10,7a), he compensates for the omission by substituting "food" for "reward."

Luke 10,7c reflects Q. The verb μεταβαίνω appears only here in Luke's gospel. Matthew omitted the clause because he took over an equivalent clause from Mark 6,10 in Matt 10,11c.

We can now display the Q house mission. The section contains three parts. Q first spells out how the missionaries are to act when they approach a house and then how they are to conduct themselves in the house. Finally, Q forbids the missionaries to change lodgings.

Q 10,5-7

5 εἰς ἣν δ' ἂν οἰκίαν εἰσέλθητε, πρῶτον λέγετε·
   εἰρήνη τῷ οἴκῳ τούτῳ.
6 καὶ ἐὰν ἐκεῖ ᾖ υἱὸς εἰρήνης,
   ἐλθάτω ἡ εἰρήνη ὑμῶν ἐπ' αὐτόν.
   εἰ δὲ μή, ἐφ' ὑμᾶς ἐπιστραφήτω.
7 ἐσθίετε τὰ παρατιθέμενα ὑμῖν,
   ἄξιος γὰρ ὁ ἐργάτης τοῦ μισθοῦ αὐτοῦ.
   μὴ μεταβαίνετε ἐξ οἰκίας εἰς οἰκίαν.

A section on reception and rejection in a city followed the house mission in Q.

Matt 10,7-8.14-15	Luke 10,8-12
	8 καὶ εἰς ἣν ἂν πόλιν εἰσέρχησθε
	καὶ δέχωνται ὑμᾶς,
	ἐσθίετε τὰ παρατιθέμενα ὑμῖν
8 ἀσθενοῦντας θεραπεύετε,	9 καὶ θεραπεύετε
	τοὺς ἐν αὐτῇ ἀσθενεῖς
νεκροὺς ἐγείρετε, λεπροὺς	
καθαρίζετε, δαιμόνια ἐκβάλλετε·	
δωρεὰν ἐλάβετε, δωρεὰν δότε.	
7 πορευόμενοι δὲ κηρύσσετε	
λέγοντες ὅτι	καὶ λέγετε αὐτοῖς·
ἤγγικεν	ἤγγικεν ἐφ' ὑμᾶς
ἡ βασιλεία τῶν οὐρανῶν.	ἡ βασιλεία τοῦ θεοῦ.
14 καὶ ὃς ἂν μὴ δέξηται ὑμᾶς	10 εἰς ἣν δ' ἂν πόλιν εἰσέλθητε
μηδὲ ἀκούσῃ τοὺς λόγους ὑμῶν,	καὶ μὴ δέχωνται ὑμᾶς,
ἐξερχόμενοι ἔξω τῆς	ἐξελθόντες εἰς τὰς

48. Matt 5,12; 6,1; 10,41bis.42; 20,8.

οἰκίας ἢ τῆς πόλεως

ἐκείνης ἐκτινάξατε
τὸν κονιορτὸν τῶν ποδῶν ὑμῶν.

15 ἀμὴν λέγω ὑμῖν, ἀνεκτότερον
ἔσται γῇ Σοδόμων καὶ Γομόρρων
ἐν ἡμέρᾳ κρίσεως
ἢ τῇ πόλει ἐκείνῃ.

πλατείας αὐτῆς εἴπατε·
11 καὶ τὸν κονιορτὸν τὸν
κολληθέντα ἡμῖν ἐκ τῆς
πόλεως ὑμῶν εἰς τοὺς
πόδας ἀπομασσόμεθα ὑμῖν·
πλὴν τοῦτο γινώσκετε ὅτι
ἤγγικεν ἡ βασιλεία τοῦ θεοῦ.
12 λέγω ὑμῖν ὅτι Σοδόμοις
ἐν τῇ ἡμέρᾳ ἐκείνῃ
ἀνεκτότερον ἔσται
ἢ τῇ πόλει ἐκείνῃ.

According to Hoffmann, Luke 10,8 is redactional. He argues that there is no real Matthean parallel to this verse. Matthew's εἰς ἣν δ᾽ ἂν πόλιν ἢ κώμην εἰσέλθητε (Matt 10,11a) is no exception for it is closer to Luke 10,5 than to Luke 10,8. The use of "city or village" reflects Matt 9,35 and results from Matthew's desire to parallel the mission of the disciples and the mission of Jesus. Luke elsewhere shows considerable interest in the city, so he introduced a section on the mission to the city into the discourse. The reference to eating what is set before you (v. 8b) is also a secondary repetition of v. 7b.[49] We saw above that the reference to eating belongs in v. 7, not in v. 8, even though v. 8 preserves the original Q expression of the idea. However, Hoffmann's position fails to account for the agreements of Matthew and Luke. Matthew may have been influenced by Matt 9,35 to add "village," but both he and Luke mention the city, and it is too much of a coincidence to suspect they both introduce the city into the discourse, each following his own redactional tendency, Matthew to parallel the disciples' and Jesus' missions and Luke to pursue his special interest in the city. The differences between Luke 10,5 and 10,8 are too minor to carry the weight Hoffmann assigns to them. So except for the final clause Luke 10,8 preserves the Q text.

Luke 10,9 is also basically Q. Matthew has an expanded form in Matt 10,7-8. Luke mentions first healing, then the message. Matthew reverses the order to emphasize the primacy of teaching which is reflected elsewhere in his gospel.[50] Matthew expanded the Q reference to healing the sick to include raising the dead, cleansing lepers, and driving out demons. These additions bring the activity of the disciples into line with the messianic works of Jesus (compare Matt 11,5) and with Mark's Mission

49. P. HOFFMANN, Studien, pp. 276-283.

50. Matthew makes a similar shift in Matt 11,4 (diff. Luke 7,22). He observes the same order in two key summaries (Matt 4,23; 9,35) and in the structure of his gospel which sets teaching (chapters 5-7) before deeds (chapters 8-9). See P. HOFFMANN, Studien, p. 275 n. 126.

Discourse (compare Mark 6,7.13).[51] Matthew's participle ἀσθενοῦντας is original. It does not fit in well with the adjective and nouns "dead," "lepers," "demons." Matthew would scarcely have changed ἀσθενεῖς if he had read it in Q.[52] Matthew dropped the article. Luke added καί to join the verse to his redactional v. 8b, and he is probably responsible for inserting ἐν αὐτῇ between the article and the adjective.[53] Otherwise, Luke's word order is original. The Q introduction to the kingdom proclamation is difficult. Matthew's πορευόμενοι δέ picks up πορεύεσθε δέ from the preceding verse (Matt 10,6) which Matthew added to the discourse so it is redactional. Matthew's κηρύσσετε might appear to be redactional also,[54] but it is supported by Luke 9,2.[55] Matthew's λέγοντες has some support in Luke's λέγετε. Luke's ἐφ᾽ ὑμᾶς is original. Matthew omits it to bring the command into line with the summaries of the preaching of John and Jesus in Matt 3,2 and 4,17. Q uses the phrase elsewhere in connection with the kingdom (Q 11,20).[56] Because Matthew drops ἐφ᾽ ὑμᾶς he also drops αὐτοῖς. Finally, Matthew adds ὅτι.[57]

Luke 10,10a is a secondary attempt to parallel vv. 5 and 8. Luke 10,10b is also Lucan redaction. Here Luke changes a gesture into a warning in direct address.[58] Luke likes to present the mission as taking place in the full light of day, hence his reference to πλατείας.[59] We can compare the Lucan redaction of the Wedding Feast where the servants go out "to the streets (πλατείας) and lanes of the city" (Luke 14,21).[60] Luke 9,5a probably contains the Q introduction to the gesture.[61] Matt 10,14 partially confirms this conclusion even though the verse depends heavily on Mark 6,11. For instance, Matthew's μηδὲ ἀκούσῃ τοὺς λόγους ὑμῶν develops Mark's μηδὲ ἀκούσωσιν ὑμῶν, but Matthew

51. G. N. STANTON, *A Gospel for a New People: Studies in Matthew*, Edinburgh: Clark, 1992, p. 335.

52. On ἀσθενής in Luke, see Acts 4,9; 5,15.16. See P. HOFFMANN, *Studien*, pp. 275-276.

53. Luke likes to insert words between the article and the noun. Compare Luke 1,70; 6,42; 9,12.37; 16,10.15; 19,30; Acts 5,16; 8,14; 10,45; 13,42; 15,23; 16,2; 17,13.28; 19,25.38; 20,21.26; 21,21.27; 22,1; 23,21; 25,27; 26,3.11; 27,2. See J. C. HAWKINS, *Horae Synopticae*, pp. 27, 50.

54. Compare Matt 3,1; 4,17.23; 9,35; 10,27; 11,1; 24,14; 26,13.

55. The verb appears also in Q 12,3 and the noun κήρυγμα in Q 11,32.

56. P. HOFFMANN, *Studien*, p. 275.

57. Compare λέγοντες ὅτι in Matt 14,26 (diff. Mark 6,49); 16,7 (diff. Mark 8,16).

58. For a parallel, see Acts 18,6 where Paul explains a gesture with a speech. See P. HOFFMANN, *Studien*, p. 270.

59. Compare especially Acts 26,26.

60. Compare also Luke 13,26; Acts 5,15.

61. καὶ ὅσοι ἂν μὴ δέχωνται ὑμᾶς, ἐξερχόμενοι ἀπὸ τῆς πόλεως ἐκείνης (Luke 9,5a).

drops Mark's "place" which might indicate that in Q the people, not the place, reject the missionaries as Luke 9,5 states. Luke 9,5a and Matt 10,14 share the participle ἐξερχόμενοι and the genitive τῆς πόλεως ἐκείνης. Luke's ἀπό is original. Although Luke likes the combination of ἐξέρχομαι ἀπό,[62] the expression appears also in Q 11,24. The compound verb influenced Matthew's ἔξω. Matthew also clarified Mark's "place" by removing it from the relative clause and substituting "outside of the house and that city" in the main clause. "That city" comes from Q (compare Luke 9,5), but Matthew added "house" to link up with the preceding section (Matt 10,11-13). In the description of the gesture Matthew and Luke agree in using κονιορτόν.[63] In Luke 10,11 the verbs κολλάω and ἀπομάσσω point to Lucan redaction.[64] The phrase ἐκ τῆς πόλεως is also Lucan.[65] Matthew's ἐκτινάξατε τὸν κονιορτὸν τῶν ποδῶν ὑμῶν is original. It lacks the small clarifying additions that characterize Luke's text, and it is confirmed by Acts 13,51 (ἐκτιναξάμενοι τὸν κονιορτὸν τῶν ποδῶν). Luke's final sentence, "but know this that the kingdom of God has drawn near," is redactional. The expressions πλήν[66] and γινώσκετε[67] are Lucan, and the kingdom proclamation simply repeats the earlier proclamation without ἐφ᾽ ὑμᾶς.[68]

Matthew introduced "amen" in the saying on the Sodomites. The same sentence structure appears in the closely related saying Q 10,14 where we find πλήν in both Matthew and Luke. Luke has drawn the πλήν forward to his redactional v. 11b, so he omits it here. Luke's ὅτι preserves Q as Matthew has the conjunction in his repetition of the saying in Matt 11,24. Matthew added γῆ[69] and Γομόρρων.[70] Hoffmann claims that Matthew's "on the day of judgment" combines two Q expressions – ἐν τῇ ἡμέρᾳ ἐκείνῃ (Luke 10,12) and ἐν τῇ κρίσει (Luke 10,14).[71] However,

62. Luke 4,35bis.41; 5,8; 8.2.29.33.35.38.46; 9,5; 11,24; 17,29; Acts 16,18.40; 28,3. See J. C. HAWKINS, Horae Synopticae, pp. 18, 40.

63. Matt 10,14; Luke 9,5; 10,11; Acts 13,51; compare also Acts 22,23.

64. For κολλάω compare Luke 15,15; Acts 5,13; 8,29; 9,26; 10,28; 17,34. P. HOFF-MANN, Studien, p. 271.

65. The prepositional phrase originally fit after the participle in v. 10 (compare Matt 10,14 and Luke 9,5), but Luke's εἰς τὰς πλατείας αὐτῆς displaced it there so Luke shifted it to the warning where it clarifies Luke's redactional κολληθέντα.

66. 5 1 15 4. See J. C. HAWKINS, Horae Synopticae, p. 21.

67. Luke 8,10.17; 19,42.44; 21,20.30-31; Acts 2,36; 22,14. See P. HOFFMANN, Studien, p. 272.

68. P. HOFFMANN, Studien, p. 272.

69. Compare Matt 2,6.20.21; 4,15bis; 10,15; 11,24. See P. HOFFMANN, Studien, p. 284 n. 148.

70. See the parallel in Matt 11,23-24 where only the Sodomites are mentioned.

71. P. HOFFMANN, Studien, p. 284.

more probably Matthew's "on the day of judgment" reflects Q, and Luke split the expression. Although Hawkins lists "on the day of judgment" as a typically Matthean expression, Matthew only uses it four times and three of the four occurrences fall in these closely related texts (Matt 10,15; 11,22.24).[72] Matthew takes over ἐν τῇ κρίσει twice from Q in Matt 12,41-42 (compare Luke 11,31-32) so he shows no aversion to the phrase. Furthermore, Luke uses "that day" redactionally in Luke 17,31 (diff. Mark 13,15) and 21,34. The position of the prepositional phrase in Matthew also reflects Q as the parallel shows (Q 10,14). Luke shifted the phrase forward to separate his two uses of "that." Luke, though, preserves the position of the noun "Sodomites." Again the parallel verse, Q 10,14, confirms the position.[73]

The Q section on the city advances the discourse in several ways. It describes the healing activity of the missionaries and summarizes their proclamation. In this way it picks up and unfolds the peace greeting of the house mission. It further dictates the action the missionaries must take when they meet with rejection. The house mission also hinted at rejection when it mentioned the possibility that the peace greeting might return to those who gave it.

Q 10,8-12

8 καὶ εἰς ἢν ἂν πόλιν εἰσέρχησθε καὶ δέχωνται ὑμᾶς,
9 θεραπεύετε τοὺς ἀσθενοῦντας ἐν αὐτῇ
    καὶ κηρύσσετε λέγοντες αὐτοῖς·
    ἤγγικεν ἐφ' ὑμᾶς ἡ βασιλεία τοῦ θεοῦ.
10 καὶ ὅσοι ἂν μὴ δέχωνται ὑμᾶς,
    ἐξερχόμενοι ἀπὸ τῆς πόλεως ἐκείνης
11 ἐκτινάξατε τὸν κονιορτὸν τῶν ποδῶν ὑμῶν.
12 πλὴν λέγω ὑμῖν ὅτι Σοδόμοις ἀνεκτότερον ἔσται
    ἐν ἡμέρᾳ κρίσεως ἢ τῇ πόλει ἐκείνῃ.

Luke follows the section on the city with the Woes against the Galilean Cities (Luke 10,13-15) and a final closing saying (Luke 10,16). Matthew has a parallel to Luke 10,16 toward the end of the Mission Discourse (Matt 10,40), but he transfers the Woes to the pericope on John's Question (Matt 11,21-23). The Woes fit snugly in their Lucan position, and they undoubtedly formed part of the Q Mission Discourse. When Matthew moved the Woes he adapted the saying in Q 10,12 to provide a conclusion to the cluster: πλὴν λέγω ὑμῖν ὅτι γῇ Σοδόμων ἀνεκτότερον ἔσται ἐν ἡμέρᾳ κρίσεως ἢ σοί (Matt 11,24; compare Matt 10,15). The adapted saying does not fit smoothly in its new context

72. J. C. HAWKINS, *Horae Synopticae*, pp. 5, 31.
73. Compare also Matt 11,24.

at the conclusion of the Woes. The σοί referring to Capernaum clashes with ὑμῖν, a clear sign that Matthew moved the Woes.[74]

Matt 11,21-23; 10,40	Luke 10,13-16
21 οὐαί σοι, Χοραζίν, οὐαί σοι, Βηθσαϊδά· ὅτι εἰ ἐν Τύρῳ καὶ Σιδῶνι ἐγένοντο αἱ δυνάμεις αἱ γενόμεναι ἐν ὑμῖν, πάλαι ἂν ἐν σάκκῳ καὶ σποδῷ μετενόησαν. 22 πλὴν λέγω ὑμῖν, Τύρῳ καὶ Σιδῶνι ἀνεκτότερον ἔσται ἐν ἡμέρᾳ κρίσεως ἢ ὑμῖν. 23 καὶ σύ, Καφαρναούμ, μὴ ἕως οὐρανοῦ ὑψωθήσῃ; ἕως ᾅδου καταβήσῃ· ὅτι εἰ ἐν Σοδόμοις ἐγενήθησαν αἱ δυνάμεις αἱ γενόμεναι ἐν σοί, ἔμεινεν ἂν μέχρι τῆς σήμερον. 40 ὁ δεχόμενος ὑμᾶς ἐμὲ δέχεται, καὶ ὁ ἐμὲ δεχόμενος δέχεται τὸν ἀποστείλαντά με.	13 οὐαί σοι, Χοραζίν, οὐαί σοι, Βηθσαϊδά· ὅτι εἰ ἐν Τύρῳ καὶ Σιδῶνι ἐγενήθησαν αἱ δυνάμεις αἱ γενόμεναι ἐν ὑμῖν, πάλαι ἂν ἐν σάκκῳ καὶ σποδῷ καθήμενοι μετενόησαν. 14 πλὴν Τύρῳ καὶ Σιδῶνι ἀνεκτότερον ἔσται ἐν τῇ κρίσει ἢ ὑμῖν. 15 καὶ σύ, Καφαρναούμ, μὴ ἕως οὐρανοῦ ὑψωθήσῃ; ἕως τοῦ ᾅδου καταβήσῃ. 16 ὁ ἀκούων ὑμῶν ἐμοῦ ἀκούει, καὶ ὁ ἀθετῶν ὑμᾶς ἐμὲ ἀθετεῖ· ὁ δὲ ἐμὲ ἀθετῶν ἀθετεῖ τὸν ἀποστείλαντά με.

Matthew and Luke agree very closely in the Woes. Luke changed an original ἐγένοντο to ἐγενήθησαν and added a clarifying participle καθήμενοι.[75] Interestingly enough, when writing on his own Matthew once repeats the Q expression ἐγένοντο (Matt 11,20) and once, like Luke, improves the style by using the form ἐγενήθησαν (Matt 11,23b).[76] In Q 10,14 Luke omitted λέγω ὑμῖν to avoid confusion, since in v. 12 the phrase refers to the disciples and not Jesus' adversaries.[77] Matthew's ἐν ἡμέρᾳ κρίσεως preserves the Q wording. As we noted above in discussing Q 10,12, "day" is confirmed by Luke 10,12 and "judgment" by Luke 10,14. In v. 15 Luke added the article τοῦ. Matthew's parallel formulation ἕως οὐρανοῦ ... ἕως ᾅδου is original. Matthew added the

---

74. J. SCHMID, Matthäus und Lukas, p. 287; P. HOFFMANN, Studien, pp. 284-285.

75. A. HARNACK, Sprüche und Reden, p. 18; ET: Sayings of Jesus, p. 19; S. SCHULZ, Q, p. 360.

76. See further, S. SCHULZ, Q, p. 360 n. 243.

77. I. H. MARSHALL, Luke, p. 425; F. NEIRYNCK, "Recent Developments," pp. 437-438.

ὅτι-clause at the end of the Capernaum saying to parallel the woe against Chorazin and Bethsaida.[78] Except for this final additional clause Matthew took over the Woes against the Galilean Cities unchanged from Q.

Matthew also preserves the original form of the Saying on Accepting (Q 10,16). A detailed discussion of this verse follows in Chapter VII. The Woes against the Galilean cities and the Saying on Accepting bring the Q Mission Discourse to an end.

Q 10,13-16

13 οὐαί σοι, Χοραζίν, οὐαί σοι, Βηθσαϊδά·
   ὅτι εἰ ἐν Τύρῳ καὶ Σιδῶνι ἐγένοντο αἱ δυνάμεις
   αἱ γενόμεναι ἐν ὑμῖν,
   πάλαι ἂν ἐν σάκκῳ καὶ σποδῷ μετενόησαν.
14 πλὴν λέγω ὑμῖν, Τύρῳ καὶ Σιδῶνι
   ἀνεκτότερον ἔσται ἐν ἡμέρᾳ κρίσεως ἢ ὑμῖν.
15 καὶ σύ, Καφαρναούμ, μὴ ἕως οὐρανοῦ ὑψωθήσῃ;
   ἕως ᾅδου καταβήσῃ.
16 ὁ δεχόμενος ὑμᾶς ἐμὲ δέχεται,
   καὶ ὁ ἐμὲ δεχόμενος δέχεται τὸν ἀποστείλαντά με.

We can now compare Mark and Q.

Q 10,2-16	Mark 6,7-13
	7 καὶ προσκαλεῖται τοὺς δώδεκα
	καὶ ἤρξατο αὐτοὺς
	ἀποστέλλειν δύο δύο
	καὶ ἐδίδου αὐτοῖς ἐξουσίαν
	τῶν πνευμάτων τῶν ἀκαθάρτων,
2 καὶ εἶπεν τοῖς μαθηταῖς αὐτοῦ·	8 καὶ παρήγγειλεν αὐτοῖς
ὁ μὲν θερισμὸς πολύς,	
οἱ δὲ ἐργάται ὀλίγοι·	
δεήθητε οὖν	
τοῦ κυρίου τοῦ θερισμοῦ	
ὅπως ἐκβάλῃ ἐργάτας	
εἰς τὸν θερισμὸν αὐτοῦ.	
3 ὑπάγετε· ἰδοὺ ἀποστέλλω ὑμᾶς	
ὡς ἄρνας ἐν μέσῳ λύκων.	
4 μὴ λαμβάνετε ἄργυρον,	ἵνα μηδὲν αἴρωσιν εἰς ὁδὸν
μὴ πήραν, μὴ ὑποδήματα,	εἰ μὴ ῥάβδον μόνον,
μὴ ῥάβδον·	μὴ ἄρτον, μὴ πήραν,
καὶ μηδένα	μὴ εἰς τὴν ζώνην χαλκόν,
κατὰ τὴν ὁδὸν ἀσπάσησθε.	9 ἀλλὰ ὑποδεδεμένους
	σανδάλια, καὶ μὴ
	ἐνδύσησθε δύο χιτῶνας.
	10 καὶ ἔλεγεν αὐτοῖς·
5 εἰς ἣν δ' ἂν οἰκίαν εἰσέλθητε,	ὅπου ἐὰν εἰσέλθητε εἰς οἰκίαν,

---

78. P. HOFFMANN, *Studien*, p. 284.

πρῶτον λέγετε· εἰρήνη
6 τῷ οἴκῳ τούτῳ. καὶ ἐὰν ἐκεῖ
ἦ υἱὸς εἰρήνης, ἐλθάτω
ἡ εἰρήνη ὑμῶν ἐπ' αὐτόν.
εἰ δὲ μή, ἐφ' ὑμᾶς
ἐπιστραφήτω.
7 ἐσθίετε τὰ παρατιθέμενα ὑμῖν,
ἄξιος γὰρ ὁ ἐργάτης
τοῦ μισθοῦ αὐτοῦ.
μὴ μεταβαίνετε ἐξ οἰκίας   ἐκεῖ μένετε ἕως ἂν
εἰς οἰκίαν.   ἐξέλθητε ἐκεῖθεν.
8 καὶ εἰς ἣν ἂν πόλιν
εἰσέρχησθε καὶ δέχωνται ὑμᾶς,
9 θεραπεύετε τοὺς ἀσθενοῦντας
ἐν αὐτῇ καὶ κηρύσσετε
λέγοντες αὐτοῖς· ἤγγικεν ἐφ'
ὑμᾶς ἡ βασιλεία τοῦ θεοῦ.
10 καὶ ὅσοι ἂν μὴ δέχωνται ὑμᾶς,   11 καὶ ὃς ἂν τόπος μὴ
    δέξηται ὑμᾶς
    μηδὲ ἀκούσωσιν ὑμῶν,
ἐξερχόμενοι ἀπὸ τῆς πόλεως   ἐκπορευόμενοι ἐκεῖθεν
11 ἐκείνης ἐκτινάξατε τὸν   ἐκτινάξατε τὸν χοῦν τὸν
κονιορτὸν τῶν ποδῶν ὑμῶν.   ὑποκάτω τῶν ποδῶν ὑμῶν
    εἰς μαρτύριον αὐτοῖς.
12 πλὴν λέγω ὑμῖν ὅτι Σοδόμοις
ἀνεκτότερον ἔσται ἐν ἡμέρᾳ
κρίσεως ἢ τῇ πόλει ἐκείνῃ.
13 οὐαί σοι, Χοραζίν,
οὐαί σοι, Βηθσαϊδά·
ὅτι εἰ ἐν Τύρῳ καὶ Σιδῶνι
ἐγένοντο αἱ δυνάμεις
αἱ γενόμεναι ἐν ὑμῖν,
πάλαι ἂν ἐν σάκκῳ
καὶ σποδῷ μετενόησαν.
14 πλὴν λέγω ὑμῖν, Τύρῳ καὶ
Σιδῶνι ἀνεκτότερον ἔσται
ἐν ἡμέρᾳ κρίσεως ἢ ὑμῖν.
15 καὶ σύ, Καφαρναούμ,
μὴ ἕως οὐρανοῦ ὑψωθήσῃ;
ἕως ᾅδου καταβήσῃ.
16 ὁ δεχόμενος ὑμᾶς ἐμὲ δέχεται,
καὶ ὁ ἐμὲ δεχόμενος δέχεται
τὸν ἀποστείλαντά με.

12 καὶ ἐξελθόντες
ἐκήρυξαν ἵνα μετανοῶσιν,
13 καὶ δαιμόνια πολλὰ
ἐξέβαλλον,
καὶ ἤλειφον ἐλαίῳ πολλοὺς
ἀρρώστους καὶ ἐθεράπευον.

There are several indications that Mark is secondary. First, disregarding for the moment Mark's introduction (v. 7) and conclusion (vv. 12-13) and looking just at the discourse material, Mark appears to be a summary of Q. All the topics of Mark's discourse appear in Q, and Mark has them in the same order as Q. However, Mark's text appears sketchy. For example, Mark coordinates vv. 10 and 11. Where the disciples are accepted they are to remain (v. 10), but where they aren't they are to shake the dust from their feet (v. 11). Mark provides few details. How are the disciples to find a house? What are they to do in the house? Furthermore, in v. 10 Mark speaks of a house, in v. 11 of a place. In v. 11 Mark indirectly mentions the purpose of the mission – "and will not listen to you" – but the clause sounds like an afterthought. Mark does not communicate the content of the disciples' preaching, and even the fact that they will say anything has to be deduced from the verb ἀποστέλλω by way of Mark 3,14.[79] The whole section appears condensed like a sketchy excerpt of a longer composition.[80] Second, Q consistently uses direct discourse. Mark begins with indirect discourse in v. 8, but switches to direct discourse in v. 9. Mark appears to adapt original discourse material to a narrative frame. Third, the Equipment Rule in Mark consciously corrects the Q Equipment Rule. In Q Jesus forbids the disciples to take silver, knapsack, shoes, and staff. In Mark Jesus allows some exceptions including a staff and sandals. A staff and sandals belonged so essentially to the provisions of wandering preachers that we can explain their mention as exceptions only as a deliberate modification of a previous ban on them.[81] Lührmann aptly characterizes Mark's exceptions as "denials of denials," and he sees them as a sign that Mark is later.[82]

Albert Fuchs denies that Mark's text is later. As we have seen, Fuchs accepts one part of the two-source theory, the priority of Mark, but he has problems with the Q hypothesis. According to Fuchs Matthew and Luke agree against Mark in the Mission Discourse because they depend

79. "And he appointed the twelve to be with him and to be sent out to preach..." (Mark 3,14).

80. R. BULTMANN, *Die Geschichte der synoptischen Tradition*, Göttingen: Vandenhoeck & Ruprecht, [4]1958, pp. 155-156; ET: *The History of the Synoptic Tradition*, trans. J. Marsh, New York/Evanston: Harper & Row, 1963, p. 145; F. W. BEARE, "The Mission of the Disciples and the Mission Charge: Matthew 10 and Parallels," in *JBL* 89 (1970) 1-13, esp. p. 13; P. HOFFMANN, *Studien*, p. 242.

81. Best explains the change as pre-Marcan, and he attributes it either to a change in geography (Italy instead of the Middle East) or to the length of the journey or to Q's asceticism. See E. BEST, *Following Jesus: Discipleship in the Gospel of Mark* (JSNT SS, 4), Sheffield: JSOT, 1981, p. 190. Hoffmann (*Studien*, p. 240) correctly sees the change as a deliberate modification of the Q Equipment Rule.

82. D. LÜHRMANN, "Gospel of Mark and the Sayings Collection Q," p. 63.

on a later redaction of Mark, Deutero-Markus, which improved Mark's text.[83] For example, Fuchs proposes a different tradition history for the Equipment Rule. For Fuchs Mark does not allow the missionaries to take a staff and sandals as exceptions to Q's strict ban, but Deutero-Markus forbids a staff and shoes to sharpen the demands on the missionaries.[84] A staff and sandals, though, probably would never appear in the instructions as permissible equipment unless they were forbidden at one point. Lührmann's "denials of denials" explains the texts better than Fuchs' interpretation. Furthermore, it is not so easy to dispense with Q in the mission instructions. In the various forms of the Mission Discourse Matthew and Luke contain much non-Marcan material like the Harvest Saying (Matt 9,37-38 par. Luke 10,2), the Commission (Matt 10,16 par. Luke 10,3), and the Woes against the Galilean Cities (Matt 11,21-23 par. Luke 10,13-15). Matthew and Luke incorporate this additional material into their gospels in such different ways that independent use of Q explains the data better than Deutero-Markus. Instead of depending on Deutero-Markus Matthew and Luke used Mark and Q; and, as we have just seen, Mark's text is later than Q.

Mark may be secondary to Q, but does Mark depend on Q? An objection often lodged against this conclusion comes from Mark's brevity. Why would Mark eliminate so much of the Q discourse? For example, Uro and Schüling claim that Mark would not have passed over such sayings as the announcement of the kingdom (Q 10,9).[85] Mark's text is much shorter than Q's. Mark's brevity, though, need not prevent us from seeing Mark as dependent on Q if we can explain why Mark omitted so much Q material.

The context in Mark's gospel demanded that Mark shorten the Q discourse drastically. Mark uses the Mission of the Twelve as a frame for John's Death:

(A) Mission of the Twelve (Mark 6,7-13)
    (B) John's Death (Mark 6,14-29)
(A′) Mission of the Twelve (Mark 6,30)

This framing technique appears often in Mark.[86] For the technique to work, the outside frame must be kept short. To see the problems Mark

---

83. A. FUCHS, "Die synoptische Aussendungsrede in quellenkritischer und traditionsgeschichtlicher Sicht," in *SNTU* 17 (1992) 77-168, esp. pp. 80-115.

84. *Ibid.*, pp. 95-98.

85. R. URO, *Sheep Among the Wolves*, pp. 36-37; J. SCHÜLING, *Studien*, pp. 19, 21.

86. Besides the Mission of the Twelve and John's Death, Mark employs the technique five times: Jesus' Relatives and the Beelzebul Controversy (Mark 3,20-35); Jairus' Daughter and the Hemorrhaging Woman (Mark 5,21-43); Cursing of the Fig Tree and the Cleansing of the Temple (Mark 11,12-25); Plot against Jesus and Jesus' Anointing (Mark 14,1-11); Jesus' Trial and Peter's Denial (Mark 14,53-72). See F. NEIRYNCK, *Duality in Mark*, p. 133.

faced, we can compare Matthew's Mission Discourse. In the beginning
of the discourse Jesus calls the twelve disciples and sends them out
to preach and heal (Matt 10,1-8), but then Matthew so lengthens the
discourse that both he and the reader forget about the actual mission.
The disciples never return, and the story moves on as if they had never
been sent out.[87] To avoid this problem, Mark shortens the Q discourse.

Furthermore, Mark's omissions make sense. To abbreviate the discourse
Mark eliminates sections that do not fit his literary or theological
conception, he transfers one verse to another context, and he reduces the
rest of the discourse to two of its essential themes. First Mark eliminates
eight verses from the Q discourse (Q 10,2-3.8-9.12-15). The narrative
and theological structure of his gospel make the omissions necessary. In
Q the Mission Discourse is a sermon of Jesus to the disciples. Mark turns
the discourse into an event in Jesus' ministry. The actual commission
which Q mentions twice (Q 10,3.8-9) Mark transfers to the narrative
introduction and conclusion of his section (Mark 6,7.12-13), so the three
Q verses that center on the commission drop out. Putting the commission
in the narrative frame also leaves no place for the Harvest Saying (Q 10,2)
which motivates the commission in Q. Mark already used the kingdom
saying in a programmatic summary (Mark 1,14-15). Mark further drops
the entire section on the Galilean cities (Q 10,12-15) because for Mark
Galilee is the place of discipleship. Opposition to Jesus centers on
Jerusalem while Galilee contrasts with Jerusalem by accepting Jesus.
Only Jesus' native place (Mark 6,1-6a) constitutes an exception. Elsewhere Galilee accepts Jesus.[88] Mark could not fit the Woes against the
Galilean Cities into his view of Galilee. Second, besides eliminating
eight verses (Q 10,2-3.8-9.12-15) Mark transfers the final saying (Q
10,16) to the Discipleship Discourse (Mark 9,33-50).[89] Third, Mark
reduces the rest of the Q discourse to two themes. He takes over and
modifies the Equipment Rule (Mark 6,8-9; compare Q 10,4) to show the
rigors of the mission, and he extracts from the Q instructions on the
house and the city (Q 10,5-11) the theme of acceptance and rejection. He
uses the house ministry to express how the disciples are to behave when

---

87. P. WERNLE, *Synoptische Frage*, p. 164.

88. In Galilee some groups oppose Jesus like the scribes (Mark 1,22; 2,6.16; 3,22;
7,1.5), the Pharisees (Mark 2,16.18.24; 3,6; 7,1.3.5; 8,11.15), and the Herodians (Mark
3,6; compare also Mark 8,15). The Galilean crowds, though, throng to Jesus (Mark
1,22.27-28.32-34.37.45; 2,1-2.12.13; 3,7-12.20; 4,1; 5,21; 6,31.33-34.53-56; 8,1).
Twice Mark goes out of his way to show that opposition to Jesus comes from Jerusalem,
not Galilee (Mark 3,22; 7,1). The Woes against the Galilean Cities would not fit in
Mark's conception of Galilee.

89. Mark 9,37 overlaps Q 10,16. See Chapter VII below.

they are accepted (Mark 6,10) and the city (place) ministry to express how they are to behave when they are rejected (Mark 6,11). In each case he selects one feature from Q to make his point. From Q's section on the house ministry, he chooses the command not to change lodging; from Q's city ministry, he selects the gesture of shaking the dust from the feet. Once we understand why Mark made the changes he made, Mark's brevity no longer prevents us from seeing that Mark depends on Q in the Mission Discourse.

We turn to the details of Mark's redaction. In v. 7 the verb προσκαλέομαι,[90] the auxiliary verb ἄρχομαι[91], and "the Twelve"[92] are Marcan. The distributive repetition of a word (δύο δύο) occurs elsewhere in Mark.[93] Mark also emphasizes the demon expulsions in Jesus' work, and he places exorcisms at the end of two important summaries (Mark 1,32-34; 3,7-12). In particular Mark 6,7 corresponds closely to Mark 3,13-15. In both texts Jesus summons (προσκαλέομαι) the disciples; both involve a mission; both mention the Twelve; and both times the disciples receive authority over unclean spirits. These two texts are the only places in which the disciples receive power to exorcise.[94] Marcan style and the similarity to Mark 3,13-15 prove that v. 7 is completely redactional. The only term that might reflect Q is ἀποστέλλειν (compare Q 10,3), but this word also appears in Mark 3,13-15.

In the place of Q's direct address, Mark begins the instructions in indirect discourse (v. 8). It is typical for Mark to use indirect discourse and especially for him to introduce a command or wish with ἵνα rather than the infinitive as in classical Greek.[95] He switches to the accusative with the infinitive in v. 9a and to direct address in v. 9b.[96] With μηδὲν

---

90. Mark 3,13.23; 6,7; 7,14; 8,1.34; 10,42; 12,43; 15,44. Mark 3,13 is a very close redactional parallel.

91. Mark 1,45; 2,23; 4,1; 5,17.20; 6,2.7.34.55; 8,11.31.32; 10,28.32.41.47; 11,15; 12,1; 13,5; 14,19.33.65.69.71; 15,8.18. See J. W. HUNKIN, "'Pleonastic' ἄρχομαι in the New Testament," in *JTS* 25 (1923-24) 390-402; C. H. TURNER, "Marcan Usage: Notes, Critical and Exegetical, on the Second Gospel," in *JTS* 28 (1926-27) 349-362, esp. pp. 352-353; J. C. DOUDNA, *The Greek of the Gospel of Mark* (JBL MS, 12), Philadelphia: Society of Biblical Literature and Exegesis, 1961, pp. 51-53, 111-117.

92. Mark 3,14.16; 4,10; 6,7; 9,35; 10,32; 11,11; 14,10.17.20.43. See J. GNILKA, *Die Verstockung Israels: Isaias 6,9-10 in der Theologie der Synoptiker* (SANT, 3), Munich: Kösel, 1961, p. 59.

93. Compare Mark 6,39.40.

94. R. LAUFEN, *Doppelüberlieferungen*, p. 519 n. 314.

95. See Mark 3,9; 5,18.43; 6,12; 7,26.32.36; 8,22.30; 9,9.12.18; 10,48; 13,34; 14,35. See P. HOFFMANN, *Studien*, p. 238.

96. Broken constructions are fairly common in Mark (Mark 3,16-17; 4,26.31-32; 12,19.38-40; 14,49). See J. C. HAWKINS, *Horae Synopticae*, pp. 135-137; V. TAYLOR, *Mark*, p. 50.

αἴρωσιν εἰς ὁδόν Mark gives a generalizing introduction to the list of forbidden objects. It serves as a summary and title for the rest.[97] The phrase εἰς ὁδόν further connects the mission with Mark's discipleship theme.[98] Q simply lists the objects the missionaries were forbidden to take with them. Mark introduces some changes in the list. The most striking are the two exceptions – a staff and sandals – that Mark allows the missionaries. The introduction of these exceptions causes the shifting of the grammatical construction. The words μόνον and ὑποδεδεμένους also show conscious redactional activity.[99] Mark also adds "and do not wear two coats." This clause marks the shift to direct discourse. It also continues Mark's lifting of the strict Q ban on provisions, for Mark allows the missionaries to take one coat with them. When Q forbids even a staff and shoes, the ban makes a theological point – the missionaries are to trust entirely in God even to the exclusion of any provision. In Mark we see the later lifting of the stringent ban for the sake of the mission. The tendency to tone down extreme statements of Q characterizes Mark's treatment of the overlap texts. In the Unforgivable Sin Mark eliminates the reference to the Son of Man because he cannot imagine that blasphemy against the Son of Man can be forgiven. Mark also tones down a Q exaggeration in the parable of the Mustard Seed where Q calls the grown mustard a "tree" and Mark corrects this to "the largest of the shrubs." The tendency to tone down an extreme statement will crop up again in the Cross Saying (Mark 8,34b) and the Saying on Tolerance (Mark 9,40).

Besides allowing a staff, sandals, and a coat Mark also introduced "bread" into the list. The addition makes sense in the framework of Mark's gospel because the provision of bread is an important theme in Mark. By adding bread to the list Mark steers toward the Bread Section (Mark 6,32-8,26) which centers on the two feeding miracles (Mark 6,32-44; 8,1-9). One of the section's themes focuses on the disciples' lack of understanding, specifically their lack of understanding about the loaves of bread (Mark 6,52; 8,14-21). In Mark 8,14 the disciples have not taken bread with them. They do not understand that Jesus would provide for them as he did for the crowd. To anticipate this theme Mark introduces bread into the list of forbidden objects. Finally, Mark substitutes "copper" for "silver" (compare Mark 12,41). Perhaps he did not think that the early missionaries had silver. The phrase εἰς τὴν ζώνην is a clarifying addition.

97. Compare "we have left all things" (Mark 10,28). See further Mark 1,16-20. See P. HOFFMANN, *Studien*, p. 241.
98. Compare Mark 1,2; 8,27; 9,33.34; 10,17.32.46.52; 12,14.
99. P. HOFFMANN, *Studien*, p. 240.

In v. 10 Mark drastically shortened the Q section of the mission in the house. After providing a new introduction ("and he said to them"),[100] Mark rewrites the first clause slightly, but he then omits everything except the injunction not to change houses. In rewriting the first clause Mark introduces ὅπου ἐάν with the aorist subjunctive, a construction that appears almost exclusively in Mark in the NT.[101] Mark formulates the command positively, "remain," instead of using Q's negative formulation, "do not move from house to house" (Q 10,7). For "house" he substitutes "there" as Q had done earlier (Q 10,6). He draws on Q elements to formulate the until-clause, picking up the Q verb ἐξέρχομαι (Q 10,10) and using ἐκεῖθεν to refer back to ἐκεῖ. So in v. 10 Mark summarizes the entire Q House Mission.

Although Mark apparently passes over Q 10,8-9, he actually transfers many of the Q motifs to his concluding summary (Mark 6,12-13) as we shall see. In v. 11 Mark edits the Q statement on the procedure the missionaries are to follow when they are not received. He rewrites the indefinite clause (Q 10,10), drawing the reference to the place into the initial clause and generalizing it ("place" instead of "city"). Mark adds "nor hear you" to the Q text, picking up a familiar Marcan theme. For example, he strongly emphasizes hearing the word in the Parable Discourse.[102] While he has not mentioned preaching as one of the goals of the mission up to this point, he will return to this theme in v. 12. Because Mark drew the reference to the place into the initial clause he substitutes ἐκεῖθεν for ἀπὸ τῆς πόλεως ἐκείνης in the main clause. He also substitutes ἐκπορευόμενοι for ἐξερχόμενοι[103] and χοῦν for κονιορτόν, and he further specifies the object by adding τὸν ὑποκάτω before τῶν ποδῶν ὑμῶν. He also adds a clarifying phrase "as a witness to them" (compare Mark 1,44; 13,9).

In v. 12 Mark mentions that the disciples preached,[104] and he introduces the theme of repentance to bring the preaching of the disciples into line with that of Jesus and John (compare Mark 1,4.15). The

---

100. As we saw above in discussing the Lamp Saying, καὶ ἔλεγεν αὐτοῖς is Marcan (Mark 2,27; 4,2.11.21.24; 6,4.10; 7,9; 8,21; 9,1.31; 11,17).

101. Mark uses the construction three more times (Mark 9,18; 14,9.14). Elsewhere it appears only in Matt 26,13 in dependence on Mark 14,9. See P. DSCHULNIGG, *Sprache*, p. 93.

102. Mark 4,3.9.11-12.20.23-24.33-34.

103. For the participle of ἐκπορεύομαι compare Mark 7,15.20; 10,17.46; 13,1. Mark will use the aorist participle of ἐξέρχομαι in the following verse.

104. The verb κηρύσσω appears in the Q discourse (Q 10,9). It is also Marcan (Mark 1,4.7.14.38.39.45; 3,14; 5,20; 6,12; 7,36; 13,10; 14,9). See E. SCHWEIZER, "Anmerkungen zur Theologie des Markus" (1962), in ID., *Neotestamentica*, 1963, pp. 93-104, esp. pp. 93-95.

proclamation of the kingdom is not mentioned just as Mark omits it in his redaction of John's preaching (Mark 1,4-8). Only Jesus proclaims the coming of the kingdom in Mark, and this proclamation coincides with the preaching of the gospel (Mark 1,14-15). The disciples stand between the proclamation of John and Jesus and the proclamation of the church which centers on the gospel (Mark 13,10; 14,9).[105] The reference to casting out demons in v. 13 ties the conclusion to the introduction (v. 7). The notice that the twelve healed the sick picks up the Q command to heal the sick (Q 10,9), but Mark uses his own word ἀρρώστους (compare Mark 6,5). Only here does Mark refer to anointing with oil, but the statement is not unusual for him as he elsewhere mentions the use of spit and manipulation (Mark 7,33; 8,23.25). In particular the healing of the sick reminds the reader of the cures in the previous Nazareth pericope (Mark 6,5).

So Mark 6,7-13 makes sense as a Marcan redactional reformulation of the Q Mission Discourse. Again, though, some would question whether we must attribute the differences between Mark and Q to Mark's literary activity. Couldn't a pre-Marcan redactor have modified the material before Mark encountered it? Did Mark have to derive the discourse from Q? What I have described as Mark's rewriting parallels in many ways his redaction of the Beelzebul Controversy. In both cases the passage falls in one of the framing sections of Mark's gospel. Jesus' True Family (Mark 3,20-21.31-35) frames the Beelzebul Controversy (Mark 3,22-30), and the Mission of the Twelve (Mark 6,7-13.30) frames the Death of John (Mark 6,14-29). The framing technique carries Mark's signature. To attribute it to a pre-Marcan redactor makes no sense. In both the Beelzebul Controversy and the Mission Discourse Mark shortens the Q passage, but the material Mark shares with Q appears in the Q order. Mark also uses Q elements to create new sections. In the Beelzebul Controversy, for instance, he constructs the parable of the divided house out of a detail of Q's divided kingdom. In the Mission Discourse Mark creates a narrative frame out of motifs he omitted from the Q discourse. Mark also separates out a saying from both passages that he will use later in the Discipleship Discourse (Mark 9,33-50). He saves the Saying on Tolerance from the Beelzebul Controversy and the Saying on Accepting from the Mission Discourse.[106] Whoever saved out the Saying on Tolerance and the Saying on Accepting had the overall compositional needs of Mark's whole gospel in mind. In other words the Beelzebul Controversy and the Mission Discourse show a consistent editing hand that can only be Mark's.

105. P. HOFFMANN, *Studien*, p. 239.
106. Compare Mark 9,40 with Q 11,23 and Mark 9,37 with Q 10,16.

According to Dale C. Allison, Paul knew the Mission Discourse.[107] Tuckett has shown, however, that the parallels Allison alleges do not carry much weight except for the saying on support (1 Cor 9,14; compare Q 10,7).[108] Even in this saying, though, the Pauline parallel shows no verbal contact with the Q saying.

οὕτως καὶ ὁ κύριος διέταξεν τοῖς τὸ εὐαγγέλιον καταγγέλλουσιν ἐκ τοῦ εὐαγγελίου ζῆν (1 Cor 9,14).
ἄξιος γὰρ ὁ ἐργάτης τοῦ μισθοῦ αὐτοῦ (Q 10,7).

Paul did not know the Mission Discourse.[109]

The Gospel of Thomas has two parallels to the Mission Discourse. Th 73 reproduces the Harvest Saying (Q 10,2) closely.

Jesus said, "The harvest is indeed (μέν) great, but the laborers (ἐργάτης) are few; but (δέ) pray the Lord to send laborers (ἐργάτης) into the harvest."

The Thomas saying reflects the synoptic saying closely. Thomas has "the Lord" instead of "the Lord of the harvest," and correspondingly writes "into the harvest" instead of "into his harvest." Thomas replaces οὖν with a second δέ and ὅπως with ἵνα. The last two changes show that the Thomas version is more recent than the synoptic saying, for the δέ is more easily understood than οὖν and ἵνα is more common than ὅπως.[110] The omission of the two genitives is somewhat puzzling. "The Lord of the harvest" is a striking phrase that shifts the center of the synoptic saying from the harvest to God who controls the harvest. By eliminating the genitives the author of Thomas concentrates the saying on the harvest itself perhaps to underline the urgency of the gnostic mission.

Th 14 has links to three synoptic passages.

Jesus said to them, "If you fast (νηστεύειν), you will beget sin for yourselves, and if you pray, you will be condemned (κατακρίνειν), and if you give alms (ἐλεημοσύνη), you will do evil (κακόν) to your spirits (πνεῦμα). And if you go into any land and travel in the regions (χώρα), if they receive (παραδέχεσθαι) they, eat what they set before you. Heal (θεραπεύειν) the sick who are among them. For (γάρ) what will go into your mouth will not defile you, but (ἀλλά) what comes out of your mouth, that is what will defile you."

---

107. D. C. ALLISON, "The Pauline Epistles and the Synoptic Gospels: The Pattern of the Parallels," in *NTS* 28 (1982) 1-32, esp. pp. 12-13.

108. C. M. TUCKETT, "1 Corinthians and Q," in *JBL* 102 (1983) 607-619, esp. p. 612; ID., "Paul and the Synoptic Mission Discourse?," in *ETL* 60 (1984) 376-381.

109. See further, F. NEIRYNCK, "Paul and the Sayings of Jesus" (1986), in ID., *Evangelica II*, 1991, pp. 511-568, esp. pp. 550-552.

110. J.-É. MÉNARD, *L'évangile selon Thomas*, pp. 173-174.

Th 14 is a composite saying made up of three parts. In the first part
Jesus rejects the traditional Jewish pious practices of fasting, prayer, and
almsgiving. The three practices appear in Matt 6,1-18, but in the order
almsgiving, prayer, and fasting. Thomas' order is probably secondary.
The author of Thomas switched the first and third elements to move fasting
to the front because it forms the theme for the whole logion. The second
part parallels Luke 10,8-9. Here, too, Thomas depends on the synoptics.
The juxtaposition of "eat what they set before you" and "heal the sick
who are among them" reflects Luke 10,8-9. This juxtaposition is Lucan
redaction. In Q the command to eat what is served appeared earlier in v.
7. Luke reformulated the command to eat in v. 7 in his own words and
then transferred the original command to v. 8 where the command to heal
followed. Thomas, then, reflects the redactional text of Luke. The third part
of Th 14 reflects Matt 15,11 which corresponds to Mark 7,15. Thomas
agrees with Matthew against Mark in using a singular subject in both
halves of the saying whereas Mark has a plural in the second half. Thomas
also agrees with Matthew against Mark in specifying that what goes in and
out passes through the mouth. So Thomas agrees with redactional
Matthew.

Neither of the two Thomas sayings preserves an independent tradition
of the sayings of Jesus. Th 73 does not reflect the redactional text of the
synoptic gospels, but neither does it show original features. Th 14 reflects
the redactional text of both Luke and Matthew. It clearly depends on the
synoptic sayings.

§ 11. Demand for a Sign

Mark 8,11-13 (Matt 12,38-42 par. Luke 11,16.29-32)

In Q the Demand for a Sign followed immediately after the Beelzebul
Controversy. In Mark five chapters separate the passages. The Q passage
falls into two parts, a first section on the sign of Jonah (Q 11,16.29-30)
and a second part on the Queen of the South and the Ninevites (Q 11,31-
32). The reconstruction is fairly straightforward except at the beginning
of the pericope where Matthew and Luke diverge sharply.

Matt 12,38-40	Luke 11,16.29-30
38 τότε ἀπεκρίθησαν αὐτῷ τινες τῶν γραμματέων καὶ Φαρισαίων λέγοντες· διδάσκαλε, θέλομεν ἀπὸ σοῦ σημεῖον ἰδεῖν.	16 ἕτεροι δὲ πειράζοντες σημεῖον ἐξ οὐρανοῦ ἐζήτουν παρ' αὐτοῦ. ...

39 ὁ δὲ ἀποκριθεὶς εἶπεν
αὐτοῖς·
γενεὰ πονηρὰ καὶ μοιχαλὶς
σημεῖον ἐπιζητεῖ,
καὶ σημεῖον οὐ δοθήσεται αὐτῇ
εἰ μὴ τὸ σημεῖον Ἰωνᾶ
τοῦ προφήτου.
40 ὥσπερ γὰρ ἦν Ἰωνᾶς
ἐν τῇ κοιλίᾳ τοῦ κήτους
τρεῖς ἡμέρας καὶ τρεῖς νύκτας,

οὕτως ἔσται
ὁ υἱὸς τοῦ ἀνθρώπου
ἐν τῇ καρδίᾳ τῆς γῆς
τρεῖς ἡμέρας κὰι τρεῖς νύκτας.

29 τῶν δὲ ὄχλων ἐπαθροιζομένων
ἤρξατο λέγειν·
ἡ γενεὰ αὕτη γενεὰ πονηρά ἐστιν·
σημεῖον ζητεῖ,
καὶ σημεῖον οὐ δοθήσεται αὐτῇ
εἰ μὴ τὸ σημεῖον Ἰωνᾶ.

30 καθὼς γὰρ ἐγένετο Ἰωνᾶς

τοῖς Νινευίταις σημεῖον,
οὕτως ἔσται καὶ
ὁ υἱὸς τοῦ ἀνθρώπου

τῇ γενεᾷ ταύτῃ.

Matthew has the demand for a sign (Matt 12,38) right before Jesus' answer (Matt 12,39-42). Luke places the demand (Luke 11,16) immediately after the charge that Jesus casts out demons by Beelzebul (Luke 11,15). What about Q? Did Matthew delay the demand or did Luke anticipate it? Two considerations show that Luke moved the demand forward. First, Luke likes to construct complex introductions that cover two pericopes.[111] He moves the introduction to the Demand for a Sign forward to combine it with the introduction to the Beelzebul Controversy (Luke 11,15-16). Second, Luke 11,29a, the clause that forms the transition between the two pericopes, shows signs of Luke's hand. Luke uses the genitive absolute often as well as ὄχλος and ἤρξατο λέγειν.[112] Although the verb ἐπαθροίζω is a *hapax legomenon*, it shouldn't stand in the way of seeing the clause as redactional.[113]

Matthew redacts the Marcan version of the Demand for a Sign in Matt 16,1-4. Although Luke omits the Marcan form as part of his great omission, the Marcan overlap text influenced the introduction of Luke as well as Matthew. Matt 16,1 is a redaction of Mark 8,11. Matt 12,38 has the greatest claim to preserve the Q introduction. However, even

---

111. See Luke 5,17; 8,1; 9,51; 12,1; 13,22-23; 17,11-12a; 19,11-12a. See A. DENAUX, "Het lucaanse reisverhaal (Lc. 9,51-19,44)," in *Collationes Brugenses et Gandavenses* 14 (1968) 214-242; 15 (1969) 464-501, esp. p. 481 n. 37.

112. Luke introduces genitive absolutes into Marcan material in Luke 3,21; 4,42; 8,4.23.45; 9,34.42.43; 18,40; 19,33.36.37; 20,45; 21,5; 22,10.53.55.60; 24,5. See H. J. CADBURY, *Style*, pp. 133-134; H. T. FLEDDERMANN, "Demands of Discipleship," p. 544 n. 11. Luke introduces ὄχλος into Marcan material in Luke 4,42; 5,15.29; 6,17.19; 9,11.12.16.18; 18,36; 22,6; 23,4.48. Luke uses ἄρχομαι with the infinitive 27 times in the gospel.

113. P. WERNLE, *Synoptische Frage*, p. 70; S. SCHULZ, *Q*, p. 251.

here Matthew introduced some changes. The τότε is Matthean.[114] The reference to the scribes and Pharisees is also Matthean.[115] Luke's ἕτεροι δέ is probably the Q phrase designating the speakers. In the Beelzebul Controversy Jesus' adversaries were designated by the indefinite τινες. The coordinated pair εἷς ... ἕτερος pops up from time to time in Q, and τινες ... ἕτεροι is the plural form.[116] Luke's πειράζοντες, ἐξ οὐρανοῦ, and ἐζήτουν παρ' αὐτοῦ all come from Mark 8,11.[117] Matthew's ἀπεκρίθησαν is redactional.[118] The Q verb was probably εἶπον, followed by the indirect object.[119] The Q introductory phrase would be: ἕτεροι δέ εἶπον αὐτῷ. Matthew preserves the Q request, διδάσκαλε, θέλομεν ἀπὸ σοῦ σημεῖον ἰδεῖν.[120] When Luke moved the introduction forward, he switched from direct discourse to a simple report of the request because in the next verse (Luke 11,17) Jesus begins by answering the Beelzebul charge, not the demand for a sign.

Matthew's ὁ δὲ ἀποκριθεὶς εἶπεν αὐτοῖς is probably the Q introduction to Jesus' reply.[121] In the reply itself Matthew preserves the Q sentence structure. Luke combines Mark's γενεὰ αὕτη and Q's γενεὰ πονηρά. To fit them both in he had to reformulate the sentence. Matthew added καὶ μοιχαλίς[122] and τοῦ προφήτου.[123] Matthew's compound verb ἐπιζητεῖ is original. The verb is attested in Q (Q 12,30), and Luke's verb comes from Mark.

The following verse compares the Son of Man and "this generation" to Jonah and the Ninevites.[124] Matthew's ὥσπερ γὰρ ἦν preserves the Q wording. In Q 17,24 Matthew and Luke agree in writing ὥσπερ; then in Q 17,26 Luke alters a second ὥσπερ γάρ to καὶ καθὼς ἐγένετο.

---

114. See note 3 above.

115. Matthew uses the stereotyped phrase "scribes and Pharisees" eleven times (Matt 5,20; 12,38; 15,1; 23,2.13.14.15.23.25.27.29).

116. See the discussion of the Beelzebul Controversy above.

117. Luke substituted ἐξ οὐρανοῦ for Mark's ἀπὸ τοῦ οὐρανοῦ. Compare Luke 3,22 diff. Mark 1,11.

118. Compare the combination of τότε and ἀποκρίνομαι in Matt 25,37.44.45.

119. The aorist εἶπον occurs often in the introductions of Q pericopes. See, for example, Q 9,57.59; 13,18.20. See H. T. FLEDDERMANN, "Demands of Discipleship," pp. 542-544, 547-548; ID., "Mustard Seed," pp. 217-219.

120. Schulz (Q, p. 251 n. 509) claims that διδάσκαλε is redactional. However, Matthew nowhere else introduces the vocative "teacher" on his own. See H. T. FLEDDERMANN, "Demands of Discipleship," pp. 544-545.

121. S. SCHULZ, Q, p. 251.

122. Matthew added the words also to his redaction of Mark 8,12 in Matt 16,4.

123. S. SCHULZ, Q, p. 251 n. 518.

124. On the form of the saying see R. A. EDWARDS, "The Eschatological Correlative as a Gattung in the New Testament," in ZNW 60 (1969) 9-20; D. SCHMIDT, "The LXX Gattung 'Prophetic Correlative'," in JBL 96 (1977) 517-522; A. D. JACOBSON, First Gospel, p. 63.

Matthew, though, imports into the saying the developed Jonah typology with its three days and three nights in the belly of the whale.[125] Luke reflects the Q wording in τοῖς Νινευίταις σημεῖον and in the οὕτως clause. Luke, though, has added a καί in the apodosis.[126]

Q 11,16.29-30

16 ἕτεροι δὲ εἶπον αὐτῷ· διδάσκαλε, θέλομεν ἀπὸ σοῦ σημεῖον ἰδεῖν.
29 ὁ δὲ ἀποκριθεὶς εἶπεν αὐτοῖς·
   γενεὰ πονηρὰ σημεῖον ἐπιζητεῖ, καὶ σημεῖον οὐ δοθήσεται αὐτῇ
   εἰ μὴ τὸ σημεῖον Ἰωνᾶ.
30 ὥσπερ γὰρ ἦν Ἰωνᾶς τοῖς Νινευίταις σημεῖον,
   οὕτως ἔσται ὁ υἱὸς τοῦ ἀνθρώπου τῇ γενεᾷ ταύτῃ.

The sayings about the Queen of the South and the Ninevites form the second half of the pericope.

Matt 12,41-42	Luke 11,31-32
42 βασίλισσα νότου ἐγερθήσεται	31 βασίλισσα νότου ἐγερθήσεται
ἐν τῇ κρίσει	ἐν τῇ κρίσει
μετὰ τῆς γενεᾶς ταύτης	μετὰ τῶν ἀνδρῶν τῆς γενεᾶς ταύτης
καὶ κατακρινεῖ αὐτήν	καὶ κατακρινεῖ αὐτούς,
ὅτι ἦλθεν ἐκ τῶν περάτων τῆς γῆς	ὅτι ἦλθεν ἐκ τῶν περάτων τῆς γῆς
ἀκοῦσαι τὴν σοφίαν Σολομῶνος,	ἀκοῦσαι τὴν σοφίαν Σολομῶνος,
καὶ ἰδοὺ πλεῖον Σολομῶνος ὧδε.	καὶ ἰδοὺ πλεῖον Σολομῶνος ὧδε.
41 ἄνδρες Νινευῖται ἀναστήσονται	32 ἄνδρες Νινευῖται ἀναστήσονται
ἐν τῇ κρίσει	ἐν τῇ κρίσει
μετὰ τῆς γενεᾶς ταύτης	μετὰ τῆς γενεᾶς ταύτης
καὶ κατακρινοῦσιν αὐτήν,	καὶ κατακρινοῦσιν αὐτήν,
ὅτι μετενόησαν	ὅτι μετενόησαν
εἰς τὸ κήρυγμα Ἰωνᾶ,	εἰς τὸ κήρυγμα Ἰωνᾶ,
καὶ ἰδοὺ πλεῖον Ἰωνᾶ ὧδε.	καὶ ἰδοὺ πλεῖον Ἰωνᾶ ὧδε.

Luke's order which follows the biblical sequence preserves the original order of the sayings.[127] Matthew reversed the sayings to connect the three sayings that mention Jonah (Matt 12,39-41).[128] In the saying on the Queen of the South Luke inserted τῶν ἀνδρῶν and correspondingly changed αὐτήν to αὐτούς. The ἄνδρες in the following verse suggested the insertion to Luke, and ἀνήρ is part of his characteristic vocabulary.[129] Matthew and Luke agree word for word in the saying on the Ninevites.

---

125. S. SCHULZ, Q, pp. 251-252.
126. Compare Luke 5,36 (diff. Mark 2,21); 11,34a (diff. Matt 6,22); 11,34b (diff. Matt 6,23); 17,37 (diff. Matt 24,28). See H. J. CADBURY, Style and Literary Method, pp. 146-147.
127. D. R. CATCHPOLE, "The Law and the Prophets in Q," in Tradition and Interpretation in the New Testament: FS E. Earle Ellis, 1987, pp. 95-109, esp. p. 99.
128. S. SCHULZ, Q, p. 252.
129. 8 4 27 100. See J. C. HAWKINS, Horae Synopticae, p. 16.

Q 11,31-32

31 βασίλισσα νότου ἐγερθήσεται ἐν τῇ κρίσει μετὰ τῆς γενεᾶς ταύτης
καὶ κατακρινεῖ αὐτήν, ὅτι ἦλθεν ἐκ τῶν περάτων τῆς γῆς
ἀκοῦσαι τὴν σοφίαν Σολομῶνος, καὶ ἰδοὺ πλεῖον Σολομῶνος ὧδε.
32 ἄνδρες Νινευῖται ἀναστήσονται ἐν τῇ κρίσει μετὰ τῆς γενεᾶς ταύτης
καὶ κατακρινοῦσιν αὐτήν, ὅτι μετενόησαν εἰς τὸ κήρυγμα Ἰωνᾶ,
καὶ ἰδοὺ πλεῖον Ἰωνᾶ ὧδε.

We can now compare Q and Mark.

Q 11,16.29-32	Mark 8,11-13
16 ἕτεροι δὲ εἶπον αὐτῷ·	11 καὶ ἐξῆλθον οἱ Φαρισαῖοι
	καὶ ἤρξαντο συζητεῖν αὐτῷ,
διδάσκαλε, θέλομεν ἀπὸ σοῦ	ζητοῦντες παρ' αὐτοῦ
σημεῖον ἰδεῖν.	σημεῖον ἀπὸ τοῦ οὐρανοῦ,
	πειράζοντες αὐτόν.
29 ὁ δὲ ἀποκριθεὶς	12 καὶ ἀναστενάξας τῷ
εἶπεν αὐτοῖς·	πνεύματι αὐτοῦ λέγει·
γενεὰ πονηρὰ σημεῖον ἐπιζητεῖ	τί ἡ γενεὰ αὕτη ζητεῖ σημεῖον;
καὶ σημεῖον	ἀμὴν λέγω ὑμῖν,
οὐ δοθήσεται αὐτῇ	εἰ δοθήσεται
εἰ μὴ τὸ σημεῖον Ἰωνᾶ.	τῇ γενεᾷ ταύτῃ σημεῖον.
30 ὥσπερ γὰρ ἦν Ἰωνᾶς τοῖς Νινευίταις	
σημεῖον,	
οὕτως ἔσται ὁ υἱὸς τοῦ ἀνθρώπου	
τῇ γενεᾷ ταύτῃ.	
31 βασίλισσα νότου ἐγερθήσεται	
ἐν τῇ κρίσει μετὰ τῆς γενεᾶς ταύτης	
καὶ κατακρινεῖ αὐτήν,	
ὅτι ἦλθεν ἐκ τῶν περάτων τῆς γῆς	
ἀκοῦσαι τὴν σοφίαν Σολομῶνος,	
καὶ ἰδοὺ πλεῖον Σολομῶνος ὧδε.	
32 ἄνδρες Νινευῖται ἀναστήσονται	
ἐν τῇ κρίσει μετὰ τῆς γενεᾶς ταύτης	
καὶ κατακρινοῦσιν αὐτήν,	
ὅτι μετενόησαν εἰς τὸ κήρυγμα Ἰωνᾶ,	
καὶ ἰδοὺ πλεῖον Ἰωνᾶ ὧδε.	
	13 καὶ ἀφεὶς αὐτοὺς
	πάλιν ἐμβὰς ἀπῆλθεν
	εἰς τὸ πέραν.

Initially it might appear that Mark's text is primary. In Mark Jesus
refuses to give a sign. Q provides an exception to this refusal which is
then elaborated. As a result Mark's text is considerably shorter than Q.
Tuckett also points out that Mark's oath formula using εἰ reflects a
Semitic idiom which makes it unlikely that Mark here redacts Q.[130]

---

130. C. M. TUCKETT, "Mark and Q," pp. 161-162.

However, these indications that Mark is primary do not stand up to close scrutiny. As in the case of the Mission Discourse, the Marcan context provides a reason why Mark would have had to shorten the Demand for a Sign if it came to him in a longer version like the version of Q. Mark's pericope falls toward the end of the Bread Section (Mark 6,32-8,26). The Bread Section unfolds in two parts. Each part begins with a feeding miracle and ends with a symbolic miracle.[131] In each part there is controversy with Jesus' adversaries and a passage dealing with the lack of understanding of the disciples.[132] The Bread Section brings the first half of Mark's gospel to a close and forms the transition to the second half. The climax of the Bread Section occurs immediately after the Demand for a Sign in the conversation between Jesus and the disciples over bread (Mark 8,14-21). This pericope centers on the Marcan theme of the lack of understanding of the disciples, and in it Jesus refers explicitly to both feeding miracles. Immediately after this conversation Jesus performs the symbolic opening of the eyes of the blind man. Mark needs a controversy story to balance the controversy story in the first half of the Bread Section, but he is rushing towards his conclusion so he pares the Demand for a Sign down to its essential content – Jesus in effect refuses to give a sign.

The oath formula also need not indicate that Mark is the earlier form of the saying. The oath formula using εἰ is a Septuagintism.[133] It occurs elsewhere in the New Testament, and forms part of the thought world of Mark and his readers.[134]

When we compare the two texts several features show that Mark is secondary. First, Mark specifies Jesus' opponents as the Pharisees. Q's more general "others" clearly is primary. Second, Mark fills out the context by stating that the opponents "began to dispute with him." Mark's expression specifies Q's simple "said." Third, Mark psychologizes by ascribing a motive to the Pharisees (πειράζοντες αὐτον) and an emotional response to Jesus (ἀναστενάξας τῷ πνεύματι αὐτοῦ). Fourth, Mark's "sign from heaven" obviously intensifies the demand. Q's simple "sign" is original. Fifth, Mark's use of "this generation" hangs in the air. In Q the present generation is contrasted with the Ninevites and the

---

131. The first half begins with the Feeding of the Five Thousand (Mark 6,32-44) and ends with the Cure of the Deaf Man (Mark 7,32-37). The second half begins with the Feeding of the Four Thousand (Mark 8,1-9) and ends with the Cure of the Blind Man (Mark 8,22-26).

132. In the first half Jesus argues with the Pharisees and the scribes over what is clean and unclean (Mark 7,1-23), and in the second half we find the Demand for a Sign (Mark 8,11-13). The disciples' lack of understanding surfaces in Mark 6,52; 7,17-23; 8,14-21.

133. See, for example, 3 Kgdms 2,8.35n.

134. The formula appears in a quotation of Psa 94,7 LXX in Heb 3,11; 4,3.5.

generation of the Queen of the South, so the use of "this generation" is more natural. Sixth, Jesus' refusal to give a sign in Mark is a secondary reflection on the Q text. Q gives an exception – no sign will be given except the sign of Jonah. The exception, though, is only apparently an exception because it becomes clear that the sign of Jonah is his preaching. Jesus says, in effect, that the adversaries will only receive preaching, not a sign. Mark sees that Q's exception does not constitute a true exception but really amounts to a refusal so he eliminates the superfluous exception. The secondary reflection shows that Mark is later. Seventh, the Marcan account appears so abrupt that it seems to be an excerpt from the longer Q account.

Not only is Mark secondary to Q; Mark also knows the Q redaction. "This generation" is a redactional term that the author of Q uses to link several passages (Q 7,31; 11,31.32.51). The term does not fit smoothly in Mark because unlike Q Mark does not contrast "this generation" and the generation of the Queen of the South or the Ninevites. Given the Marcan context Jesus could more naturally reply, "Why do you demand a sign? Truly I tell you, no sign will be given to you." Mark picks up "this generation" from Q where it fits naturally, and uses it instead of "you." So Mark again shows that he knows redactional Q.

If we examine the Marcan redaction, we see clearly that Mark is working with the Q text. In v. 11 ἐξῆλθον, οἱ Φαρισαῖοι, ἤρξαντο, συζητεῖν, and πειράζοντες αὐτόν are all Marcan. Mark uses ἐξέρχομαι very frequently throughout the gospel,[135] and the Pharisees surface often in Mark as Jesus' adversaries.[136] We have seen above that pleonastic ἄρχομαι with the infinitive appears often in Mark.[137] The verb συζητέω is characteristically Marcan.[138] Mark also uses πειράζοντες αὐτόν to describe the motivation of Jesus' adversaries in Mark 10,2 (compare Mark 12,15). With ζητοῦντες and σημεῖον Mark anticipates v. 12 which he has drawn from Q. Mark qualifies the sign as a sign "from heaven" to intensify the demand (compare Mark 13,25). In other words v. 11 is a Marcan redactional introduction to the demand for a sign.

In v. 12 ἀναστενάξας τῷ πνεύματι αὐτοῦ is Marcan.[139] The historical present λέγει appears very frequently in Mark.[140] Mark introduces Jesus'

---

135. Mark 1,25.26.28.29.35.38.45; 2,12.13; 3,6.21; 4,3; 5,2.8.13.30; 6,1.10.12.24.34. 54; 7,29.30.31; 8,11.27; 9,25.26.29.30; 11,11.12; 14,16.26.48.68; 16,8.

136. Mark 2,16.18*bis*.24; 3,6; 7,1.3.5; 8,11.15; 10,2; 12,13.

137. See the discussion of the Mission Discourse above.

138. 0 6 2 2. The other five occurrences are all redactional (Mark 1,27; 9,10.14.16; 12,28). See J. C. HAWKINS, *Horae Synopticae*, p. 13.

139. The compound ἀναστενάξας is a *hapax legomenon* in the NT, but Mark uses the simple verb in Mark 7,34. For τῷ πνεύματι αὐτοῦ compare Mark 2,8.

140. J. C. HAWKINS, *Horae Synopticae*, pp. 143-149.

reply with a rhetorical question to increase the liveliness of the scene.[141] Mark picks up "this generation" from Q 11,30-32 which he omits, and he introduces the solemn asseveration formula "amen, I say to you."[142] Finally, Mark transposes the refusal into the Hebrew oath formula.[143]

The concluding verse is completely redactional. Marcan expressions abound: καί-parataxis,[144] ἀφείς,[145] πάλιν,[146] ἐμβάς,[147] ἀπῆλθεν,[148] and εἰς τὸ πέραν.[149] Mark uses this verse as a transition to the climax of the Bread Section, the discussion with the disciples about bread (Mark 8,14-21).

In both the Mission Discourse and the Demand for a Sign Mark is secondary to Q. In both pericopes Mark also shows knowledge of redactional Q.

The Mission Discourse invites comparison with the Beelzebul Controversy, the only other extensive overlap text. In both cases Mark's text is considerably shorter. Mark's brevity comes from several sections in each Q pericope that have nothing corresponding in Mark. However, in the material they have in common, the sections of Mark's pericopes appear in the same order as their Q counterparts. Furthermore, we found good reasons why Mark omitted the sections he does not share with Q. In other words, the omissions are Marcan omissions. In both cases Mark edits the pericope by drawing on motifs from Q. Mark fits both pericopes into one of his framing passages, and in each case Mark saves out a saying that he will use in the Discipleship Discourse. Finally, the detailed editing reflects Marcan vocabulary and Marcan themes. The same hand edited both the Beelzebul Controversy and the Mission Discourse. Everything points to Mark as the redactor of the two passages.

In the Demand for a Sign Mark shows knowledge of redactional Q in the expression "this generation." The term does not fit smoothly in Mark's pericope because Mark does not contrast Jesus' adversaries with

141. Mark also used a rhetorical question to introduce Jesus' defense in the Beelzebul Controversy (Mark 3,23).

142. Mark also introduced "amen, I say to you" in his editing of the Q saying on the Unforgivable Sin in Mark 3,28.

143. For the construction in the NT see BDF, § 372 (4), § 454 (5). Since it is used in the Septuagint, it must have been intelligible in Greek. See further, J. C. HAWKINS, *Horae Synopticae*, p. 133; C. F. D. MOULE, *Idiom-Book*, pp. 151, 179.

144. For καί see J. C. HAWKINS, *Horae Synopticae*, pp. 150-152.

145. For ἀφείς compare Mark 1,18.20; 4,36; 7,8; 12,12.

146. The adverb πάλιν is a Marcan word (17 28 3 5). See J. C. HAWKINS, *Horae Synopticae*, p. 13.

147. For ἐμβαίνω see Mark 4,1; 5,18; 6,45; 8,10.

148. For ἀπῆλθεν see Mark 1,35; 5,20.24; 6,46; 7,24.

149. For εἰς τὸ πέραν see Mark 4,35; 5,1.21; 6,45.

the generation of the Queen of the South or with the Ninevites. Mark could much more naturally phrase his rhetorical question, "Why do you demand a sign?" "This generation" appears in the three verses that Q has over and above Mark (Q 11,30-32), showing that Mark knew the verses he omits. "This generation" comes from Q, and it has crept into Mark because Mark edits the Q pericope. The evidence continues to pile up that Mark knew Q.

VI

CAESAREA PHILIPPI

The first half of Mark's gospel leads up to the Caesarea Philippi pericope (Mark 8,27-9,1). The second half leads from Caesarea Philippi to the cross and resurrection. At the center of Mark stands Jesus' question, "But you, who do you say I am?" (Mark 8,29). After Peter's response Jesus goes on to predict his passion, death, and resurrection which triggers a sharp exchange between Peter and Jesus (Mark 8,31-33). Jesus then continues with six sayings on discipleship (Mark 8,34-9,1). Half of the sayings have Q parallels.[1] Once again we find several overlap texts in a cluster.

§ 12. THE CROSS SAYING

Mark 8,34b (Matt 10,38 par. Luke 14,27)

The Q saying follows the sayings on hating father and mother, son and daughter (Q 14,26). Matthew and Luke both redact the Marcan saying (Matt 16,24; Luke 9,23).

Matt 10,38	Luke 14,27
καὶ ὃς οὐ λαμβάνει	ὅστις οὐ βαστάζει
τὸν σταυρὸν αὐτοῦ	τὸν σταυρὸν ἑαυτοῦ
καὶ ἀκουλουθεῖ ὀπίσω μου,	καὶ ἔρχεται ὀπίσω μου,
οὐκ ἔστιν μου ἄξιος.	οὐ δύναται εἶναί μου μαθητής.

Matthew's καί is redactional. Luke in general avoids asyndeton so the lack of connection in his text reflects Q.[2] Matthew added the connective

---

1. Mark 8,34b par. Q 14,27; Mark 8,35 par. Q 17,33; Mark 8,38 par. Q 12,8-9.
2. The data has been collected and summarized by Jeremias: (1) Luke systematically eliminates Marcan asyndeta. Of forty instances of asyndeton in texts Luke takes over from Mark he supplies a connective thirty-six times. The four exceptions (Luke 5,13.23.32; 20,16) are allowed to stand for emphasis. (2) When Luke himself introduces asyndeton either into Marcan material (Luke 21,13.19.23) or in Acts (Acts 3,25.26; 7,44.52; 8,21; 10,37; 20,29. 33.34.35; 25,10b; 26,8), it is always for emphasis. (3) Because of this Lucan tendency to avoid asyndeton, the relative frequency of asyndeton in the non-Marcan material (55 times) must be due to Luke's sources. This is confirmed by Matthew's frequent agreement with Luke in not having a connective in Q material (Q 6,45; 10,22; 11,23.32.34; 12,51; 16,13 *bis*; 17,33). See J. JEREMIAS, *Sprache*, pp. 60-61. See further, J. C. HAWKINS, *Horae Synopticae*, pp. 137-138; H. J. CADBURY, *Style and Literary Method*, pp. 147-148.

to bind the saying to the preceding double saying in his gospel. Luke substituted ὅστις for Q's ὅς to underline the generalizing character of the logion. The form ὅστις is common in Matthew so there is no reason why he would have altered it if he had read it in Q.[3] The phrase λαμβάνει τὸν σταυρόν appears only here in the NT and does not occur in profane Greek. The usual expression is βαστάζει τὸν σταυρόν.[4] Luke has apparently grecized the Q expression which Matthew preserved.[5] Matthew's use of βαστάζω decides the issue. Matthew introduces βαστάζω in his redaction of the Q account of John's Preaching (Matt 3,11).[6] Since he used it redactionally, it is not likely that he would change the verb if it lay before him in a Q text. Luke substituted ἑαυτοῦ for αὐτοῦ.[7] Matthew's ἀκολουθεῖ ὀπίσω μου is a Septuagintism (compare 3 Kgdms 19,20; Hos 2,7; Isa 45,14; Ezek 29,16). Although Matthew can use ἀκολουθέω redactionally,[8] it is more probable that Luke altered the verb. Both Luke and Matthew switch from ἀκολουθέω to a form of ἔρχομαι in editing Mark 8,34 (Matt 16,24; Luke 9,23).[9]

In the main clause it is difficult to choose between Matthew's οὐκ ἔστιν μου ἄξιος and Luke's οὐ δύναται εἶναί μου μαθητής.[10] Both ἄξιος and μαθητής are attested in Q.[11] Matthew uses ἄξιος redactionally in Matt 10,11 and twice in Matt 10,13 (compare also Matt 22,8). Luke, though, is the only gospel writer to use the cognate verb ἀξιόω (Luke 7,7; Acts 15,38; 28,22) and its compound καταξιόω (Luke 20,35; Acts 5,41), and he uses the adjective ἄξιος redactionally in Acts 13,25 (compare Q 3,16). So although Matthew can use ἄξιος redactionally, Luke had no reason to avoid it. We can answer the question which is original by examining the content of the two variants and the context in Matthew. First, the content. Luke's version is absolute. Anyone not taking up the

3. See, for example, Matt 2,6; 5,39.41; 7,24*bis*.26; 10,32.33; 12,50; 13,12*bis*.52; 18,4; 19,29; 20,1; 21,33; 22,2; 23,12*bis*.

4. Compare John 19,17. See E. DINKLER, "Jesu Wort vom Kreuztragen," in *Neutestamentliche Studien für Rudolf Bultmann*, ²1957, pp. 110-129, esp. p. 112 n. 6.

5. Luke uses βαστάζω relatively frequently (3 1 5 4). See R. LAUFEN, *Doppelüberlieferungen*, p. 303.

6. See Chapter II above.

7. See Chapter IV above.

8. Matt 4,22; 8,1.23; 9,27; 14,13; 19,2; 20,29.

9. The manuscript tradition has two variants for the infinitive in Mark's conditional clause: (1) ἀκολουθεῖν P⁴⁵ C* D W Θ 0214 f¹ *et al.* and (2) ἐλθεῖν ℵ A B C² K L Γ f¹³ *et al.* Although Reading (2) has excellent attestation, it probably represents an assimilation to Matt 16,24.

10. Matthew uses οὐκ ἔστιν μου ἄξιος in Matt 10,37a.37b.38. Luke uses οὐ δύναται εἶναί μου μαθητής in Luke 14,26.27.33.

11. The adjective ἄξιος appears in Q 3,8; 10,7, and the noun μαθητής in Q 6,40; 7,18.

cross cannot be a disciple. Matthew's version is milder. Whoever does not carry the cross is not worthy of Jesus. Luke disqualifies someone from being a disciple; Matthew leaves the door open. Matthew's milder formulation seems secondary. The context in Matthew also points in the same direction. Matthew sets the saying in the Mission Discourse (Matt 9,37-11,1) which Jesus addresses to the twelve (Matt 10,5), so in Matthew the hearers are already disciples. They must, however, show themselves worthy of Jesus.[12] When we pull all of these obervations together – Matthew's fondness for ἄξιος, Matthew's milder form of the saying, and Matthew's context – it becomes obvious that Luke preserves the Q main clause.

In summary, Matthew has linked the saying to the preceding double saying in his gospel by "and." He has not intervened in the relative clause, allowing Christian and Septuagintal expressions to stand. Luke intervened repeatedly in the relative clause to improve the Greek, but he preserves the Q form of the main clause. We can now compare Q and Mark.

Q 14,27	Mark 8,34b
	εἴ τις θέλει ὀπίσω μου ἀκολουθεῖν,
	ἀπαρνησάσθω ἑαυτὸν
ὃς οὐ λαμβάνει τὸν σταυρὸν αὐτοῦ	καὶ ἀράτω τὸν σταυρὸν αὐτοῦ
καὶ ἀκολουθεῖ ὀπίσω μου,	καὶ ἀκολουθείτω μοι.
οὐ δύναται εἶναί μου μαθητής.	

The Q Cross Saying consists of a relative clause which contains two conditions of discipleship, taking up the cross and following Jesus, followed by a main clause. Both the relative clause and the main clause are negative. Mark's saying has a conditional clause followed by three imperatives, all positive. Mark's saying introduces the collection of sayings that conclude the Caesarea Philippi pericope (Mark 8,34-9,1). The Q saying forms the climax of a set of three sayings that spell out the cost of discipleship.[13]

Q 14,26-27

26 ὃς οὐ μισεῖ τὸν πατέρα αὐτοῦ καὶ τὴν μητέρα
οὐ δύναται εἶναί μου μαθητής·
ὃς οὐ μισεῖ τὸν υἱὸν αὐτοῦ καὶ τὴν θυγατέρα
οὐ δύναται εἶναί μου μαθητής·
27 ὃς οὐ λαμβάνει τὸν σταυρὸν αὐτοῦ
καὶ ἀκολουθεῖ ὀπίσω μου,
οὐ δύναται εἶναί μου μαθητής.

12. A. H. McNEILE, *Matthew*, p. 148; S. SCHULZ, *Q*, p. 447; R. LAUFEN, *Doppelüberlieferungen*, pp. 303-304.

13. For the reconstruction of the first two sayings, see H. FLEDDERMANN, "Cross and Discipleship in Q," pp. 472-477.

Repetition dominates the formulation of the Q sayings. All three have identical main clauses. Biblical and Hellenistic rhetoric often use end repetition, called epiphora or epistrophe.[14] The sentences also show initial repetition in the relative clauses (ὃς οὐ with the present indicative), again a common rhetorical technique called anaphora or epanaphora.[15] However, the combination of initial and end repetition, called symploche, does not occur often.[16] The three Q sayings use combined initial and end repetition to produce an extremely effective rhetorical unit.

There are several indications that the Q Cross Saying is prior to the Marcan saying. First, the Q context appears more original than the Marcan. The three sayings in Q 14,26-27 are related thematically and stylistically. They have identical main clauses, and each begins the same way (ὃς οὐ with the present indicative). The extensive repetition indicates that the sayings were conceived as an original unit. Although Mark's saying is related thematically to the following sayings, it does not cohere stylistically with them. Second, the Marcan saying repeats the concept of following. It appears both in the conditional clause ("If anyone wishes to follow after me...") and as the final imperative ("and follow me"). This repetition shows that the saying has been reworked. The Q saying is simpler and more straightforward. Third, Mark's "let him deny himself" appears to be an interpretative addition. It spells out in spiritualizing terms what the Q saying implies but does not state.[17] Fourth, two terms in Mark echo the passion narrative. The word "deny" plays an important role in the Peter's Denial (Mark 14,30.31.68.70.72), and the word "take up" appears in the episode of Simon of Cyrene (Mark 15,21). It is easier to imagine Mark adding the terms to the Cross Saying to bring it into line with the passion narrative than to imagine Q suppressing them. Fifth, the Q negative statement is uncompromising; Mark's positive imperatives are milder. Although the imperatives do not water down the absolute demands of the saying, the positive formulation tries to engage the hearer and win assent, whereas the negative form of the Q saying makes no concession to human weakness. It is more probable that a stern,

14. 1 Cor 7,12-13; 9,19-22; 12,4-6; 2 Cor 11,22.27; Epictetus, *Diss.* 1. 29. 10; 2. 19. 24; 3. 22. 105; 4. 1. 102, 9. 9. See R. N. SOULEN, *Handbook of Biblical Criticism*, Atlanta: John Knox, ²1981, p. 62; N. TURNER, *Handbook for Biblical Studies*, Philadelphia: Westminster, 1982, p. 68.

15. Psa 13; 29; 1 Cor 3,9; 10,21.23; 2 Cor 7,2.4; Gal 3,28; 4,4-5; 5,26; Phil 2,1; 3,6; 4,12; Epictetus 1. 4. 14, 5. 7. See R. N. SOULEN, *Handbook*, p. 18; N. TURNER, *Handbook*, p. 42.

16. R. N. SOULEN, *Handbook*, p. 186; N. TURNER, *Handbook*, p. 129.

17. See J. LAMBRECHT, "Q-Influence," p. 282.

uncompromising negative statement was turned into an imperative than that the positive formulation was changed to a negative one.

Granted that Mark's saying comes later than the Q saying, does Mark know redactional Q? To answer this question we need to pay close attention to the Q context of the Cross Saying. We saw above that the Q saying forms the climax of a series of three sayings.

Q 14,26-27

26 Whoever does not hate his father and mother
cannot be my disciple;
whoever does not hate his son and daughter
cannot be my disciple;
27 whoever does not take up his cross
and follow after me
cannot be my disciple.

The extensive repetition that dominates these sayings shows that we are dealing with an original unit. The sayings were conceived and composed together. These three sayings draw together two separate lines of thought in the Q document. The first two complete Q's treatment of the family. In the Demands of Discipleship (Q 9,57-60) Q teaches that discipleship overrides every human bond and duty, even the solemn obligation to bury a father.[18] The third saying continues Q's identification of the disciple with Jesus' suffering. In the Persecution Beatitude (Q 6,22-23) Q connects the suffering of the community with the Son of Man, and the Demands of Discipleship associate the disciple with Jesus' homelessness (Q 9,58). The Cross Saying carries this theme to its climax by demanding that the disciple take up the cross. Because Q 14,26-27 draws these two Q themes together, it comes from the pen of the author of Q. Because Mark knew this Q composition, Mark knew redactional Q.

If we examine the Marcan context of the saying, it becomes apparent that all the differences between Mark and Q result from Marcan redaction. The saying in Mark 8,34b announces the discipleship theme that dominates the sayings collection in Mark 8,34-9,1. Mark writes a special introduction for the collection: καὶ προσκαλεσάμενος τὸν ὄχλον σὺν τοῖς μαθηταῖς αὐτοῦ εἶπεν αὐτοῖς (Mark 8,34a). This introductory phrase is thoroughly Marcan. The participle προσκαλεσάμενος is common in Mark.[19] Mark uses σύν elsewhere to join two groups or individuals (compare Mark 4,10; 9,4). The linking of the crowd with the disciples is also significant. The crowd is basically friendly in Mark. The only exception occurs in

---

18. H. T. FLEDDERMANN, "Demands of Discipleship," pp. 553-555.
19. Mark 3,23; 7,14; 8,1; 10,42; 12,43; 15,44.

the passion narrative (Mark 14,43; 15,8.11.15), but this exception is only apparent, not real, for in the passion narrative everyone, including the disciples, turn on Jesus. Before the passion the crowd flocks to Jesus,[20] so much so that access to him becomes blocked (Mark 2,4), he must have recourse to a boat (Mark 3,9; 4,1), and he has no time even to eat (Mark 3,20). Jesus' enemies are afraid to arrest him because of the crowd (Mark 11,18.32; 12,12). The crowd, though friendly toward Jesus, must either choose or reject discipleship. For this reason Mark addresses two significant sections to the crowd. Mark includes the crowd with the disciples in the present section (Mark 8,34-9,1) because it sets out the conditions of discipleship. Mark also has the crowd hear Jesus' Warning about the Scribes (Mark 12,37b-40) because the scribes are Jesus' chief adversaries, the opposite of the disciples.[21] In Mark's context the uncompromising Q formulation would not be as appropriate as Mark's conditional clause followed by the three imperatives which make an appeal for acceptance. A shift from an uncompromising saying to a more tolerant one occurs elsewhere in the overlap texts and appears to be characteristic of Mark. We have seen, for example, that in the Mission Discourse Q forbids the missionaries to take anything with them on the journey, even the most basic necessities (Q 10,4). Mark, though, allows some exceptions, a staff and sandals (Mark 6,8-9).[22]

Because Mark created a new context for the saying, he doubles the statement about following Jesus. Instead of leaving the statement about following in the middle of the saying, Mark first draws it to the beginning in a conditional clause that announces the theme, "If anyone wishes to follow after me," and then he uses it again at the end to form the climax of the three imperatives – "let him follow me." The form of the conditional clause (εἴ τις θέλει followed by an infinitive) corresponds closely to another programmatic saying, Mark 9,35, which also introduces a section on discipleship;[23] and the verb θέλω links the saying to the following saying on Losing One's Life.[24] The first imperative, "let him deny himself," is an interpretative addition of Mark. The key word comes from the denial sequence of Mark's passion narrative where Peter denies Jesus.[25]

---

20. Mark 2,4.13; 3,9.20.32; 4,1; 5,21.24.31; 6,34; 8,1; 9,25; 10,1.46; 11,18; 12,37.

21. See H. FLEDDERMANN, "Warning about the Scribes," p. 61 n. 40.

22. For other examples of Mark toning down Q, see the Mustard Seed (Mark 4,30-32) and the Saying on Tolerance (Mark 9,40).

23. Mark 9,35 is a redactional reworking of Mark 10,43-44, so the conditional clause is Marcan. See H. FLEDDERMANN, "Discipleship Discourse," pp. 60-61.

24. Compare ὃς γὰρ ἐὰν θέλῃ τὴν ψυχὴν αὐτοῦ σῶσαι (Mark 8,35a).

25. In the denial sequence Mark uses both the simple verb ἀρνέομαι (Mark 14,68.70) and its compound ἀπαρνέομαι (Mark 14,30.31.72).

By introducing the term here Mark sets up a contrast between denying oneself and denying Jesus. For Mark the disciple either denies self, takes up the cross, and follows Jesus; or, like Peter, the disciple ends up denying Jesus. The second imperative, "let him take up his cross," reflects the first Q condition, but the passion narrative again influenced the formulation. Mark writes ἀράτω instead of using the Q verb λαμβάνω to bring the saying into line with the narrative of Simon of Cyrene (Mark 15,21). The third imperative, "and follow me," takes up the second Q condition, but in Mark's redaction it forms an *inclusio* with the conditional clause. It constitutes the climax of the three imperatives and resumes and summarizes the entire saying. In his redaction Mark doubled the clause on following to produce a programmatic introduction and a summarizing conclusion; he modified the saying to conform it to the passion narrative; and he recast the main clause into a series of imperatives that spell out the demands of discipleship.

The Thomas parallel (Th 55) combines the sayings on hating family and taking up the cross found in Matt 10,37-38 par. Luke 14,26-27.

> Jesus said, "Whoever does not hate his father and mother cannot be a disciple (μαθητής) to me, and whoever does not hate his brothers and sisters, and take up the cross (σταυρός) in my way, will not be worthy (ἄξιος) of me."

Thomas adds "in my way" to the Cross Saying to bind the fate of the disciple to the fate of Jesus. Thomas also adds the phrase to two other sayings.[26] Thomas reflects Luke 14,26-27 in the expressions "does not hate," "brothers and sisters," and "cannot be a disciple to me." The Thomas saying echoes Matt 10,37-38 in the phrase "will not be worthy of me." Since "worthy" is a Matthean redactional addition to the Q text, Thomas shows an awareness of redactional Matthew.[27] The original Q saying on hating relatives mentioned four relatives, "father," "mother," "son," and "daughter." Luke added "brothers and sisters" in his version (Luke 14,26), drawing the additional terms from Mark 10,29-30.[28] So Th 55 also reflects redactional Luke.[29] Not only does Th 55 reflect the redactional text of Matthew and Luke, it again shows how familiar the author of Thomas was with the synoptic gospels. As we have seen, Thomas does not just draw on a single gospel. The author compares various versions of a saying or parable available in the synoptic gospels and combines elements from more than one to arrive at a new formulation.

---

26. Th 101 *bis*, 108. See M. FIEGER, *Thomasevangelium*, pp. 165-166.
27. C. TUCKETT, "Thomas and the Synoptics," p. 148.
28. See C. TUCKETT, "Thomas and the Synoptics," p. 148; H. FLEDDERMANN, "Cross and Discipleship in Q," p. 475.
29. See H. FLEDDERMANN, "Cross and Discipleship in Q," p. 480.

§ 13. Losing One's Life

Mark 8,35 (Matt 10,39 par. Luke 17,33)

Matthew and Luke formulate the Q saying differently. Besides taking over the Q text, each also edits the Marcan saying (Matt 16,25; Luke 9,24). John also has a parallel (John 12,25). First the Q saying.

Matt 10,39	Luke 17,33
ὁ εὑρὼν τὴν ψυχὴν αὐτοῦ	ὃς ἐὰν ζητήσῃ τὴν ψυχὴν αὐτοῦ περιποιήσασθαι
ἀπολέσει αὐτήν,	ἀπολέσει αὐτήν,
καὶ ὁ ἀπολέσας τὴν ψυχὴν αὐτοῦ ἕνεκεν ἐμοῦ	ὃς δ' ἂν ἀπολέσῃ
εὑρήσει αὐτήν.	ζῳογονήσει αὐτήν.

We must first resolve the difference in form. Matthew uses substantival participles in the subordinate clause whereas Luke has relative clauses. Luke's relative clauses are original. Matthew uses substantival participles often, and he creates a stylistic unit at the end of the Mission Discourse by linking together eight substantival participles:

> 37a ὁ φιλῶν πατέρα ἢ μητέρα ὑπὲρ ἐμέ ...
> 37b ὁ φιλῶν υἱὸν ἢ θυγατέρα ὑπὲρ ἐμέ ...
> 39a ὁ εὑρὼν τὴν ψυχὴν αὐτοῦ ...
> 39b ὁ ἀπολέσας τὴν ψυχὴν αὐτοῦ ...
> 40a ὁ δεχόμενος ὑμᾶς ...
> 40b ὁ ἐμὲ δεχόμενος ...
> 41a ὁ δεχόμενος προφήτην εἰς ὄνομα προφήτου ...
> 41b ὁ δεχόμενος δίκαιον εἰς ὄνομα δικαίου ...

Matthew switched from Q's relative clauses to the substantival participles to fit the saying into this stylistic unit.

Many of the differences between Matthew and Luke stem from Luke's desire to avoid the verb εὑρίσκω which struck him as strange in this context. For the first occurrence of the verb Luke substitutes ζητέω ... περιποιήσασθαι and for the second ζῳογονέω. This vocabulary has a Lucan flavor. On four other occasions Luke introduces ζητέω with the infinitive into his sources.[30] He uses περιποιέω in Acts 20,28 and ζῳογονέω in Acts 7,19. Both verbs are Septuagintal, and they occur together in Exod 1,16-17 LXX.[31] Matthew's verb εὑρίσκω is common

---

30. Luke 5,18 (diff. Mark 2,3); 6,19 (diff. Mark 3,10); 9,9 (diff. Mark 6,16); 13,24 (diff. Matt 7,13-14). In the last instance (Luke 13,24 diff. Matt 7,13-14) Luke uses ζητέω with the infinitive to replace εὑρίσκω. See J. LAMBRECHT, "Q-Influence," p. 283 n. 33.

31. Exod 1,16-17 lies behind Acts 7,19, so it probably influenced Luke's choice of verbs in his redaction of the Q saying.

in Q.[32] Luke also drops τὴν ψυχὴν αὐτοῦ in the second half of the saying as redundant.[33]

The phrase ἕνεκεν ἐμοῦ causes special problems. Did Matthew add it or did Luke delete it? Schulz argues that Matthew preserves the original context of the saying in a Q collection of discipleship sayings where the phrase fits perfectly. According to Schulz Luke dropped the phrase when he shifted the saying to a new context in the Q apocalypse.[34] Matthew's position, however, need not be original. Matthew joined the Q sayings on the cross and losing one's life in Matt 10,38-39 because he found the overlap sayings joined in Mark 8,34-35, so Matthew does not reflect the original Q context of the saying on losing one's life.[35] Although Luke dropped the reference to "the gospel" in his redaction of Mark 8,35, he retains ἕνεκεν ἐμοῦ in Luke 9,24 so there is no reason to suspect that he dropped the phrase from the Q saying. Instead Matthew assimilated the Q saying to the Marcan saying by adding ἕνεκεν ἐμοῦ.[36] Matthew also assimilated the Marcan saying to the Q saying in Matt 16,25 by introducing the Q verb εὑρίσκω into his redaction of Mark 8,35.[37] We can now compare Mark and Q.

Q 17,33	Mark 8,35
ὃς ἐὰν εὕρῃ	ὃς γὰρ ἐὰν θέλῃ
τὴν ψυχὴν αὐτοῦ	τὴν ψυχὴν αὐτοῦ σῶσαι
ἀπολέσει αὐτήν,	ἀπολέσει αὐτήν,
ὃς δ' ἂν ἀπολέσῃ τὴν ψυχὴν αὐτοῦ	ὃς δ' ἂν ἀπολέσῃ τὴν ψυχὴν αὐτοῦ
	ἕνεκεν ἐμοῦ καὶ τοῦ εὐαγγελίου
εὑρήσει αὐτήν.	σώσει αὐτήν.

Parallelism dominates both sayings. Two opposite terms appear in the first half of each saying which are then reversed in the second half. Q uses "find" and "lose," and Mark "save" and "lose." Mark has a connective (γάρ) and an auxiliary verb (θέλῃ) in the first relative clause and a prepositional phrase (ἕνεκεν ἐμοῦ καὶ τοῦ εὐαγγελίου) in the second.

32. Q 7,9; 11,9.10.24.25; 12,43; 15,5.
33. Luke avoids superfluous repetition of nouns. Compare Luke 4,41 (diff. Mark 1,34); 5,33 (diff. Mark 2,18); 5,37 (diff Mark 2,22); 9,18 (diff. Mark 8,27); 12,58 (diff. Matt 5,25). See H. J. CADBURY, *Style and Literary Method*, p. 83.
34. S. SCHULZ, *Q*, p. 445.
35. Luke's context in the Apocalyptic Discourse may also be secondary. Since Matthew and Luke both moved the saying to a new context, its original position in Q can no longer be recovered.
36. See R. SCHNACKENBURG, "Der eschatologische Abschnitt Lk 17,20-37," in *Mélanges bibliques en hommage au R. P. Béda Rigaux*, 1970, pp. 213-234, esp. p. 224.
37. Matthew frequently assimilates the Marcan and Q forms of the overlap texts to each other. Compare Matt 5,32 and 19,9; Matt 12,39 and 16,4; Matt 13,12 and 25,29; Matt 17,20 and 21,21.

Nothing corresponding to these expressions appears in Q, so Mark's text is slightly longer than Q's.

There are three signs that Mark is secondary. First, the Q word pair "find" and "lose" is more original than Mark's "save" and "lose." "Save" is a technical theological term and is clearly secondary to the enigmatic "find." Second, Mark's θέλῃ softens the opposition between "save" and "find." The softened saying is secondary to Q's paradoxical formulation.[38] Third, the Q saying contains no christological reference. Mark's phrase "because of me and the gospel" interprets the saying in terms of the Christian proclamation about Jesus. Mark's explicitly christological saying is secondary.

Who is responsible for these differences? "Because of me and the gospel" is certainly Marcan. Mark adds an almost identical phrase, "because of me and because of the gospel," in Mark 10,29, and he has a similar expression, "if anyone is ashamed of me and my words," in Mark 8,38. The θέλῃ corresponds to the θέλει in Mark 8,34.[39] Mark connects the sayings with γάρ because v. 35 gives the motivation for v. 34.[40] The verb σῴζω is fairly common in Mark in a theological sense.[41] We need appeal to no one but Mark himself to account for the differences between his text and Q. Mark gives the theological principle behind the Cross Saying in the saying on Losing One's Life. The use of θέλω in both sayings is significant. If it is your intention to be a disciple, you must take up the cross (Mark 8,34). If it is your intention to save your life, you must lose it (Mark 8,35).

John has a parallel to the saying in John 12,25.

> ὁ φιλῶν τὴν ψυχὴν αὐτοῦ ἀπολλύει αὐτήν,
> καὶ ὁ μισῶν τὴν ψυχὴν αὐτοῦ ἐν τῷ κόσμῳ τούτῳ
> εἰς ζωὴν αἰώνιον φυλάξει αὐτήν.

John's version parallels Matthew's saying (Matt 10,39). John maintains the basic thought of the Matthean saying and much of the parallel structure, but John translated the saying into his own vocabulary. John uses substantival participles like Matthew. Matthew, though, uses a single pair of verbs "find" and "lose" in both halves of the saying, whereas John introduces two pairs, "love" – "hate" and "lose" – "guard." Both

---

38. R. LAUFEN, *Doppelüberlieferungen*, pp. 322-323; J. LAMBRECHT, "Q-Influence," p. 284.

39. Compare also Mark 9,35; 10,43.44.

40. All four γάρ's in Mark 8,35-38 are redactional (compare also Mark 4,22.25; 9,39.40.41.49). See J. LAMBRECHT, "Q-Influence," p. 284.

41. Mark 3,4; 5,23.28.34; 6,56; 10,26.52; 13,13.20; 15,30.31*bis*.

"love" and "hate" are common in John's gospel.[42] In the first half of the saying John takes over Matthew's verb "lose," but he switches to the present tense. In the second half he preserves the future tense, but introduces "guard" as the main verb. The verb φυλάσσω appears only three times in John's gospel (John 12,25.47; 17,12), but John 17,12 like the present verse contrasts the verb with ἀπόλλυμι: "While I was with them, I protected them in your name that you have given me, and I guarded (ἐφύλαξα) them, and not one of them was lost (ἀπώλετο) except the son of destruction so that the scripture might be fulfilled." In the place of Matthew's ἕνεκεν ἐμοῦ, John substitutes two prepositional phrases – one linked backward to the participle, the other linked forward to the main verb. "This world" and "eternal life" are familiar Johannine terms.[43] Most of the Johannine vocabulary recurs in John 15,18-25 which spells out the relationships between Jesus, the disciples, and the world.[44] John 12,25 makes sense as a Johannine rewriting of Matt 10,39. Since Matt 10,39 contains redactional features like the substantival participles, this saying shows that John knew the redactional text of Matthew.

§ 14. JESUS AND THE SON OF MAN

Mark 8,38 (Matt 10,32-33 par. Luke 12,8-9)

The Q logion on Confessing and Denying occurs in a long section on Fearless Preaching (Q 12,2-12). Matthew and Luke both have parallels to the Marcan saying (Matt 16,27; Luke 9,26), although Matthew's saying differs significantly from his Marcan source.[45]

Matt 10,32-33	Luke 12,8-9
	8 λέγω δὲ ὑμῖν,
32 πᾶς οὖν ὅστις ὁμολογήσει ἐν ἐμοὶ	πᾶς ὃς ἂν ὁμολογήσῃ ἐν ἐμοὶ
ἔμπροσθεν τῶν ἀνθρώπων,	ἔμπροσθεν τῶν ἀνθρώπων,

42. For φιλέω see John 5,20; 11,3.36; 12,25; 15,19; 16,27bis; 20,2; 21,15.16.17ter. For μισέω see John 3,20; 7,7bis; 12,25; 15,18bis.19.23bis.24.25; 17,14.

43. John uses κόσμος 78 times. For ὁ κόσμος οὗτος see John 8,23bis; 9,39; 11,9; 12,25.31bis; 13,1; 16,11; 18,36bis. For ζωὴ αἰώνιος see John 3,15.16.36; 4,14.36; 5,24.39; 6,27.40.47.54.68; 10,28; 12,25.50; 17,2.3. The phrase εἰς ζωὴν αἰώνιον appears in three other places (John 4,14.36; 6,27).

44. "Love" appears in v. 19, "hate" in vv. 18bis.19.23bis.24.25; and "world" in vv. 18.19 quinquies.

45. Matthew eliminates the first half of the Marcan saying and concentrates on the Son of Man's coming. For Matthew's redaction see W. D. DAVIES and D. C. ALLISON, Matthew, 2. 674-676.

ὁμολογήσω κἀγὼ ἐν αὐτῷ	καὶ ὁ υἱὸς τοῦ ἀνθρώπου
	ὁμολογήσει ἐν αὐτῷ
ἔμπροσθεν τοῦ πατρός μου	ἔμπροσθεν τῶν ἀγγέλων
τοῦ ἐν τοῖς οὐρανοῖς·	τοῦ θεοῦ·
33 ὅστις δ᾽ ἂν ἀρνήσηταί με	9 ὁ δὲ ἀρνησάμενός με
ἔμπροσθεν τῶν ἀνθρώπων,	ἐνώπιον τῶν ἀνθρώπων
ἀρνήσομαι κἀγὼ αὐτὸν	ἀπαρνηθήσεται
ἔμπροσθεν τοῦ πατρός μου	ἐνώπιον τῶν ἀγγέλων
τοῦ ἐν τοῖς οὐρανοῖς.	τοῦ θεοῦ.

Rudolf Pesch claims that originally the saying was introduced by ἀμὴν λέγω ὑμῖν which either Luke or Q altered to λέγω δὲ ὑμῖν.[46] However, neither Matthew's οὖν nor Luke's λέγω δὲ ὑμῖν goes back to Q. Luke introduces a λέγω ὑμῖν phrase three times in the Q section (Luke 12,4.5.8). We can see Luke's redactional procedure clearest in v. 4. The original Q section began with an injunction to preach publicly what the disciples have heard privately (Q 12,2-3). Luke changed the section into a warning against hypocrisy by his introduction (Luke 12,1).[47] In transforming the beginning he created more of a break between v. 3 and v. 4 than existed originally in Q, so he makes a new beginning with his first λέγω ὑμῖν phrase. He then introduces two additional λέγω ὑμῖν phrases to further structure the section.[48] Neither can we trace Matthew's οὖν back to Q. Matthew uses οὖν frequently, three times in the present section (Matt 10,26.31.32).[49]

In the first relative clause Matthew substituted ὅστις for ὅς.[50] Matthew's future ὁμολογήσει is original. As we have seen in the Un-forgivable Sin logion, the future indicative is rare in conditional relative

46. R. PESCH, "Über die Autorität Jesu: Eine Rückfrage anhand des Bekenner- und Verleugnerspruchs Lk 12,8f par.," in *Die Kirche des Anfangs: FS Heinz Schürmann*, 1977, pp. 25-55, esp. pp. 30-35.
47. D. M. SWEETLAND, "Discipleship and Persecution: A Study of Luke 12,1-12," in *Bib* 65 (1984) 61-79, esp. pp. 64-67.
48. See further F. NEIRYNCK, "Recent Developments," pp. 441-442.
49. 56 5 33 61. Matthew takes over οὖν four times from Mark (Matt 19,6; 21,25; 24,42 [25,13]; 27,22) and five times from Q (Matt 3,8.10; 6,23; 7,11; 9,38). Matthew introduces οὖν fourteen times into Marcan material (Matt 12,12; 13,18.56; 17,10; 19,7; 21,40; 22,17.21.28.43.45; 24,15; 26,54; 27,17), and he uses it seventeen times in Q texts where Luke does not (Matt 5,48; 6,9.22.31.34; 7,12.24; 10,16.26.31.32; 12,26; 18,4; 22,9; 24,26; 25,27.28). See R. PESCH, "Über die Autorität Jesu," p. 33.
50. The nominative singular masculine ὅστις is Matthean (19 1 3 0). Matthew makes a similar switch from ὅς to ὅστις in Matt 12,50 (diff. Mark 3,35); 13,12*bis* (diff. Mark 4,25); 19,29 (diff. Mark 10,29). Matthew introduces ὅστις in Matt 21,33 (diff. Mark 12,1). He writes πᾶς ὅστις in Matt 19,29, ὅστις οὖν in Matt 18,4, and πᾶς οὖν ὅστις in Matt 7,24. See S. SCHULZ, *Q*, pp. 68 n. 65, 451 n. 356; V. SPOTTORNO, "The Relative Pronoun in the New Testament," in *NTS* 28 (1982) 132-141.

clauses.[51] Luke switched to the more common subjunctive. The Unforgivable Sin logion follows the saying on Confessing and Denying in Q (Q 12,8-10). Q formulated both with the future indicative. In one case Matthew eliminated the future indicative (Matt 12,32), in the other case Luke did (Luke 12,8-9). In the first main clause Matthew changed "the Son of Man" to "I."[52] Matthew interchanges "the Son of Man" and a personal pronoun in two other passages. In the Caesarea Philippi pericope Matthew first anticipates "the Son of Man" in Jesus' question where it replaces the first personal pronoun (Matt 16,13 diff. Mark 8,27). Then in the following passion prediction Matthew replaces "the Son of Man" with "him" (Matt 16,21 diff. Mark 8,31). Matthew also replaces "the Son of Man" with "me" in the Persecution Beatitude (Matt 5,11 diff. Luke 6,22).[53] The title "Son of Man" plays on the word "men" in the saying, and it forms the catchword link to the following saying on the Unforgivable Sin (Q 12,10).[54] Matthew's ἔμπροσθεν τοῦ πατρός μου τοῦ ἐν τοῖς οὐρανοῖς is secondary to Luke's reference to the angels.[55] Luke has, though, added a clarifying τοῦ θεοῦ, so the original Q expression was ἔμπροσθεν τῶν ἀγγέλων, corresponding exactly to ἔμπροσθεν τῶν ἀνθρώπων.[56]

In the second half of the saying, Matthew offers a full parallel to the first half. Luke on the other hand, has a participial phrase in place of the relative clause and a passive verb in the main clause. Matthew reflects the Q sentence structure. Luke uses participles to replace a variety of constructions in his sources, including relative clauses.[57] Luke's passive assimilates the second half to the passive in the following saying (Luke 12,10). Matthew's simple verb is to be preferred to Luke's compound verb. Luke is partial to compound verbs, he likes the future passive, and he tends to lengthen the future passive forms by prefixing prepositions.[58]

---

51. See Chapter III above.

52. See A. J. B. HIGGINS, "'Menschensohn' oder 'ich' in Q: Lk 12,8-9 / Mt 10,32-33," in *Jesus und der Menschensohn: FS Anton Vögtle*, 1975, pp. 117-123, esp. p. 122.

53. J. S. KLOPPENBORG, "Blessing and Marginality: The 'Persecution Beatitude' in Q, Thomas & Early Christianity," in *Forum* 2/3 (1986) 36-56, esp. p. 41.

54. D. R. CATCHPOLE, "The Angelic Son of Man in Luke 12:8," in *NT* 24 (1982) 255-265, esp. p. 255.

55. S. SCHULZ, *Q*, p. 68.

56. Luke adds a clarifying τοῦ θεοῦ in several places. In redacting Peter's Confession, Luke changes Mark's "You are the Christ" (Mark 8,29) to "The Christ of God" (Luke 9,20). Compare also Luke 8,11 (diff. Mark 4,14); 11,42 (diff. Matt 23,23); 22,69 (diff. Mark 14,62); 23,35 (diff. Mark 15,32). See also Luke 11,49; 15,10; Acts 10,3; 20,28; 23,4; 27,23. See further J. JEREMIAS, *Sprache*, pp. 208-209.

57. See Chapter III above.

58. See Chapter IV above.

Finally, Luke's ἐνώπιον is secondary. Matthew and Mark avoid ἐνώπιον, but Luke uses it frequently as a substitute for ἔμπροσθεν.[59]

We can now compare Q and Mark.

Q 12,8-9	Mark 8,38
8 πᾶς ὃς ὁμολογήσει ἐν ἐμοὶ ἔμπροσθεν τῶν ἀνθρώπων, καὶ ὁ υἱὸς τοῦ ἀνθρώπου ὁμολογήσει ἐν αὐτῷ ἔμπροσθεν τῶν ἀγγέλων·	
9 ὃς δὲ ἀρνήσεταί με	ὃς γὰρ ἐὰν ἐπαισχυνθῇ με καὶ τοὺς ἐμοὺς λόγους
ἔμπροσθεν τῶν ἀνθρώπων,	ἐν τῇ γενεᾷ ταύτῃ τῇ μοιχαλίδι καὶ ἁμαρτωλῷ,
καὶ ὁ υἱὸς τοῦ ἀνθρώπου ἀρνήσεται αὐτὸν	καὶ ὁ υἱὸς τοῦ ἀνθρώπου ἐπαισχυνθήσεται αὐτόν,
ἔμπροσθεν	ὅταν ἔλθῃ ἐν τῇ δόξῃ τοῦ πατρὸς αὐτοῦ μετὰ
τῶν ἀγγέλων.	τῶν ἀγγέλων τῶν ἁγίων.

The Q statement has two parallel statements, one about confessing Jesus, the other about denying him. Mark has no parallel to the first half of the Q saying; Mark only parallels the negative half. Mark's saying, though, is quite a bit longer than the second half of the Q saying.

Kümmel maintains that the Marcan form of the saying is more original than the Q form. He argues first of all that the expression "this adulterous and sinful generation" is not Marcan. Second, Mark's verb "be ashamed" cannot be considered an improvement over the Q verb "deny," since both verbs represent good Greek style. Third, except for the phrase "Father of the Son of Man" Mark's temporal clause has greater claim to be original than the indeterminate "before the angels" of Q.[60] Mark's saying, though, contains undeniable secondary features.

In comparing the two texts we can best begin with the phrase "and my words" which looks like an interpretative addition and expansion of the Q saying. It spells out what the Q saying only implies – that if one doesn't accept Jesus' teaching, one rejects Jesus. Because it makes

---

59. 0 0 22 13. Luke introduces ἐνώπιον twice into Marcan material (Luke 5,18 diff. Mark 2,3; Luke 8,47 diff. Mark 5,33). He changes ἔμπροσθεν to ἐνώπιον (Luke 5,25 diff. Mark 2,12). Luke uses ἐνώπιον in the second half of the saying for variety. He also alternates ἔμπροσθεν and ἐνώπιον in the Cure of the Paralyzed Man (Luke 5,17-26). See J. C. HAWKINS, *Horae Synopticae*, p. 18; H. FLEDDERMANN, "Q Saying on Confessing and Denying," p. 611.

60. W. G. KÜMMEL, "Das Verhalten Jesus gegenüber und das Verhalten des Menschensohns: Markus 8,38 par und Lukas 12,3f par Mattäus 10,32f," in *Jesus und der Menschensohn: FS Anton Vögtle*, 1975, pp. 210-224, esp. pp. 216-219.

explicit what is implicit in the Q saying, Mark's saying comes later. Once we see that this phrase was added to the saying, it is easier to account for other changes. The addition of "and my words" caused the shift from "deny" to "be ashamed of" as the latter verb works much better with the expanded object "me and my words" than "deny" would.[61] Mark's verb may not represent better Greek than the Q verb, but it clearly results from a secondary expansion of the Q saying. Once the switch was made the positive half of the saying had to drop out as there is no clear opposite to "be ashamed of" that would work in the first half of the saying. Mark's "in this adulterous and sinful generation" is secondary to Q's "before men." Mark's phrase heightens the opposition to Jesus that the Q saying only hints at.[62] Mark's temporal clause clarifies Q's "before the angels." The Q phrase designates the forum for the Son of Man's action, but it remains vague. By shifting from "where" to "when" Mark spells out what the Q saying implies, that the judgment will take place at the parousia. Mark's "in the glory of his Father" is clearly secondary. It reflects the conflation of christological titles that marks the later stages in their use.

Mark's saying clearly lies downstream from the Q saying, but does Mark know redactional Q? No consensus has emerged on the origin of the Q saying. Bultmann and Tödt traced the saying back to the historical Jesus and used it to authenticate the future Son of Man sayings.[63] Vielhauer disagreed sharply, attributing the saying to the early church instead of the historical Jesus.[64] However, before making sweeping claims for the statement, we need to examine its role in Q.

Q refers ten times to the Son of Man.[65] Twice Q refers to the present activity of the Son of Man (Q 7,33-34; 9,58), but the other texts portray

---

61. The word "be ashamed of" better describes one's relationship to the gospel (compare Rom 1,16; 2 Tim 1,8.12.16). See further M. HORSTMANN, *Studien zur markinischen Christologie: Mk 8,27-9,13 als Zugang zum Christusbild des zweiten Evangeliums* (Neut-Abh, 6), Münster: Aschendorff, ²1973, pp. 44-45.

62. The OT uses the term "adultery" for faithless Israel, so its presence in Mark should cause no surprise. See Ezek 16,38; 23,45; Mal 3,5. See further F. HAUCK, "μοιχεύω," *TDNT* 4 (1967) 729-735, esp. p. 730.

63. R. BULTMANN, *Die Geschichte der synoptischen Tradition*, pp. 117, 135, 162-163; ET: *Synoptic Tradition*, pp. 112, 128, 151-152; H. E. TÖDT, *Menschensohn*, pp. 50-56, 206-207, 308-312; ET: *Son of Man*, pp. 55-60, 224-226, 339-344.

64. P. VIELHAUER, "Gottesreich und Menschensohn in der Verkündigung Jesu" (1957), in ID., *Aufsätze zum Neuen Testament*, 1965, pp. 55-91, esp. pp. 76-79; ID., "Jesus und der Menschensohn: Zur Diskussion mit Heinz Eduard Tödt und Eduard Schweizer" (1963), in ID., *Aufsätze*, 1965, pp. 92-140, esp. pp. 101-107.

65. Q 6,22-23; 7,33-34; 9,58; 11,30; 12,8-9.10.40; 17,24.26.30. See J. S. KLOPPENBORG, *Q Parallels: Synopsis, Critical Notes & Concordance*, Sonoma, CA: Polebridge, 1988, p. 238.

an eschatological figure with a well defined role.[66] The Son of Man will come in the end time to judge the wicked and save the righteous.[67] The Q saying on Confessing and Denying fits smoothly into this conception of the Son of Man. Four-part parallelism characterizes the saying.

Q 12,8-9

8 Everyone who confesses me before men,
   the Son of Man will also confess him before the angels;
9 but whoever denies me before men,
   the Son of Man will also deny him before the angels.

Bultmann and Tödt saw a distinction between Jesus and the Son of Man in this saying, and they used the distinction to argue that the saying must be authentic because the early church would never introduce such a distinction once it believed in Jesus as the Son of Man. The saying also appears to assign the Son of Man the role of advocate in the judgment.[68] However, a close study of the saying's parallelism leads to different conclusions. Complex lexical patterning dominates the saying.[69] The word pair "me" – "Son of Man" corresponds to the pair "men" – "angels." The two pairs distinguish between the time before the eschaton and the end time itself. Jesus as Son of Man will confess in the eschaton whoever confesses him in this world before the end time. The saying intends no real distinction between Jesus and the Son of Man. The saying also probably does not portray Jesus as advocate. Parallelism activates many aspects of language including its metaphorical power.[70] We can see how parallelism creates metaphors in the Q baptism saying. Although the sentence on the Coming One separates the two halves of the baptism saying, the two clauses have a parallel structure.

I baptize you in water …
He will baptize you in the Holy Spirit and in fire … (Q 3,16)

The saying uses "baptize" literally in the first clause, but metaphorically in the second. The same holds true for the Q Saying on Confessing and Denying. In the two relative clauses "confess" and "deny" literally mean confessing and denying Jesus. In the two main clauses "confess"

---

66. See I. HAVENER, *Q: The Sayings of Jesus* (Good News Studies, 19), Wilmington: Glazier, 1987, pp. 72-77.

67. Q 6,22-23; 11,30; 12,40; 17,24.26.30.

68. B. LINDARS, "Jesus as Advocate: A Contribution to the Christological Debate," in *BJRL* 62 (1979-80) 476-497.

69. On the use of word pairs in biblical parallelism see A. BERLIN, *The Dynamics of Biblical Parallelism*, Bloomington: Indiana University Press, 1985, pp. 83-85.

70. See A. BERLIN, *Dynamics*, pp. 99-102.

and "deny" are metaphors for the saving and judging activity of the end-time Son of Man.[71] In other words the Q Saying on Confessing and Denying fits seamlessly in the overall Q portrayal of the Son of Man. Since it fits so smoothly in Q's christology, the saying could well come from the Q redactor. If so, then the saying shows that Mark knew redactional Q.

Once we see that Mark is secondary to Q, we can examine the Marcan redaction. Mark is responsible for the addition "and my words." We do not have to look far to find the reason for the addition. Jesus has just predicted his passion (Mark 8,31) which Peter promptly rejected (Mark 8,32), triggering Jesus' sharp rebuke (Mark 8,33). In this context Mark equates rejection of Jesus' words with rejection of Jesus. The following Transfiguration scene reinforces this point with the Father's command, "Hear him" (Mark 9,7). The addition of "and my words" brought with it the switch from "deny" to "be ashamed of" as the latter verb works better with the expanded object. Mark replaces Q's "before men" with the fuller "in this adulterous and sinful generation." Taylor aptly characterizes the phrase as a "homiletical expansion."[72] The expansion helps balance the long temporal clause which follows. With the temporal clause Mark shifts the scene to the parousia in terms similar to those that portray the parousia in Mark 13,26-27. The phrase ἐν τῇ δόξῃ is Marcan. In Mark the title "the Son of Man" is not sufficient by itself to designate an eschatological figure. Mark adds a further qualification.[73] The reference to "his Father" is also Marcan. It reflects Mark's orchestration of the three main titles, "Christ," "Son of God," and "Son of Man." Mark combines the three titles in Jesus' confession before the Sanhedrin (Mark 14,61-62), and all three appear in the Caesarea Philippi pericope.[74] Mark also prepares for the Transfiguration scene where the voice proclaims Jesus as God's Son.[75]

The Caesarea Philippi pericope demonstrates once again that when Mark composes sayings material he reaches for Q. Three of the six sayings in Mark 8,34-9,1 come from Q, and the first two form a cluster bound together by θέλω. In taking over the sayings Mark shows that he knew redactional Q. Mark's saying on Jesus and the Son of Man may reflect

---

71. H. FLEDDERMANN, "Q Saying on Confessing and Denying," pp. 615-616.

72. V. TAYLOR, *Mark*, p. 383.

73. See Mark 13,26; 14,62 (compare also Mark 10,37). See P. HOFFMANN, "Mk 8,31: Zur Herkunft und markinischen Rezeption einer alten Überlieferung," in *Orientierung an Jesus: FS Josef Schmid*, 1973, pp. 170-204, esp. pp. 198-200.

74. Mark 8,29.31.38.

75. J. LAMBRECHT, "Q-Influence," p. 287.

redactional Q. The Son of Man dominates Q's christology, and the saying on Confessing and Denying fits perfectly into Q's theology of the Son of Man. The editor of Q could well have formulated the saying. If so, then Mark reflects redactional Q. If this remains only a possibility for the Son of Man saying, the Cross Saying definitely shows that Mark knew redactional Q. In Q the Cross Saying appears in a original composition that draws together two important lines of thought (Q 14,26-27). For Q discipleship supercedes family ties (Q 9,57-60) and unites the disciple with Jesus' suffering (Q 6,22-23). Since Q 14,26-27 combines these two separate Q themes, it could only go back to the Q redactor. Because Mark knows this composition, he knows redactional Q.

THE DISCIPLESHIP DISCOURSE

In the last chapter I discussed the three overlap texts that appear in the Caesarea Philippi pericope which opens the Discipleship Section of Mark's gospel (Mark 8,27-10,52). The Discipleship Section contains six more overlap texts, four concentrated in the Discipleship Discourse (Mark 9,33-50). The present chapter will present the texts in the Discipleship Discourse and an additional text from the passion narrative (Mark 14,21) that overlaps the same Q text as Mark's Scandal Saying (Mark 9,42). Once again the overlap texts appear in a group in Mark.

§ 15. On Accepting

Mark 9,37 (Matt 10,40 par. Luke 10,16)

The Marcan saying in the Discipleship Discourse has synoptic parallels in Matt 18,5 and Luke 9,48. The Q saying concludes the Mission Discourse.[1]

Matt 10,40	Luke 10,16
ὁ δεχόμενος ὑμᾶς ἐμὲ δέχεται, καὶ ὁ ἐμὲ δεχόμενος δέχεται	ὁ ἀκούων ὑμῶν ἐμοῦ ἀκούει,
	καὶ ὁ ἀθετῶν ὑμᾶς ἐμὲ ἀθετεῖ· ὁ δὲ ἐμὲ ἀθετῶν ἀθετεῖ
τὸν ἀποστείλαντά με.	τὸν ἀποστείλαντά με.

Some argue that Luke preserves the Q wording because it is against Luke's style to introduce parallelism and Matthew's verb "receive" comes from Mark.[2] However, the parallelism is not carried through completely which could indicate that Luke introduced it, and the verb "receive" occurs elsewhere in the Q Mission Discourse (Q 10,8.10). There are signs that Luke redacted the saying. The verb ἀκούω is a

---

1. A slightly different form of the saying is found in John 13,20 (compare also John 12,44-45).
2. J. Schmid, *Matthäus und Lukas*, pp. 278-279; S. Schulz, *Q*, pp. 457-458.

favorite Lucan term,[3] but it is especially the use of the verb pair "hear" and "reject" that points to Lucan redaction. Luke used the pair in Luke 7,29-30 to show how the tax-collectors and the people listened to John and were baptized whereas the Pharisees and the scribes rejected God's plan by not being baptized. Luke worked over this passage redactionally, so it is probable that he also introduced the same verb pair in Luke 10,16. Luke has just drawn a strong contrast between those who accept the disciples and their message and those who do not (Luke 10,8-15). He therefore makes the verb "receive" more precise by substituting the verb pair "hear" and "reject."[4] A further factor could be Luke's use of δέχομαι in the Mission Discourse. Although in Q it meant to receive the messengers and accept their message, Luke seems to have narrowed it to "receive in hospitality" (Luke 10,8). He needed something stronger for his climactic closing statement.[5] Matthew, then, preserves the original Q wording.

Q 10,16	Mark 9,37
ὁ δεχόμενος ὑμᾶς	ὃς ἂν ἓν τῶν τοιούτων παιδίων δέξηται ἐπὶ τῷ ὀνόματί μου,
ἐμὲ δέχεται,	ἐμὲ δέχεται·
καὶ ὁ ἐμὲ δεχόμενος	καὶ ὃς ἂν ἐμὲ δέχηται,
δέχεται	οὐκ ἐμὲ δέχεται
τὸν ἀποστείλαντά με.	ἀλλὰ τὸν ἀποστείλαντά με.

There are several indications that the Q saying is the original one. First, the Q saying is a self-contained logion that is capable of being handed on independently. The Marcan saying with its reference to "one such child as this" points beyond itself to a particular context. Second, the Q saying is a straightforward example of step parallelism constructed with the verb "receive" and the three objects "you," "me," and "the one who sent me." In contrast the Marcan saying is not well balanced. The first clause is overloaded with "one such child as this" and "in my name." Third, in the Q saying the verb δέχομαι has a consistent meaning. In the first part of the saying it means the acceptance of the messengers

3. Compare especially Luke 8,15 with Mark 4,20; Luke 8,21 with Mark 3,35. See further Luke 5,1.15; 6,18.27; 8,8.10.12.13.14.18; 9,35; 10,39; 11,28.31; 14,35; 15,1; 16,29.31; 19,48; 21,38; Acts 2,22.37; 3,22-23; 4,4.19; 7,2; 8,6; 10,22.33.44; 13,7.16.44; 15,7; 16,14; 18,8.26; 19,5.10; 28,26-27.28. See. P. HOFFMANN, *Studien*, pp. 285-286 n. 154.

4. P. HOFFMANN, *Studien*, pp. 285-286. For Luke's intention compare the comment of Fitzmyer: "It is, however, only the Lucan Jesus who during the ministry explicitly begins to train his disciples to carry on his own proclamation, when he says, 'Whoever listens to you listens to me' (Luke 10:16). Here Luke has cast the saying, preserved elsewhere in the Synoptic tradition in terms of reception, explicitly in terms of hearing the proclamation" (*Luke*, 1. 150).

5. P. HOFFMANN, *Studien*, p. 281.

and belief in their message. In the second half of the saying it means belief in Jesus and the one who sent him. The meaning "to believe" is also found in the second half of the Marcan saying, but in the first half of Mark's saying "receive" seems to mean "to accept," "to protect."[6] This tension in the meaning of the verb "receive" indicates a secondary development of the saying. Finally, "in my name" appears to be a clarifying addition to the saying.[7]

When we examine the differences between the Q saying and the Marcan saying, we find that they all result from Marcan redaction. First, the phrase "one such child as this" comes from the new context Mark created for the saying. In Mark 9,36 Mark constructed the scene of a child in the middle of the disciples by drawing elements from the Blessing of the Children (Mark 10,13-16).[8] The phrase "one such child as this" refers to this redactional scene and is Marcan. Since the child symbolizes the believer, the phrase "in my name" links the child to Jesus.[9] In v. 42 Mark refers to "one of these little believers." The "little" refers to the child in v. 37, identifying the child with the believer. Later in Mark Jesus states that the child possesses the kingdom (Mark 10,14). Mark wishes to present the child as a symbol of the lowly believer and to define discipleship in terms of accepting such a one, so to fit the saying into the Discipleship Discourse Mark made two qualifying additions, "one such child as this" and "in my name." These additions would have overloaded the participial phrase so Mark switched to an indefinite relative clause. This shift from participles to relative clauses occurs elsewhere in the overlap texts.[10] Mark continued the indefinite relative construction in the second half of the saying and introduced his οὐκ ... ἀλλά construction.[11]

6. R. SCHNACKENBURG, "Mk 9,33-50," in *Synoptische Studien: FS Alfred Wikenhauser*, 1953, pp. 184-206, esp. p. 186; J. SCHMID, *Das Evangelium nach Markus* (Regensburger Neues Testament, 2), Regensburg: Pustet, ⁴1958, p. 179; ET: *The Gospel according to Mark*, trans. K. Condon, Staten Island, NY: Alba, 1968, p. 179.

7. For the meaning of the phrase see H. KOSMALA, "'In my Name,'" in *ASTI* 5 (1966-67) 87-109.

8. The same word for child (παιδίον) is used in both places. The verb ἐναγκαλίζο-μαι occurs only in these two places in the entire NT. See H. FLEDDERMANN, "Discipleship Discourse," p. 61.

9. "In the name" (Mark 9,37.38.39.41) is one of the catchwords around which the Discipleship Discourse is built. The other catchwords are "to cause to sin" (Mark 9,42.43.45.47), "fire" (Mark 9,43.48.49), and "salt" (Mark 9,49.50).

10. Compare Mark 4,25 with Q 19,26, Mark 9,40 with Q 11,23, Mark 10,11-12 with Q 16,18.

11. R. Pesch (*Markusevangelium*, 2. 106) maintains that the dialectical οὐκ ... ἀλλά formulation of the saying is the original one. But the formulation points rather to Marcan redaction. See, for example, Mark 2,17; 3,29; 4,17; 5,39; 8,33; 10,45; 12,27; 14,36. See further F. NEIRYNCK, *Duality in Mark*, pp. 90-94.

Thus the differences between Mark and Q all result from Marcan redaction. At the beginning of the tradition stands Matthew's form of the saying (Matt 10,40) which preserves the Q saying unchanged. Both Luke (Luke 10,16) and Mark (Mark 9,37) redacted the Q saying, and both Matthew (Matt 18,5) and Luke (Luke 9,48) redacted Mark's saying.

John also records a form of the saying (John 13,20) that closely mirrors Matt 10,40.

> ἀμὴν ἀμὴν λέγω ὑμῖν, ὁ λαμβάνων ἄν τινα πέμψω ἐμὲ λαμβάνει,
> ὁ δὲ ἐμὲ λαμβάνων λαμβάνει τὸν πέμψαντά με.

Peder Borgen claims that John's saying is a variation of the Jesus logion that was transmitted and interpreted in the community, independently of the synoptic gospels. He argues that the Johannine logion uses different vocabulary, that it does not reflect the synoptic context of the saying, and that John's treatment parallels Paul's treatment of Jesus' sayings.[12] Borgen's arguments, though, fail to convince. The formal parallel with Paul does not really apply to this Johannine saying. Borgen discusses Paul's use of the divorce saying where Paul inserts a parenthesis in the saying (1 Cor 7,11) and appends a commentary (1 Cor 7,12-14), but preserves formal elements of the Jesus saying. The situation is different in John 13,20 because John's saying much more closely approximates Matt 10,40 than Paul's saying approaches Jesus' divorce saying found in the synoptics. We cannot attach much weight to the different context in John, for John could easily have moved the saying to a new context. The key lies in the vocabulary, and the vocabulary points to a conclusion directly opposed to Borgen's.

John has a solemn introduction to the saying (ἀμὴν ἀμὴν λέγω ὑμῖν); and his saying employs λαμβάνω instead of δέχομαι, πέμπω instead of ἀποστέλλω, and an indefinite third person expression ἄν τινα πέμψω instead of ὑμᾶς. John alone uses the introductory phrase ἀμὴν ἀμὴν λέγω ὑμῖν with its double ἀμήν.[13] John carefully distinguishes between πέμπω and ἀποστέλλω.[14] He uses the verbs in two different meanings, and he prefers certain grammatical forms for each verb. In particular he uses the substantival aorist active participle of πέμπω as a stereotyped expression to identify the sender. This substantival expression accounts for twenty-seven of the thirty-two occurrences of πέμπω in

---

12. P. BORGEN, "The Independence of the Gospel of John: Some Observations," in *The Four Gospels 1992: Festschrift Frans Neirynck*, 1992, 3. 1815-1833, esp. pp. 1820-1823.

13. John 1,51; 3,3.5.11; 5,19.24.25.26.32.47.53; 8,34.51.58; 10,1.7; 12,24; 13,16.20. 21.38; 14,12; 16,20.23; 21,18.

14. C. MERCER, "ἀποστέλλειν and πέμπειν in John," in *NTS* 36 (1990) 619-624.

John.[15] Although John uses ἀποστέλλω twenty-eight times, he never uses the aorist active participle. So following his normal usage, John replaced τὸν ἀποστείλαντά με with τὸν πέμψαντά με. In the first half of the saying John switches from the second person plural (ὑμᾶς) to an indefinite third person singular expression which uses the same verb πέμπω for symmetry (ἄν τινα πέμψω). John only uses δέχομαι once (John 4,45). He much prefers λαμβάνω, so he substitutes the latter for the former throughout the saying.[16] John's saying basically translates the saying found in Matt 10,40 into Johannine terms. Since Matthew reproduces the Q saying exactly, John's saying depends either on Matthew's gospel or on Q.

§ 16. On Tolerance

Mark 9,40 (Matt 12,30 par. Luke 11,23)

In Q the saying occurs in the Beelzebul Controversy. Mark does not record the saying in his version of the Beelzebul Controversy but in the Discipleship Discourse where it comments on the Strange Exorcist (Mark 9,38-39).[17] Luke redacts Mark's version in Luke 9,50, but Matthew passes over the saying as well as the Strange Exorcist. Laufen does not include the Saying on Tolerance in his list of overlap texts because he doubts that the Marcan and Q sayings are variants of one logion. Even if they both go back to a single source, Laufen claims we cannot determine which is more original.[18] However, the first half of the Q saying and the Marcan saying have enough common elements to speak of a true overlap. Each begins with a negative participial phrase or relative clause; each has a main clause with ἔστιν; each uses the preposition κατά. Furthermore, the two sayings have similar subject matter. Each deals with the relationship of an outsider to Jesus or the disciples. As we shall see, we can also determine which is prior.

---

15. John uses the substantival aorist active participle in John 1,22.33; 4,34; 5,23.24. 30.37; 6,38.39.44; 7,16.18.28.33; 8,16.18.26.29; 9,4; 12,44.45.49; 13,16.20b; 14,24; 15,21; 16,5. John uses the future indicative four times (John 13,20a; 14,26; 15,26; 16,7) and the present indicative once (John 20,21). See further C. C. TARELLI, "Johannine Synonyms," in *JTS* 47 (1946) 175-177, esp. p. 175.

16. John uses λαμβάνω forty-six times.

17. E. WILHELMS, "Der fremde Exorzist: Eine Studie über Mark. 9,38 ff.," in *Stud Theol* 3 (1949) 162-171, esp. p. 163.

18. R. LAUFEN, *Doppelüberlieferungen*, p. 87.

Matt 12,30	Luke 11,23
ὁ μὴ ὢν μετ᾽ ἐμοῦ	ὁ μὴ ὢν μετ᾽ ἐμοῦ
κατ᾽ ἐμοῦ ἐστιν,	κατ᾽ ἐμοῦ ἐστιν,
καὶ ὁ μὴ συνάγων μετ᾽ ἐμοῦ	καὶ ὁ μὴ συνάγων μετ᾽ ἐμοῦ
σκορπίζει.	σκορπίζει.

Matthew and Luke agree word for word even though the saying is somewhat long, fifteen words in Greek.[19] We compare this saying with Mark.

Q 11,23	Mark 9,40
ὁ μὴ ὢν μετ᾽ ἐμοῦ	ὃς γὰρ οὐκ ἔστιν καθ᾽ ἡμῶν,
κατ᾽ ἐμοῦ ἐστιν,	ὑπὲρ ἡμῶν ἐστιν.
καὶ ὁ μὴ συνάγων μετ᾽ ἐμοῦ	
σκορπίζει.	

Three considerations show that Mark is secondary. First, the Q saying makes a general statement which a harvest image then illustrates. "Gathering with me" interprets "with me," and "scatters" interprets "against me." Mark offers only a general statement without an image. The image appears original; it is hard to conceive of someone adding it. Second, the Q saying demands solidarity; Mark allows a looser bond. Instead of "with" (μετά) demanding personal attachment, he has "for" (ὑπέρ) requiring only support. The Q saying is exclusive and intolerant – not to be with Jesus is to be against him. The Marcan saying is inclusive and tolerant – not to be opposed is to be in favor. It is more probable that an intolerant saying has been softened than that a tolerant one has been sharpened. Third, the Q saying demands personal attachment to Jesus; the Marcan saying requires support of the community. Again, it is easier to imagine a statement about Jesus being broadened to a statement about the community than to imagine the opposite development. These considerations show that the Q saying is original.[20]

The differences between Mark and Q make sense when we investigate the Marcan context. Mark uses the saying to comment on the Strange Exorcist (Mark 9,38-39), and he connects it to the pericope with the conjunction γάρ.[21] The saying offers a theoretical reason for the tolerant stance advocated in the pericope. To adapt the saying to this new context

19. For other instances of very close verbal agreement in Q texts see Q 3,7b-9; 6,41-42; 7,6b-9.22-23.24b-28.31-35; 9,58; 10,2-3.13-15.21-22; 11,9-13.19-20.24-26.31-32; 12,2. 22-31.39-40.42b-46; 13,21.34-35; 16,13. See P. WERNLE, *Synoptische Frage*, p. 81; J. A. FITZMYER, *Luke*, 1. 76.

20. R. PESCH, *Markusevangelium*, 2. 110.

21. In Mark Jesus makes three comments on the Strange Exorcist, all linked by γάρ (Mark 9,39.40.41).

Mark reverses the Q saying and expands it to include the disciples (ἡμῶν instead of ἐμοῦ). He also weakens the bond from personal attachment to general support (ὑπέρ instead of μετά). Personal attachment is not required. Jesus extends to this outsider the blessing of fellowship.[22] Mark shifted the participial construction to a relative clause as he does elsewhere in the overlap texts.[23] He also drops the image half of the Q saying because he could not adapt it to his thought. We can thus easily explain the differences between Mark and Q by observing the context Mark fits the saying into.

Mark's saying is much more tolerant than the Q saying, but it is not uncommon in the overlap texts for Mark to tone down Q. In the Mustard Seed Mark calls the mustard "the largest of the shrubs" (Mark 4,32), correcting Q's exaggerated "tree" (Q 13,19). The Q Mission Discourse forbids the missionaries to take anything with them (Q 10,4), but Mark allows some exceptions, including a staff and sandals (Mark 6,8-9). In the Cross Saying he substitutes more exhortatory imperatives for Q's harsh negatives (Mark 8,34 diff. Q 14,27). The Saying on Tolerance reflects Marcan redactional tendencies in the overlap texts.

§ 17. On Scandal

Mark 9,42 (Matt 18,6-7 par. Luke 17,1b-2)

In Luke's gospel the Saying on Scandal has its own introduction – "But he said to his disciples" (Luke 17,1a) – which shows that it originally appeared as an independent saying without a specific setting in Q. Both Luke and Matthew conflated the Q saying with Mark 9,42.

Matt 18,6-7	Luke 17,1b-2
6 ὃς δ᾽ ἂν σκανδαλίσῃ ἕνα τῶν μικρῶν τούτων τῶν πιστευόντων εἰς ἐμέ,	
	1b ἀνένδεκτόν ἐστιν τοῦ τὰ σκάνδαλα μὴ ἐλθεῖν, πλὴν οὐαὶ δι᾽ οὗ ἔρχεται·
συμφέρει αὐτῷ ἵνα κρεμασθῇ μύλος ὀνικὸς	2 λυσιτελεῖ αὐτῷ εἰ λίθος μυλικὸς περίκειται

22. For a Marcan parallel see Mark 3,31-35. For a non-biblical parallel from Cicero's *Pro Q. Ligario*, see W. NESTLE, "'Wer nicht mit mir ist, der ist wider mich.,'" in *ZNW* 13 (1912) 84-87; A. FRIDRICHSEN, "'Wer nicht mit mir ist, ist wider mich.,'" in *ZNW* 13 (1912) 273-280.

23. See Mark 4,25; 9,37; 10,11-12.

περὶ τὸν τράχηλον αὐτοῦ
καὶ καταποντισθῇ
ἐν τῷ πελάγει τῆς θαλάσσης.

περὶ τὸν τράχηλον αὐτοῦ
καὶ ἔρριπται
εἰς τὴν θάλασσαν
ἢ ἵνα σκανδαλίσῃ
τῶν μικρῶν τούτων ἕνα.

7 οὐαὶ τῷ κόσμῳ ἀπὸ τῶν σκανδάλων·
ἀνάγκη γὰρ ἐλθεῖν τὰ σκάνδαλα,
πλὴν οὐαὶ τῷ ἀνθρώπῳ
δι' οὗ τὸ σκάνδαλον ἔρχεται.

Although both Matthew and Luke conflated Mark and Q, the extent of the conflation is disputed. Laufen does not include Mark 9,42 in his list of overlap texts because he remains uncertain whether a true Q parallel to Mark 9,42 exists.[24] Frans Neirynck traces only Luke 17,1b to Q; he attributes all of Luke 17,2 to Lucan redaction of Mark 9,42.[25] However, Neirynck cuts too deeply. Luke's last clause ("...than that he scandalize one of these little ones") comes from Mark. It limps behind badly in Luke, and it awkwardly introduces a new grammatical construction. But something closely corresponding to λυσιτελεῖ αὐτῷ and the if-clause probably stood in Q. First, Matthew's and Luke's redactional procedures make it probable that Luke 17,2 stood in Q. If Q contained Luke 17,2, then Q overlaps here with Mark 9,42, and it is obvious why Matthew and Luke conflated Mark and Q. They found in their Marcan source a saying that resembled the Q saying. But if Q did not contain Luke 17,2, then no overlap exists, and this passage is the only place outside the Baptist and Temptation episodes where Matthew and Luke have independently combined a Q passage – the Scandal Saying – with the same Marcan passage. Such coincident editing of Mark and Q seems improbable. Second, the thought of Luke 17,2 fits comfortably in Q. Q threatens evil-doers with a whole series of frightening punishments. The chaff will be burned with unquenchable fire (Q 3,17); the Lord will cut in two the servant who mistreats his fellow workers (Q 12,46); those cast out of the kingdom into the outer darkness will weep and gnash their teeth (Q 13,28). To have a millstone tied around one's neck and be cast into the sea mirrors the kind of punishment Q holds out to those who refuse to enter the kingdom. Third, the language and imagery of the saying reflect the Faith Saying (Q 17,6) which follows the Scandal Saying closely in

24. R. LAUFEN, *Doppelüberlieferungen*, p. 87.
25. F. NEIRYNCK, "Recent Developments," p. 432. In his synopsis Neirynck prints only Matt 18,7 par. Luke 17,1b. See F. NEIRYNCK, *Q-Synopsis: The Double Tradition Passages in Greek* (Studiorum Novi Testamenti Auxilia, 13), Leuven: University Press – Peeters, 1988, pp. 56-57; ID., "A Synopsis of Q" (1988), in ID., *Evangelica II*, 1991, pp. 465-474, esp. p. 471.

Q.[26] The Faith Saying states, "If you have faith like a mustard seed, you would say to this mulberry tree, 'Be uprooted and planted in the sea,' and it would obey you." The Faith Saying and the Scandal Saying are the only two passages in the synoptics in which someone or something other than a net or a hook is forcibly removed to the sea. Finally, Matthew agrees with Luke in having a finite verb instead of Mark's καλόν ἐστιν. Matthew makes a similar shift in Matt 5,29-30, but it could be that the Q verbal form prompted Matthew to make the change in both places. There is no reason why Luke would want to avoid the Marcan phrase (compare Luke 9,33). So although Luke conflated Mark and Q, the Q saying extends into Luke 17,2. Only the final part of Luke 17,2 ("...than that he scandalize one of these little ones") comes from Mark 9,42.

Matthew also conflated Mark and Q. Except for minor differences Matthew's first clause repeats Mark 9,42. Because Matthew added the relative clause at the beginning, he shifts the woe saying and the clause on the necessity of scandal to the end. Luke preserves the original Q order of the saying. In Q the woe was directed against the man through whom scandals come. Matthew added a second woe, "woe to the world because of scandals." This second woe is a redactional addition of Matthew. The words κόσμος and σκάνδαλον are Matthean. Matthew uses κόσμος nine times.[27] He introduces it redactionally in Matt 24,21 (diff. Mark 13,19), and it is probably also redactional in Matt 5,14. Both κόσμος and σκάνδαλον appear in Matthew's redactional explanation of the parable of the Wheat and the Tares (Matt 13,37-43). Matthew also uses causal ἀπό elsewhere.[28]

The clause on the necessity or inevitability of scandal is difficult. Luke's ἀνένδεκτόν ἐστιν is a *hapax legomenon* in the NT, but on the other hand Matthew nowhere else uses ἀνάγκη. There are several indications that Luke has changed the Q expression. Although the expression ἀνένδεκτόν ἐστιν occurs only here in the NT, Luke uses an equivalent expression οὐκ ἐνδέχεται in Luke 13,33.[29] To this formal consideration we can add one of content. There is a slight difference in meaning between Matthew's "it is necessary that scandals come" and Luke's "it is impossible that scandals not come." Luke's expression tries to avoid divine responsibility for scandals. So Matthew's ἀνάγκη reflects Q.

---

26. Only the Saying on Forgiveness (Q 17,3-4) separates the two sayings.
27. Matt 4,8; 5,14; 13,35.38; 16,26; 18,7; 24,21; 25,34; 26,13.
28. Compare Matt 13,44. See BDF, § 176 (1), § 210 (1).
29. Compare also the use of δεκτός in Luke 4,19.24; Acts 10,35.

Matthew's γάρ links the saying to his redactional woe saying so it is redactional. In introducing γάρ Matthew probably surpressed the ἔστιν that Luke has in the first clause. Matthew drew the infinitive forward to compensate for the elipsis. Luke added τοῦ.[30] The Q clause would have been ἀνάγκη ἐστιν τὰ σκάνδαλα ἐλθεῖν.

Matthew's πλὴν οὐαὶ τῷ ἀνθρώπῳ probably preserves the Q beginning of the following clause. Luke omits the antecedent to the relative clause to obtain a more compact sentence.[31] In the relative clause Matthew added τὸ σκάνδαλον. The Q saying originally spoke in general of scandals. Matthew, though, introduced the special case of scandalizing a little believer from Mark (Matt 18,6a). Therefore he inserts the singular τὸ σκάνδαλον as the subject of ἔρχεται.

Luke's λυσιτελεῖ, a *hapax legomenon*, is original.[32] The verb συμφέρω, on the other hand, is characteristically Matthean.[33] Matthew assimilates the saying to Matt 5,29-30 by the use of συμφέρει ... ἵνα.[34] Luke's εἰ comes from Q. Matthew's verb κρεμάννυμι also does not go back to Q, for Matthew uses it redactionally in Matt 22,40. Luke's περίκειται is original.[35] Luke moved the subject of the if-clause forward to obtain a more normal word order, and he substituted λίθος μυλικός for the more difficult μύλος ὀνικός. The verb ἔρριπται is also redactional. Luke uses it redactionally in Luke 4,35 (diff. Mark 1,26), and he uses it twice in Acts for throwing something into the sea (Acts 27,19.21). Elsewhere Matthew uses Luke's verb, so he had no reason to alter the verb if he had read it in Q.[36] Matthew alone of NT writers uses καταποντίζω (compare Matt 14,30). Q commonly uses βάλλω for throwing, so the original verb was probably βέβληται.[37] We can now compare Mark and Q.

---

30. The τοῦ before infinitives is Lucan (6 0 20 18). See J. C. HAWKINS, *Horae Synopticae*, pp. 22, 48.

31. For Luke's making sentences more compact, see Chapter IV above on Mark 4,25.

32. J. SCHLOSSER, "Lk 17,2 und die Logienquelle," in *SNTU* 8 (1983) 70-78, esp. p. 77.

33. 4 0 0 2. At least two of the other three uses are redactional (compare Matt 5,29-30 with Mark 9,43-47). See J. C. HAWKINS, *Horae Synopticae*, pp. 7, 33.

34. W. C. ALLEN, *Matthew*, p. xxx.

35. Luke uses κρεμάννυμι in Luke 23,39 (diff. Mark 15,32b); Acts 5,30; 10,39; 28,4. He had no reason to avoid Matthew's verb. See J. SCHLOSSER, "Lk 17,2 und die Logienquelle," pp. 77-78.

36. Matthew uses ῥίπτω in Matt 9,36 (diff. Mark 6,34); 15,30; 27,5.

37. See Q 3,9; 4,9; 12,28.58; 14,35.

Q 17,1b-2   Mark 9,42

                                    καὶ ὃς ἂν σκανδαλίσῃ
                                    ἕνα τῶν μικρῶν τούτων
                                    τῶν πιστευόντων,

1b ἀνάγκη ἐστιν τὰ σκάνδαλα ἐλθεῖν,
   πλὴν οὐαὶ τῷ ἀνθρώπῳ
   δι' οὗ ἔρχεται·
2 λυσιτελεῖ αὐτῷ   καλόν ἐστιν αὐτῷ μᾶλλον
   εἰ περίκειται μύλος ὀνικὸς   εἰ περίκειται μύλος ὀνικὸς
   περὶ τὸν τράχηλον αὐτοῦ   περὶ τὸν τράχηλον αὐτοῦ
   καὶ βέβληται εἰς τὴν θάλασσαν.   καὶ βέβληται εἰς τὴν θάλασσαν.

Mark's saying is secondary to the Q saying. First, the Q saying is self-contained. It makes a general statement about the necessity of scandal and the dire consequences that will result for the one who causes scandal. Mark, on the other hand, opens with a relative clause, "and whoever scandalizes one of these little believers..." "One of these little believers" refers back to the child in Mark 9,37. Since Mark 9,33-50 is a secondary Marcan composition, this reference to what precedes is secondary. The self-contained Q logion is primary. Second, λυσιτελεῖ αὐτῷ is a NT *hapax legomenon*. Mark's καλόν ἐστιν αὐτῷ reflects the most common introduction to the *Tobspruch* form, so it is secondary to the Q form.[38]

Once we see that Mark is secondary to Q, we can turn to study the Marcan redaction. Mark composed the initial relative clause from the Q saying and elements drawn from other parts of the Discipleship Discourse.[39] The ὃς ἂν construction picks up a construction used in v. 37. The verb "scandalize" comes from the noun "scandal" in the Q saying, and it echoes the verb in the following sayings (vv. 43, 45, and 47). The expression "one of these little ones" reflects "one such child as this" in v. 37. Since the child symbolizes the believer, Mark adds the further qualification τῶν πιστευόντων. The clause on the necessity of scandal would no longer fit after the relative clause, so Mark eliminated it. Matthew faces the same problem once he took over Mark's relative clause (Matt 18,6), and he solves it by transposing the clause on the necessity of scandal to the end (Matt 18,7). Such a solution would not appeal to Mark. He dropped the clause because for him scandal means falling into unbelief so he could never admit that scandals were necessary.[40] Mark

38. See Matt 18,8.9; 26,24; Mark 9,43.45.47; 14,21. On the form see G. F. SNYDER, "The *Tobspruch* in the New Testament," in *NTS* 23 (1976-77) 117-120.
39. The reading εἰς ἐμέ is an assimilation to Matt 18,6. See B. M. METZGER, *Textual Commentary*, pp. 101-102.
40. Compare Mark 4,17; 6,3; 14,27. See H. FLEDDERMANN, "Discipleship Discourse," p. 68 n. 56.

uses the woe in Mark 14,21 so he passes over it here. In the second half of the saying Mark introduced only a few stylistic improvements. Instead of λυσιτελεῖ αὐτῷ Mark anticipates the *Tobspruch* form of the scandal sayings he records in vv. 43, 45, and 47. Mark 9,42 contrasts with two other verses in the Discipleship Discourse, v. 37 and v. 41. One who receives a child receives Jesus and the one who sent him (Mark 9,37); but one who scandalizes a child draws terrible punishment on himself. The least service done to a disciple will be rewarded (Mark 9,41); but any harm done a disciple will be severely punished.

According to Dale C. Allison, Paul echoes Mark 9,42 in Rom 14,13 and 1 Cor 8,13, picking up the saying from a pre-Marcan collection of logia.[41] However, neither parallel follows the Marcan wording closely,[42] and the extent of any pre-Marcan collection behind Mark 9,33-50 remains disputed.[43]

In the passion narrative Mark has another parallel to Q 17,1b-2. I will treat this further parallel before concluding the discussion of the overlap texts in the Discipleship Discourse.

§ 17a. THE SON OF MAN AND THAT MAN

Mark 14,21 (Matt 18,6-7 par. Luke 17,1b-2)

Mark has a second overlap with the Q Scandal Saying in the passion narrative. Laufen does not even mention this text in his discussion of the extent of the Mark-Q overlap.[44] However, Mark 14,21 shares several features with the Q Scandal Saying and deserves inclusion in the overlap texts. Both texts combine a woe against the man through whom something occurs (οὐαὶ τῷ ἀνθρώπῳ δι' οὗ) with a *Tobspruch* that leads into a conditional clause (λυσιτελεῖ αὐτῷ εἰ / καλὸν αὐτῷ εἰ).

Q 17,1b-2	Mark 14,21
	ὅτι ὁ μὲν υἱὸς τοῦ ἀνθρώπου ὑπάγει καθὼς γέγραπται περὶ αὐτοῦ·
1b ἀνάγκη ἐστιν τὰ σκάνδαλα ἐλθεῖν, πλὴν οὐαὶ τῷ ἀνθρώπῳ δι' οὗ ἔρχεται·	οὐαὶ δὲ τῷ ἀνθρώπῳ ἐκείνῳ δι' οὗ ὁ υἱὸς τοῦ ἀνθρώπου παραδίδοται·

---

41. D. C. ALLISON, "Pauline Epistles and the Synoptic Gospels," pp. 14-15.
42. Compare τὸ μὴ τιθέναι πρόσκομμα τῷ ἀδελφῷ ἢ σκάνδαλον (Rom 14,13) and εἰ ... σκανδαλίζει τὸν ἀδελφόν μου, ... ἵνα μὴ τὸν ἀδελφόν μου σκανδαλίσω (1 Cor 8,13).
43. See F. NEIRYNCK, "Paul and the Sayings of Jesus," pp. 528-532.
44. R. LAUFEN, *Doppelüberlieferungen*, pp. 81-92.

2 λυσιτελεῖ αὐτῷ   καλὸν αὐτῷ
   εἰ περίκειται μύλος ὀνικὸς   εἰ οὐκ ἐγεννήθη
   περὶ τὸν τράχηλον αὐτοῦ   ὁ ἄνθρωπος ἐκεῖνος.
   καὶ βέβληται εἰς τὴν θάλασσαν.

The Q saying appears to be original for three reasons. First, as was pointed out above, the Q saying is a self-contained unit on the necessity of scandal and the consequences to the one through whom scandals come. The Marcan saying is completely dominated by the opposition between the Son of Man and "that man," but it is not clear from the saying who "that man" is. Only the wider context of Mark's gospel with its theme of the betrayer clarifies who "that man" refers to.[45] Second, Mark's καλὸν αὐτῷ reflects the most common introduction to the *Tobspruch*. Q's λυσιτελεῖ is original. Third, the two if-clauses also show that the Q saying is original. The graphic image of the millstone being hung around the neck and being hurled into the sea is more original than the rather common "not be born."[46]

We turn now to the Marcan redaction. The opposition between the Son of Man and "that man" dominates Mark's saying. Both the Son of Man and "that man" are mentioned twice. Repetition of the antecedent is a feature of Marcan duality, and it indicates that Mark is responsible for the wording.[47] The use of μὲν … δέ highlights the opposition between the two figures.

Mark introduces the saying with a ὅτι-*recitativum*.[48] The first clause, "the Son of Man goes as it is written about him," picks up several themes of Mark's portrayal of the Son of Man. The verb ὑπάγει corresponds to the many references to Jesus' going his way.[49] Although Jesus follows God's will, he freely goes toward his death. The scriptural necessity of the passion is brought out explicitly in the phrase "as it is written about him,"[50] and a scripture allusion appears in the immediate

45. Mark refers to the betrayer in Mark 3,19; 9,31; 10,33-34; 14,10-11.18-21.41. 42.44.

46. Compare Jer 20,14-18; Job 3,1-26; 1 Enoch 38,2. See further H. L. STRACK and P. BILLERBECK, *Kommentar zum Neuen Testament aus Talmud und Midrasch*, vol. 1, Munich: Beck, 1922, pp. 989-990.

47. F. NEIRYNCK, *Duality in Mark*, pp. 85-87.

48. Either the reader must supply καὶ εἶπεν at the beginning of v. 21, or, more probably, the ὅτι reaches back to ὁ δὲ εἶπεν in v. 20. See L. SCHENKE, *Studien zur Passionsgeschichte des Markus: Tradition und Redaktion in Markus 14,1-42* (FzB, 4), Würzburg: Echter / Stuttgart: Katholisches Bibelwerk, 1971, pp. 237-238.

49. Compare ὁδός (Mark 8,27; 9,33.34; 10,17.32.46.52; 11,8) and προάγω (Mark 10,32; 14,28; 16,7). See P. HOFFMANN, "Mk 8,31," p. 190 n. 71.

50. The expression is found in the redactional verses Mark 1,2 and 9,12b (compare also Mark 8,31; 9,11.13; 14,27.49).

context (Mark 14,18, compare Psa 40,10 LXX).[51] Mark announced the theme of the scriptural necessity of the passion at the beginning of the passion predictions (Mark 8,31; 9,12).[52] He welds the statement about scriptural necessity to the woe against "that man" by introducing μὲν ... δέ and by repeating "Son of Man" and "that man." The contrast between "men" and "the Son of Man" is a feature of Mark's understanding of the Son of Man.[53] The expression "that man" means one who thinks human thoughts and not the thoughts of God, one who is not prepared to believe.[54] Humans radically reject the will of God which Jesus announced in Mark 8,31. The disciples with their flight (Mark 14,50-52) and Peter with his denial (Mark 14,54.66-72) further typify human rejection of God's will.[55] God's will, though, does not absolve humans of responsibility, so opposition to the Son of Man turns into disaster for those who oppose him. Since Mark used the millstone image in the Discipleship Discourse (Mark 9,42), he substitutes the common "not be born" in the if-clause to characterize the severity of the punishment.[56] In this saying Mark impressively holds together the will of God expressed in scripture, Jesus' free acceptance of God's will, and human guilt in rejecting it.

§ 18. On Salt

Mark 9,50a (Matt 5,13 par. Luke 14,34-35a)

Each synoptic writer records a single Salt Saying, but Matthew-Luke agreements show that Q contained a version of the saying. Despite the agreements against Mark, Matthew and Luke diverge sharply in formulating the Salt Saying.

Matt 5,13	Luke 14,34-35a
ὑμεῖς ἐστε τὸ ἅλας τῆς γῆς·	34 καλὸν οὖν τὸ ἅλας·
ἐὰν δὲ τὸ ἅλας μωρανθῇ,	ἐὰν δὲ καὶ τὸ ἅλας μωρανθῇ,
ἐν τίνι ἁλισθήσεται;	ἐν τίνι ἀρτυθήσεται;
εἰς οὐδὲν	35 οὔτε εἰς γῆν οὔτε εἰς κοπρίαν
ἰσχύει ἔτι	εὔθετόν ἐστιν,
εἰ μὴ βληθὲν ἔξω καταπατεῖσθαι	ἔξω βάλλουσιν αὐτό.
ὑπὸ τῶν ἀνθρώπων.	

51. P. HOFFMANN, "Mk 8,31," p. 188.
52. O. J. F. SEITZ, "Rejection of the Son of Man," pp. 451-455.
53. Compare Mark 2,27-28; 8,27-33; 9,31; and Mark's redaction of the Unforgivable Sin saying in Mark 3,28-29.
54. Compare Mark 8,33. See P. HOFFMANN, "Mk 8,31," p. 186.
55. P. HOFFMANN, "Mk 8,31," p. 191.
56. The threat implied in Mark 14,21 is present also in Mark 8,38 and 14,62.

Matthew's phrase "you are the salt of the earth" assimilates this saying to Matt 5,14, "you are the light of the world."[57] Formally it picks up the "blessed are you" of the last beatitude (Matt 5,11).[58] Matthew draws γῆ from the second half of the Q saying (Q 14,35a). Luke preserves the Q introduction of the saying, but he adds οὖν.[59] Luke also added καί in the conditional clause.[60] Matthew's ἁλισθήσεται assimilates the verb to the noun ἅλας, whereas Luke's verb is rare in the NT.[61] It undoubtedly reflects Q. There are several indications that Luke preserves the Q form of the second half of the saying. Luke's vocabulary has some unusual features. The noun κοπρία is a *hapax legomenon* in the NT; εὔθετος is rare.[62] Matthew's vocabulary, on the other hand, shows some Matthean features. The construction οὐδὲν ... εἰ μή is not unusual in Matthew.[63] The verb καταπατέω appears also in Matt 7,6. Luke introduces the verb into his Marcan source in Luke 8,5 (diff. Mark 4,4) and Luke 12,1 (diff. Mark 8,14), so there is no reason Luke would want to avoid it. Luke's impersonal third plural βάλλουσιν is more original than Matthew's passive participle. Matthew uses ἰσχύω four times. The other instances come from Mark, but Luke uses the verb frequently so again there is nothing in Matthew's vocabulary that would cause Luke problems.[64] Finally, Matthew's εἰς οὐδὲν ἰσχύει appears to be a summary of a fuller expression like the one Luke offers.[65] Matthew simplified the image as he has done elsewhere in the overlap texts.[66] We can now compare the Q saying with Mark.

---

57. See R. SCHNACKENBURG, "'Ihr seid das Salz der Erde, das Licht der Welt': Zu Mt 5,13-16" (1964), in ID., *Schriften zum Neuen Testament*, 1971, pp. 177-200, esp. p. 180; H.-T. WREGE, *Die Überlieferungsgeschichte der Bergpredigt* (WUNT, 9) Tübingen: Mohr – Siebeck, 1968, p. 28; G. N. STANTON, *Gospel for a New People*, p. 338.

58. See G. SCHNEIDER, "Bildwort von der Lampe," p. 134 n. 88.

59. See Chapter IV above on Mark 4,30-32.

60. Luke likes to use δὲ καί (3 2 25 7). See J. C. HAWKINS, *Horae Synopticae*, pp. 17, 37; H. J. CADBURY, *Style and Literary Method*, p. 146.

61. It occurs only in Mark 9,50; Luke 14,34; Col 4,6.

62. Besides the present verse it occurs only in Luke 9,62; Heb 6,7 (compare ἀνεύθετος in Acts 27,12).

63. Compare Matt 12,24 with Mark 3,22 and Luke 11,15; Matt 14,17 with Mark 6,38. See J. LAMBRECHT, *Marcus Interpretator*, p. 34.

64. Matthew takes over ἰσχύω from Mark in Matt 8,28 (par. Mark 5,4), Matt 9,12 (par. Mark 2,17), and Matt 26,40 (par. Mark 14,37). Luke uses the verb in Luke 6,48; 8,43; 13,24; 14,6.29.30; 16,3; 20,26; Acts 6,10; 15,10; 19,16.20; 25,7; 27,16.

65. S. SCHULZ, *Q*, p. 471.

66. See Chapter II above on Mark 1,7-8.

Q 14,34-35a	Mark 9,50

34 καλὸν τὸ ἅλας·   καλὸν τὸ ἅλας·
  ἐὰν δὲ τὸ ἅλας μωρανθῇ,   ἐὰν δὲ τὸ ἅλας ἄναλον γένηται,
  ἐν τίνι ἀρτυθήσεται;   ἐν τίνι αὐτὸ ἀρτύσετε;
35 οὔτε εἰς γῆν οὔτε εἰς κοπρίαν
  εὐθετόν ἐστιν,
  ἔξω βάλλουσιν αὐτό.

The two sayings are obviously related, but there are just as obviously differences between them. The Q saying is about twice as long as the Marcan saying because it includes a reflection on the fate of the salt that has no parallel in Mark. The Q saying remains impersonal throughout. Mark's saying, on the other hand, directly addresses the readers with the second person plural verb in the last clause. There is also a slight difference in wording. Mark has ἄναλον γένηται where Q has μωρανθῇ.

Schnackenburg claims that Mark preserves the earliest form of the saying.[67] However, the differences between the two sayings point in the opposite direction and show that Mark is later than Q. First, Mark makes explicit the hortatory element that is only implied in the Q saying. The Q saying centers exclusively on the salt, and it avoids any direct appeal to the hearer. However, an implied parenesis lies behind the rhetorical question and the graphic description of useless salt's fate. Mark makes this implied parenesis explicit with the second person plural ἀρτύσετε. This is a sign that Mark is secondary. Second, the explicit parenesis of Mark shifts the focus of the saying from the salt to the people who use the salt. The description of the fate of the salt loses its meaning in the process, so the fact that it does not appear in Mark further demonstrates the secondary character of Mark's saying. Third, the Q word μωρανθῇ is somewhat confusing in this context. The verb basically means "to make foolish" (1 Cor 1,20) or, in the passive, "to become foolish" (Rom 1,22). Mark's ἄναλον γένηται clarifies an ambiguous μωρανθῇ, again showing that Mark is later.[68]

The differences between Mark and Q result from Marcan redaction. Mark uses ἄναλον γένηται to clarify Q's μωρανθῇ. The change reflects Mark's style, for he likes alpha-privative adjectives.[69] Mark also

67. R. SCHNACKENBURG, "'Ihr seid das Salz der Erde,'" p. 179.

68. Perry Kea argues that Mark's ἄναλον γένηται is original. However, Mark almost certainly improves Q's ambiguous term μωρανθῇ, and ἄναλον reflects his fondness for alpha-privative adjectives (see following note). See P. V. KEA, "Salting the Salt: Q 14: 34-35 and Mark 9:49-50," in *Forum* 6/3-4 (1990) 239-244.

69. Compare ἀκάθαρτος (11 times); ἄκαρπος (Mark 4,19); ἄλαλος (Mark 7,37; 9,17.25); ἄνιπτος (Mark 7,2); ἄσβεστος (Mark 9,43); ἀσύνετος (Mark 7,18); ἄτιμος (Mark 6,4). See E. WENDLING, *Entstehung*, p. 107 n. 2; H. FLEDDERMANN, "Discipleship Discourse," p. 69 n. 60.

substitutes the active expression αὐτὸ ἀρτύσετε for the passive ἀρτυθήσεται to make the saying explicitly parenetic. He uses the active form
to lead into his climax in v. 50b which he formulates in the imperative.
The αὐτό focuses the saying even more strongly on the power of the
salt. This change helps orient the thought of v. 50a completely to that of
v. 50b: "Have salt within you, and be at peace with one another." In v. 50b
salt is a symbol of covenant fellowship.[70] The Salt Saying (v. 50a) demands
that this salt be genuine. Mark drops the second half of the saying because
the fate of the salt does not fit in the explicit parenetic reformulation. He
wants to move on to his conclusion.

As in other chapters Mark again clustered Q sayings in the Discipleship Discourse. The discourse, though, gives us new insight into how
Mark incorporated Q material into his gospel. The overlap texts consist
primarily of short sayings and parables. However, Mark and Q do share
two extended texts – the Beelzebul Controversy and the Mission
Discourse. Earlier in the gospel Mark edited the Q Beelzebul Controversy
and the Q Mission Discourse, but in each case he saved a saying for the
Discipleship Discourse (Mark 9,40 par. Q 11,23; Mark 9,37 par. Q
10,16). Mark mined Q for material just like Matthew and Luke mined
Mark. In the Measure Saying we saw Mark conflate two Q texts (Q
6,38c; 12,31). In the Scandal Saying we encounter the opposite development. Mark twice redacts the Q Scandal Saying (Q 17,1b-2), once in the
Discipleship Discourse (Mark 9,42) and once in the passion narrative
(Mark 14,21). Mark redacts Q with techniques similar to those Matthew
and Luke use to edit Mark.

---

70. No consensus has emerged on the symbolism of the salt. For example, Soucek and
Cullmann maintain that it refers to the disciples' willingness to suffer. See J. B. SOUCEK,
"Salz der Erde und Licht der Welt: Zur Exegese von Matth. 5,13-17," in *TZ* 19 (1963)
169-179, esp. pp. 174-175; O. CULLMANN, "Das Gleichnis vom Salz: Zur frühesten Kommentierung eines Herrenworts durch die Evangelisten" (1957), in ID., *Vorträge und Aufsätze 1925-1962*, 1966, pp. 192-201, esp. pp. 197-199. However, in the OT salt is a symbol
of the covenant (Lev 2,13; Num 18,19; 2 Chr 13,5; Ezra 4,14). This symbolism fits perfectly
with the parallel clause "be at peace with one another." See H. FLEDDERMANN, "Discipleship
Discourse," p. 73.

VIII

TOWARD THE PASSION

After the Discipleship Discourse we find the next major cluster of overlap texts in the Eschatological Discourse. Between the two clusters lie several chapters (Mark 10-12) that comprise the end of Mark's Discipleship Section (Mark 8,27-10,52) and the beginning of the Jerusalem Section (Mark 11,1-13,37). Five overlap texts fall in these chapters. Two of them follow one another in a small cluster on faith and prayer (Mark 11,22-23.24), but the other three appear widely scattered (Mark 10,11-12.31; 12,38-39). In these chapters Jesus continues to instruct the crowds and the disciples, and opposition to him continues to mount. Mark's story moves toward the passion.

§ 19. ON DIVORCE

Mark 10,11-12 (Matt 5,32 par. Luke 16,18)

Matthew works the Q divorce saying into the antitheses of the Sermon on the Mount (Matt 5,32), and he edits the Marcan saying in Matt 19,9. In Luke, as in Q, the divorce saying concludes a cluster of three sayings on the law (Luke 16,16-18).

Matt 5,32	Luke 16,18
ἐγὼ δὲ λέγω ὑμῖν ὅτι	
πᾶς ὁ ἀπολύων τὴν γυναῖκα αὐτοῦ	πᾶς ὁ ἀπολύων τὴν γυναῖκα αὐτοῦ
παρεκτὸς λόγου πορνείας	
	καὶ γαμῶν ἑτέραν
ποιεῖ αὐτὴν μοιχευθῆναι,	μοιχεύει,
καὶ ὃς ἐὰν ἀπολελυμένην γαμήσῃ,	καὶ ὁ ἀπολελυμένην ἀπὸ ἀνδρὸς γαμῶν
μοιχᾶται.	μοιχεύει.

Matthew's ἐγὼ δὲ λέγω ὑμῖν ὅτι is redactional since Matthew uses it in all the antitheses.[1] His παρεκτὸς λόγου πορνείας is also redactional. Matthew uses an equivalent expression (μὴ ἐπὶ πορνείᾳ) in his redaction

---

1. Matt 5,22.28.32.34.39.44 (the last three verses omit ὅτι).

of Mark 10,11 in Matt 19,9.[2] Matthew and Luke differ in the formulation of the first main clause. Matthew writes "causes her to commit adultery." Luke has a second participial phrase καὶ γαμῶν ἑτέραν and a simple verb μοιχεύει. Some scholars like Schneider and Zmijewski claim that Luke added καὶ γαμῶν ἑτέραν under the influence of Mark 10,11.[3] However, dependence on Mark can not be demonstrated.[4] A decision on this point demands a close look at the difference in thought between Matthew and Luke. In Luke both parts of the saying state that remarriage after divorce constitutes adultery so the phrase καὶ γαμῶν ἑτέραν is demanded by the symmetry of the saying. Matthew's saying is less unified. In Matthew's first clause the divorce itself causes the woman to commit adultery. Matthew has adapted the saying to the context of the antitheses. He already dealt with adultery in the second antithesis (Matt 5,27-28). In the third (Matt 5,31-32) he wants to focus on divorce, so he recasts the Q saying to make it castigate the divorce directly and not the remarriage and adultery which follows from the divorce. This Matthean refocusing clearly adapts the saying to the context in Matthew's gospel. Luke therefore basically preserves the Q form of the saying. A change on Luke's part cannot be explained.[5] In the second part of the saying Matthew adopted the conditional relative construction and the verb μοιχᾶται from Mark. Luke reflects Q except for the phrase ἀπὸ ἀνδρός which is a clarifying addition. Luke uses ἀπό with ἀπολύω in Acts 15,33, and ἀνήρ is very common in Luke.[6] Neirynck also traces ἑτέραν to Luke's redaction, but ἕτερος is a good Q word.[7] We can now compare the Marcan saying.

---

2. According to Fitzmyer the two clauses allow divorce in the case of marriages within certain degrees of kinship that Jewish law would forbid. See the discussion of CD 4:12b-5:14a in J. A. FITZMYER, "The Matthean Divorce Texts and Some New Palestinian Evidence" (1976), in ID., *To Advance the Gospel*, 1981, pp. 79-111, esp. pp. 87-89, 91-99. Neirynck disputes this interpretation. See F. NEIRYNCK, "De Jesuswoorden over echtscheiding" (1972), in ID., *Evangelica*, 1982, pp. 821-834, esp. pp. 833-834.

3. G. SCHNEIDER, "Jesu Wort über die Ehescheidung in der Überlieferung des Neuen Testaments" (1971), in ID., *Jesusüberlieferung und Christologie*, 1992, pp. 187-209, esp. p. 192; J. ZMIJEWSKI, "Neutestamentliche Weisungen für Ehe und Familie," in *SNTU* 9 (1984) 31-78, esp. p. 52.

4. F. NEIRYNCK, "Jesuswoorden over echtscheiding," p. 826.

5. R. LAUFEN, *Doppelüberlieferungen*, pp. 345-346; J. A. FITZMYER, "Matthean Divorce Texts," pp. 82-83.

6. Statistics on ἀνήρ: 8 4 27 100. See further S. SCHULZ, *Q*, p. 116; R. LAUFEN, *Doppelüberlieferungen*, p. 347; J. JEREMIAS, *Sprache*, p. 259; F. NEIRYNCK, "Jesuswoorden over echtscheiding," p. 826.

7. For Neirynck's position, see "Jesuswoorden over echtscheiding," p. 826. However, Matthew and Luke both attest ἕτερος in Q texts four times (Q 9,59; 11,26; 16,13*bis*) and ἄλλος only twice (Q 6,29; 7,8). Furthermore, ἕτερος probably should be restored in seven other Q texts (Q 7,19.32; 11,16; 14,19.20; 17,34.35).

Q 16,18	Mark 10,11-12
	11 καὶ λέγει αὐτοῖς·
πᾶς ὁ ἀπολύων	ὃς ἂν ἀπολύσῃ
τὴν γυναῖκα αὐτοῦ	τὴν γυναῖκα αὐτοῦ
καὶ γαμῶν ἑτέραν	καὶ γαμήσῃ ἄλλην
μοιχεύει,	μοιχᾶται ἐπ' αὐτήν·
καὶ ὁ ἀπολελυμένην	12 καὶ ἐὰν αὐτὴ ἀπολύσασα
	τὸν ἄνδρα αὐτῆς
γαμῶν μοιχεύει.	γαμήσῃ ἄλλον μοιχᾶται.

Laufen claims that both Mark and Q show original elements in the Divorce Saying. According to Laufen casuistic legal sayings are frequently formulated with conditional relative clauses so Mark's form lies closer to the original, and he considers the dualistic ἑτέραν secondary to the more correct ἄλλην.[8] Neither of these arguments hold up under closer scrutiny. We have frequently seen that Mark has relative clauses where Q has participles. The relative clauses go back to Mark not to the original sayings.[9] In the NT ἕτερος has lost its duality and appears interchangeably with ἄλλος, so no argument for originality can be based on a difference in meaning between the two words.[10]

The most striking difference between the two sayings is that the Q saying reflects Palestinian conditions in which only the man could initiate a divorce. Mark reflects Greek and Roman law according to which the woman also had the right to initiate a divorce. This shows that the Q saying is the original one, and that the Marcan saying adapts the thought to the changed circumstances of the gentile mission.[11] Further, Mark's ἐπ' αὐτήν in the first main clause is a secondary addition which reflects the new emphasis on the woman.[12]

---

8. R. LAUFEN, Doppelüberlieferungen, p. 347.

9. Compare Mark 4,25 (diff. Q 19,26); Mark 9,37 (diff. Q 10,16); Mark 9,40 (diff. Q 11,23).

10. J. H. MOULTON, W. F. HOWARD, and N. TURNER, Grammar, 1. 79-80, 2. 182, 3. 197-198.

11. J. A. FITZMYER, "Matthean Divorce Texts," pp. 85-86; J. S. KLOPPENBORG, "Alms, Debt and Divorce: Jesus' Ethics in their Mediterranean Context," in Toronto Journal of Theology 6 (1990) 182-200, esp. p. 193.

12. Arguing that Mark's saying goes back to an Aramaic original, Berndt Schaller refers the ἐπ' αὐτήν to the second woman and translates the clause "commits adultery with her." See B. SCHALLER, "Die Sprüche über Ehescheidung und Wiederheirat in der synoptischen Überlieferung," in Der Ruf Jesu und die Antwort der Gemeinde: FS Joachim Jeremias, 1970, pp. 226-246, esp. pp. 238-245. More probably Mark's prepositional phrase secondarily interprets a Greek original and should be referred to the first woman ("commits adultery against her"). See G. DELLING, "Das Logion Markus 10,11 und seine Abwandlungen im Neuen Testament" (1956), in ID., Studien zum Neuen Testament, 1970, pp. 226-235 esp. p. 232; J. A. FITZMYER, "Matthean Divorce Texts," p. 85.

Mark's redaction confirms this conclusion, for we can easily derive Mark's saying from the Q saying. Mark links the Divorce Saying to the preceding pericope with a typical introductory phrase καὶ λέγει αὐτοῖς.[13] He changes Q's participial construction to a conditional relative clause, as he does in other overlap texts, and he replaces ἑτέραν, a word he never uses, with his familiar ἄλλην.[14] Mark also adds ἐπ' αὐτήν as a clarifying addition,[15] and he substitutes μοιχᾶται for μοιχεύει.[16] Mark then formulates a parallel second sentence (v. 12) which extends the principle to cover the woman's action possible under Greek and Roman law. He avoids monotony by proceding with a conditional and a participle instead of the relative conditional with two coordinated verbs as in v. 11.

Paul quotes a saying of the Lord on divorce in 1 Cor 7,10-11.

> τοῖς δὲ γεγαμηκόσιν παραγγέλλω, οὐκ ἐγὼ ἀλλὰ ὁ κύριος, γυναῖκα ἀπὸ ἀνδρὸς μὴ χωρισθῆναι, – ἐὰν δὲ καὶ χωρισθῇ, μενέτω ἄγαμος ἢ τῷ ἀνδρὶ καταλλαγήτω, – καὶ ἄνδρα γυναῖκα μὴ ἀφιέναι.

Paul's saying resembles Mark 10,11-12 reflecting Greco-Roman law which allowed the woman as well as the man to initiate divorce,[17] but it is not close enough to the synoptic sayings for us to conclude that Paul knew any synoptic formulation.[18]

§ 20. THE FIRST AND THE LAST

Mark 10,31 (Matt 20,16 par. Luke 13,30)

Laufen does not include Mark 10,31 in his list of overlap texts because he doubts the saying appeared in Q.[19] However, Matthew records two forms of the saying (Matt 19,30; 20,16), and the Matthean sayings follow the classic pattern of a source doublet. One saying (Matt 19,30) agrees closely with the Marcan saying, and it occurs in the Marcan context at the conclusion of the discussion on riches (Matt 19,23-30 par. Mark 10,23-31). Matthew's second saying (Matt 20,16) agrees with Luke

---

13. Mark 1,38; 3,4; 4,13; 6,31; 7,18; 9,35; 12,16; 14,34.
14. Mark uses ἄλλος 22 times.
15. For ἐπί with the accusative meaning "against" compare Mark 3,24.25.26; 13,8.12; 14,48.
16. Both verbs are Septuagintal; see F. HAUCK, "μοιχεύω," pp. 729-735.
17. N. WALTER, "Paul and the Early Christian Jesus-Tradition," in *Paul and Jesus: Collected Essays*, 1989, pp. 51-80, esp. p. 69.
18. F. NEIRYNCK, "Paul and the Sayings of Jesus," pp. 557-567.
19. R. LAUFEN, *Doppelüberlieferungen*, pp. 88-89.

13,30 against Mark in initially placing "last" before "first."[20] Moreover, Luke 13,30 concludes a section (Luke 13,22-30) that formed a unit in Q.[21] The saying appeared in Q and Mark, and it deserves a place among the overlap texts. We begin by comparing Matthew and Luke.

Matt 20,16	Luke 13,30
οὕτως ἔσονται οἱ ἔσχατοι	καὶ ἰδού εἰσιν ἔσχατοι
πρῶτοι	οἳ ἔσονται πρῶτοι,
καὶ οἱ πρῶτοι	καὶ εἰσιν πρῶτοι
ἔσχατοι.	οἳ ἔσονται ἔσχατοι.

Matthew's οὕτως is attested in Q,[22] but Matthew uses it frequently and so it reflects his redactional style.[23] Matthew uses the Marcan and Q sayings as an *inclusio* to frame the parable of the Laborers in the Vineyard (Matt 20,1-15), and the inferential οὕτως fits perfectly in the concluding member of the *inclusio*.[24] Luke's καὶ ἰδού is also attested in Q, but it too is redactional.[25] Luke uses καὶ ἰδού often in narrative, but he also introduces it into sayings material.[26] The original Q connective was probably a simple καί. Matthew's form of the saying has a single future verb. Luke has three additional forms of the copula, a second future and two presents. Matthew preserves the Q form of the saying since Luke often adds the copula to elliptical sentences to make them fuller.[27] We can now compare Q and Mark.

---

20. J. C. HAWKINS, *Horae Synopticae*, pp. 90-91.

21. Mussner considers Luke 13,22-30 a Lucan composition. See F. MUSSNER, "Das 'Gleichnis' vom gestrengen Mahlherrn (Lk 13,22-30): Ein Beitrag zum Redaktionsverfahren und zur Theologie des Lukas" (1956), in ID., *Praesentia Salutis*, 1967, pp. 113-124. Although Mussner convincingly lays out the evidence for intense Lucan redaction in the section, an original Q composition probably lies behind vv. 24-30. Two features of the text – the use of catchwords and the order of the sayings – prove that the passage already formed a unit in Q. Two catchwords, θύρα and πολύς, connect the sayings, but catchword composition characterizes Q rather than Luke. See H. T. FLEDDERMANN, "Demands of Discipleship," p. 553 n. 44. Matthew's parallel sayings for the most part appear in the same order as in Luke:
(1) Matt 7,13-14 (par. Luke 13,24)
(2) Matt 7,22-23 (par. Luke 13,26-27)
(3) Matt 8,11-12 (par. Luke 13,28-29)
(4) Matt 20,16 (par. Luke 13,30).

22. Q 10,21; 11,30; 12,28.43; 15,7; 17,24.26.

23. Matthew uses οὕτως very frequently (32 10 21 27), and he introduces it into his Marcan source in Matt 17,12 (diff. Mark 9,13); 19,8 (diff. Mark 10,6); 26,40 (diff. Mark 14,37). See U. LUZ, *Evangelium nach Matthäus*, 1. 47; ET: *Matthew 1-7*, p. 64.

24. R. B. VINSON, "A Study of Matthean Doublets with Marcan Parallels," in *SBT* 12 (1982) 239-259, esp. p. 254.

25. Q 11,31.32.

26. Luke introduces καὶ ἰδού into sayings material in Luke 11,41 (diff. Matt 23,26); 23,14.15; 24,49.

27. See Luke 8,30 (diff. Mark 5,9); 17,35 (diff. Matt 24,41); 18,27 (diff. Mark 10,27). See H. J. CADBURY, *Style and Literary Method*, p. 149.

Q 13,30	Mark 10,31
καὶ ἔσονται οἱ ἔσχατοι πρῶτοι καὶ οἱ πρῶτοι ἔσχατοι.	πολλοὶ δὲ ἔσονται πρῶτοι ἔσχατοι καὶ οἱ ἔσχατοι πρῶτοι.

Two considerations show that the Q saying is original. First, the Q statement is a double maxim that reverses the fate of two groups designated by the terms "last" and "first." After καὶ ἔσονται the two halves are formulated identically – the article οἱ appears with the first term followed immediately by the second term without the article. Mark's saying is less symmetrical. In the first half of the saying the first term is modified by "many" while in the second half the first term has the article. The more symmetrical saying is probably original. This is all the more likely because in Mark's form the copula awkwardly separates "many" from the term "first" which it modifies. Second, as with many maxims Q formulates the saying in absolute terms. The two groups experience a complete reversal in their fates – the last will be first and the first last. Mark's form backs away somewhat from the absolute reversal of the two groups. The adjective "many" moderates the reversal, rendering it less absolute. We have seen elsewhere in the overlap texts that Mark frequently has a milder form of a saying than Q, and that the milder formulation betrays Mark's saying as secondary.[28]

Mark's saying is a redaction of the Q saying. Mark uses the saying to conclude the pericope on riches (Mark 10,23-31). He substitutes δέ for καί to provide a better connection to the preceding sayings, and he introduces "many" to soften the Q saying. Because he introduced "many" he drops the article in the first half of the saying. He reverses "last" and "first" to adapt the saying to the context of his gospel. Jesus has just told the disiciples that those who leave all to follow him will receive a hundredfold in this life and everlasting life in the next (Mark 10,29-30). To drive home this point he wants to end with the last being first, so he reverses the order of the two terms to make the saying climax in the last being first. By switching the terms Mark assimilates the saying to a related saying, Mark 9,35, which also begins with "first." Because the differences between Mark and Q can all be traced back to Marcan redaction, Mark's saying is not an independent saying, nor is it a variant that goes back to the oral tradition. Mark depends on Q.

---

28. See the Equipment Rule (Mark 6,8-9), the Cross Saying (Mark 8,34), and the Saying on Tolerance (Mark 9,40).

The saying on the first and the last also appears in the Gospel of Thomas. Th 4 reads:

> Jesus said, "The person old in days will not hesitate to ask an infant of seven days concerning the place (τόπος) of life, and he will live. For many of the first will be last, and they will become a single one."

The synoptic form uses "first" and "last" in both halves of the saying. Thomas' saying only uses the two terms in the first half; in the second half Thomas continues with "and they will become a single one." The second half expresses a familiar theme in Thomas that centers on the "single one." In Thomas' gnostic theology salvation involves a return to the beginning and a return to an original "oneness" symbolized by a child.[29] The Thomas saying reflects Mark's version in two ways. First, Thomas has the terms "first" and "last" in the same order as Mark. Second, Thomas, like Mark, has the adjective "many." Since both features reflect Mark's redaction, Thomas depends on redactional Mark and is secondary to the synoptics. A Greek version of the Thomas saying appears in P. Oxy. 654.21-27.[30]

> [λέγει Ἰη(σοῦ)ς]· οὐκ ἀποκνήσει ἄνθ[ρωπος παλαιὸς ἡμε]ρῶν ἐπερωτῆσε πα[ιδίον ἑπτὰ ἡμε]ρῶν περὶ τοῦ τόπου τῆ[ς ζωῆς καὶ ζή]σετε· ὅτι πολλοὶ ἔσονται π[ρῶτοι ἔσχατοι καὶ] οἱ ἔσχατοι πρῶτοι, καὶ [εἰς ἓν καταντήσου]σιν.

Except for the conjunction δέ the Greek fragment of the saying agrees word for word with Mark's text including Mark's second clause which drops out in the Coptic saying. Since the Greek version preserves the earliest form of the Gospel of Thomas that has survived, it proves that dependence on the synoptics does not represent a later stage in the development of Thomas. We can trace dependence on the synoptics as far back as we can trace Thomas. The saying also gives us a rare glimpse into Thomas' use of canonical sayings. The author of Thomas often selected synoptic sayings for inclusion in the gospel because they allowed a gnostic interpretation to be added. Once added, though, the gnostic interpretation tended to take over as in the present case where Mark's second clause drops out between the Greek original and the Coptic translation.

---

29. See Th 11, 16, 22, 23, 49, 75, 106. See further A. F. J. KLIJN, "The 'Single One' in the Gospel of Thomas," in *JBL* 81 (1962) 271-278; H. C. KEE, "'Becoming a Child' in the Gospel of Thomas," in *JBL* 82 (1963) 307-314.

30. J. A. FITZMYER, "Oxyrhynchus Logoi," pp. 378-381; M. MARCOVICH, "Textual Criticism on the *Gospel of Thomas*," in *JTS* 20 (1969) 53-74, esp. pp. 60-61.

§ 21. On Faith

Mark 11,22-23 (Matt 17,20 par. Luke 17,6)

Matthew records two forms of the Faith Saying. In redacting the Cursing of the Fig Tree, Matthew edits Mark's version of the saying in Matt 21,21 (compare Mark 11,22-23). He attaches the Q Faith Saying to the end of the Cure of the Possessed Boy (Matt 17,20). Since Luke drops the Cursing of the Fig Tree, he uses only the Q saying, incorporating it into a loose collection of sayings on various topics (Luke 17,1-6) which conclude with a parable (Luke 17,7-10). He introduces the saying with "And the apostles said to the Lord, 'Increase our faith'" (Luke 17,5). Even though Matthew and Luke differ considerably in formulating the saying, the main contours of the Q saying emerge fairly easily.[31]

Matt 17,20	Luke 17,6
ἀμὴν γὰρ λέγω ὑμῖν,	εἶπεν δὲ ὁ κύριος·
ἐὰν ἔχητε πίστιν	εἰ ἔχετε πίστιν
ὡς κόκκον σινάπεως,	ὡς κόκκον σινάπεως,
ἐρεῖτε τῷ ὄρει τούτῳ·	ἐλέγετε ἂν τῇ συκαμίνῳ ταύτῃ·
μετάβα ἔνθεν	ἐκριζώθητι
ἐκεῖ,	καὶ φυτεύθητι ἐν τῇ θαλάσσῃ·
καὶ μεταβήσεται·	καὶ ὑπήκουσεν ἂν ὑμῖν.
καὶ οὐδὲν ἀδυνατήσει ὑμῖν.	

Matthew draws ἀμὴν γὰρ λέγω ὑμῖν from Mark 11,23.[32] Luke's εἶπεν δὲ ὁ κύριος is also redactional. Luke uses εἶπεν δέ / εἶπαν δέ fifty-nine times in the Gospel and sixteen times in Acts[33] and ὁ κύριος for Jesus in narrative fourteen times.[34] The full expression εἶπεν δὲ ὁ κύριος occurs in Luke 11,39 and 18,6. The syntax of the saying differs in Matthew and Luke. Matthew has ἐάν with the subjunctive in the protasis and the future in the apodosis. Luke on the other hand has the present

---

31. Günther Schwarz tries to reach behind the four synoptic sayings for an Aramaic original. See G. Schwarz, "Πίστιν ὡς κόκκον σινάπεως," in *BibNot* 25 (1984) 27-35. However, he does not explore the literary relationships between the sayings. They are not four primary witnesses to a source text that lies behind them. Furthermore, it is not certain that an Aramaic original ever existed. Even Q does not give us access to an Aramaic original, for Q's Greek is not translation Greek. See N. Turner, "Q in Recent Thought," in *ExpT* 80 (1968-69) 824-828.

32. S. Schulz, *Q*, p. 466.

33. Luke 1,13.34.38; 4,3.24; 6,8.9.39; 7,48.50; 8,25; 9,9.13.14.20.50.59.60.61.62; 10,18.28; 11,2.39; 12,13.15.16.20.22.41; 13,7.23; 15,3.11.21.22; 16,3.25.27.31; 17,1.6.22; 18,6.9.19.26.28; 19,9.19; 20,13.41; 22,36.52.60.67.70; 24,17.44; Acts 1,7; 3,6; 5,3; 7,1.33; 8,29; 9,5.15; 10,4; 11,12; 12,8; 18,9; 19,4; 21,39; 23,20; 25,10. See J. C. Hawkins, *Horae Synopticae*, pp. 17, 39.

34. Luke 7,13.19; 10,1.39.41; 11,39; 12,42; 13,15; 17,5.6; 18,6; 19,8; 22,61*bis*. See J. C. Hawkins, *Horae Synopticae*, pp. 20, 43.

indicative for a real condition in the protasis, but the imperfect indicative for an unreal condition in the apodosis.[35] The thought is, "If you really have faith like a mustard seed, you would say to this mulberry tree, 'Be uprooted and planted in the sea,' and it would obey you." Schulz and Zmijewski claim that Matthew's ἐάν reproduces Q because Luke often substitutes εἰ for ἐάν.[36] However, no such Lucan tendency can be demonstrated. Luke never substitutes εἰ for ἐάν in editing Mark.[37] Matthew introduced an identical clause, ἐὰν ἔχητε πίστιν (Matt 21,21), in editing Mark's form of the Faith Saying. He introduces the same clause in the Q saying to assimilate the sayings to one another.[38] Matthew's ἐάν with the subjunctive is the most common conditional in the NT.[39] Zmijewski also claims that Matthew's future tenses in the apodosis come from Q. Here again, Zmijewski does not reckon with Matthew's assimilation of the Marcan and Q sayings to each other. The futures come from Mark 11,23 where the final verb is in the future (ἔσται ὑμῖν). In editing Mark 11,23 Matthew recasts the saying and in the process he creates two main clauses. He extends Mark's future to both of these clauses (ποιήσετε ... γενήσεται [Matt 21,21]). He carries over the future tense to the Q saying (ἐρεῖτε ... μεταβήσεται ... ἀδυνατήσει [Matt 17,20]) just as he carried over ἀμὴν λέγω ὑμῖν and ἐὰν ἔχητε πίστιν. On the other hand, the tenses in Luke are used in a very sophisticated way; they clearly reflect the Q original.

The most important difference between Matthew and Luke concerns the underlying image. Matthew speaks of a "mountain" and Luke of a "mulberry tree."[40] Here again Luke reflects Q. Matthew has taken the mountain from Mark. His μετάβα ἔνθεν ἐκεῖ is a simplifying adaptation of either Mark's ἄρθητι καὶ βλήθητι εἰς τὴν θάλασσαν or Luke's ἐκριζώθητι καὶ φυτεύθητι ἐν τῇ θαλάσσῃ, and καὶ μεταβήσεται is a rewriting of Luke's more expressive καὶ ὑπήκουσεν ἂν ὑμῖν.[41] The

---

35. See BDF, § 372 (1); M. ZERWICK, Graecitas Biblica, pp. 90-91; ET: Biblical Greek, pp. 105-106.

36. S. SCHULZ, Q, p. 466; J. ZMIJEWSKI, "Der Glaube und seine Macht: Eine traditions-geschichtliche Untersuchung zu Mt 17,20; 21,21; Mk 11,23; Lk 17,6" (1980), in ID., Das Neue Testament – Quelle christlicher Theologie und Glaubenspraxis, 1986, pp. 265-292, esp. p. 272.

37. H. J. CADBURY, Style and Literary Method, pp. 141-142.

38. W. C. ALLEN, Matthew, p. xxx.

39. BDF, § 371.

40. Luke may not have distinguished the "mulberry tree" (συκάμινος) from the "sycamore tree" (συκαμορέα [Luke 19,4]). See J. A. FITZMYER, Luke, 2. 1143-1144.

41. The verb "obey" is firmly rooted in the synoptic miracle tradition (compare Mark 1,27; 4,41). Although the word does not appear in Q's only full miracle, the concept dominates the account (Q 7,1-10).

verb μεταβαίνω[42] and the adverb ἐκεῖ[43] are Matthean. Matthew's last clause καὶ οὐδὲν ἀδυνατήσει ὑμῖν is a generalizing conclusion that refers to the disciples' inability to cure the afflicted boy (Matt 17,16.19).[44] It is redactional. Matthew simplified the imagery and at the same time radicalized it by taking over Mark's mountain. We have already seen Matthew simplifying the imagery in John's Preaching (Matt 3,11) and the Salt Saying (Matt 5,13). In radicalizing the imagery, though, Matthew disturbed it. Q contrasts the tiny mustard seed with the huge mulberry tree. The mountain disturbs this plant imagery.

So Luke preserves the Q saying unchanged. Matthew intervened repeatedly to assimilate the Q saying to his version of the Marcan saying. He carries over from Matt 21,21 the introductory amen-clause, the conditional ἐὰν ἔχητε πίστιν, the future tense, and the mountain image. He further simplifies the imagery and adapts the saying to the cure of the afflicted boy (Matt 17,14-20). We can now compare Mark and Q.

Q 17,6	Mark 11,22-23
	22 καὶ ἀποκριθεὶς ὁ Ἰησοῦς λέγει αὐτοῖς·
εἰ ἔχετε πίστιν ὡς κόκκον σινάπεως,	ἔχετε πίστιν θεοῦ.
	23 ἀμὴν λέγω ὑμῖν ὅτι
ἐλέγετε ἂν τῇ συκαμίνῳ ταύτῃ· ἐκριζώθητι καὶ φυτεύθητι ἐν τῇ θαλάσσῃ·	ὃς ἂν εἴπῃ τῷ ὄρει τούτῳ· ἄρθητι καὶ βλήθητι εἰς τὴν θάλασσαν, καὶ μὴ διακριθῇ ἐν τῇ καρδίᾳ αὐτοῦ ἀλλὰ πιστεύῃ ὅτι ὃ λαλεῖ γίνεται,
καὶ ὑπήκουσεν ἂν ὑμῖν.	ἔσται αὐτῷ.

Four points prove Mark secondary. First, both sayings contain parenesis, but the Q saying is implicit whereas Mark's saying is explicit. Q's complex conditional sentence contains a promise that implies a parenesis. Mark's imperative "have faith in God" turns the promise into an exhortation and makes explicit what the Q saying only implies.[45] Second, Mark's saying heightens the miraculous. Q talks about transplanting a tree;

---

42. 6 0 1 1. Of the six times Matthew uses the verb, two occur here in the Faith Saying. Once Matthew uses the verb in a redactional summary (Matt 11,1) and three times he introduces the verb into his Marcan source: Matt 8,34 (diff. Mark 5,17); 12,9 (diff. Mark 3,1); 15,29 (diff. Mark 7,31). So all six uses are redactional. See J. C. HAWKINS, Horae Synopticae, p. 6.

43. 31 12 16 11. See U. LUZ, Evangelium nach Matthäus, 1. 40; ET: Matthew 1-7, 58.

44. Compare καὶ οὐκ ἠδυνήθησαν αὐτὸν θεραπεῦσαι (Matt 17,16 diff. Mark 9,18) and διὰ τί ἡμεῖς οὐκ ἠδυνήθημεν ἐκβαλεῖν αὐτό; (Matt 17,19 diff. Mark 9,28).

45. V. HASLER, Amen: Redaktionsgeschichtliche Untersuchung zur Einführungsformel der Herrenworte "Wahrlich ich sage euch", Zürich/Stuttgart: Gotthelf, 1969, p. 43.

Mark about moving a mountain. The change from a mulberry tree to a mountain is intelligible, but it is inconceivable that anyone would change a mountain to a mulberry tree. Third, Q's saying is more graphic than Mark's. The Q verbs "be uprooted" and "be planted" are more picturesque than Mark's common "be taken up" and "be thrown." Q's "and it will obey you" is more striking than Mark's bland "it will be to him." Fourth, Mark's "and does not doubt in his heart but believes that what he says happens" is an interpretative addition. It contains a further reflection on the theme of the saying and betrays Mark's saying as a later development.

We turn now to examine the Marcan redaction. The introductory phrase καὶ ἀποκριθεὶς ὁ Ἰησοῦς is Marcan.[46] Mark takes over the phrase ἔχετε πίστιν from Q, but he turns it into an imperative and adds a genitive θεοῦ – "Have faith in God." In this way he forges a general command that announces the theme of the parenetic section Mark 11,22-25.[47] The addition of the genitive displaces the Q phrase "like a mustard seed." The phrase would have to go in any case because Mark switches to the mountain image. Mark then adds the solemn asseveration formula "amen I say to you." The formula is redactional at least at Mark 3,28. Mark recasts Q's apodosis into a conditional relative clause followed by a future. Since he uses the Faith Saying to comment on the Cursing of the Fig Tree, Q's mulberry tree would clash with the fig tree. Mark had to switch the imagery, but he took the opportunity to heighten the miraculous nature of faith by introducing the mountain. The verbs αἴρω and βάλλω that Mark substitutes for the Q verbs appear often in Mark.[48] The insertion "and does not doubt in his heart but believes that what he says happens" shows several Marcan stylistic features. The μὴ ... ἀλλά construction is Marcan.[49] For "in his heart" compare "in their hearts" (Mark 2,6) and "in your hearts" (Mark 2,8).[50] The insertion picks up the faith theme announced in the introductory verse (Mark 11,22), and it points forward to the following saying.[51] In Mark Jesus commonly insists on the necessity of believing without any hesitation. Jesus rebukes the disciples at the

---

46. Compare Mark 3,33; 9,5; 10,51; 11,14.22; 12,35; 14,48.

47. We have seen other instances of Mark fashioning an introduction in his editing of the overlap texts. In the Beelzebul Controversy Mark introduces his version with a rhetorical question, "How can Satan cast out Satan?" (Mark 3,23). In editing the Cross Saying Mark draws the Q clause on following forward ("If anyone wishes to follow after me..." [Mark 8,34b]) to introduce the theme of the whole section (Mark 8,34-9,1).

48. Statistics for αἴρω: 19 19 20 9; for βάλλω: 34 18 18 5.

49. See Chapter VII above on Mark 9,37.

50. Compare also Mark 3,5; 6,52; 7,6.19.21; 8,17; 12,30.33.

51. Compare "believe that you have received it" (Mark 11,24).

Stilling of the Storm, "Why are you so foolish? Do you not yet have faith?" (Mark 4,40). He tells Jairus, "Do not fear, only believe" (Mark 5,36). The thought is expressed positively in the pericope of the possessed boy, "All things are possible to one who believes" (Mark 9,23). The insertion clearly articulates a favorite Marcan theme. The final phrase ἔσται αὐτῷ assimilates the saying to the following one.[52] The differences between Mark and Q make sense as Marcan changes.

Two closely parallel sayings in the Gospel of Thomas (Th 48, 106) echo the Faith Saying.[53] Th 48 reads:

> Jesus said, "If two make peace with each other in a single house, they will say to the mountain, 'Move from here!' and it will move."

Th 48 reflects Matthew's formulation of the saying in the futures "they will say" and "it will move" and in using the verb "move."

Th 106 is a variant form of the same saying:

> Jesus said, "When you make the two one, you will become the sons of man, and when you say, 'Mountain, move away,' it will move away."

Like Th 48, this saying also reflects Matthew's formulation by using "move" and the future "it will move." Since "move" and the futures are Matthean additions to the saying, both of the Thomas sayings depend on the redactional text of the synoptics.

§ 22. On Asking and Receiving

Mark 11,24 (Matt 7,8 par. Luke 11,10)

In Q a short teaching on the Efficacy of Prayer (Q 11,9-13) follows the Lord's Prayer (Q 11,2-4).[54] The second proverb in the collection overlaps Mark 11,24. Matthew works the Q teaching into the Sermon on the Mount (Matt 7,7-11), and he edits the Marcan saying in Matt 21,22.

Matt 7,8	Luke 11,10
πᾶς γὰρ ὁ αἰτῶν λαμβάνει	πᾶς γὰρ ὁ αἰτῶν λαμβάνει
καὶ ὁ ζητῶν εὑρίσκει	καὶ ὁ ζητῶν εὑρίσκει
καὶ τῷ κρούοντι	καὶ τῷ κρούοντι
ἀνοιγήσεται.	ἀνοιγήσεται.

---

52. Compare ἔσται ὑμῖν (Mark 11,24).
53. M. Fieger, *Thomasevangelium*, pp. 4, 153-155, 263-265.
54. For the structure of the section see R. A. Piper, "Matthew 7,7-11 par. Luke 11,9-13: Evidence of Design and Argument in the Collection of Jesus' Sayings," in J. Delobel (ed.), *Logia*, 1982, pp. 411-418; Id., *Wisdom in the Q-Tradition*, pp. 15-24.

The manuscripts offer three readings for the last verb in Luke 11,10:

(1) ἀνοίγεται   P[75] B D *et al.*
(2) ἀνοιγήσεται   P[45] ℵ C L X θ ψ *et al.*
(3) ἀνοιχθήσεται   A K W Δ Π *et al.*

The choice is between the present and the future (Readings 1 and 2). Since the manuscript evidence doesn't decide the issue, internal arguments must determine the original reading. But here, too, arguments can be found for both readings. The future could assimilate the verse to the future in Luke 11,9, and the present might assimilate the final verb to the other presents in v. 10. As a result the editors of the United Bible Societies' *The Greek New Testament* print both readings.[55] We can only talk of probabilities in a difficult case like this one, but it seems more likely that one future would be changed to conform to the two presents than that a single future would be introduced into a string of presents. If we read ἀνοιγήσεται, then Matthew and Luke agree word for word.

Q 11,10	Mark 11,24
	διὰ τοῦτο λέγω ὑμῖν,
	πάντα ὅσα προσεύχεσθε
πᾶς γὰρ ὁ αἰτῶν	καὶ αἰτεῖσθε,
λαμβάνει	πιστεύετε ὅτι ἐλάβετε,
	καὶ ἔσται ὑμῖν.
καὶ ὁ ζητῶν εὑρίσκει	
καὶ τῷ κρούοντι ἀνοιγήσεται.	

The Q saying grounds (γάρ) the preceding saying that opens the small collection in Q 11,9-13.[56] The proverb uses three metaphors from daily life to show that effort always attains its end. Each metaphor involves a pair of terms – "ask/receive," "seek/find," and "knock/open." The initial πᾶς makes the saying extremely general. Q seems to say that asking inevitably leads to receiving. "For everyone who asks receives and the one who seeks finds and to the one knocking, it will be opened." Although the saying does not mention prayer, the author of Q understood it to refer to prayer as the context shows. Q joins the collection of sayings in Q 11,9-13 to the Lord's Prayer (Q 11,2-4), and the final saying in the collection (Q 11,13) refers "asking" to the heavenly Father.[57]

55. B. M. METZGER, *Textual Commentary*, pp. 156-157. See also J. A. FITZMYER, *Luke*, 2. 915.
56. "Ask and it will be given to you; seek and you will find; knock and it will be opened to you" (Q 11,9).
57. See R. A. PIPER, "Matthew 7,7-11 par. Luke 11,9-13," p. 414; ID., *Wisdom in the Q-Tradition*, p. 19.

In comparing Mark and Q two points stand out. First, the Q saying, as we have seen, uses three pairs of metaphorical terms taken from daily life. Mark's saying uses only one pair of terms from daily life, "ask" and "receive." The Marcan saying, though, also has a pair of theological terms, "pray" and "believe," that interpret the everyday terms. The interpretative terms are secondary. Second, not only do the theological terms interpret the metaphor, they also forestall a possible misunderstanding. Mark's saying initially appears as general as the Q saying. Mark begins with "everything (πάντα) which you pray for and ask for ..." (v. 24a), but he goes on to limit the asking, "believe that you have received it ..." (v. 24b). Not every asking leads to receiving. Receiving comes from believing. We have seen elsewhere other examples of Mark's version of an overlap text toning down extreme statements in Q.[58] So also in the Saying on Asking and Receiving Mark's carefully nuanced text interprets the metaphor, explicitly theologizes, and avoids any misunderstanding by limiting extreme claims. It is clearly secondary to the Q saying.

Granted that Mark is secondary to Q, does Mark reflect redactional Q? Could not Mark have received the saying from the oral tradition? We can rule out the oral tradition in this instance because Mark's interpretation shows that he knows the Q context of the saying. The Q saying itself only presents three metaphors that extol the value of effort. The context in Q, not the saying itself, applies the metaphors to prayer. By elaborating this interpretation that centers on prayer, Mark shows that he knows the setting of the saying in Q.

The Faith Saying (Mark 11,22-23) and the Saying on Asking and Receiving (Mark 11,24) form a cluster in Mark.[59] Mark uses the second saying to comment on the first, and he partially assimilates the sayings to each other. He also introduces the second saying with a formula (διὰ τοῦτο λέγω ὑμῖν) that links the two. The phrase διὰ τοῦτο does not occur frequently in Mark (elsewhere only Mark 6,14; 12,24); however, the context demands it here because Mark wants to generalize what he has said about mountain-moving faith and to further link faith with prayer. To generalize Mark interprets Q's "asking" with πάντα ὅσα προσεύχεσθε καὶ αἰτεῖσθε.[60] The πάντα comes from Q's πᾶς, and

---

58. See the Mustard Seed (Mark 4,30-32), the Equipment Rule (Mark 6,8), the Cross Saying (Mark 8,34), and the Saying on Tolerance (Mark 9,40).

59. We have seen that Mark clusters two overlap texts in Chapter 3, five in the Parable Discourse, three in the Caesarea Philippi pericope, and four in the Discipleship Discourse. We will see that he also collects five overlap texts in the Eschatological Discourse.

60. Compare Q's πᾶς (Q 11,10a).

αἰτέω picks up the verb from the first Q pair. Prayer comes from the context of the Q saying, and it further develops a Marcan interest. Mark insists on prayer also in the Cure of the Possessed Boy (Mark 9,29). Mark interprets Q's "receiving" by introducing the concept of faith, πιστεύετε ὅτι ἐλάβετε. The first verb, πιστεύω, picks up Mark's introductory exhortation "Have faith in God" (Mark 11,22). The second verb is the second member of the first Q pair "ask/receive." Mark corrects Q. Not all asking will result in receiving, but only an asking accompanied by prayer and a receiving conditioned by faith. Since Mark has drawn "receive" into a ὅτι-clause, he ends the statement with καὶ ἔσται ὑμῖν. This last clause and the ὅτι-clause assimilate the end of v. 24 to the end of v. 23.[61] This is not the first time we have found Mark as-similating one Q text to another. In the Parable Discourse he assimilates the Lamp Saying and the saying on revealing what is hidden to one another (Mark 4,21-22). He also assimilates the Cross Saying and the saying on Losing One's Life (Mark 8,34-35).

The tiny cluster comprised of the Faith Saying and the Saying on Asking and Receiving combines two themes – faith and prayer – that Mark also combines in the Cure of the Possessed Boy (Mark 9,14-29). The cure itself centers on faith (vv. 19, 23, 24); but when the disciples question Jesus about their inability to expel the spirit, Jesus' reply insists on prayer (Mark 9,28-29). Mark, not some pre-Marcan redactor, drew together the two Q texts that make up this cluster.

The Gospel of Thomas contains parallels to the Q Saying on Asking and Receiving in Th 2 and 94.[62] The Coptic text of Th 2 reads:

> Jesus said, "Let him who seeks not stop seeking until he finds. When he finds, he will be disturbed. When he is disturbed, he will marvel, and will reign over all."

A different form of this saying is preserved in *P. Oxy.* 654.5-9:[63]

> [λέγει Ἰη(σοῦ)ς·] μὴ παυσάσθω ὁ ζη[τῶν τοῦ ζητεῖν ἕως ἂν] εὕρῃ, καὶ ὅταν εὕρῃ, [θαμβηθήσεται καὶ θαμ]βηθεὶς βασιλεύσῃ κα[ὶ βασι-λεύσας ἀναπα]ήσεται.

The underlying form of both sayings is the chain saying. A chain saying begins with a pair of terms, but then the second member of the pair forms the first member of a new pair and so on. The Coptic form is

---

61. Compare πιστεύετε ὅτι ἐλάβετε, καὶ ἔσται ὑμῖν (v. 24) with ἀλλὰ πιστεύῃ ὅτι ὃ λαλεῖ γίνεται, ἔσται αὐτῷ (v. 23).

62. A closely related saying appears in Th 92. However, Th 92 is formulated in the second person plural rather than the third person singular, so it parallels Q 11,9 rather than Q 11,10.

63. J. A. FITZMYER, "Oxyrhynchus Logoi," pp. 370-373.

somewhat longer and contains a different ending than the Greek saying. The Greek form uses five terms – seek, find, marvel, rule, rest. The Coptic saying adds "be disturbed" before "marvel," and the final clause does not pick up "marvel" before concluding with "and will reign over all." Neither form of the saying reflects Mark's text, and the contact with Q 11,10 is limited to the terms "seek" and "find." The synoptic saying provided only the first pair of terms which Thomas used to begin the chain which develops gnostic ideology.[64]

Th 94 contains a second parallel:

> Jesus [said], "One who seeks will find, and to [one who knocks] it will be opened."

This text is much closer to the Q saying. It picks up the second and third metaphors of the Q saying. Matthew and Luke agree word for word in this saying, and Thomas shows no peculiarities, so it is not possible to draw any conclusions from this saying about the dependence or in-dependence of the tradition underlying Thomas.

§ 23. First Places

Mark 12,38-39 (Matt 23,6-7 par. Luke 11,43)

The Woes against the Pharisees (Q 11,39-44.46-52) followed the Say-ings on Light (Q 11,33-35) in Q. Luke takes over the Q saying in the Woes, and he edits Mark's saying in Luke 20,46. Matthew delayed the Woes to conflate them with Mark's Warning about the Scribes (Mark 12,37b-40). Matthew's conflation complicates the reconstruction of the original Q text.

Matt 23,6-7	Luke 11,43
	οὐαὶ ὑμιν τοῖς Φαρισαίοις,
6 φιλοῦσιν δὲ τὴν πρωτοκλισίαν	ὅτι ἀγαπᾶτε
ἐν τοῖς δείπνοις	
καὶ τὰς πρωτοκαθεδρίας	τὴν πρωτοκαθεδρίαν
ἐν ταῖς συναγωγαῖς	ἐν ταῖς συναγωγαῖς
7 καὶ τοὺς ἀσπασμοὺς	καὶ τοὺς ἀσπασμοὺς
ἐν ταῖς ἀγοραῖς	ἐν ταῖς ἀγοραῖς.
καὶ καλεῖσθαι	
ὑπὸ τῶν ἀνθρώπων ῥαββί.	

Luke's saying appears in a series of woes (Luke 11,42-52). Since Matthew himself soon breaks into a series of woes (Matt 23,13-33), the

---

64. M. Fieger, *Thomasevangelium*, p. 22.

saying was probably a woe saying in Q. Luke addresses the woe to the Pharisees whereas Matthew throughout Chapter 23 refers to the "scribes and Pharisees."[65] Since Matthew has brought the Q saying to the place of Mark's Warning about the Scribes, he combines Mark's scribes and Q's Pharisees. Luke can also link the scribes and Pharisees so he had no reason to avoid the combination here.[66] The Q woe was probably directed to the Pharisees. In Q "Pharisees" was probably in the vocative case instead of Luke's dative since Matthew's woes (Matt 23,13-36) all use the vocative whereas Luke vacillates between the dative and the vocative in Luke 6,24-26. Matthew preserves the original main verb φιλέω, although the verb would have been in the second person plural in Q. Luke introduces φιλούντων in his redaction of Mark 12,38 in Luke 20,46. The word could be a reminiscence of Q since Luke frequently exchanges words between Q and Mark in the overlap texts.[67] Luke's own ἀγαπᾶτε is an assimilation to ἀγάπην in Luke 11,42. The phrase "the first seat at the feasts" is found in Matthew but not in Luke. It probably stood in Q, for if Matthew had borrowed it from Mark it would appear in the plural. Luke gives a fuller treatment of the first seat in Luke 14,7-14 so he passes over it here. Luke's singular πρωτοκαθεδρίαν preserves the Q form of the second object; Matthew's plural is an assimilation to Mark. So in Q the first two objects were in the singular. Matthew's last phrase "and be called 'Rabbi' by men," is probably a Matthean addition. It is true that Luke avoids the title "Rabbi" consistently.[68] However, the infinitive phrase interrupts the sequence of simple noun objects; it is an intrusion, a Matthean preparation of the discussion that follows in Matt 23,8-12. We can now compare Mark and Q.

Q 11,43	Mark 12,38-39
οὐαὶ ὑμῖν, Φαρισαίοι,	38 βλέπετε ἀπὸ τῶν γραμματέων
ὅτι φιλεῖτε	τῶν θελόντων ἐν στολαῖς περιπατεῖν
τὴν πρωτοκλισίαν ἐν τοῖς δείπνοις	καὶ ἀσπασμοὺς ἐν ταῖς ἀγοραῖς
καὶ τὴν πρωτοκαθεδρίαν	39 καὶ πρωτοκαθεδρίας
ἐν ταῖς συναγωγαῖς	ἐν ταῖς συναγωγαῖς
καὶ τοὺς ἀσπασμοὺς ἐν ταῖς ἀγοραῖς.	καὶ πρωτοκλισίας ἐν τοῖς δείπνοις.

65. Matthew uses the stereotyped phrase "scribes and Pharisees" nine times (Matt 5,20; 12,38; 23,2.13.15.23.25.27.29). All nine passages name the scribes first. The reverse order is found only in Matt 15,1 in dependence on Mark 7,1.

66. Luke 5,21.30; 6,7; 11,53; 15,2; compare Acts 23,9. See J. SCHMID, *Matthäus und Lukas*, p. 325.

67. For example, Luke picks up "silver" from the Q Equipment Rule (compare Matt 10,9) and introduces it into his redaction of Mark in Luke 9,3.

68. J. SCHMID, *Matthäus und Lukas*, p. 323.

There are several indications that the Q saying is original. First, the Q saying shows a nice climax. The Pharisees seek places of honor in the private domain of the house, in the religious public domain of the synagogue, and in the general public domain of the market place. In Mark this climax is destroyed. Second, the Q saying is a woe addressed to the Pharisees. In Mark the saying is a warning addressed to the crowds. The Q audience and form are original. It is easier to imagine Mark changing a woe addressed to the Pharisees into a warning about the scribes than the reverse, especially since the scribes are the chief adversaries of Jesus in Mark.[69] Third, Q's singulars are more plausible than Mark's plurals. How many first places can there be? Fourth, the grammar of the Q saying is straightforward. A woe leads into an explanatory ὅτι-clause with the verb in the indicative and three object phrases. Mark's grammar is awkward. His θελόντων works well with the infinitive object but is less appropriate with the noun objects. Luke sensed the difficulty and cleared it up by introducing φιλούντων in his redaction of Mark's saying (Luke 20,46). All of these considerations throw Mark downstream from Q.

We turn to Mark's redaction. Mark transformed the woe addressed to the Pharisees into a warning to the crowd about the scribes. He begins with an imperative, "Beware of the scribes who are fond of walking around in long robes..." (Mark 12,38b). He introduces the warning with βλέπετε, an expression he uses on three other occasions.[70] Before introducing the Q objects Mark proceeds with the participle θελόντων and an infinitive phrase "to walk in long robes." The verb θέλω with an infinitive occurs often in Mark.[71] The long robes characterize the scribes as seeking honor as στολαί is often used in the Septuagint to refer to particularly splendid clothing.[72] After describing the scribes' clothing,

---

69. Mark refers to the scribes 21 times (Mark 1,22; 2,6.16; 3,22; 7,1.5; 8,31; 9,11.14; 10,33; 11,18.27; 12,28.32.35.38; 14,1.43.53; 15,1.31), to the high priests 14 times (Mark 8,31; 10,33; 11,18.27; 14,1.10.43.53.55; 15,1.3.10.11.31), the Pharisees 12 times (Mark 2,16.18*bis*.24; 3,6; 7,1.3.5; 8,11.15; 10,2; 12,13), the elders 5 times (Mark 8,31; 11,27; 14,43.53: 15,1), and the Herodians twice (Mark 3,6; 12,13). See A. F. J. KLIJN, "Scribes Pharisees Highpriests and Elders in the New Testament," in *NT* 3 (1959) 260-267; J. C. WEBER, JR., "Jesus' Opponents in the Gospel of Mark," in *JBR* 34 (1966) 214-222; M. J. COOK, *Mark's Treatment of the Jewish Leaders* (NTSup, 51), Leiden: Brill, 1978, pp. 63-67; H. FLEDDERMANN, "Warning about the Scribes," p. 53 n. 4.

70. Mark 8,15 (with ἀπό); 13,5.9. See T. J. WEEDEN, "The Heresy that Necessitated Mark's Gospel," in *ZNW* 59 (1968) 145-158, esp. p. 151 n. 15.

71. Mark 6,19.26.48; 7,24; 8,34.35; 9,35; 10,44. Two of these texts are overlap texts in which Mark introduced the construction redactionally (Mark 8,34.35).

72. Gen 41,42; Exod 28,2; 29,21; 31,10; 2 Chr 18,9; 23,13; Esth 6,8; 8,15; 1 Macc 6,15; Jonah 3,6. Rengstorf refers στολαί to a special sabbath clothing, but Mark usually explains Jewish customs to his non-Jewish readers, so Rengstorf's interpretation appears improbable. See K. H. RENGSTORF, "Die στολαί der Schriftgelehrten: Eine Erläuterung

Mark characterizes their behavior by picking up the three objects from the Q saying. He switches the first and third objects to fit his new context. Greetings in the market places are brought into contact with walking around in long robes. Neither of the other two noun objects would have worked as well. The switch also brings the first places at the feasts into contact with the further charge that the scribes devour widows' houses (Mark 12,40). Mark changed the singulars to plurals and dropped the article with the objects. Mark does not use the article in lists, and he tends to group singulars and plurals in lists.[73]

The five sayings in Mark 10-12 fit what by now has become a familiar pattern. All five Marcan sayings appear later than their Q counterparts. We can trace the differences between Mark and Q to Mark's redaction. At no point do we need the oral tradition to account for the differences. The Saying on Asking and Receiving (Mark 11,24) also shows that Mark knew the Q redaction because Mark interprets the saying by centering it on prayer, an interpretation that comes from the Q context of the saying not the saying itself. Two of the sayings appear joined together and assimilated to one another in a small cluster on faith and prayer (Mark 11,22-24). The assimilation articulates a familiar Marcan theme – the necessity of faith – so we can trace the cluster to Mark and rule out a pre-Marcan redactor.

zu Mark. 12,38," in *Abraham unser Vater: FS Otto Michel*, 1963, pp. 383-404; H. FLED-DERMANN, "Warning about the Scribes," pp. 54-57.
    73. Mark 7,21-22; 10,29-30. See H. FLEDDERMANN, "Warning about the Scribes," p. 60 n. 39.

THE ESCHATOLOGICAL DISCOURSE

In Mark's Eschatological Discourse (Mark 13,1-37) we encounter the final cluster of overlap texts. Five overlap texts exploring a variety of themes punctuate the discourse and lead the reader to the brink of the passion. The first two texts follow one another immediately, forming a smaller cluster within the larger grouping of overlap texts.

§ 24. ON CONFESSING

Mark 13,11 (Matt 10,19-20 par. Luke 12,11-12)

The Q saying originally concluded the section on Fearless Confession (Q 12,2-12). Matthew transferred Mark 13,9-13 to the Mission Discourse (compare Matt 10,17-22), and in the process he conflated the Marcan and Q sayings.

Matt 10,19-20	Luke 12,11-12
19 ὅταν δὲ παραδῶσιν ὑμᾶς,	11 ὅταν δὲ εἰσφέρωσιν ὑμᾶς ἐπὶ τὰς συναγωγὰς καὶ τὰς ἀρχὰς καὶ τὰς ἐξουσίας,
μὴ μεριμνήσητε πῶς	μὴ μεριμνήσητε πῶς ἢ τί ἀπολογήσησθε
ἢ τί λαλήσητε· δοθήσεται γὰρ ὑμῖν	ἢ τί εἴπητε· 12 τὸ γὰρ ἅγιον πνεῦμα διδάξει ὑμᾶς
ἐν ἐκείνῃ τῇ ὥρᾳ τί λαλήσητε·	ἐν αὐτῇ τῇ ὥρᾳ ἃ δεῖ εἰπεῖν.
20 οὐ γὰρ ὑμεῖς ἐστε οἱ λαλοῦντες ἀλλὰ τὸ πνεῦμα τοῦ πατρὸς ὑμῶν τὸ λαλοῦν ἐν ὑμῖν.	

Matthew's παραδῶσιν comes from Mark (compare Matt 10,17 par. Mark 13,9). Luke's εἰσφέρωσιν comes from Q. The verb is attested in Q (Q 11,4), and it is somewhat unusual for Luke. Luke uses εἰσφέρω twice for carrying the paralytic (Luke 5,18.19) and once for bringing in ideas (Acts 17,20), but only in this passage and in the other Q passage (Q 11,4) does it have the meaning "to lead into." Although Luke on occasion uses φέρω with the meaning "to lead" (Luke 15,23; Acts 14,13), he usually prefers ἄγω or one of its compounds. Mark regularly uses φέρω to mean "lead," and Luke usually changes the verb when he edits Mark.[1] The verb "to lead into" demands a prepositional phrase. Luke's ἐπὶ τὰς συναγωγάς poses no problems because the noun is attested in Q (Q 11,43). Luke probably added the other two objects. In Luke 20,20 Luke introduces ἀρχή and ἐξουσία into the Marcan context (compare Mark 12,13). The additions make sense. Luke expands the Q reference to synagogues to include also pagan courts. Matthew dispenses with the prepositional phrase because he follows Mark, and in Mark the context already specified where the disciples would be handed over (Matt 10,17-18 par. Mark 13,9).

With ἢ τί ἀπολογήσησθε Luke doubles the original Q formulation. Luke alone of the gospel writers uses the verb ἀπολογέομαι and the noun ἀπολογία,[2] and he introduces the verb into Marcan material in Luke 21,14 (diff. Mark 13,11).[3] Matthew's λαλήσητε comes from Mark. Luke shows no tendency to avoid λαλέω and he even favors it for prophetic speech, so Luke's εἴπητε preserves the Q verb.[4]

The second half of the saying is difficult to reconstruct. Schulz claims that Luke's τὸ γὰρ ἅγιον πνεῦμα διδάξει ὑμᾶς ἐν αὐτῇ τῇ ὥρᾳ preserves the original Q text. He points out among other things that, although διδάσκω is common in Luke, only in this verse does the Holy Spirit appear as subject.[5] Luke, though, probably introduced the Holy Spirit into the Q saying under the influence of Mark. The style, vocabulary, and content of v. 12 are Lucan. Luke also introduced the Holy Spirit into another Q text (Q 11,13), and he omits a second article frequently in referring to the Holy Spirit.[6] Luke uses διδάσκω often;[7] the expression αὐτὸς ὁ with a noun denoting time is found only in Luke-Acts in the

---

1. See Luke 4,40 (diff. Mark 1,32); 9,28 (diff. Mark 9,2); 9,38 (diff. Mark 9,17); 9,41 (diff. Mark 9,19); 9,42 (diff. Mark 9,20); 19,30 (diff. Mark 11,2); 19,35 (diff. Mark 11,7); 23,1 (diff. Mark 15,1); 23,33 (diff. Mark 15,22). See H. J. CADBURY, *Style and Literary Method*, p. 174; C. H. TURNER, "Marcan Usage: Notes, Critical and Exegetical, on the Second Gospel," in *JTS* 26 (1924-25) 12-20, esp. pp. 12-14; F. NEIRYNCK, *Minor Agreements*, p. 279; J. A. FITZMYER, "The Use of *Agein* and *Pherein* in the Synoptic Gospels," in *Festschrift to Honor F. Wilbur Gingrich*, 1972, pp. 147-160.

2. Statistics for ἀπολογέομαι: 0 0 2 6; for ἀπολογία: 0 0 0 2. See J. C. HAWKINS, *Horae Synopticae*, p. 28.

3. See J. LAMBRECHT, *Redaktion*, p. 117.

4. *Ibid.*, p. 118. Statistics on λαλέω: 26 19 31 59. On Luke's use of the verb, see H. JASCHKE, "'λαλεῖν' bei Lukas: Ein Beitrag zur lukanischen Theologie," in *BZ* 15 (1971) 109-114.

5. S. SCHULZ, *Q*, p. 443.

6. See Chapter III above on Mark 3,28-30.

7. 14 17 17 16.

NT;[8] and δεῖ is characteristic of Luke.[9] The thought of the sentence has a close parallel in Acts 2,4: "as the Spirit gave them ability." So Luke's v. 12 is redactional. Matthew's v. 19b essentially preserves the Q text. The form δοθήσεται appears in three other Q texts (Q 11,9.29; 19,26), and in Q 11,9 it appears with ὑμῖν. The only change Matthew introduced is again to switch to Mark's verb λαλέω. Matthew's v. 20 comes from Mark 13,11.

Q 12,11-12	Mark 13,11
11 ὅταν δὲ εἰσφέρωσιν ὑμᾶς ἐπὶ τὰς συναγωγάς, μὴ μεριμνήσητε πῶς ἢ τί εἴπητε·	καὶ ὅταν ἄγωσιν ὑμᾶς παραδιδόντες, μὴ προμεριμνᾶτε τί λαλήσητε,
12 δοθήσεται γὰρ ὑμῖν ἐν ἐκείνῃ τῇ ὥρᾳ τί εἴπητε.	ἀλλ᾽ ὃ ἐὰν δοθῇ ὑμῖν ἐν ἐκείνῃ τῇ ὥρᾳ τοῦτο λαλεῖτε· οὐ γάρ ἐστε ὑμεῖς οἱ λαλοῦντες ἀλλὰ τὸ πνεῦμα τὸ ἅγιον.

There are several signs that Mark is secondary. First, Q's ὅταν-clause specifies where the persons addressed will be taken; Mark's clause leaves this open because Mark has designated the venue in v. 9. Without any reference to a specific forum like the synagogues, Mark's clause betrays itself as a secondary reworking to fit an already developed context. Second, in the ὅταν-clause Mark's participle παραδιδόντες clarifies why those addressed are being led. Third, in the main clause Mark's verb προμεριμνᾶτε makes explicit a nuance implied in the Q main verb, and his construction is simpler. Fourth, the Q γάρ-clause states that the disciples will be inspired, but the source of the inspiration is only implied in the passive verb form (theological passive). Mark's text makes the source of inspiration explicit with a further clause.

Mark is secondary to Q, but does Mark depend on Q? Neither form of the saying is an aphorism that could be handed on separately. Both forms begin with a ὅταν-clause which presupposes that the context has described some situation of persecution or witnessing which the ὅταν-clause resumes. The Q saying appears in such a context in the section on Fearless Confessing (Q 12,2-12). Three other Marcan overlap texts have Q parallels from this section.[10] In each case Mark's text was secondary

---

8. Luke 2,38; 10,21; 12,12; 13,1.31; 20,19; 23,12; 24,13.33; Acts 16,18; 22,13. In Luke 20,19 Luke adds the expression in redacting Mark 12,12. See J. C. HAWKINS, *Horae Synopticae*, p. 16; J. JEREMIAS, *Sprache*, p. 98.
9. 8 6 18 22.
10. See Mark 3,28-30 (par. Q 12,10); 4,22 (par. Q 12,2); 8,38 (par. Q 12,8-9).

to the Q text. But the Q section is itself a composite made up of various sayings. The conclusion seems inevitable. Mark had the Q section on Fearless Confessing before him when he composed his gospel, and he drew on it repeatedly for material in his own sayings compositions. Mark knew and used Q.

If we now examine the saying phrase by phrase, the Marcan redaction will become clear. Mark joins the saying to the preceding by the co-ordinating καί. Q's δέ would be more appropriate, but parataxis is so common in Mark that we must see his hand here. Mark anticipated the logion in v. 9.[11] With the ὅταν-clause he reaches back to v. 9 and sum-marizes it.[12] Since he has already specified where the disciples will wit-ness in v. 9, Mark can dispense with a description of the forum in v. 11. As a result he has to abandon Q's εἰσφέρωσιν. He substitutes ἄγωσιν and adds the participle παραδιδόντες which connects the verse to the handing over theme that runs through his gospel.[13] The participle παρα-διδόντες especially reaches back to v. 9 and forward to v. 12. Mark switches from μεριμνήσητε to προμεριμνᾶτε to draw out an implied nuance. His present emphasizes repeated action. He also simplifies the construction by dropping πῶς ἤ, and he substitutes λαλήσητε for εἴπητε. The witness theme dominates the whole section Mark 13,9-11, and Mark's λαλέω fits this theme better than Q's λέγω.[14] To further emphasize the theme Mark continues the imperative "do not worry beforehand" with a second imperative "say this." To make room for this imperative Mark must abandon Q's future passive δοθήσεται for a con-ditional relative clause – "but whatever is given to you in that hour." The resumptive pronoun τοῦτο leads into the second imperative which again employs λαλέω. The new clause enables Mark to continue with "for it is not you who will be speaking, but the Holy Spirit." Q provided the γάρ, and Mark uses λαλέω for the third time in the verse, this time as a participle. The Holy Spirit specifies the source of inspiration which the Q saying concealed in a theological passive. Clearly Marcan is the double use of the dual terms μή ... ἀλλά and οὐ ... ἀλλά.[15] Again when we compare Mark's text and the Q saying, the differences between them all stem from Mark's redaction. Furthermore, by using a form of παραδίδωμι

---

11. "As for yourselves, beware; for they will hand you over to councils; and you will be beaten in synagogues; and you will stand before governors and kings because of me, as a testimony to them" (Mark 13,9).

12. J. LAMBRECHT, *Redaktion*, p. 119.

13. Mark 1,14; 3,19; 9,31; 10,33; 13,9.11.12; 14,10.11.18.21.41.42.44; 15,1.10.15.

14. Compare 1 Thess 2,2.4.16. Mark uses λαλέω mostly in redactional verses (Mark 1,34; 2,2; 4,33-34; 5,35-36; 8,32; 11,23; 12,1; 14,9.43).

15. F. NEIRYNCK, *Duality in Mark*, pp. 90-94.

Mark links this verse to the immediately following verse which also has a Q overlap.

§ 25. FAMILY DIVISION

Mark 13,12 (Matt 10,34-36 par. Luke 12,51-53)

Matthew works the Q section into the Mission Discourse. Luke creates a special introduction for the section (Luke 12,49-50) and fits the new unit into the Journey Narrative.

Matt 10,34-36	Luke 12,51-53
34 μὴ νομίσητε ὅτι ἦλθον βαλεῖν εἰρήνην ἐπὶ τὴν γῆν· οὐκ ἦλθον βαλεῖν εἰρήνην ἀλλὰ μάχαιραν.	51 δοκεῖτε ὅτι εἰρήνην παρεγενόμην δοῦναι ἐν τῇ γῇ; οὐχί, λέγω ὑμῖν, ἀλλ᾽ ἢ διαμερισμόν.
	52 ἔσονται γὰρ ἀπὸ τοῦ νῦν πέντε ἐν ἑνὶ οἴκῳ διαμεμερισμένοι, τρεῖς ἐπὶ δυσὶν καὶ δύο ἐπὶ τρισίν,
35 ἦλθον γὰρ διχάσαι ἄνθρωπον κατὰ τοῦ πατρὸς αὐτοῦ	53 διαμερισθήσονται πατὴρ ἐπὶ υἱῷ καὶ υἱὸς ἐπὶ πατρί,
καὶ θυγατέρα κατὰ τῆς μητρὸς αὐτῆς καὶ νύμφην κατὰ τῆς πενθερᾶς αὐτῆς, 36 καὶ ἐχθροὶ τοῦ ἀνθρώπου οἱ οἰκιακοὶ αὐτοῦ.	μήτηρ ἐπὶ τὴν θυγατέρα καὶ θυγάτηρ ἐπὶ τὴν μητέρα πενθερὰ ἐπὶ τὴν νύμφην αὐτῆς καὶ νύμφη ἐπὶ τὴν πενθεράν.

Although Matthew and Luke express the same thought, they differ greatly in the construction and wording of the passage. Matthew and Luke cast the first sentence into patterns that each uses in his *Sondergut*. Matthew has already used μὴ νομίσητε ὅτι ἦλθον ... οὐκ ἦλθον ... ἀλλά in Matt 5,17, a passage that is almost certainly redactional; and Luke's δοκεῖτε ὅτι ... οὐχί, λέγω ὑμῖν ... ἀλλά recurs in Luke 13,2-3.4-5. Matthew's μὴ νομίσητε is probably redactional as the parallel with Matt 5,17 suggests.[16] Luke uses νομίζω nine times in Luke-Acts (with ὅτι in Acts 21,29), so he had no reason to eliminate it.[17] Luke uses δοκέω ten times in his gospel and nine times in Acts, but the word is found twice in Q,[18] and δοκεῖτε is a

---

16. Compare also Matt 20,10 where Matthew uses νομίζω with ὅτι.

17. Luke 2,44; 3,23; Acts 7,25; 8,20; 14,19; 16,13.27; 17,29; 21,29.

18. Compare Q 3,8; 12,40. Luke dropped the word from John's Preaching, but Matthew almost certainly preserves the Q text. See H. FLEDDERMANN, "Beginning of Q," p. 156.

catchword linking this pericope to the preceding one in Q.[19] Luke usually avoids rhetorical questions, so his question is probably original, especially since rhetorical questions appear regularly in Q.[20] Several considerations demonstrate that Matthew preserves the Q ὅτι-clause. Luke shows that he knows Matthew's clause in Luke 12,49 (πῦρ ἦλθον βαλεῖν ἐπὶ τὴν γῆν). In his own ὅτι-clause Luke substituted παρεγενόμην for ἦλθον,[21] and he softened the Semitizing βαλεῖν to the less graphic δοῦναι. This last change led him to switch ἐπὶ τὴν γῆν to ἐν τῇ γῇ. In both v. 49 and v. 51 Luke moved the object forward for emphasis.[22] Matthew preserves the original word order.

Matt 10,34b also preserves the Q wording of the next clause. Luke frequently uses the construction οὐχί ... ἀλλά, and he inserts λέγω ὑμῖν for emphasis.[23] He also softens μάχαιραν to διαμερισμόν. The noun διαμερισμός depends on the verb διαμερίζω Luke introduces in vv. 52-53, and it reflects his fondness for nouns ending in -μός.[24]

The second part of the passage (Matt 10,35-36 par. Luke 12,52-53) presents enormous difficulties. Matt 10,36 and Luke 12,52 agree roughly in thought. It might seem that Luke 12,52 is the original Q wording and that Matthew has altered Q to conform it more closely to Micah 7,6 LXX. However, Matthew is not that close to the Septuagint, and the wording of Luke 12,52 suggests that the verse is a Lucan redactional formulation. Luke uses a periphrastic construction with the perfect participle forty-five times in Luke-Acts.[25] The phrase ἀπὸ τοῦ νῦν is Lucan, appearing

19. The catchwords δοκέω, ἐπί, and ἔρχομαι link Q 12,39-40.42b-46 to Q 12,51-53 (compare v. 40 with v. 51; vv. 42b.44 with vv. 51.53; vv. 39.40.43 with vv. 51.52).

20. See the discussion of the Mustard Seed in Chapter IV above.

21. The verb παραγίνομαι is characteristic of Luke (3 1 8 20). He introduces παραγίνομαι into his Marcan source in Luke 22,52 (diff. Mark 14,48), and he replaces ἔρχομαι with παραγίνομαι in Luke 8,19 (compare Mark 3,31) and Luke 19,16 (compare Matt 25,20 and Q 19,18.20). See J. C. Hawkins, *Horae Synopticae*, p. 21; H. J. Cadbury, *Style and Literary Method*, pp. 177-178; J. Jeremias, *Sprache*, pp. 152-153.

22. See E. Haenchen, *Apostelgeschichte*, pp. 70-71; ET: *Acts*, pp. 78-79.

23. Luke uses οὐχί ... ἀλλά in Luke 1,60; 12,51; 13,3.5; 16,30, and he joins it with λέγω ὑμῖν in Luke 12,51; 13,3.5. Matthew and Mark never use the construction. See J. C. Hawkins, *Horae Synopticae*, pp. 21, 45. On λέγω ὑμῖν see F. Neirynck, "Recent Developments," pp. 436-449.

24. Compare ἁγνισμός (Acts 21,26), ἀπαρτισμός (Luke 14,28), γογγυσμός (Acts 6,1), διαλογισμός (Luke 2,35; 5,22; 6,8; 9,46.47; 24,38), ἐπισιτισμός (Luke 9,12), ἱματισμός (Luke 7,25; 9,29; Acts 20,33), πειρασμός (Luke 4,13; 8,13; 11,4; 22,28. 40.46; Acts 20,19). The nouns ἁγνισμός, ἀπαρτισμός, διαμερισμός, and ἐπισιτισμός are *hapax legomena* in the NT. See J. C. Hawkins, *Horae Synopticae*, pp. 17, 21; J. Schmid, *Matthäus und Lukas*, p. 276 n. 2.

25. Luke 1,7; 2,26; 4,16.17; 5,1.17.18; 8,2; 9,32.45; 12,2.6.35.52; 14,8; 15,24.32; 18,34; 20,6; 23,15.51.53.55; 24,38; Acts 1,17; 2,13; 4,31; 5,25; 8,16; 9,33; 12,12; 13,48; 14,26; 16,9; 18,25; 19,32; 20,8.13; 21,29.33; 22,20.29; 25,10.14; 26,26. See J. Jeremias, *Sprache*, p. 24.

six times in the Luke-Acts and nowhere else in the gospels.[26] Luke uses it to refer to a new age,[27] and it occurs with the periphrastic future in two important redactional verses.[28] The verb which Luke uses in vv. 52 and 53, διαμερίζω, is redactional.[29] Furthermore, the numbers two and five recur in Luke 12,6 where Luke probably introduced them into another Q text (contrast Matt 10,29). So v. 52 represents a Lucan transformation of the Q ending (Matt 10,36) which Luke moved forward. To complete his rewriting Luke reworked v. 53 to bring it into line with v. 52. Matthew and Micah speak of the division of the younger generation against the older whereas Luke heightens the split by portraying the two generations as mutually hostile. So Luke is responsible for the doubling "father against son," "mother against daughter," and "mother-in-law against her daughter-in-law." He anticipated the doubling in v. 52 with "three against two and two against three." Matt 10,35-36 is therefore very close to the Q wording, but Matthew introduced some slight changes.

Matthew preserves the original verb διχάσαι, a NT *hapax legomenon*.[30] In v. 35 Matthew replaced an original υἱόν with ἄνθρωπον, anticipating the use of "man" in the climactic summary in v. 36. Matthew substituted κατά for ἐπί throughout v. 35. He made a similar substitution in the Beelzebul Controversy.[31] The preposition governed the accusative in Q. In the redactional v. 52 Luke uses the dative, but he switches to the accusative in the middle of v. 53. The use of ἐπί with the accusative in the first part of the saying confirms this conclusion.[32] Matthew's γάρ (compare Luke 12,52) and the possessive pronouns (compare Luke's lone αὐτῆς in v. 53) are original. Luke also omitted the article in the

26. Luke 1,48; 5,10; 12,52; 22,18.69; Acts 18,6. See J. C. HAWKINS, *Horae Synopticae*, pp. 16, 36. The phrase is common in the Septuagint. See, for example, Gen 46,30; Psa 112,2; 113,26; 120,8; 124,2; 130,3; Isa 9,6. See A. PLUMMER, *A Critical and Exegetical Commentary on the Gospel according to S. Luke* (International Critical Commentary), Edinburgh: Clark, 1896, p. 335.

27. J. A. FITZMYER, *Luke*, 1. 367.

28. "From now on you will be catching people" (Luke 5,10 diff. Mark 1,17) and "From now on the Son of Man will be seated at the right of the power of God" (Luke 22,69 diff. Mark 14,62).

29. Matthew and Mark use the verb only once of Jesus' garments (Matt 27,35 par. Mark 15,24), but Luke uses it eight times (Luke 11,17.18; 12,52.53; 22,17; 23,34; Acts 2,3.45). Luke introduced it twice in the Beelzebul Controversy for Q's μερίζω (Luke 11,17.18 diff. Matt 12,25.26).

30. Luke's future passive διαμερισθήσονται corresponds to three tendencies of his style, his fondness for compound verbs, for future passives, and for lengthening the future passive forms. See H. FLEDDERMANN, "The Q Saying on Confessing and Denying," pp. 611-612.

31. Compare Matt 12,25-28 with Luke 11,17-20. The original ἐπί appears in Matt 12,26 par. Luke 11,18. Compare also Matthew's substitution of κατά for εἰς in Q 12,10.

32. Compare Matt 10,34 with Luke 12,49.51.

first two prepositional phrases.[33] He agrees with Matthew in using it in the final four. It appeared in Q throughout the prepositional phrases. Finally we can compare Mark and Q.

Q 12,51-53	Mark 13,12
51 δοκεῖτε ὅτι ἦλθον βαλεῖν εἰρήνην ἐπὶ τὴν γῆν; οὐκ ἦλθον βαλεῖν εἰρήνην ἀλλὰ μάχαιραν. 53 ἦλθον γὰρ διχάσαι υἱὸν ἐπὶ τὸν πατέρα αὐτοῦ καὶ θυγατέρα ἐπὶ τὴν μητέρα αὐτῆς καὶ νύμφην ἐπὶ τὴν πενθερὰν αὐτῆς 52 καὶ ἐχθροὶ τοῦ ἀνθρώπου οἱ οἰκιακοὶ αὐτοῦ.	καὶ παραδώσει ἀδελφὸς ἀδελφὸν εἰς θάνατον καὶ πατὴρ τέκνον, καὶ ἐπαναστήσονται τέκνα ἐπὶ γονεῖς καὶ θανατώσουσιν αὐτούς·...

When we compare Q and Mark, we find two phenomena that indicate that Mark is secondary. First, the Q saying centers on division within families, and it uses "sword" as a metaphor for this division. Mark's saying describes literal warfare between and among generations. It is easier to imagine a writer like Mark taking a metaphor and interpreting it literally than to imagine the opposite movement from a situation of violence like the one Mark describes to the metaphor of Q. Second, Mark's statement is broader than the Q statement. The Q saying pits the younger generation against the older. The Marcan saying not only opposes children to parents, but parents to children, and it extends the opposition further to include siblings. Mark's statement generalizes and radicalizes the Q saying. It clearly lies downstream from Q in the tradition-historical development of the saying.

Mark's redaction centers on the concept of "handing over" and the resultant death. The verb "hand over" picks up the theme that Mark already emphasized in vv. 9 and 11. The mission will result in the disciples being handed over to death. This fate conforms their lives to the life of the Son of Man. Just as Jesus' family opposed him (Mark 3,20-21.31-35), so too the Christian must expect opposition from family members. The theme of putting to death comes from Mark's literal reading of the Q "sword" metaphor. Although Mark preserves the Q word πατήρ, he generalizes the saying by introducing τέκνον and γονεῖς, and he extends the opposition to siblings by adding the clause on brother handing over brother. Mark took over the verb ἐπαναστήσονται from Micah 7,6

---

33. See H. J. CADBURY, *Style and Literary Method*, pp. 197-199.

LXX. In redacting the Q saying Mark draws on the underlying Micah text, and he ties the saying into the terms and the themes of his Eschatological Discourse. In particular, vv. 11 and 12 form a tight unit joined together by the catchword "hand over." Once again Mark has drawn two overlap texts together into a cluster.

Th 16 contains a related saying:

> Jesus said, "Perhaps people think that I have come to cast peace upon the world. They do not know that I have come to cast divisions upon the earth: fire, sword, war. For there will be five in a house; they will be three against two and two against three, father against son and son against father, and they will stand alone."

In reconstructing the Q text we saw that Luke 12,52 is Lucan. Th 16 depends on the redactional text of Luke because it reproduces this redactional verse. Thomas also shows knowledge of the Matthean form of the saying by mentioning "sword," and he draws on Luke's introductory verses for "fire" (Luke 12,49-50), so the Thomas saying is a secondary hybrid. The final phrase "they will stand alone" is a gnostic interpretative addition to the saying.[34]

§ 26. RUMORS OF THE COMING

Mark 13,21 (Matt 24,26 par. Luke 17,23)

Both Matthew and Luke connect the Q saying closely with the Marcan saying. In Q the saying opens the Apocalyptic Discourse (Q 17,23-24. 26-30.33-35.37). Luke fits the Q discourse into his gospel by formulating a redactional introductory verse (Luke 17,22).[35] Immediately before this introductory verse the Pharisees ask Jesus when the kingdom is coming, and Jesus' response contains an echo of Mark's saying (Luke 17,20-21).[36] Matthew incorporates the Q saying into his redaction of Mark's Eschatological Discourse, adding it shortly after he redacted the Marcan saying in Matt 24,23.

---

34. J. A. FITZMYER, *Luke*, 2. 994.

35. "He said to the disciples, 'Days will come when you will desire to see one of the days of the Son of Man and you will not see it'" (Luke 17,22).

36. Included in Jesus' answer is the clause "nor will they say, 'Behold here or there'" which contains ὧδε and ἐκεῖ in the same order they appear in in Mark 13,21.

Matt 24,26	Luke 17,23
ἐὰν οὖν εἴπωσιν ὑμῖν·	καὶ ἐροῦσιν ὑμῖν·
ἰδοὺ ἐν τῇ ἐρήμῳ ἐστίν,	ἰδοὺ ἐκεῖ, ἤ·
μὴ ἐξέλθητε·	
ἰδοὺ ἐν τοῖς ταμείοις,	ἰδοὺ ὧδε·
μὴ πιστεύσητε·...	μὴ ἀπέλθητε μηδὲ διώξητε.

The connective οὖν is very common in Matthew,[37] so Luke's "and" is probably the original Q conjunction. Luke's future ἐροῦσιν assimilates the verb to the futures in Luke's redactional introductory verse (Luke 17,22), so Matthew's conditional clause reflects Q. Matthew's prepositional phrases "in the desert" and "in the innermost rooms" are original. Luke borrows "there ... here" from Mark, but he reverses the order of the words to bring them into harmony with the longer Q form preserved in Matthew. "There" corresponds to "in the desert," and "here" to "in the innermost rooms."[38] Matthew's verbs are also original. Q uses ἐξέρχομαι three times in connection with the desert (Q 7,24. 25.26). Matthew's second verb is more difficult, but neither of Luke's verbs would work with "in the innermost rooms" which is certainly original. Moreover, both of Luke's verbs are common in Luke and even more common in Matthew, so Matthew had no reason to avoid them.[39] So except for the original connective, Matthew preserves the Q text.

Q 17,23	Mark 13,21
καὶ ἐὰν εἴπωσιν ὑμῖν·	καὶ τότε ἐάν τις ὑμῖν εἴπῃ·
ἰδοὺ ἐν τῇ ἐρήμῳ ἐστίν,	ἴδε ὧδε ὁ χριστός,
μὴ ἐξέλθητε·	
ἰδοὺ ἐν τοῖς ταμείοις,	ἴδε ἐκεῖ,
μὴ πιστεύσητε.	μὴ πιστεύετε·...

Two observations show that Mark is secondary. First, the Q statement does not specify the person sought. Only the context (Q 17,24) clarifies who the saying refers to. Mark makes the saying explicit by adding "the Christ." Second, Mark also generalizes the references to the resting place. In this way Mark breaks the bounds of the Q saying which he considered too narrow. The Christ can appear anywhere, not just in the desert or the innermost rooms.

Mark's redaction is straightforward. The καὶ τότε is demanded by the place of the saying in the total discourse so it is redactional.[40] Instead of

37. 56 5 33 61.
38. J. LAMBRECHT, *Redaktion*, p. 101.
39. Statistics: ἀπέρχομαι (35 22 20 7); διώκω (6 0 3 9).
40. Compare also Mark 13,14 (τότε).26 (καὶ τότε).27 (καὶ τότε). See J. LAMBRECHT, *Redaktion*, pp. 102-103.

using the plural in the conditional clause Mark writes an indefinite singular as he does elsewhere.[41] From v. 22 it is evident that for Mark the τις refers to the false prophets.[42] The word ἴδε is the Marcan equivalent of ἰδού.[43] Mark replaced the two prepositional phrases "in the desert" and "in the innermost rooms" with "here" and "there" to generalize the saying. Mark sets "the Christ" equal to the Son of Man who was intended by the Q saying (Q 17,24), but Mark's discourse elsewhere presupposes this identification (Mark 13,24-27). Finally, Mark shifts to the present imperative to denote continuous action.[44] Thus the Marcan saying derives easily from the Q saying.

The Gospel of Thomas has a parallel in Th 113.

> His disciples said to him, "When will the kingdom come?" (Jesus said,) "It will not come by looking for it. They will not say, 'Behold, over here!' or 'Behold, over there!' Rather, the kingdom of the Father is spread out on the earth, but people do not see it."

The Thomas saying parallels Luke 17,20-21. In Luke the Pharisees pose the question, "When will the kingdom come?" In Thomas the disciples ask Jesus. In Luke Jesus answers, "The kingdom of God is not coming with observation; nor will they say, 'Look, here it is, or there!' For, in fact, the kingdom of God is among you."[45] Luke here presents the abbreviated form of the saying that Mark offers in Mark 13,21. In reflecting Luke Thomas again presupposes the redactional text of the evangelists and is secondary.

§ 27. JESUS' WORDS

Mark 13,31 (Matt 5,18 par. Luke 16,17)

Laufen does not include Mark 13,31 in his list of overlap texts because the content of Mark's saying differs too much from the Q saying. Mark's saying centers on Jesus' words whereas the Q saying focuses on the law.[46] However, Mark and Q show striking similarities in language.

---

41. See, for example, Mark 8,34.

42. J. LAMBRECHT, *Redaktion*, p. 104.

43. 4 9 0 0. See J. LAMBRECHT, *Redaktion*, p. 103.

44. For other examples of negative present imperatives in Mark see Mark 5,36; 6,50; 9,39; 10,9.14; 13,11; 16,6.

45. The last clause is paralleled in both the Coptic and Greek forms of the Gospel of Thomas. See Th 3 and *P. Oxy.* 654. 9-21. See J. A. FITZMYER, "Oxyrhynchus Logoi," pp. 374-378.

46. R. LAUFEN, *Doppelüberlieferungen*, pp. 90-91.

Both sayings use the same pair of nouns "heaven and earth" and the same verb "to pass away." Both discuss the validity of normative statements – the law on the one hand and Jesus' words on the other. We are dealing with variants of a single saying, not two sayings as Laufen suspects.

Luke 16,17 is the middle saying of a group of three sayings on the Law (Luke 16,16-18) which were originally independent of each other and also independent of the material that precedes and follows them in Luke's gospel.[47] Matt 5,18, on the other hand, appears in a group of four sayings that deal with the same theme, the abiding validity of the law (Matt 5,17-20).[48] Matthew and Luke both take over Mark 13,31, but each edits the verse slightly (Matt 24,35; Luke 21,33).[49]

Matt 5,18	Luke 16,17
ἀμὴν γὰρ λέγω ὑμῖν·	
ἕως ἂν παρέλθῃ	εὐκοπώτερον δέ ἐστιν
ὁ οὐρανὸς καὶ ἡ γῆ,	τὸν οὐρανὸν καὶ τὴν γῆν παρελθεῖν
ἰῶτα ἓν ἢ μία κεραία	ἢ τοῦ νόμου μίαν κεραίαν
οὐ μὴ παρέλθῃ ἀπὸ τοῦ νόμου,	πεσεῖν.
ἕως ἂν πάντα γένηται.	

At first glance Matthew and Luke appear to diverge sharply in their formulation of this saying, but closer examination reveals that most of the differences come from their use of two different sentence patterns, both with parallels in the synoptic tradition. Matthew offers a variation of a common pattern that begins with a solemn asseveration (ἀμὴν λέγω ὑμῖν/σοι) followed by an emphatic negative future (οὐ μή with the aorist subjunctive) leading into a clause beginning with ἕως or μέχρις οὗ. This sentence pattern is a solemn negative prediction that states that something will not happen until an eschatological condition is met. The pattern occurs both in the triple tradition and in Q,[50] and Matthew uses it once in his *Sondergut* (Matt 10,23). Matt 5,18 develops this pattern except that a second ἕως-clause appears between the asseveration and the emphatic negative future. Luke 16,17 also follows a pattern that is attested elsewhere in the synoptic tradition – εὐκοπώτερόν ἐστιν followed

47. J. LAMBRECHT, *Redaktion*, pp. 212-213.

48. *Ibid.*, p. 213.

49. Thus Mark 13,31 and parallels form a double doublet even though Van Dulmen does not include this example in his list of double doublets. See A. VAN DULMEN, *Doubletten*, pp. xvi-xvii.

50. The triple tradition has two examples: (1) Mark 9,1 par. Matt 16,28; Luke 9,27, and (2) Mark 13,30 par. Matt 24,34; Luke 21,32. There are also two examples in Q: (1) Matt 5,26 par. Luke 12,59, and (2) Matt 23,39 par. Luke 13,35.

by two infinitive phrases joined by ἤ.[51] So if we want to reconstruct the Q saying we must first decide which sentence pattern stems from Q.

Matthew's second ἕως-clause is commonly considered to be redactional.[52] It is borrowed from Matt 24,34 and functions as a parallel to πληρῶσαι in the preceding verse (Matt 5,17).[53] If this second clause is redactional, then the first one must be traditional (Q), since, it is argued, Matthew would not have introduced two ἕως-clauses.[54] But there are problems with this line of argument. The position of the first ἕως-clause is unusual. There is no other example of a ἕως-clause before the main clause in the gospels, and there is only one other example in the NT (1 Tim 4,13). The unusual position of the ἕως-clause would be easily explained if Luke preserved the original Q sentence pattern, for the first ἕως-clause would be Matthew's attempt to force the first infinitive phrase into his new sentence pattern. A further consideration bolsters this conclusion. Matthew's solemn asseveration with the emphatic negative future is a stronger statement than Luke's sentence. It is easier to conceive of Matthew's strengthening the statement than of Luke's toning it down. If Matthew's form were the Q form it is difficult to imagine why Luke would have changed it. He takes over a similar sentence pattern twice from Mark and twice from Q.[55]

Once the question of the sentence pattern has been resolved, the other questions are easier to answer. Luke's connective particle, δέ, could be the original link to the preceding saying. Matthew elsewhere introduces ἀμὴν λέγω ὑμῖν,[56] and the combination with γάρ is typically Matthean.[57] Here Matthew has possibly introduced the phrase under the influence of Matt 24,34-35.[58] It is true that Luke has a tendency to avoid the phrase, but he usually varies it rather than eliminate it completely,[59] and he also uses the expression three times on his own (Luke 4,24; 12,37; 23,43).

---

51. This pattern is found twice in the triple tradition: (1) Mark 2,9 par. Matt 9,5; Luke 5,23, and (2) Mark 10,25 par. Matt 19,24; Luke 18,25.

52. S. SCHULZ, *Q*, p. 114; J. P. MEIER, *Law and History in Matthew's Gospel: A Redactional Study of Mt. 5:17-48* (AnBib, 71), Rome: Biblical Institute, 1976, p. 58.

53. J. LAMBRECHT, *Redaktion*, pp. 214-215.

54. S. SCHULZ, *Q*, p. 114.

55. See note 50 above.

56. See Matt 19,23 (diff. Mark 10,23); 24,2 (diff. Mark 13,2).

57. Matt 5,18; 10,23; 13,17; 17,20. See J. LAMBRECHT, *Redaktion*, p. 213.

58. *Ibid.*, pp. 214-215.

59. Luke omits only the ἀμήν or he substitutes for it ναί or ἀληθῶς. See Luke 7,9 (diff. Matt 8,10); 7,28 (diff. Matt 11,11); 10,24 (diff. Matt 13,17); 11,51 (diff. Matt 23,36); 12,44 (diff. Matt 24,47); 12,59 (diff. Matt 5,26); 15,7 (diff. Matt 18,13); 21,3 (diff. Mark 12,43); 22,34 (diff. Mark 14,30). See further H. J. CADBURY, *Style and Literary Method*, pp. 157-158; J. JEREMIAS, *Sprache*, pp. 125-126.

So Luke's main clause and first infinitive phrase probably reflect Q. In the second infinitive phrase Luke has πεσεῖν, but Matthew's corresponding verb is παρέλθῃ. Granted that Luke's construction is original, is his verb? Has he varied the expression?[60] In the two similar sayings (Luke 5,23; 18,25) Luke shows no inclination to avoid a repetition of the verb.[61] Matthew repeated the verb to bring the saying closer to Matt 24,34-35. In repeating the verb he also shifted its meaning. In the first clause the word means "pass away." If it were not for the phrase ἀπὸ τοῦ νόμου, this could also be the meaning of the word in the second clause. However, the presence of the prepositional phrase shifts the meaning slightly to "fall out." This last meaning is found only here in Matthew.[62] Luke shows no tendency to avoid παρέρχομαι and even introduces it twice into his sources.[63] So Luke's πεσεῖν reflects Q. In Matthew the saying speaks of the least thing falling out of the law (ἀπὸ τοῦ νόμου). In the Lucan version "the law" is a possessive genitive. Matthew's prepositional phrase is probably original. In the Septuagint (δια)πίπτω is usually followed by an ἀπό-phrase.[64] Luke shifted the reference to the law to obtain a tighter sentence structure.[65] In tightening the sentence Luke also felt it necessary to drop the reference to "one iota."[66] We can now compare Mark and Q.

Q 16,17	Mark 13,31
εὐκοπώτερον δέ ἐστιν	
τὸν οὐρανὸν καὶ τὴν γῆν παρελθεῖν	ὁ οὐρανὸς καὶ ἡ γῆ παρελεύσονται,
ἢ ἰῶτα ἓν ἢ μίαν κεραίαν	οἱ δὲ λόγοι μου οὐ μὴ παρελεύσονται.
πεσεῖν ἀπὸ τοῦ νόμου.	

Two main lines of thought show that the Q saying is original. First, the Q logion states that the law will not pass away. Mark's saying maintains that Jesus' words will not pass away. An original word about the abiding validity of the law, a saying that was potentially embarrassing to the early church, has been transformed into a word about the abiding validity of Jesus' words. Since Jesus' words take the place of the law, Mark's saying displays secondary Christianizing tendencies. Second, the structure of the two sayings and the vocabulary show that the Q saying is earlier. The Q

---

60. S. SCHULZ, Q, p. 114.
61. J. LAMBRECHT, Redaktion, pp. 218-219.
62. Ibid., p. 218.
63. See Luke 11,42 (diff. Matt 23,23); 18,37 (diff. Mark 10,47).
64. Jos 21,45; 23,14; 1 Kgdms 3,19; 4 Kgdms 10,10. See J. LAMBRECHT, Redaktion, p. 220.
65. See Chapter IV above on Mark 4,25.
66. J. LAMBRECHT, Redaktion, p. 220.

saying shows a nice variation in the two infinitive phrases with graphic images in both. Mark's second verb simply negates the first, and in the place of ἰῶτα and κεραία which are found only here in the NT, Mark has the plural of λόγος, a word that appears over three hundred times in the NT. The variation and graphic images show that the Q saying is original.

We turn now to Mark's redaction. The expression "my words" is Marcan.[67] The closest parallel is "me and my words" in Mark 8,38 which echoes "me and the Gospel" in Mark 8,35. Since the phrase is redactional in Mark 8,38, it should not surprise us that Mark uses it redactionally in this verse. Mark takes over "heaven and earth will pass away" from the Q saying. He formulates a parallel clause around the expression "my words" which uses the same main verb. The multiplication of cognate verbs, the use of οὐ μή, and the combination of a positive expression followed by a negative one are all instances of Marcan duality.[68] The close parallelism that Mark creates means that he must drop the construction "it is easier ... than" which appears in the Q saying. In this final part of the Eschatological Discourse Mark wants to emphasize the abiding validity of the statements (prophecies) of Jesus about the signs, the final trials, and the coming of the Son of Man.[69] The prophecies detail the passing away of heaven and earth so Mark's redaction expresses a major theme of the Eschatological Discourse in a simple, beautifully constructed parallel sentence.

An echo of the saying appears in Th 11:

> Jesus said, "This heaven will pass away, and the one above it will pass away. The dead are not alive, and the living will not die. During the days when you ate what is dead, you made it alive. When you are in the light, what will you do? On the day when you were one, you became two. But when you become two, what will you do?"

The saying reflects the synoptic sayings only at the beginning, and the contact is so slight that Fieger denies that the Thomas saying has anything to do with the synoptic sayings.[70] In any case the Thomas saying does not reflect any redactional features of the synoptics, so it does not

---

67. Mark uses both the singular and the plural of λόγος. He uses the singular in three senses: (1) absolutely with the definite article as equivalent to "the Gospel" (Mark 2,2; 4,14.15*bis*.16.17.18.19.20.33); (2) referring to something that has occurred earlier as equivalent to an event, the thing that was said, the occurrence (Mark 1,45; 5,36; 7,29; 8,32; 9,10; 10,22; 11,29; 12,13; 14,39); (3) the word of God (Mark 7,13). The plural occurs in Mark 8,38; 10,24; 13,31. See J. LAMBRECHT, *Redaktion*, p. 221 n. 2.

68. F. NEIRYNCK, *Duality in Mark*, pp. 77-82, 88, 89-94.

69. J. LAMBRECHT, *Redaktion*, p. 223.

70. M. FIEGER, *Thomasevangelium*, p. 59.

help us resolve the question of the relationship of Thomas and the synoptics. The saying, though, illustrates several gnostic themes like the transformation of dead food, the light, and the ideal of an original unity.[71]

§ 28. UNCERTAINTY OF THE HOUR

Mark 13,35 (Matt 24,44 par. Luke 12,40)

The Q saying comes at the end of the parable of the Householder (Q 12,39-40). Matthew and Luke agree closely in the wording of the saying.

Matt 24,44	Luke 12,40
διὰ τοῦτο	
καὶ ὑμεῖς γίνεσθε ἕτοιμοι,	καὶ ὑμεῖς γίνεσθε ἕτοιμοι,
ὅτι ᾗ οὐ δοκεῖτε ὥρᾳ	ὅτι ᾗ ὥρᾳ οὐ δοκεῖτε
ὁ υἱὸς τοῦ ἀνθρώπου	ὁ υἱὸς τοῦ ἀνθρώπου
ἔρχεται.	ἔρχεται.

Matthew and Luke only show two slight variations in the saying. The transitional phrase διὰ τοῦτο appears in Matthew, but not in Luke. The phrase is attested in Q (Q 11,19.49; 12,22), and Mark uses the phrase three times (Mark 6,14; 11,24; 12,24). In the parallels to Mark 6,14 Matthew takes over the phrase, Luke omits the whole clause. In the second instance (Mark 11,24) Matthew omits the phrase, Luke the whole passage. In the third case (Mark 12,24) Matthew omits the phrase, Luke the whole sentence. Matthew introduces the phrase into a Marcan context in Matt 12,31 (diff. Mark 3,28) and Matt 13,13 (diff. Mark 4,12). He uses it three times in his special material (Matt 13,52; 18,23; 21,43). Besides taking over the phrase three times from Q, Luke uses it in Luke 14,20 (Q context) and Acts 2,26 (Psalm quotation). On balance it seems best to consider the phrase a Matthean addition as we have clear evidence that Matthew uses it redactionally and no clear evidence that Luke eliminates the phrase.[72]

Besides the initial phrase Matthew and Luke only differ in the word order. The attraction of the relative to the case of the antecedent is characteristic of Luke. The noun is occasionally drawn into the relative clause, and when this occurs with temporal expressions Luke places the

---

71. J.-É. MÉNARD, L'évangile selon Thomas, pp. 95-97.
72. H. FLEDDERMANN, "The Householder and the Servant Left in Charge," SBL 1986 Seminar Papers, 1986, pp. 17-26, esp. p. 19.

noun immediately after the relative.[73] So Matthew preserves the Q word order.

Q 12,40	Mark 13,35
καὶ ὑμεῖς γίνεσθε ἕτοιμοι,	γρηγορεῖτε οὖν·
ὅτι ᾗ οὐ δοκεῖτε ὥρᾳ	οὐκ οἴδατε γὰρ πότε
ὁ υἱὸς τοῦ ἀνθρώπου ἔρχεται.	ὁ κύριος τῆς οἰκίας ἔρχεται,
	ἢ ὀψὲ ἢ μεσονύκτιον
	ἢ ἀλεκτοροφωνίας ἢ πρωΐ, ...

There are two indications that the Q saying is original. First, the Q temporal expression is simpler than Mark's. Q states simply "the Son of Man comes at an hour you do not expect." Mark initially has a more general expression, "you do not know when the Lord of the house returns," but Mark goes on to add, "whether in the evening or at midnight or at cockcrow or at dawn." Mark's expression expands and develops the simpler "hour." Second, the Q saying is self-contained. It grounds a call to be ready in a ὅτι-clause that describes the sudden coming of the Son of Man. The coming of the Son of Man is readily intelligible because the motif of coming appears closely associated with the Son of Man in Dan 7,13. Mark's saying is more firmly bound to the context. It is not immediately clear who the Lord of the house is. It is easier to imagine a self-contained saying being adapted to a specific context than a specific saying being reformulated in general terms.

Mark not only is secondary to Q, Mark also shows knowledge of redactional Q. The Q saying forms part of the parable of the Householder. The Householder consists of a brief parable (Q 12,39) followed by its application (Q 12,40). The application parallels a line in the parable of the Servant Left in Charge which follows the Householder in Q. The Householder urges vigilance "because the Son of Man comes at an hour you do not expect" (Q 12,40). The Servant Left in Charge states that "the master of that servant will come on a day he does not expect and at an hour he does not know" (Q 12,46a). The two statements are not independent. The second one is firmly rooted in the Servant Left in Charge because the master's return takes the servant by surprise. This means that the statement in the Householder is a secondary formulation designed to introduce the Servant Left in Charge. The Servant Left in Charge needs an introduction for two reasons. First, the Servant Left in

---

73. Luke 1,20; 17,27.29.30; Acts 1,2; 7,20. See J. JEREMIAS, *Sprache*, p. 88; BDF, § 294 (5).

Charge contains an implied parenesis. It warns the reader against wrong-doing, and encourages fidelity. The Householder makes the implied parenesis explicit by formulating an admonition in the second person plural, "You also be prepared" (Q 12,40). Second, since Q centers so much attention on the Son of Man, the reader would probably identify the returning Lord in the Servant Left in Charge with the Son of Man. The author of the Householder makes the identification certain. So the Householder is a Q redactional formulation. It is not an independent parable, but a complex introduction to the Servant Left in Charge.[74] By showing knowledge of the Householder, Mark shows knowledge of redactional Q.

Mark's "watch, therefore," is redactional. Mark picks up the word that dominates the end of the Eschatological Discourse (Mark 13,34.37). With the explanatory clause he reaches back to v. 32.[75] He has already stated that no one knows the day or the hour except the Father. Now he spells out just how uncertain the hour remains. The Lord can return "in the evening, or at midnight, or at cockcrow, or at dawn." Mark sub-stitutes "the Lord of the house" for Q's "the Son of Man" to adapt the saying to the context of the end of the discourse where it follows the parable of the Man on a Journey (Mark 13,34).

The five sayings in this chapter provide additional evidence to confirm the conclusions we have come to. In each case Mark's form appears secondary to the Q form. Furthermore, the clustering of five sayings in Mark's Eschatological Discourse demonstrates once again that Mark composes discourse material with Q in front of him. The first two sayings follow one another immediately, and Mark edited each to articulate the handing over theme that he develops in vv. 9-13. Finally, the last saying, the Uncertainty of the Hour, again shows that Mark knew redactional Q.

---

74. H. FLEDDERMANN, "Householder and the Servant Left in Charge," pp. 24-25.
75. These γάρ-clauses are very common in Mark. See above on Mark 4,22.

THE RELATIONSHIP OF MARK AND Q

We have now studied all of the overlap texts. The first part of this final chapter will summarize the results of the investigation, and the second part will sketch its implications.

1. RESULTS OF THE STUDY

I will summarize the results of the study in three propositions which establish the conclusion of the study.

1. *Everywhere in the overlap texts Mark is secondary to Q.*

Scholars who maintain that Mark and Q are independent often appeal to the so-called priority discrepancy to prove their position. According to these scholars at times Q shows the prior form of the overlap texts, at times Mark does. The present study disputes this claim. When we used tradition history to compare Mark and Q, we never found Mark original, for everywhere the Q text proved to be earlier. In other words, the so-called priority discrepancy does not exist.

The signs that Mark is secondary vary from text to text, but certain patterns kept surfacing. The Q sayings and parables contain a number of exaggerations; Mark eliminates them. Q makes some harsh demands on the reader; Mark softens them. Some examples. In the Mustard Seed Q calls the mustard a tree to exploit the OT tree imagery. Mark corrects the exaggeration by referring to the mustard as the largest of the shrubs. Mark tones down the Q Equipment Rule. Q forbids the missionaries to wear shoes or carry a staff; Mark allows both. Mark softens Q's radical Cross Saying by shifting from the uncompromising negative statement to a positive exhortation. He turns Q's intolerant "Whoever is not with me is against me ..." (Q 11,23) into "Whoever is not against you is for you" (Mark 9,40).

Often Q remains content to understate a point or to leave it implicit; Mark makes the point explicit. Again the Mustard Seed serves as a good example. The Q parable implies a contrast between the tiny seed and the large tree. Mark makes the contrast explicit by spelling it out in a special clause (Mark 4,31). Compared with Q Mark shows a more developed or a

more strongly emphasized christology. The saying on John and the Coming
One provides a good example. The Q saying contrasts John and Jesus, but
also strongly emphasizes the coming judgment. In Mark judgment drops
out, concentrating the saying more strongly on christology. In the Unforgivable Sin Q states that a word against the Son of Man can be forgiven. Mark with his developed Son of Man christology cannot accept this
statement, so he completely reformulates the saying to eliminate the offen-
sive clause. In the saying on Losing One's Life Mark adds a christological
reference, "because of me and the gospel," to a saying that originally
contained no explicit christology.

In three places individual vocabulary words change meaning in the
overlap texts, showing that Mark's text is secondary. In the Q version the
word has a single meaning, but in the Marcan version the word has more
than one meaning. In the Q Beelzebul Controversy "house" designates a
"building" throughout the pericope; in Mark "house" means both
"building" and "family." In the Measure Saying the word "measure"
consistently means "judge" in Q. In Mark the word means "accept the
Word" in first part of the saying, but "judge" in the second half. In the
Saying on Accepting Q uses "receive" to mean "believe." In Mark the
same word means "to accept," "to protect" in one part of the saying but
"believe" in the other. The shift in meaning in Mark creates tension in
the sayings, a tension that arises because Mark stretches the passages to
fit new situations. In these sayings Mark is clearly secondary to Q.

Before passing on to the second finding of the present study, we should
weigh the impact of this first finding. The overlap texts are extensive.
They do not represent an isolated phenomenon that crops up sporadically in
Mark's gospel or in Q. The twenty-nine overlap texts stretch from the
opening verses of Mark's gospel all the way into the passion narrative.
They comprise fifty verses of Mark. Their Q counterparts also run from
the opening section of Q to the cluster of pericopes that close Q with
stops in between in all the major sections of Q. In studying the overlap
texts we have reconstructed sixty-five of Q's two hundred and twenty
verses. The overlap of Mark and Q is extensive whether we look at it
from the side of Mark or the side of Q. If Mark and Q were independent
of one another, we would expect that at times Mark would show the
more original text and at times Q, especially since the two documents
overlap so extensively. In other words, if the two were independent we
would expect to find a priority discrepancy. The fact that it does not
occur indicates that one of the documents depends on the other. Since
Mark is consistently secondary, Mark must depend on Q. The second
finding points unmistakably in this direction.

2. *In the overlap texts Mark reflects the redactional text of Q.*

In several places in the overlap texts Mark knows the Q redaction. We found two kinds of evidence. On the one hand, individual Marcan sayings reflect redactional features of Q. On the other hand, although the overlap texts appear throughout Mark, we found most of them concentrated in clusters. Some of these clusters consist entirely of Q texts assembled into new units.

Several Marcan texts reflect redactional Q elements. In the first overlap text we studied we saw that the author of Q altered the text of Malachi by twice introducing the singular pronoun "you." The double use of the pronoun adapts the Malachi text both to the previous quotation from Exodus and to the situation in Q in which Jesus answers the messengers from John by quoting the OT as if God were talking to Jesus about John. Mark reflects this redactional "you" of Q.[1]

In the Demand for a Sign Mark refers to "this generation." The expression "this generation" is a key redactional expression in Q, and it does not fit naturally in Mark's passage. Mark could easily have written, "No sign will be given to you." "This generation" in Mark's text comes from Q's Sign of Jonah which contrasts "this generation" with the generation of the Ninevites and the Queen of the South.[2]

The Cross Saying is a Q construction. It occurs in a cluster of sayings (Q 14,26-27) that form an original stylistic and conceptual unit. The three Q sayings on hating parents and children and bearing the cross have similar relative clauses and identical main clauses. They draw together two important lines of thought in Q, the overriding demands of discipleship and the identity of Jesus and the disciple. We cannot trace the Cross Saying any further back in the tradition than the Q cluster. Since Mark knows the saying, he knows redactional Q.[3]

Mark interprets the Saying on Asking and Receiving by applying it to prayer, an interpretation that arises from the context of the saying in Q. By applying the saying to prayer Mark shows that he knows the Q context of the saying.

In the saying on the Uncertainty of the Hour Mark reflects the text of the Q parable of the Householder. The Householder, though, is not an independent parable, but an elaborate introduction to the Servant Left in Charge. The author of Q composed the Householder to make explicit the

---

1. See above on Mark 1,2, pp. 25-31.
2. See above on Mark 8,11-13, pp. 126-133.
3. See above on Mark 8,34b, pp. 135-141.

implicit parenesis of the Servant Left in Charge and to identify the returning Lord of the second parable with the Son of Man.[4]

Evidence in one text of the redactional text of a second writing is the clearest proof that the first depends on the second. Since Mark knows the redactional text of Q, Mark depends on Q.

The distribution of the overlap texts also shows that Mark knew redactional Q. Mark clusters the overlap texts in several places in his gospel. We find five overlap texts grouped together in the Parable Discourse and another five in the Eschatological Discourse.[5] Four overlap texts appear in the Discipleship Discourse and three in the Caesarea Philippi pericope.[6] The Beelzebul Controversy and the Unforgivable Sin are joined together to form parts of one complex controversy (Mark 3,22-30). We also found three smaller clusters, each consisting of two sayings. The saying on Losing One's Life follows the Cross Saying immediately (Mark 8,34-35). Mark joins the Faith Saying to the saying on Asking and Receiving (Mark 11,22-24), and he connects the saying on Confessing with the saying on Family Division (Mark 13,11-12). To a certain extent this clustering should come as no surprise. Q consists almost entirely of sayings and discourses; Mark contains primarily narrative. If the two overlap, they can only overlap in the few narrative sections of Q or in the discourse sections of Mark. However, we cannot dismiss the clusters so easily. Two of the clusters show clearly that Mark had the entire Q document in front of him as he wrote.

Mark frames the Beelzebul Controversy with the pericope of Jesus' True Family (Mark 3,20-21.31-35). Mark condenses the Beelzebul Controversy to fit it within the frame, but he also expands the condensed controversy to adapt it to the framing pericope. For each expansion Mark draws on Q. To the charge that Jesus drives out demons by Beelzebul Mark adds a second charge that Jesus is possessed. The second charge comes from the Q pericope on John and Jesus where John's adversaries claim he is possessed (Q 7,33). Mark also adds an initial rhetorical question ("How can Satan cast out Satan?") to Jesus' answer. The question pieces together features of the Q controversy.[7] Mark also takes a detail of Q's parable of the Divided Kingdom and builds it into a second parable of

---

4. See above on Mark 13,35, pp. 206-208.
5. For the Parable Discourse see Mark 4,21.22.24cd.25.30-32; for the Eschatological Discourse see Mark 13,11.12.21.31.35.
6. For the Discipleship Discourse See Mark 9,37.40.42.50a; for the Caesarea Philippi pericope see Mark 8,34b.35.38.
7. For πῶς δύναται see Q 11,21; for σατανᾶς see Q 11,18; for ἐκβάλλω see Q 11,15.

the Divided House (Mark 3,25) to further connect the Beelzebul Controversy with the framing pericope of Jesus' Family. Finally, Mark joins an edited Unforgivable Sin logion (Mark 3,28-30) as a comment on both the scribes and Jesus' family. If Mark were drawing on the oral tradition, we would expect to find some non-Q material in the composition. Instead everything comes from Q. We can also rule out a pre-Marcan redactor because the techniques, especially the framing technique, are characteristically Marcan. Mark's text only makes sense if he had the complete Q document in front of him as he composed the section. We observed the same phenomenon in the Parable Discourse. Mark reached out to various parts of Q to pull together the five sayings he used in Mark 4,21-25, and he further drew on Q for the Mustard Seed. In the cluster of sayings in Mark 4,21-25 we find five Q sayings joined together. If Mark were drawing on the oral tradition, we would expect to find some non-Q material mixed in. The sayings also develop Mark's parable theory which forms part of his main theme, the messianic secret, so we can rule out a pre-Marcan redactor. The clusters of sayings in the Caesarea Philippi pericope (Mark 8,34-9,1), the Discipleship Discourse (Mark 9,33-50), the sayings on Faith (Mark 11,22-24), and the Eschatological Discourse (Mark 13,1-37) confirm this analysis. In each case Mark composed with knowledge of the whole Q document.

The third proposition completes the summary of the findings of this study.

3. *The differences between Mark and Q in the overlap texts stem from Marcan redaction.*

Everywhere in the overlap texts we have seen that starting from the Q text we can explain the Marcan text using the redactional techniques of Mark. In no case did we find it necessary to appeal to the oral tradition to explain Mark's text. Not only is the oral tradition not necessary, we can positively rule out the oral tradition as Mark's source in the two longest overlap texts, the Beelzebul Controversy and the Mission Discourse. A single editing hand redacted both texts. In both cases Mark's text is shorter than the Q text. The omissions, though, are Marcan omissions, they reflect known Marcan concerns. What Mark and Q have in common appears in the same order in the two documents. Furthermore, both texts make up part of a section that utilizes Mark's framing technique, and in each case Mark saves out a saying to incorporate later in the Discipleship Discourse. A consistent editing technique underlies both texts, and we can only identify the editor as Mark himself.

In the smaller clusters of sayings we found that often the overlap texts had been assimilated to one another. The Cross Saying and the saying on Losing One's Life follow one another immediately in Mark, and a Marcan verb, θέλω, ties them together. Similarly, a Marcan παραδίδωμι links the saying on Confessing and the saying on Family Division in the Eschatological Discourse. An editor assimilated the Faith Saying and the saying on Asking and Receiving to connect faith and prayer, a common theme in the gospel; and someone drew five Q texts together in Mark 4,21-25 to develop the central theme of the gospel – the messianic secret. In short, we found in the smaller clusters an editor who uses Marcan vocabulary and style to express Marcan themes. The editor can only be Mark.

The three propositions lead to the major finding of this study.

Conclusion: Mark knew and used Q.

Nowhere did we need to appeal to an edition of Mark or an edition of Q to explain the overlap texts. Mark knew and used final Q.

2. Implications of the Study

The study has implications for the two-source theory, for the sayings gospel Q, for Mark, for Thomas, and for the historical Jesus.

1. *The Two-Source Theory*

This study introduces a refinement into the two-source theory. The two-source theory explains the triple tradition by the priority of Mark and the double tradition by the Q hypothesis. In other words Matthew and Luke used two main sources, Mark and Q, in writing their gospels. A simple diagram sets out the relationships.

The relationship between Mark and Q remained a problem for the two-source theory that never found a solution that satisfied everyone. This study demonstrated that Mark also used Q so we need to adjust the diagram to show the relationship of Mark and Q.

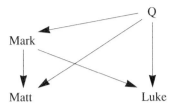

Not only does this study introduce a refinement in the two-source theory; it also provides additional support for the theory. The study confirms the ability of the two-source theory to explain the synoptic problem. The two-source theory has always striven for a comprehensive explanation of the data. The doublets form part of the data that any synoptic theory must explain, and the classic two-source theory put forward a reasonably complete explanation. Some doublets resulted from the redactional work of the gospel writers, but the majority arose because Matthew and Luke used two different sources – Mark and Q. We can now go one step further and explain why the two sources have overlapping material in the first place. Matthew and Luke found two different accounts in their sources because Mark knew and used Q. Mark adapted several Q sayings, parables, and discourses in composing his gospel, so the two later evangelists, Matthew and Luke, encountered both versions in their sources, the original Q version and Mark's adaptation. At times they took over both texts, at times they chose between them, at times they conflated them.

Other synoptic theories cannot explain the overlap texts as well as the two-source theory. For example, the texts pose insuperable problems for the Griesbach hypothesis. According to the Griesbach hypothesis Mark would have had to have picked the Lucan elements out of the Matthean text of the Beelzebul Controversy to arrive at his version. But this procedure runs counter to all we know about ancient writers.[8] We can explain the texts much more satisfactorily using the two-source theory.

2. *The Sayings Gospel Q*

The study enhances the position of Q as the earliest gospel writing. Q stands at the beginning of the synoptic tradition as the first example of the gospel genre. Any study of the tradition must start with a discussion of Q. Furthermore, Mark becomes a third witness alongside Matthew and Luke to the text of Q. For obvious methodological reasons, I have

---

8. F. G. Downing, "Compositional Conventions and the Synoptic Problem," in *JBL* 107 (1988) 69-85.

not used Mark to reconstruct the original text of Q, but this procedure now becomes legitimate.

The study of earlier stages of Q becomes more difficult. As we have seen, the relationship between Mark and Q acts like a toggle switch in interpreting the overlap texts. As long as Mark and Q were considered independent, then scholars like Risto Uro could use Mark to study the development of the Q discourses.[9] Since the study has demonstrated that Mark knew and used Q, we can no longer justify this procedure. We have thrown the toggle. No longer can Mark serve as a control to study the development of Q discourses like the Mission Discourse. We only have access to earlier stages of Q through close literary analysis of the final text, but such analysis rarely leads to consensus in the absence of external controls.

3. *The Gospel of Mark*

This study has enormous implications for the gospel of Mark. Since we have thrown the toggle, we can no longer use Mark to study the prehistory of Q, but we can use Q to study Mark. Redaction criticism has been able to make important contributions to our understanding of Matthew and Luke by comparing these later gospels with their source Mark. The lack of a source to compare Mark with has made it much more difficult to reach any consensus on the gospel of Mark. We can now compare Mark directly with one of the sources he used – Q.

When we compare Mark and Q, we find that Mark uses Q just as freely as Matthew and Luke use Mark. Mark never takes over a Q passage unchanged. He tones down radical Q statements. He abbreviates Q discourses. He can take a Q text and split it, using it in two different contexts.[10] Mark mines the Q section on Fearless Preaching for four sayings that he uses in four different contexts.[11] He conflates Q.[12] He takes over a Q discourse, but saves a verse for another context.[13] Mark alters his source Q just as radically as Matthew and Luke change Mark. Mark's extensive reworking of Q undermines Pesch's claim that Mark is a conservative redactor.[14] In the one place where we can check Mark's redaction, in his use of Q, we find that he is not conservative at all.

---

9. See Chapter I above.

10. Compare Q 17,1b-2 and Mark 9,42; 14,21.

11. Mark 3,28-30 (par. Q 12,10); 4,22 (par. Q 12,2); 8,38 (par. Q 12,8-9); 13,11 (par. Q 12,11-12).

12. Compare Mark 4,24cd and Q 6,38c; 12,31b.

13. Mark uses the Beelzebul Controversy in Mark 3,22-27 and the Mission Discourse in Mark 6,7-13, but each times he saves a saying for the Discipleship Discourse (Mark 9,40 par. Q 11,23; Mark 9,37 par. Q 10,16).

14. R. PESCH, *Markusevangelium*, 1. 15-32.

4. The Gospel of Thomas

The overlap texts present a unique opportunity to study the sources of the Gospel of Thomas because the overlap texts are the most intensely worked texts in the synoptic gospels. Not only do we possess a Q version and a Marcan version of these texts, but frequently Matthew and Luke redact the Marcan form as well. The later writers leave a complex redactional trail that enables us to reconstruct the tradition history of the texts. The Gospel of Thomas overlaps the overlap texts extensively. Fourteen overlap texts have have at least one and sometimes two parallels in the Gospel of Thomas.[15] A total of eighteen Thomas sayings parallel the overlap texts.[16] These texts show over and over again that Thomas knew the redactional text of the synoptic gospels. Thomas reflects redactional Matthew seven times,[17] redactional Mark four times,[18] redactional Luke seven times,[19] and either redactional Mark or redactional Luke once.[20] This widespread knowledge of the redactional text of all three synoptic writers proves that Thomas depends on the synoptic gospels.[21] Furthermore, Greek versions exist for three of the Thomas sayings, and two of these Greek versions also contain redactional elements of the synoptics so it is not possible to argue that dependence on the synoptics dates only from the Coptic translation.[22] As far back as we can trace Thomas, we can trace knowledge of the redactional text of the synoptics. Thomas does not give us independent access to the sayings of the historical Jesus as Stephen J. Patterson argues.[23] Nor does Thomas help us reconstruct Q. Helmut Koester claims that Thomas preserves original Q readings which can be used to reconstruct Q.[24] However, when we reconstruct Q,

---

15. Mark 3,22-27.28-30; 4,21.22.25.30-32; 6,7-13; 8,34b; 10,31; 11,22-23.24; 13,12. 21.31.

16. Th 2, 4, 5, 6b, 11, 14, 16, 20, 33, 35, 41, 44, 48, 55, 73, 94, 106, 113.

17. Th 14, 20, 33, 44, 48, 55, 106.

18. Th 4, 20, 35, 41.

19. Th 5, 6b, 14, 16, 33, 55, 113.

20. Th 44 reflects either redactional Mark or redactional Luke in using "blaspheme."

21. Even though Crossan maintains that Thomas is independent of the canonical gospels, he acknowledges that the presence of redactional elements from the synoptics in Thomas would show that Thomas depends on the synoptics. The overlap texts provide just this evidence of synoptic redactional features in Thomas. See J. D. CROSSAN, *Four Other Gospels: Shadows on the Contours of Canon*, Minneapolis: Winston, 1985, pp. 36-37.

22. Greek versions exist for Th 2 (*P. Oxy.* 654. 5-9), Th 4 (*P. Oxy.* 654. 21-27), and Th 5 (*P. Oxy.* 654. 27-31). The Greek text of Th 4 reflects redactional Mark, and the Greek text of Th 5 reflects redactional Luke.

23. See S. J. PATTERSON, *The Gospel of Thomas and Jesus* (Foundations & Facets), Sonoma, CA: Polebridge, 1993, pp. 217-241.

24. H. KOESTER, "Q and its Relatives," in *Gospel Origins and Christian Beginnings: FS James M. Robinson*, 1990, pp. 49-63, esp. pp. 61-63.

we have to eliminate Matthew's and Luke's alterations to arrive at the original Q wording. When Q reconstructions fail, they fail because not all Matthean and Lucan redactional features have been removed. Since Thomas reflects the redactional text of the synoptics, any use of Thomas to reconstruct Q will inevitably reintroduce redactional elements of Matthew and Luke into the reconstruction. What we strive to push out the front door will come in through the back. Using Thomas to reconstruct Q will only distort Q. The Gospel of Thomas helps us understand the later gnostic reception of the gospel tradition, but it does not help us with the historical Jesus, with the synoptic problem, or with the reconstruction of Q.

5. *The Historical Jesus*

This study of the overlap texts primarily clarifies the development of early Christian literature by working out the relationship of Mark and Q, but it also contributes to the study of Christian origins and the historical Jesus although some of the contributions are negative.

The conclusion of this study makes the quest for the historical Jesus more difficult because it shows that our sources are more intertwined than many scholars realized. Multiple attestation has always played an important role in the quest for authentic sayings of Jesus. A saying had a greater claim to be original if it appeared in several sources, especially if both Mark and Q recorded it. But this study has shown that Mark and Q are not independent witnesses to the Jesus tradition. Mark drew on Q, so Mark and Q cannot be used to drive a saying further back in the tradition to the ministry and teaching of Jesus. Because a saying or concept occurs in Mark and Q could mean only that it originated with Q.

Take the Son of Man problem, for example. Did Jesus speak of the Son of Man either as a distinct figure or in referring to himself? Matthew and Luke derive the concept from Mark and Q, but it now appears that Mark received the concept from Q. We cannot trace the concept further back than Q with any certainty at all.

Although the overlap texts seem to present only a minor problem for the great synoptic source theories, they hold important clues for any resolution of the synoptic problem, for they contain the evidence that enables us to determine the origins of the synoptic tradition. This study has shown that Q stands at the beginning of the gospel tradition and that Q represents the first example of the gospel genre that we can identify. Any attempt to understand the tradition or the genre must begin with Q. The second gospel, Mark, knew and used Q, and the next two gospels, Matthew and Luke, used both of the first two gospels.

ABBREVIATIONS

AASF	Annales Academiae Scientiarum Finnicae (Helsinki)
AB	Anchor Bible (Garden City, NY)
AnBib	Analecta Biblica (Rome)
ANRW	Aufstieg und Niedergang der römischen Welt (Berlin – New York)
ASTI	Annual of the Swedish Theological Institute (Leiden)
ATR	Anglican Theological Review (Evanston, IL)
BBB	Bonner biblische Beiträge (Bonn)
BDF	Blass, Debrunner, Funk, *Greek Grammar*
BETL	Bibliotheca Ephemeridum Theologicarum Lovaniensium (Leuven)
Bib	Biblica (Rome)
BibNot	Biblische Notizen (München)
BJRL	Bulletin of the John Rylands University Library (Manchester)
BR	Biblical Research (Chicago, IL)
BZ	Biblische Zeitschrift (Paderborn)
BZNW	Beihefte zur ZNW (Berlin)
CBQ	Catholic Biblical Quarterly (Washington, DC)
DeltBM	Deltion biblikôn meletôn (Athena)
EKK NT	Evangelisch-Katholischer Kommentar zum Neuen Testament (Neukirchen – Einsiedeln)
ErfTS	Erfurter theologische Studien (Leipzig)
ETL	Ephemerides Theologicae Lovanienses (Leuven)
EvT	Evangelische Theologie (München)
ExpT	Expository Times (Banstead, Surrey)
FzB	Forschung zur Bibel (Stuttgart)
Greg	Gregorianum (Rome)
HibbJourn	The Hibbert Journal (London)
HTKNT	Herders theologischer Kommentar zum Neuen Testament (Freiburg/B)
HTR	Harvard Theological Review (Cambridge, MA)
JBL	Journal of Biblical Literature (Atlanta, GA)
JBL MS	Journal of Biblical Literature Monograph Series (Atlanta, GA)
JBR	Journal of Bible and Religion (Brattleboro, VT)
JSNT	Journal for the Study of the New Testament (Sheffield)
JSNT SS	Journal for the Study of the New Testament Supplement Series (Sheffield)
JTS	Journal of Theological Studies (Oxford)
NeutAbh	Neutestamentliche Abhandlungen (Münster)
NRT	Nouvelle revue théologique (Tournai)
NT	Novum Testamentum (Leiden)
NTS	New Testament Studies (Cambridge)
NTSup	Novum Testamentum Supplements (Leiden)
RHPR	Revue d'histoire et de philosophie religieuses (Strasbourg)
SANT	Studien zum Alten und Neuen Testament (München)

SBS	Stuttgarter Bibelstudien (Stuttgart)
ScEccl	Sciences ecclésiastiques (Montréal)
ScotJT	Scottish Journal of Theology (Edinburgh)
SNTS MS	Society for New Testament Studies Monograph Series (Cambridge)
SNTU	Studien zum Neuen Testament und seiner Umwelt (Linz)
StudTheol	Studia Theologica (Oslo)
TDNT	Theological Dictionary of the New Testament
TR	Theologische Rundschau (Tübingen)
TS	Theological Studies (Washington, DC)
TTZ	Trierer theologische Zeitschrift (Trier)
TU	Texte und Untersuchungen (Berlin)
TWNT	Theologisches Wörterbuch zum Neuen Testament (Stuttgart)
TZ	Theologische Zeitschrift (Basel)
WMANT	Wissenschaftliche Monographien zum Alten und Neuen Testament (Neukirchen)
WUNT	Wissenschaftliche Untersuchungen zum Neuen Testament (Tübingen)
ZNW	Zeitschrift für die neutestamentliche Wissenschaft und die Kunde der älteren Kirche (Berlin)
ZTK	Zeitschrift für Theologie und Kirche (Tübingen)

BIBLIOGRAPHY

ALAND, K. *Vollständige Konkordanz zum griechischen Neuen Testament*: Band *II: Spezialübersichten*, Berlin/New York: de Gruyter, 1978.

ALLEN, W.C. *A Critical and Exegetical Commentary on the Gospel according to S. Matthew* (International Critical Commentary), Edinburgh: Clark, ³1912.

ALLISON, D. C. "The Pauline Epistles and the Synoptic Gospels: The Pattern of the Parallels," *NTS* 28 (1982) 1-32.

ARGYLE, A. W. "The Accounts of the Temptations of Jesus in Relation to the Q Hypothesis," *ExpT* 64 (1952-53) 382.

— "Scriptural Quotations in Q Material," *ExpT* 65 (1953-54) 285-286.

BACON, B. W. "The Prologue of Mark: A Study of Sources and Structure," *JBL* 26 (1907) 84-106.

— *The Beginnings of the Gospel Story*, New Haven: Yale, 1909.

— *The Making of the New Testament*, New York: Holt, 1912.

— "The Nature and Design of Q, the Second Synoptic Source," *HibbJourn* 22 (1923-24) 674-688.

— *The Gospel of Mark: Its Composition and Date*, New Haven: Yale, 1925.

BARTH, F. *Einleitung in das Neue Testament*, Gütersloh: Bertelsmann, ⁵1921.

BEARDSLEE, W. A. "Proverbs in the Gospel of Thomas," in D. E. AUNE (ed.), *Studies in New Testament and Early Christian Literature: Essays in Honor of Allen P. Wikgren* (NTSup, 33), Leiden: Brill, 1972, pp. 92-103.

BEARE, F. W. "The Mission of the Disciples and the Mission Charge: Matthew 10 and Parallels," *JBL* 89 (1970) 1-13.

BEASLEY-MURRAY, G. R. *Jesus and the Future*, London: Macmillan, 1954.

BERGER, K. *Die Amen-Worte Jesu: Eine Untersuchung zum Problem der Legitimation in apokalyptischer Rede* (BZNW, 39), Berlin: Walter de Gruyter, 1970.

BERLIN, A. *The Dynamics of Biblical Parallelism*, Bloomington: Indiana University Press, 1985.

BEST, E. "Spirit-Baptism," *NT* 4 (1960) 236-243.

— "Discipleship in Mark: Mark 8:22-10:52," *ScotJT* 23 (1970) 323-337; = ID., *Disciples and Discipleship: Studies in the Gospel according to Mark*, Edinburgh: Clark, 1986, pp. 1-16.

— "Mark's Preservation of the Tradition," in M. SABBE (ed.), *L'Évangile selon Marc: Tradition et rédaction* (BETL, 34), Gembloux: Duculot; Leuven: University Press, 1974, pp. 21-34; = ID., *Disciples and Discipleship*, 1986, pp. 31-48.

— "Mark III. 20, 21, 31-35," *NTS* 22 (1975-76) 309-319; = ID., *Disciples and Discipleship*, 1986, pp. 49-63.

— "An Early Sayings Collection," *NT* 18 (1976) 1-16; = ID., *Disciples and Discipleship*, 1986, pp. 64-79.

— *Following Jesus: Discipleship in the Gospel of Mark* (JSNT SS, 4), Sheffield: JSOT, 1981.

BLASS, F., A. DEBRUNNER, R. W. FUNK. *A Greek Grammar of the New Testament and Other Early Christian Literature*, Chicago/London: University of Chicago, 1961 (= BDF).

BLOMBERG, C. L. "Tradition and Redaction in the Parables of the Gospel of Thomas," in D. WENHAM (ed.), *The Jesus Tradition outside the Gospels* (Gospel Perspectives, 5), Sheffield: JSOT, 1985, pp. 177-205.

BOISMARD, M.-É. *Synopse des quatre Évangiles en français: Tome II: Commentaire*, Paris: Cerf, 1972.

BORGEN, P. "The Independence of the Gospel of John: Some Observations," in F. VAN SEGBROECK, C. M. TUCKETT, G. VAN BELLE, J. VERHEYDEN (eds.) *The Four Gospels 1992: Festschrift Frans Neirynck* (BETL, 100), 3 vols., Leuven: University Press – Peeters, 1992, 3. 1815-1833.

BORING, M. E. "The Unforgivable Sin Logion Mark iii 28-29 / Matt xii 31-32 / Luke xii 10: Formal Analysis and History of the Tradition," *NT* 18 (1976) 258-279.

— "Criteria of Authenticity: The Lucan Beatitudes as a Test Case," *Forum* 1/4 (1985) 3-38.

— "The Historical-Critical Method's 'Criteria of Authenticity': The Beatitudes in Q and Thomas as a Test Case," *Semeia* 44 (1988) 9-44.

— "The Synoptic Problem, 'Minor' Agreements, and the Beelzebul Pericope," in F. VAN SEGBROECK, C. M. TUCKETT, G. VAN BELLE, J. VERHEYDEN (eds.), *The Four Gospels 1992: Festschrift Frans Neirynck* (BETL, 100), 3 vols., Leuven: University Press – Peeters, 1992, 1. 587-619.

BOUSSET, W. "Wellhausens Evangelienkritik," *TR* 9 (1906) 1-14, 43-51.

BRIGGS, C. A. "The Use of the Logia of Matthew in the Gospel of Mark," *JBL* 23 (1904) 191-210.

BROWN, J. P. "Mark as Witness to an Edited Form of Q," *JBL* 80 (1961) 29-44.

— "The Form of 'Q' Known to Matthew," *NTS* 8 (1961-62) 27-42.

BROWN, R. E. *The Gospel according to John* (AB, 29 & 29A), 2 vols., Garden City, NY: Doubleday, 1966, 1970.

BULTMANN, R. *Die Geschichte der synoptischen Tradition*, Göttingen: Vandenhoeck & Ruprecht, ⁴1958; ET: *The History of the Synoptic Tradition*, trans. J. Marsh, New York/Evanston: Harper & Row, 1963.

BURKITT, F. C. *The Gospel History and its Transmission*, Edinburgh: Clark, ²1907.

BURNEY, C. F. *The Poetry of Our Lord: An Examination of the Formal Elements of Hebrew Poetry in the Discourses of Jesus Christ*, Oxford: Clarendon, 1925.

BUSSMANN, W. *Synoptische Studien: 2. Zur Redenquelle*, Halle: Waisenhaus, 1929.

CADBURY, H. J. *The Style and Literary Method of Luke*, Cambridge: Harvard University Press, 1920.

CADOUX, A. T. *The Sources of the Second Gospel*, London: Clarke, 1935.

CASTOR, G. D. "The Relationship of Mark to the Source Q," *JBL* 31 (1912) 82-91.

CATCHPOLE, D. R. "Tradition History," in I. H. MARSHALL (ed.), *New Testament Interpretation: Essays on Principles and Methods*, Grand Rapids, MI: Eerdmans, 1977, pp. 165-180.

— "The Angelic Son of Man in Luke 12:8," *NT* 24 (1982) 255-265.

— "The Law and the Prophets in Q," in G. F. HAWTHORNE with O. BETZ (eds.), *Tradition and Interpretation in the New Testament: Essays in Honor of E. Earle Ellis for His 60th Birthday*, Grand Rapids, MI: Eerdmans / Tübingen: Mohr – Siebeck, 1987, pp. 95-109.

— "The Mission Charge in Q," *Semeia* 55 (1992) 147-174.
— "The Beginning of Q: A Proposal," *NTS* 38 (1992) 205-221.
— *The Quest for Q*, Edinburgh: Clark, 1993.
CONZELMANN, H., and A. LINDEMANN. *Arbeitsbuch zum Neuen Testament*, Tübingen: Mohr – Siebeck, ³1977; ET: *Interpreting the New Testament: An Introduction to the Principles and Methods of N. T. Exegesis*, trans. S. S. Schatzmann, Peabody, MA: Hendrickson, 1988.
COOK, M. J. *Mark's Treatment of the Jewish Leaders* (NTSup, 51), Leiden: Brill, 1978.
CROSSAN, J. D. "Mark and the Relatives of Jesus," *NT* 15 (1973) 81-113.
— *Four Other Gospels: Shadows on the Contours of Canon*, Minneapolis: Winston, 1985.
CRUM, J. M. C. "Mark and 'Q'," *Theology* 12 (1926) 275-282.
— *The Original Jerusalem Gospel: Being Essays on the Document Q*, New York: Macmillan, 1927.
CULLMANN, O. "Das Gleichnis vom Salz: Zur frühesten Kommentierung eines Herrenworts durch die Evangelisten," *RHPR* 37 (1957) 36-43; = ID., *Vorträge und Aufsätze 1925-1962*, Tübingen: Mohr – Siebeck / Zürich: Zwingli, 1966, pp. 192-201.
DAVIES, S. "The Christology and Protology of the *Gospel of Thomas*," *JBL* 111 (1992) 663-682.
DAVIES, W. D., and D. C. ALLISON. *The Gospel according to Saint Matthew* (International Critical Commentary), 3 vols., Edinburgh: Clark, 1988 (vol. 1), 1991 (vol. 2).
DEHANDSCHUTTER, B. "Recent Research on the Gospel of Thomas," in F. VAN SEGBROECK, C. M. TUCKETT, G. VAN BELLE, J. VERHEYDEN (eds.), *The Four Gospels 1992: Festschrift Frans Neirynck* (BETL, 100), 3 vols., Leuven: University Press / Peeters, 1992, 3. 2257-2262.
DELLING, G. "Das Logion Markus 10,11 und seine Abwandlungen im Neuen Testament," *NT* 1 (1956) 263-274; = ID., *Studien zum Neuen Testament und zum hellenistischen Judentum: Gesammelte Aufsätze 1950-1968*, Göttingen: Vandenhoeck & Ruprecht, 1970, pp. 226-235.
DENAUX, A. "Het lucaanse reisverhaal (Lc. 9,51-19,44)," *Collationes Brugenses et Gandavenses* 14 (1968) 214-242; 15 (1969) 464-501.
DEVISCH, M. "Le document Q, source de Matthieu: Problématique actuelle," in M. DIDIER (ed.), *L'Évangile selon Matthieu: Rédaction et théologie* (BETL, 29), Gembloux: Duculot, 1972, pp. 71-97.
— "La relation entre l'évangile de Marc et le document Q," in M. SABBE (ed.), *L'Évangile selon Marc: Tradition et rédaction* (BETL, 34), Leuven: University Press – Peeters, 1974, ²1988, pp. 59-91.
— *De geschiedenis van de Quelle-hypothese: I. Inleiding; II. Van J. G. Eichhorn tot B. H. Streeter; III. De recente exegese*, unpublished doctoral dissertation, 3 vols., Leuven: Katholieke Universiteit te Leuven, 1975.
DINKLER, E. "Jesu Wort vom Kreuztragen," in W. ELTESTER (ed.), *Neutestamentliche Studien für Rudolf Bultmann* (BZNW, 21), Berlin: Töpelmann, ²1957, pp. 110-129; = ID., *Signum Crucis: Aufsätze zum Neuen Testament und zur Christlichen Archäologie*, Tübingen, Mohr, 1967, pp. 77-98.
DODD, C. H. *The Parables of the Kingdom*, New York: Charles Scribner's Sons, 1961.

DOUDNA, J. C. *The Greek of the Gospel of Mark* (JBL MS, 12), Philadelphia: Society of Biblical Literature and Exegesis, 1961.

DOWNING, F. G. "Towards the Rehabilitation of Q," *NTS* 11 (1964-65) 169-181.

— "Compositional Conventions and the Synoptic Problem," *JBL* 107 (1988) 69-85.

DSCHULNIGG, P. *Sprache, Redaktion und Intention des Markus-Evangeliums: Eigentümlichkeiten der Sprache des Markus-Evangeliums und ihre Bedeutung für die Redaktionskritik* (SBB, 11), Stuttgart: Katholisches Bibelwerk, 1984.

DUNGAN, D. L. (ed.). *The Interrelations of the Gospels: A Symposium Led by M.-É. Boismard – W. R. Farmer – F. Neirynck, Jerusalem, 1984* (BETL, 95), Leuven: University Press – Peeters, 1990.

DUPONT, J. "Les paraboles du sénevé et du levain (Mt 13,31-33; Lc 13,18-21)," *NRT* 89 (1967) 897-913; = ID., *Études sur les Évangiles synoptiques* (BETL, 70), 2 vols., Leuven: University Press – Peeters, 1985, 2. 592-608.

— "La lampe sur le lampadaire dans l'évangile de saint Luc (Lc 8,16; 11,33)," in *Au service de la Parole de Dieu: Mélanges A.-M. Charue*, Gembloux: Duculot, 1969, pp. 43-59; = ID., *Études sur les Évangiles synoptiques*, 1985, 2. 1032-1048.

— "Renoncer à tous ses biens (Lc 14,33)," *NRT* 93 (1971) 561-582; = ID., *Études sur les Évangiles synoptiques*, 1985, 2. 1076-1097.

— "Le couple parabolique du sénevé et du levain: Mt 13,31-33; Lc 13,18-21," in G. STRECKER (ed.), *Jesus Christus in Historie und Theologie: Neutestamentliche Festschrift für H. Conzelmann*, Tübingen, Mohr, 1975, pp. 331-345; = ID., *Études sur les Évangiles synoptiques*, 1985, 2. 609-623.

— "La transmission des paroles de Jésus sur la lampe et la mesure dans Marc 4,21-25 et dans la tradition Q," in J. DELOBEL (ed.), *Logia: Les paroles de Jésus – The Sayings of Jesus: Mémorial J. Coppens* (BETL, 59), Leuven: University Press – Peeters, 1982, pp. 201-236; = ID., *Études sur les Évangiles synoptiques*, 1985, 1. 259-294.

EDWARDS, R. A. "The Eschatological Correlative as a *Gattung* in the New Testament," *ZNW* 60 (1969) 9-20.

FALLON, F. T., and R. CAMERON. "The Gospel of Thomas: A *Forschungsbericht* and Analysis," *ANRW* 2. 25. 6 (1988) 4195-4251.

FARMER, W. R. *The Synoptic Problem: A Critical Analysis*, New York: Macmillan, 1964.

FEINE, P. *Einleitung in das Neue Testament*, Leipzig; Quelle & Meyer, ³1923.

FEINE, P., and J. BEHM. *Einleitung in das Neue Testament*, Leipzig: Quelle & Meyer, ⁸1936.

FIEGER, M. *Das Thomasevangelium: Einleitung, Kommentar und Systematik* (NeutAbh, 22), Münster: Aschendorff, 1991.

FITZMYER, J. A. "The Oxyrhynchus Logoi of Jesus and the Coptic Gospel according to Thomas," *TS* 20 (1959) 505-560; = ID., *Essays on the Semitic Background of the New Testament* (SBL Sources for Biblical Study, 5), Missoula: Society of Biblical Literature – Scholars Press, 1974, pp. 355-433.

— "The Use of Explicit Old Testament Quotations in Qumran Literature and in the New Testament," *NTS* 7 (1960-61) 297-333; = ID., *Essays on the Semitic Background*, 1974, pp. 3-58.

— "The Priority of Mark and the 'Q' Source in Luke," in D. G. MILLER (ed.), *Jesus and Man's Hope: Vol. 1*, Pittsburgh: Pittsburgh Theological Seminary, 1970, pp. 131-170; = ID., *To Advance the Gospel: New Testament Studies*, New York: Crossroad, 1981, pp. 3-40.

— "The Use of *Agein* and *Pherein* in the Synoptic Gospels," in E. H. BARTH & R. E. COCROFT (eds.), *Festschrift to Honor F. Wilbur Gingrich, Lexicographer, Scholar, Teacher, and Committed Christian Layman*, Leiden: Brill, 1972, pp. 147-160.

— "The Matthean Divorce Texts and Some New Palestinian Evidence," *TS* 37 (1976) 197-226; = ID., *To Advance the Gospel*, 1981, pp. 79-111.

— *The Gospel according to Luke* (AB, 28, 28A), 2 vols., Garden City, NY: Doubleday, 1981, 1985.

FLEDDERMANN, H. T. "The Discipleship Discourse (Mark 9:33-50)," *CBQ* 43 (1981) 57-75.

— "A Warning about the Scribes (Mark 12:37b-40)," *CBQ* 44 (1982) 52-67.

— "John and the Coming One (Matt 3:11-12 // Luke 3:16-17)," *SBL 1984 Seminar Papers*, pp. 377-384.

— "The Beginning of Q," *SBL 1985 Seminar Papers*, pp. 153-159.

— "The Householder and the Servant Left in Charge," *SBL 1986 Seminar Papers*, pp. 17-26.

— "The Q Saying on Confessing and Denying," *SBL 1987 Seminar Papers*, pp. 606-616.

— "The Cross and Discipleship in Q," *SBL 1988 Seminar Papers*, pp. 472-482.

— "The Mustard Seed and the Leaven in Q, the Synoptics, and Thomas," *SBL 1989 Seminar Papers*, pp. 216-236.

— "The Demands of Discipleship: Matt 8,19-22 par. Luke 9,57-62," in F. VAN SEGBROECK, C. M. TUCKETT, G. VAN BELLE, J. VERHEYDEN (eds.), *The Four Gospels 1992: Festschrift Frans Neirynck* (BETL, 100), 3 vols., Leuven: University Press – Peeters, 1992, 1. 541-561.

FRIDRICHSEN, A. "'Wer nicht mit mir ist, ist wider mich,'" *ZNW* 13 (1912) 273-280.

FRIEDRICHSEN, T. A. "'Minor' and 'Major' Matthew-Luke Agreements against Mk 4,30-32," in F. VAN SEGBROECK, C. M. TUCKETT, G. VAN BELLE, J. VERHEYDEN (eds.), *The Four Gospels 1992: Festschrift Frans Neirynck* (BETL, 100), 3 vols., Leuven: University Press – Peeters, 1992, 1. 649-676.

FUCHS, A. *Die Entwicklung der Beelzebulkontroverse bei den Synoptikern: Traditionsgeschichtliche und redaktionsgeschichtliche Untersuchung von Mk 3,22-27 und Parallelen, verbunden mit der Rückfrage nach Jesus* (SNTU, B5), Linz: SNTU, 1980.

— "Die synoptische Aussendungsrede in quellenkritischer und traditionsgeschichtlicher Sicht," *SNTU* 17 (1992) 77-168.

GARDNER-SMITH, P. *Saint John and the Synoptic Gospels*, Cambridge: University Press, 1938.

GARRETT, S. R. "'Lest the Light in You be Darkness': Luke 11:33-36 and the Question of Commitment," *JBL* 110 (1991) 93-105.

GEORGE, A. "Note sur quelques traits lucaniens de l'expression 'Par le doigt de Dieu' (Luc XI,20)," *ScEccl* 18 (1966) 461-466.

GNILKA, J. *Die Verstockung Israels: Isaias 6,9-10 in der Theologie der Synoptiker* (SANT, 3), Munich: Kösel, 1961.

GOGUEL, M. *Introduction au Nouveau Testament: Tome I: Les évangiles synoptiques*, Paris: Leroux, 1923.

GOODSPEED, E. J. *An Introduction to the New Testament*, Chicago: University of Chicago, 1937.

GOULDER, M. D. "On Putting Q to the Test," *NTS* 24 (1977-78) 218-234.

GRANT, F. C. "The Mission of the Disciples: Mt. 9:35-11:1 and Parallels," *JBL* 35 (1916) 293-314.

— *The Growth of the Gospels*, New York: Abingdon, 1933.

— *The Earliest Gospel*, New York: Abingdon – Cokesbury, 1943.

— *The Gospels: Their Origin and their Growth*, New York: Harper & Brothers, 1957.

GRIESBACH, J. J. "A Demonstration that Mark was Written after Matthew and Luke," in B. ORCHARD & T. R. W. LONGSTAFF (eds.), *J. J. Griesbach: Synoptic and Text-Critical Studies 1776-1976* (SNTS MS, 34), Cambridge: University Press, 1978, pp. 103-135.

GRUNDMANN, W. *Das Evangelium nach Markus* (Theologischer Handkommentar zum Neuen Testament, 2), Berlin: Evangelische Verlagsanstalt, [3]1965.

GUTHRIE, D. *New Testament Introduction*, Leicester: Apollos / Downers Grove, IL: Intervarsity, [4]1990.

GÜTTGEMANNS, E. *Candid Questions Concerning Gospel Form Criticism* (Pittsburgh Theological Monograph Series, 26), Pittsburgh: Pickwick, 1979.

GUY, H. A. *The Synoptic Gospels*, London: Macmillan, 1960.

HAENCHEN, E. *Die Apostelgeschichte* (Kritisch-exegetischer Kommentar über das Neue Testament, 3), Göttingen: Vandenhoeck & Ruprecht, [15]1958; ET: *The Acts of the Apostles: A Commentary*, trans. R. McL. Wilson, Philadelphia: Westminster, 1971.

HAHN, F. "Die Bildworte vom neuen Flicken und vom jungen Wein (Mk. 2,21f parr)," *EvT* 31 (1971) 357-375.

— "Die Worte vom Licht Lk 11,33-36," in P. HOFFMANN with N. BROX & W. PESCH (eds.), *Orientierung an Jesus: Zur Theologie der Synoptiker: Für Josef Schmid*, Freiburg/Basel/Vienna: Herder, 1973, pp. 107-138.

HALVERSON, J. "Oral and Written Gospel: A Critique of Werner Kelber," *NTS* 40 (1994) 180-195.

HAMERTON-KELLY, R. G. "A Note on Matthew xii.28 par. Luke xi.20," *NTS* 11 (1964-65) 167-169.

HARNACK, A. *Sprüche und Reden Jesu: Die zweite Quelle des Matthäus und Lukas* (Beiträge zur Einleitung in das Neue Testament, 2), Leipzig: Hinrichs, 1907; ET: *The Sayings of Jesus: The Second Source of St. Matthew and St. Luke*, trans. J. R. Wilkinson, London: Williams & Norgate / New York: G. P. Putnam's Sons, 1908.

HASLER, V. *Amen: Redaktionsgeschichtliche Untersuchung zur Einführungsformel der Herrenworte "Wahrlich ich sage euch"*, Zürich/Stuttgart: Gotthelf, 1969.

HAUCK, F. "μοιχεύω," *TWNT* 4 (1942) 737-743; ET: *TDNT* 4 (1967) 729-735.

HAVENER, I. *Q: The Sayings of Jesus* (Good News Studies, 19), Wilmington: Glazier, 1987.

HAWKINS, J. C. *Horae Synopticae: Contributions to the Study of the Synoptic Problem*, Oxford: Clarendon, [2]1909.

— "Probabilities as to the So-Called Double Tradition of St. Matthew and St. Luke," in W. SANDAY (ed.), *Studies in the Synoptic Problem by Members of the University of Oxford*, Oxford: Clarendon, 1911, pp. 95-138.

— "Three Limitations to St. Luke's Use of St. Mark's Gospel," in W. SANDAY (ed.), *Studies in the Synoptic Problem*, 1911, pp. 27-94.

HEIL, J. P. "Reader-Response and the Narrative Context of the Parables about Growing Seed in Mark 4:1-34," *CBQ* 54 (1992) 271-286.

HIGGINS, A. J. B. "'Menschensohn' oder 'ich' in Q: Lk 12,8-9 / Mt 10,32-33," in R. PESCH & R. SCHNACKENBURG with O. KAISER (eds.), *Jesus und der Menschensohn: Für Anton Vögtle*, Freiburg: Herder, 1975, pp. 117-123.

HOFFMANN, P. "Lk 10,5-11 in der Instruktionsrede der Logienquelle," *Evangelisch-Katholischer Kommentar zum Neuen Testament: Vorarbeiten Heft 3*, Neukirchen-Vluyn: Neukirchener Verlag / Zürich: Benziger, 1971, pp. 37-53.

— "Mk 8,31: Zur Herkunft und markinischen Rezeption einer alten Überlieferung," in P. HOFFMANN with N. BROX & W. PESCH (eds.), *Orientierung an Jesus: Zur Theologie der Synoptiker: Für Josef Schmid*, Freiburg/Basel/Vienna: Herder, 1973, pp. 170-204.

— *Studien zur Theologie der Logienquelle* (NeutAbh, 8), Münster: Aschendorff, 1972, [3]1982.

— "Der Q-Text der Sprüche vom Sorgen: Mt 6,25-33 / Lk 12,22-31: Eine Rekonstruktionsversuch," in L. SCHENKE (ed.), *Studien zum Matthäusevangelium: Festschrift für Wilhelm Pesch* (SBS), Stuttgart: Katholisches Bibelwerk, 1988, pp. 127-155.

HOLST, R. "Reexamining Mk 3:28f. and Its Parallels," *ZNW* 63 (1972) 122-124.

HONEY, T. E. F. "Did Mark Use Q?," *JBL* 62 (1943) 319-331.

HORSLEY, R. "Logoi Propheton?: Reflections on the Genre of Q," in B. A. PEARSON with A. T. KRAABEL, G. W. E. NICKELSBURG, N. R. PETERSEN (eds.), *The Future of Early Christianity: Essays in Honor of Helmut Koester*, Minneapolis: Fortress, 1991, pp. 195-209.

HORSTMANN, M. *Studien zur markinischen Christologie: Mk 8,27-9,13 als Zugang zum Christusbild des zweiten Evangeliums* (NeutAbh, 6), Münster: Aschendorff, [2]1973.

HUNKIN, J. W. "'Pleonastic' ἄρχομαι in the New Testament," *JTS* 25 (1923-24) 390-402.

JACOBSON, A. D. "The Literary Unity of Q: Lc 10,2-16 and Parallels as a Test Case," in J. DELOBEL (ed.), *Logia: Les paroles de Jésus – The Sayings of Jesus: Mémorial Joseph Coppens* (BETL, 59), Leuven: University Press – Peeters, 1982, pp. 419-423.

— *The First Gospel: An Introduction to Q* (Foundations & Facets), Sonoma, CA: Polebridge, 1992.

JASCHKE, H. "'λαλεῖν' bei Lukas: Ein Beitrag zur lukanischen Theologie," *BZ* 15 (1971) 109-114.

JEREMIAS, J. *Die Gleichnisse Jesu*, Göttingen: Vandenhoeck & Ruprecht, [8]1970; ET: *The Parables of Jesus*, trans. S. H. Hooke, New York: Charles Scribner's Sons, [2]1963.

— *Die Sprache des Lukasevangeliums: Redaktion und Tradition im Nicht-Markusstoff des dritten Evangeliums* (Kritisch-exegetischer Kommentar über das Neue Testament), Göttingen: Vandenhoeck & Ruprecht, 1980.

JOHNSON, S. E. "The Biblical Quotations in Matthew," *HTR* 36 (1943) 135-153.

JÜLICHER, A., with E. FASCHER. *Einleitung in das Neue Testament*, Tübingen: Mohr – Siebeck, [7]1931.

KEA, P. V. "Salting the Salt: Q 14:34-35 and Mark 9:49-50," *Forum* 6/3-4 (1990) 239-244.

KEE, H. C. "'Becoming a Child' in the Gospel of Thomas," *JBL* 82 (1963) 307-314.

— "The Function of Scriptural Quotations and Allusions in Mark 11-16," in E. E. ELLIS & E. GRÄSSER (eds.), *Jesus und Paulus: Festschrift für Werner Georg Kümmel zum 70. Geburtstag*, Göttingen: Vandenhoeck & Ruprecht, 1975, pp. 165-188.

KELBER, W. H. *The Oral and the Written Gospel: The Hermeneutics of Speaking and Writing in the Synoptic Tradition, Mark, Paul, and Q*, Philadelphia: Fortress, 1983.

KENNEDY, H. A. A. "The Composition of Mark iv. 21-25: A Study in the Synoptic Problem," *ExpT* 25 (1913-14) 301-305.

KEYLOCK, L. R. "Bultmann's Law of Increasing Distinctness," in G. F. HAWTHORNE (ed.), *Current Issues in Biblical and Patristic Interpretation: Studies in Honor of Merrill C. Tenney Presented by his Former Students*, Grand Rapids, MI: Eerdmans, 1975, pp. 193-210.

KING, K. "Kingdom in the Gospel of Thomas," *Forum* 3/1 (1987) 48-97.

KLIJN, A. F. J. "Scribes Pharisees Highpriests and Elders in the New Testament," *NT* 3 (1959) 260-267.

— "The 'Single One' in the Gospel of Thomas," *JBL* 81 (1962) 271-278.

KLOPPENBORG, J. S. "Blessing and Marginality: The 'Persecution Beatitude' in Q, Thomas & Early Christianity," *Forum* 2/3 (1986) 36-56.

— *The Formation of Q: Trajectories in Ancient Wisdom Collections* (Studies in Antiquity & Christianity), Philadelphia: Fortress, 1987.

— *Q Parallels: Synopsis, Critical Notes & Concordance*, Sonoma, CA: Polebridge, 1988.

— "Alms, Debt and Divorce: Jesus' Ethics in their Mediterranean Context," *Toronto Journal of Theology* 6 (1990) 182-200.

— "City and Wasteland: Narrative World and the Beginning of the Sayings Gospel (Q)," *Semeia* 52 (1990) 145-160.

KNOPF, R., H. LIETZMANN, and R. WEINEL. *Einführung in das Neue Testament*, Berlin: Töpelmann, [5]1949.

KOESTER, H. *Ancient Christian Gospels: Their History and Development*, London: SCM / Philadelphia: Trinity Press International, 1990.

— "Q and its Relatives," in J. E. GOEHRING, C. W. HEDRICK, J. T. SANDERS, with H. D. BETZ (eds.), *Gospel Origins and Christian Beginnings: In Honor of James M. Robinson* (Forum Fascicles), Sonoma, CA: Polebridge, 1990, pp. 49-63.

KOGLER, F. *Das Doppelgleichnis vom Senfkorn und vom Sauerteig in seiner traditionsgeschichtlichen Entwicklung: Zur Reich-Gottes-Vorstellung Jesu und ihren Aktualisierungen in der Urkirche* (FzB, 59), Würzburg: Echter, 1988.

KOSMALA, H. "'In my Name,'" *ASTI* 5 (1966-67) 87-109.

KÜMMEL, W. G. *Einleitung in das Neue Testament*, Heidelberg: Quelle & Meyer, [17]1973; ET: *Introduction to the New Testament*, trans. H. C. Kee, Nashville: Abingdon, 1975.

— "Das Verhalten Jesus gegenüber und das Verhalten des Menschensohns: Markus 8,38 par und Lukas 12,3f par Mattäus 10,32f," in R. PESCH & R. SCHNACKENBURG with O. KAISER (eds.), *Jesus und der Menschensohn: Für Anton Vögtle*, Freiburg: Herder, 1975, pp. 210-224.

LAMBRECHT, J. "Die Logia-Quellen von Markus 13," *Bib* 47 (1966) 321-360.

— *Die Redaktion der Markus-Apokalypse: Literarische Analyse und Struktur-untersuchung* (AnBib, 28), Rome: Pontifical Biblical Institute, 1967.

— *Marcus Interpretator: Stijl en boodschap in Mc. 3,20-4,34*, Brugge/Utrecht: Desclée de Brouwer, 1969.

— "Redaction and Theology in Mk., IV," in M. SABBE (ed.), *L'évangile selon Marc: Tradition et rédaction* (BETL, 34), Gembloux: Duculot / Leuven: University Press, 1974; Leuven: University Press – Peeters, ²1988, pp. 269-308.

— "Q-Influence on Mark 8,34-9,1," in J. DELOBEL (ed.), *Logia: Les paroles de Jésus – The Sayings of Jesus: Mémorial Joseph Coppens* (BETL, 59), Leuven: University Press – Peeters, 1982, pp. 277-304.

— *Once More Astonished: The Parables of Jesus*, New York: Crossroad, 1983.

— "John the Baptist and Jesus in Mark 1.1-15: Markan Redaction of Q?," *NTS* 38 (1992) 357-384.

LARFELD, W. *Die neutestamentliche Evangelien nach ihrer Eigenart und Abhängigkeit untersucht*, Gütersloh: Bertelsmann, 1925.

LATOURELLE, R. "Critères d'authenticité historique des Évangiles," *Greg* 55 (1974) 609-638.

LAUFEN, R. *Die Doppelüberlieferungen der Logienquelle und des Markusevangeliums* (BBB, 54), Bonn: Hanstein, 1980.

— "ΒΑΣΙΛΕΙΑ und ΕΚΚΛΗΣΙΑ: Eine traditions- und redaktionsge-schichtliche Untersuchung des Gleichnisses vom Senfkorn," in J. ZMIJEW-SKI & E. NELLESEN (eds.), *Begegnung mit dem Wort: Festschrift für Heinrich Zimmermann* (BBB, 53), Bonn: Hanstein, 1980, pp. 105-140; = ID., *Doppelüberlieferungen*, 1980, pp. 174-200.

LÉGASSE, S. "L''homme fort' de Luc xi 21-22," *NT* 5 (1962) 5-9.

LINDARS, B. "Jesus as Advocate: A Contribution to the Christological Debate," *BJRL* 62 (1979-80) 476-497.

LOISY, A. *Les évangiles synoptiques*, 2 vols., Ceffonds: Privately published, 1907, 1908.

LONGENECKER, R. N. "Literary Criteria in Life of Jesus Research: An Evaluation and Proposal," in G. F. HAWTHORNE (ed.), *Current Issues in Biblical and Patristic Interpretation: Studies in Honor of Merrill C. Tenney Presented by his Former Students*, Grand Rapids, MI: Eerdmans, 1975, pp. 217-229.

LORENZMEIER, T. "Zum Logion Mt 12,28; Lk 11,20," in H. D. BETZ & L. SCHOTTROFF (eds.), *Neues Testament und christliche Existenz: Festschrift für Herbert Braun zum 70. Geburtstag am 4. Mai 1973*, Tübingen: Mohr – Siebeck, 1973, pp. 289-304.

LÜHRMANN, D. *Die Redaktion der Logienquelle* (WMANT, 33), Neukirchen-Vluyn: Neukirchener Verlag, 1969.

— "The Gospel of Mark and the Sayings Collection Q," *JBL* 108 (1989) 51-71.

LUZ, U. "Q 3-4," *SBL 1984 Seminar Papers*, pp. 375-376.

— *Das Evangelium nach Matthäus: 1. Teilband: Mt 1-7* (EKK NT, 1), Zürich/ Einsiedeln/Cologne: Benziger – Neukirchen-Vluyn: Neukirchener Verlag, 1985; ET: *Matthew 1-7: A Commentary*, trans. W. C. Linss, Minneapolis: Augsburg, 1989.

MACK, B. "Q and the Gospel of Mark: Revising Christian Origins," *Semeia* 55 (1992) 15-39.

MANSON, T. W. *The Teaching of Jesus: Studies in its Form and Content*, Cambridge: University Press, ²1935.

— *The Sayings of Jesus*, London: SCM, 1949.

MARCOVICH, M. "Textual Criticism on the *Gospel of Thomas*," *JTS* 20 (1969) 53-74.

MARSHALL, I. H. *The Gospel of Luke: A Commentary on the Greek Text* (New International Greek Testament Commentary), Exeter: Paternoster / Grand Rapids, MI: Eerdmans, 1978.

MCARTHUR, H. K. "The Parable of the Mustard Seed," *CBQ* 33 (1971) 198-210.

MCELENEY, N. J. "Authenticating Criteria and Mark 7:1-23," *CBQ* 34 (1972) 431-460.

MCNEILE, A. H. *The Gospel according to St. Matthew*, London: Macmillan, 1915.

— "Τότε in St. Matthew," *ExpT* 12 (1910-11) 127-128.

MCNEILE, A. H., with C. S. C. WILLIAMS. *An Introduction to the Study of the New Testament*, Oxford: Clarendon, ²1953.

MEIER, J. P. *Law and History in Matthew's Gospel: A Redactional Study of Mt. 5:17-48* (AnBib, 71), Rome: Biblical Institute, 1976.

MÉNARD, J.-É. *L'évangile selon Thomas* (Nag Hammadi Studies, 5), Leiden: Brill, 1975.

MERCER, C. "ἀποστέλλειν and πέμπειν in John," *NTS* 36 (1990) 619-624.

METZGER, B. M. *A Textual Commentary on the Greek New Testament*, London/ New York: United Bible Societies, 1971.

MEYER, E. *Ursprung und Anfänge des Christentums: I. Die Evangelien*, Stuttgart: Cotta, 1962 (reprint of 4th and 5th editions, 1924).

MOFFATT, J. *An Introduction to the Literature of the New Testament*, New York: Charles Scribner's Sons, 1911.

MOULE, C. F. D. *An Idiom-Book of New Testament Greek*, Cambridge: University Press, ²1959.

MOULTON, J. H., W. F. HOWARD, and N. TURNER. *A Grammar of New Testament Greek*, 4 vols., Edinburgh: Clark, 1906, 1929, 1963, 1976.

MOULTON, J. H., and G. MILLIGAN. *The Vocabulary of the Greek Testament Illustrated from the Papyri and Other Non-Literary Sources*, Grand Rapids, MI: Eerdmans, 1930.

MOWERY, R. L. "The Articular References to the Holy Spirit in the Synoptic Gospels and Acts," *BR* 31 (1986) 26-45.

MUSSNER, F. "Das 'Gleichnis' vom gestrengen Mahlherrn (Lk 13,22-30): Ein Beitrag zum Redaktionsverfahren und zur Theologie des Lukas," in *TTZ* 65 (1956) 129-143; = ID., *Praesentia Salutis: Gesammelte Studien zu Fragen und Themen des Neuen Testamentes* (Kommentare und Beiträge zum Alten und Neuen Testament), Düsseldorf: Patmos, 1967, pp. 113-124.

NEIRYNCK, F. "Hawkins's Additional Notes to his 'Horae Synopticae,'" *ETL* 46 (1970) 78-111.

— *Duality in Mark: Contributions to the Study of the Markan Redaction* (BETL, 31), Leuven: University Press, 1972; Leuven: University Press – Peeters, ²1988.

— "De Jezuswoorden over echtscheiding," in V. HEYLEN (ed.), *Mislukt huwelijk en echtscheiding: Een multi-disciplinaire verkenning* (Sociologische verkenningen, 2), Leuven: University Press, 1972, pp. 127-142; = ID., *Evangelica: Gospel Studies–Études d'évangile: Collected Essays* (BETL, 60), Leuven: University Press – Peeters, 1982, pp. 821-834.

— *The Minor Agreements of Matthew and Luke against Mark* (BETL, 37), Leuven: University Press, 1974.

— "John and the Synoptics," in M. DE JONGE (ed.), *L'évangile de Jean: Sources, rédaction, théologie* (BETL, 44), Leuven: University Press, 1977, pp. 73-106; = ID., *Evangelica*, 1982, pp. 365-400.

— "L'édition du texte de Q," *ETL* 55 (1979) 373-381; = ID., *Evangelica*, 1982, pp. 925-933.

— "Deuteromarcus et les accords Matthieu-Luc," *ETL* 56 (1980) 397-408; = ID., *Evangelica*, 1982, pp. 769-780.

— "Recent Developments in the Study of Q," in J. DELOBEL (ed.), *Logia: Les paroles de Jésus – The Sayings of Jesus: Mémorial J. Coppens* (BETL, 59), Leuven: University Press – Peeters, 1982, pp. 29-75; = ID., *Evangelica II: 1982-1991: Collected Essays* (BETL, 99), Leuven: University Press – Peeters, 1991, pp. 409-464.

— "Le texte des Actes des Apôtres et les caractéristiques stylistiques lucaniennes," *ETL* 61 (1985) 304-339; = ID., *Evangelica II*, 1991, pp. 243-278.

— "Paul and the Sayings of Jesus," in A. VANHOYE (ed.), *L'Apôtre Paul: Personnalité, style et conception du ministère* (BETL, 73), Leuven: University Press – Peeters, 1986, pp. 265-321; = ID., *Evangelica II*, 1991, pp. 511-568.

— "Mt 12,25a / Lc 11,17a et la rédaction des évangiles," *ETL* 62 (1986) 122-133; = ID., *Evangelica II*, 1991, pp. 481-492.

— *Q-Synopsis: The Double Tradition Passages in Greek* (Studiorum Novi Testamenti Auxilia, 13), Leuven: University Press – Peeters, 1988; ²1995.

— "A Synopsis of Q," *ETL* 64 (1988) 441-449; = ID., *Evangelica II*, 1991, pp. 465-474.

— "The Apocryphal Gospels and the Gospel of Mark," in J.-M. SEVRIN (ed.), *The New Testament in Early Christianity* (BETL, 86), Leuven: University Press – Peeters, 1989, pp. 123-175; = ID., *Evangelica II*, 1991, pp. 715-772.

— "The Two-Source Hypothesis: Introduction," in D. L. DUNGAN (ed.), *The Interrelations of the Gospels: A Symposium Led by M.-É. Boismard – W. R. Farmer – F. Neirynck, Jerusalem, 1984* (BETL, 95), Leuven: University Press – Peeters, 1990, pp. 3-22.

— "Synoptic Problem," in R. E. BROWN, J. A. FITZMYER, R. E. MURPHY (eds.), *The New Jerome Biblical Commentary*, Englewood Cliffs, NJ: Prentice Hall, 1990, pp. 587-595.

— *The Minor Agreements in a Horizontal-Line Synopsis* (Studiorum Novi Testamenti Auxilia, 15), Leuven: University Press – Peeters, 1991.

— "The Minor Agreements and the Two-Source Theory," in ID., *Evangelica II*, 1991, pp. 3-42.

— "John and the Synoptics: 1975-1990," in A. DENAUX (ed.), *John and the Synoptics* (BETL, 101), Leuven: University Press – Peeters, 1992, pp. 3-62.

— "The International Q Project," *ETL* 69 (1993) 221-225.

— "Literary Criticism, Old and New," in C. FOCANT (ed.), *The Synoptic Gospels: Source Criticism and the New Literary Criticism* (BETL, 110), Leuven: University Press – Peeters, 1993, pp. 13-38.

NEIRYNCK, F., with J. DELOBEL, T. SNOY, G. VAN BELLE, F. VAN SEGBROECK, *Jean et les Synoptiques: Examen critique de l'exégèse de M.-É. Boismard* (BETL, 49), Leuven: University Press, 1979.

NEIRYNCK, F., and F. VAN SEGBROECK, with H. LECLERCQ, *New Testament Vocabulary: A Companion Volume to the Concordance* (BETL, 65), Leuven: University Press – Peeters, 1984.

NESTLE, W. "'Wer nicht mit mir ist, der ist wider mich.,'" *ZNW* 13 (1912) 84-87.

NEW, D. S. *Old Testament Quotations in the Synoptic Gospels, and the Two-Document Hypothesis* (SBL Septuagint and Cognate Studies Series, 37), Atlanta: Scholars Press, 1993.

NICOLARDOT, F. *Les procédés de rédaction des trois premiers évangélistes*, Paris: Fischbacher, 1908.

NIELSEN, H. K. "Kriterien zur Bestimmung authentischer Jesusworte," *SNTU* 4 (1979) 5-26.

NUNN, H. P. V. *A Short Syntax of New Testament Greek*, Cambridge: University Press, [5]1938.

PATTERSON, S. J. "Introduction," in J. S. KLOPPENBORG, M. W. MEYER, S. J. PATTERSON, M. G. STEINHAUSER, *Q-Thomas Reader*, Sonoma, CA: Polebridge, 1990, pp. 77-123.

— *The Gospel of Thomas and Jesus* (Foundations & Facets), Sonoma, CA: Polebridge, 1993.

PATTON, C. S. "Did Mark Use Q? Or Did Q Use Mark?," *American Journal of Theology* 16 (1912) 634-642.

PEABODY, D. B. *Mark as Composer* (New Gospel Studies, 1), Macon, GA: Mercer University Press, 1987.

PESCH, R. "Anfang des Evangeliums Jesu Christi: Eine Studie zum Prolog des Markusevangeliums (Mk 1,1-15)," in G. BORNKAMM and K. RAHNER (eds.), *Die Zeit Jesu: Festschrift für Heinz Schlier*, Freiburg/Basel/Vienna: Herder, 1970, pp. 108-144.

— *Das Markusevangelium* (HTKNT, 2). 2 vols.; Freiburg/Basel/Vienna: Herder, 1976, 1977.

— "Über die Autorität Jesu: Eine Rückfrage anhand des Bekenner- und Verleugnerspruchs Lk 12,8f par.," in R. SCHNACKENBURG, J. ERNST, J. WANKE (eds.), *Die Kirche des Anfangs: Festschrift für Heinz Schürmann zum 65. Geburtstag* (ErfTSt, 38), Leipzig: St. Benno-Verlag, 1977, pp. 25-55.

PIPER, R. A. "Matthew 7,7-11 par. Luke 11,9-13: Evidence of Design and Argument in the Collection of Jesus' Sayings," in J. DELOBEL (ed.), *Logia: Les paroles de Jésus – The Sayings of Jesus: Mémorial Joseph Coppens* (BETL, 59), Leuven: University Press – Peeters, 1982, pp. 411-418.

— *Wisdom in the Q-Tradition: The Aphoristic Teaching of Jesus* (SNTS MS, 61), Cambridge: University Press, 1989.

PLUMMER, A. *A Critical and Exegetical Commentary on the Gospel according to S. Luke* (International Critical Commentary), Edinburgh: Clark, 1896.

POLAG, A. *Fragmenta Q: Textheft zur Logienquelle*, Neukirchen-Vluyn: Neu-kirchener Verlag, [2]1982.

POLKOW, D. "Method and Criteria for Historical Jesus Research," *SBL 1987 Seminar Papers*, pp. 336-356.

PRYKE, E. J. *Redactional Style in the Marcan Gospel: A Study of Syntax and Vocabulary as Guides to Redaction in Mark* (SNTS MS, 33), Cambridge: University Press, 1978.

RAWLINSON, A. E. J. *St. Mark: With Introduction, Commentary and Additional Notes* (Westminster Commentaries), London: Methuen, 1925.

RENGSTORF, K. H. "Die στολαί der Schriftgelehrten: Eine Erläuterung zu Mark. 12,38," in O. BETZ, M. HENGEL, P. SCHMIDT (eds.), *Abraham unser Vater: Juden und Christen im Gespräch über die Bibel: Festschrift für Otto Michel zum 60. Geburtstag* (Arbeiten zur Geschichte des Spätjudentums und Urchristentums, 5), Leiden/Cologne: Brill, 1963, pp. 383-404.

ROBBINS, V. K. "*Dynameis* and *Semeia* in Mark," *BR* 18 (1973) 5-20.

ROBINSON, J. M. "ΛΟΓΟΙ ΣΟΦΩΝ: Zur Gattung der Spruchquelle Q," in E. DINKLER (ed.), *Zeit und Geschichte: Dankesgabe an Rudolf Bultmann zum 80. Geburtstag*, Tübingen: Mohr – Siebeck, 1964, pp. 77-96; = "LOGOI SOPHON: On the Gattung of Q," in J. M. ROBINSON and H. KOESTER, *Trajectories through Early Christianity*, Philadelphia: Fortress, 1971, pp. 71-113.

— "The Sayings Gospel Q," in F. VAN SEGBROECK, C. M. TUCKETT, G. VAN BELLE, J. VERHEYDEN (eds.), *The Four Gospels 1992: Festschrift Frans Neirynck* (BETL, 100), 3 vols., Leuven: University Press – Peeters, 1992, 1. 361-388.

RODD, C. S. "Spirit or Finger," *ExpT* 72 (1960-61) 157-158.

SANDAY, W. "The Conditions under which the Gospels were written, in their bearing upon some Difficulties of the Synoptic Problem," in ID., *Studies in the Synoptic Problem by Members of the University of Oxford*, Oxford: Clarendon, 1911, pp. 1-26.

— "Introductory," in ID., *Studies in the Synoptic Problem*, 1911, pp. vii-xxvii.

SANDERS, E. P. *The Tendencies of the Synoptic Tradition* (SNTS MS, 9), Cambridge: University Press, 1969.

SCHALLER, B. "Die Sprüche über Ehescheidung und Wiederheirat in der synoptischen Überlieferung," in E. LOHSE with C. BURCHARD & B. SCHALLER (eds.), *Der Ruf Jesu und die Antwort der Gemeinde: Exegetische Untersuchungen Joachim Jeremias zum 70. Geburtstag gewidmet von seinen Schülern*, Göttingen: Vandenhoeck & Ruprecht, 1970, pp. 226-246.

SCHENK, W. "Das Präsens Historicum als makrosyntaktisches Gliederungssignal im Matthäusevangelium," *NTS* 22 (1975-76) 464-475.

— "Der Einfluss der Logienquelle auf das Markusevangelium," *ZNW* 70 (1979) 141-165.

SCHENKE, L. *Studien zur Passionsgeschichte des Markus: Tradition und Redaktion in Markus 14,1-42* (FzB, 4), Würzburg: Echter / Stuttgart: Katholisches Bibelwerk, 1971.

SCHLOSSER, J. "Lk 17,2 und die Logienquelle," *SNTU* 8 (1983) 70-78.

SCHMID, J. *Matthäus und Lukas: Eine Untersuchung des Verhältnisses ihrer Evangelien* (Biblische Studien, 23/2-4), Freiburg: Herder, 1930.

— *Das Evangelium nach Markus* (Regensburger Neues Testament, 2), Regensburg: Pustet, ⁴1958; ET: *The Gospel according to Mark*, trans. K. Condon, Staten Island, NY: Alba, 1968.

SCHMIDT, D. "The LXX *Gattung* 'Prophetic Correlative'," *JBL* 96 (1977) 517-522.

SCHMITHALS, W. "Die Worte vom leidenden Menschensohn: Ein Schlüssel zur Lösung des Menschensohn-Problems," in C. ANDRESEN & G. KLEIN (eds.), *Theologia Crucis – Signum Crucis: Festschrift für Erich Dinkler zum 70. Geburtstag*, Tübingen: Mohr – Siebeck, 1979, pp. 417-445.

SCHNACKENBURG, R. "Mk 9,33-50," in J. SCHMID & A. VÖGTLE (eds.), *Synoptische Studien Alfred Wikenhauser zum siebzigsten Geburtstag am 22. Februar 1953 dargebracht von Freunden, Kollegen und Schülern*, Munich: Zink, 1953, pp. 184-206; = ID., *Schriften zum Neuen Testament: Exegese in Fortschritt und Wandel*, Munich: Kösel-Verlag, 1971, pp. 129-154

— "'Ihr seid das Salz der Erde, das Licht der Welt': Zu Mt 5,13-16," *Mélanges Eugène Tisserant: Vol. I* (Studi e Testi, 231), Rome: Bibliotheca Apostolica Vaticana, 1964, pp. 365-387; = ID., *Schriften zum Neuen Testament*, 1971, pp. 177-200.

— "Der eschatologische Abschnitt Lk 17,20-37," in A. DESCAMPS & A. DE HALLEUX (eds.), *Mélanges bibliques en hommage au R. P. Béda Rigaux*, Gembloux: Duculot, 1970, pp. 213-234; = ID., *Schriften zum Neuen Testament*, 1971, pp. 220-243.

— "Tradition und Interpretation im Spruchgut des Johannesevangeliums," in J. ZMIJEWSKI & E. NELLESEN (eds.), *Begegnung mit dem Wort: Festschrift für Heinrich Zimmermann* (BBB, 53), Bonn: Hanstein, 1980, pp. 141-159.

SCHNEIDER, G. "Das Bildwort von der Lampe: Zur Traditionsgeschichte eines Jesus-Wortes," *ZNW* 61 (1970) 183-209; = ID., *Jesusüberlieferung und Christologie: Neutestamentliche Aufsätze 1970-1990* (NTSup, 67), Leiden: Brill, 1992, pp. 116-142.

— "Jesu Wort über die Ehescheidung in der Überlieferung des Neuen Testaments," *TTZ* 80 (1971) 65-87; = ID., *Jesusüberlieferung und Christologie*, 1992, pp. 187-209.

SCHNEIDER, J. "ἔρχομαι," *TWNT* 2 (1935) 662-682; ET: *TDNT* 2 (1964) 666-684.

SCHRAGE, W. *Das Verhältnis des Thomas-Evangeliums zur synoptischen Tradition und zu den koptischen Evangelienübersetzungen: Zugleich ein Beitrag zur gnostischen Synoptikerdeutung* (BZNW, 29), Berlin: Töpelmann, 1964.

SCHÜLING, J. *Studien zum Verhältnis von Logienquelle und Markusevangelium* (FzB, 65), Würzburg: Echter, 1991.

SCHÜRMANN, H. *Das Lukasevangelium: Erster Teil: Kommentar zu Kap. 1,1-9,50* (HTKNT, 3), Freiburg/Basel/Vienna: Herder, 1969.

SCHWARZ, G. "Πίστιν ὡς κόκκον σινάπεως," *BibNot* 25 (1984) 27-35.

SCHWEIZER, E. "Anmerkungen zur Theologie des Markus," in *Neotestamentica et Patristica: FS Oscar Cullmann* (NTSup, 6), Leiden: Brill, 1962, pp. 35-46; = ID., *Neotestamentica: German and English Essays 1951-1963*, Zürich/Stuttgart: Zwingli, 1963, pp. 93-104.

SEITZ, O. J. F. "The Rejection of the Son of Man: Mark Compared with Q," in E. A. LIVINGSTONE (ed.), *Studia Evangelica: Vol. VII* (TU, 126), Berlin: Akademie, 1982, pp. 451-465.

SHIROCK, R. "Whose Exorcists are They?: The Referents of οἱ υἱοὶ ὑμῶν at Matthew 12.27/Luke 11.19," *JSNT* 46 (1992) 41-51.

SIEBER, J. H. *A Redactional Analysis of the Synoptic Gospels with Regard to the Question of the Sources of the Gospel according to Thomas*, unpublished doctoral dissertation, Claremont, CA: Claremont Graduate School, 1966.

— "The Gospel of Thomas and the New Testament," in J. E. GOEHRING, C. W. HEDRICK, J. T. SANDERS, with H. D. BETZ (eds.), *Gospel Origins and Christian Beginnings: In Honor of James M. Robinson*, Sonoma, CA: Polebridge, 1990, pp. 64-73.

SIMPSON, R. T. "The Major Agreements of Matthew and Luke against Mark," *NTS* 12 (1965-66) 273-284.

SNOY, T. "La rédaction marcienne de la marche sur les eaux (Mc., VI,45-52)," *ETL* 44 (1968) 205-241, 433-481.

SNYDER, G. F. "The *Tobspruch* in the New Testament," *NTS* 23 (1976-77) 117-120.

SOIRON, T. *Die Logia Jesu: Eine literarkritische und literargeschichtliche Untersuchung zum synoptischen Problem* (NeutAbh, 6/4), Münster: Aschendorff, 1916.

SOUCEK, J. B. "Salz der Erde und Licht der Welt: Zur Exegese von Matth. 5,13-17," *TZ* 19 (1963) 169-179.

SOULEN, R. N. *Handbook of Biblical Criticism*, Atlanta: John Knox, ²1981.

SPOTTORNO, V. "The Relative Pronoun in the New Testament," *NTS* 28 (1982) 132-141.

STANTON, G. N. *A Gospel for a New People: Studies in Matthew*, Edinburgh: Clark, 1992.

STANTON, V. H. *The Gospels as Historical Documents: Part II: The Synoptic Gospels*, Cambridge: University Press, 1909.

STEIN, R. H. "The 'Criteria' for Authenticity," in R. T. FRANCE & D. WENHAM (eds.), *Gospel Perspectives: Vol. I: Studies of History and Tradition in the Four Gospels*, Sheffield: JSOT, 1980, pp. 225-263.

STEINHAUSER, M. G. "The Sayings of Jesus in Mark 4:21-22, 24b-25," *Forum* 6/3-4 (1990) 197-217.

STENDAHL, K. *The School of St. Matthew*, Lund: Gleerup, ²1968.

STEPHENSON, T. "The Classification of Doublets in the Synoptic Gospels," *JTS* 20 (1918-19) 1-8.

— "The Overlapping of Sources in Matthew and Luke," *JTS* 21 (1919-20) 127-145.

STRACK, H. L., and P. BILLERBECK, *Kommentar zum Neuen Testament aus Talmud und Midrash*, vol. 1, Munich: Beck, 1922.

STREETER, B. H. "St. Mark's Knowledge and Use of Q," in W. SANDAY (ed.), *Studies in the Synoptic Problem by Members of the University of Oxford*, Oxford: Clarendon, 1911, pp. 165-183.

— *The Four Gospels: A Study of Origins*, London: Macmillan, 1924.

STYLER, G. M. "The Priority of Mark," in C. F. D. MOULE, *The Birth of the New Testament*, San Francisco: Harper & Row, ³1982, pp. 285-316.

SWEETLAND, D. M. "Discipleship and Persecution: A Study of Luke 12,1-12," *Bib* 65 (1984) 61-79.

TARELLI, C. C. "Johannine Synonyms," *JTS* 47 (1946) 175-177.

TAYLOR, V. *The Gospels: A Short Introduction*, London: Epworth, ⁷1952.

— *The Gospel according to St. Mark*, London: Macmillan, 1952, ²1966.
— "The Order of Q," *JTS* 4 (1953) 27-31; = ID., *New Testament Essays*, Grand Rapids, MI: Eerdmans, 1972, pp. 90-94.
— "The Original Order of Q," in A. J. B. HIGGINS (ed.), *New Testament Essays: Studies in Memory of T. W. Manson*, Manchester: University Press, 1959, pp. 246-269; = ID., *New Testament Essays*, 1972, pp. 95-118.
THROCKMORTON, B. H. "Did Mark Know Q?," *JBL* 67 (1948) 319-329.
TITIUS, A. "Das Verhältnis der Herrnworte im Markusevangelium zu den Logia des Matthäus," *Theologische Studien: Professor D. Bernhard Weiss zu seinem 70. Geburtstage dargebracht*, Göttingen: Vandenhoeck & Ruprecht, 1897, pp. 284-331.
TÖDT, H. E. *Der Menschensohn in der synoptischen Überlieferung*, Gütersloh: Mohn, ²1963; ET: *The Son of Man in the Synoptic Tradition*, trans. D. M. Barton, Philadelphia: Westminster, 1965.
TRILLING, W. "Zur Überlieferungsgeschichte des Gleichnisses vom Hochzeitsmahl Mt 22,1-14," *BZ* 4 (1960) 251-265.
TUCKETT, C. M. "1 Corinthians and Q," *JBL* 102 (1983) 607-619.
— "On the Relationship between Matthew and Luke," *NTS* 30 (1984) 130-142.
— "Paul and the Synoptic Mission Discourse?," *ETL* 60 (1984) 376-381.
— "Thomas and the Synoptics," *NT* 30 (1988) 132-157.
— "Q and Thomas: Evidence of a Primitive 'Wisdom Gospel'?: A Response to H. Koester," *ETL* 67 (1991) 346-360.
— "Mark and Q," in C. FOCANT (ed.), *The Synoptic Gospels: Source Criticism and the New Literary Criticism* (BETL, 110), Leuven: University Press – Peeters, 1993, pp. 149-175.
TURNER, C. H. "Marcan Usage: Notes, Critical and Exegetical, on the Second Gospel," *JTS* 25 (1923-24) 377-386; 26 (1924-25) 12-20, 145-156, 225-240, 337-346; 27 (1925-26) 58-62; 28 (1926-27) 9-30, 349-362; 29 (1927-28) 275-289, 346-361.
TURNER, Nicholas. *Handbook for Biblical Studies*, Philadelphia: Westminster, 1982.
TURNER, Nigel. "Q in Recent Thought," *ExpT* 80 (1968-69) 824-828.
URO, R. *Sheep Among the Wolves: A Study on the Mission Instructions of Q* (AASF, Dissertationes Humanarum Litterarum, 47), Helsinki: Suomalainen Tiedeakatemia, 1987.
VAGANAY, L. *Le problème synoptique: Une hypothèse de travail* (Bibliothèque de Théologie, 3/1), Paris/Tournai: Desclée, 1954.
VAN CANGH, J.-M. "'Par l'esprit de Dieu – par le doigt de Dieu' Mt 12,28 par. Lc 11,20," in J. DELOBEL (ed.), *Logia: Les paroles de Jésus – The Sayings of Jesus: Mémorial Joseph Coppens* (BETL, 59), Leuven: University Press – Peeters, 1982, pp. 337-342.
VAN DULMEN, A. *De doubletten in het evangelie van Lucas*, unpublished Licentiate dissertation, Leuven: Katholieke Universiteit, 1966.
VASSILIADIS, P. "Prolegomena to a Discussion on the Relationship between Mark and the Q-Document," *DeltBM* 3 (1975) 31-46.
— "The Original Order of Q: Some Residual Cases," in J. DELOBEL (ed.), *Logia: Les paroles de Jésus – The Sayings of Jesus: Mémorial Joseph Coppens* (BETL, 59), Leuven: University Press – Peeters, 1982, pp. 379-387.

VIELHAUER, P. "Gottesreich und Menschensohn in der Verkündigung Jesu," in W. SCHNEEMELCHER (ed.), *Festschrift für Günther Dehn zum 75. Geburtstag am 18. April 1957 dargebracht von der Evangelisch-Theologischen Fakultät der Rheinischen Friedrich Wilhelms-Universität zu Bonn*, Neukirchen: Verlag der Buchhandlung des Erziehungsvereins, 1957, pp. 51-79; = ID., *Aufsätze zum Neuen Testament* (Theologische Bücherei, 31), Munich: Kaiser, 1965, pp. 55-91.

— "Jesus und der Menschensohn: Zur Diskussion mit Heinz Eduard Tödt und Eduard Schweizer," *ZTK* 60 (1963) 133-177; = ID., *Aufsätze zum Neuen Testament*, 1965, pp. 92-140.

— *Geschichte der urchristlichen Literatur: Einleitung in das Neue Testament, die Apokryphen und die Apostolischen Väter*, Berlin/New York: de Gruyter, 1975.

VINSON, R. B. "A Study of Matthean Doublets with Marcan Parallels," *Studia biblica et theologica* 12 (1982) 239-259.

WALKER, W. O. "The Quest for the Historical Jesus: A Discussion of Methodology," *ATR* 51 (1969) 38-56.

WALTER, N. "Paul and the Early Christian Jesus-Tradition," in A. J. M. WEDDERBURN (ed.), *Paul and Jesus: Collected Essays* (JSNT SS, 37), Sheffield: JSNT, 1989, pp. 51-80.

WEBER, J. C. "Jesus' Opponents in the Gospel of Mark," *JBR* 34 (1966) 214-222.

WEEDEN, T. J. "The Heresy that Necessitated Mark's Gospel," *ZNW* 59 (1968) 145-158.

WEISS, B. *Lehrbuch der Einleitung in das Neue Testament*, Berlin: Hertz, 1886; ET: *A Manual of Introduction to the New Testament*, trans. A. J. K. Davidson, 2 vols, New York: Funk & Wagnalls, 1889.

— *Die Quellen des Lukasevangeliums*, Stuttgart/Berlin: Cotta, 1907.

WEISS, J. *Das älteste Evangelium*, Göttingen: Vandenhoeck und Ruprecht, 1903.

WELLHAUSEN, J. *Einleitung in die drei ersten Evangelien*, Berlin: Reimer, 1905.

WENDLING, E. *Die Entstehung des Marcus-Evangeliums: Philologische Untersuchungen*, Tübingen: Mohr – Siebeck, 1908.

— "Neuere Schriften zu den synoptischen Evangelien und zur Apostelgeschichte," *ZNW* (1909) 135-168.

WERNLE, P. *Die synoptische Frage*, Freiburg i. B.: Mohr – Siebeck, 1899.

WIKENHAUSER, A. *Einleitung in das Neue Testament*, Freiburg/Basel/Vienna: Herder, [4]1961.

WILHELMS, E. "Der fremde Exorzist: Eine Studie über Mark. 9,38 ff.," *Stud Theol* 3 (1949) 162-171.

WOOD, H. G. "The Priority of Mark," *ExpT* 65 (1953-54) 17-19.

WREDE, W. *Das Messiasgeheimnis in den Evangelien: Zugleich ein Beitrag zum Verständnis des Markusevangeliums*, Göttingen: Vandenhoeck & Ruprecht, 1901, [3]1965; ET: *The Messianic Secret*, trans. J. C. G. Grieg, Greenwood, SC: Attic, 1971.

WREGE, H.-T. *Die Überlieferungsgeschichte der Bergpredigt* (WUNT, 9), Tübingen: Mohr – Siebeck, 1968.

YATES, J. E. "Luke's Pneumatology and Lk. 11,20," in F. L. CROSS (ed.), *Studia Evangelica: Vol. II* (TU, 87), Berlin: Akademie Verlag, 1964, pp. 295-299.

ZELLER, D. *Kommentar zur Logienquelle* (Stuttgarter kleiner Kommentar: Neues Testament, 21), Stuttgart: Katholisches Bibelwerk, 1984.

ZERWICK, M. *Graecitas Biblica Exemplis Illustratur*, Rome: Biblical Institute, [3]1955; ET: *Biblical Greek Illustrated by Examples*, trans. J. Smith, Rome: Biblical Institute, 1963.

ZIMMERMANN, H. *Neutestamentliche Methodenlehre: Darstellung der historisch-kritischen Methode*, Stuttgart: Katholisches Bibelwerk, [3]1970.

ZMIJEWSKI, J. "Der Glaube und seine Macht: Eine traditionsgeschichtliche Untersuchung zu Mt 17,20; 21,21; Mk 11,23; Lk 17,6," in J. ZMIJEWSKI & E. NELLESEN (eds.), *Begegnung mit dem Wort: Festschrift für Heinrich Zimmermann* (BBB, 53), Bonn: Hanstein, 1980, pp. 81-103; = ID., *Das Neue Testament – Quelle christlicher Theologie und Glaubenspraxis: Aufsätze zum Neuen Testament und seiner Auslegung*, Stuttgart: Katholisches Bibelwerk, 1986, pp. 265-292.

— "Neutestamentliche Weisungen für Ehe und Familie," *SNTU* 9 (1984) 31-78.

INDEX OF BIBLICAL REFERENCES

3,10	146	6,1-18	126	9,6	102
3,11-12	31-39	6,1	86 110	9,9	102
3,11	136 180	6,9	146	9,10	42
3,15	81 86	6,22	129 146	9,12	167
4,8	161	6,23	129 146	9,16-17	76
4,9	91	6,24	55	9,18	42
4,10	102	6,25	92	9,27	44 136
4,15	113	6,26	92	9,28	102
4,17	32 93 112	6,30	92 107	9,31	42
4,19	102	6,31	146	9,32-34	41-45
4,22	136	6,32	50	9,35	43 48 106 111 112
4,23	43 111 112	6,33	85-87	9,36-11,1	101
4,24	42 43	6,34	146	9,36	101 103 162
5,1	42	7,1	85	9,37-11,1	137
5,3	51	7,2	85-87	9,37-	2
5,6	86	7,4	54	10,42	
5,10	86	7,6	167	9,37-38	101-126
5,11	147 167	7,7-11	182	9,38	146
5,12	110	7,8	182-186	10,1-8	120
5,13-16	80	7,11	146	10,1	43 47
5,13	7 33 45 91 166-	7,12	67 146	10,5-6	101
	169 180	7,13-14	142 175	10,5	137
5,14	80 161 167	7,16	92	10,6	112
5,15	75-80	7,21	98	10,7-16	101-126
5,17-20	202	7,22-23	175	10,7	51
5,17	195 203	7,22	109	10,9	68 187
5,18	201-206	7,24	136 146	10,11	48 67 136
5,19	67	7,26	136	10,12	33
5,20	86 98 128 187	8,1-9,34	44	10,13	136
5,21	67	8,1	42 136	10,14	67
5,22	25 67 171	8,4	102	10,16	25 146
5,23	107	8,5	42	10,17-25	81 103
5,25	143	8,7	43 102	10,17-22	191
5,26	202 203	8,10	203	10,17-18	192
5,27-28	172	8,11-12	175	10,19-20	191-195
5,28	25 171	8,11	51	10,21	6
5,29-30	5 161 162	8,12	107	10,23	202 203
5,31	67 172	8,16	42 43	10,26	6 81-84 146
5,32	7 25 67 143 171-	8,20	98 102	10,27	80 81 112
	174	8,22	102	10,29	196
5,34	25 171	8,23	136	10,30	81
5,39	25 136 171	8,26	102 107	10,31	25 146
5,40	88	8,28	42 43 167	10,32-33	6 145-152
5,41	67 136	8,33	43	10,32	25 67 136
5,42	88	8,34	48 180	10,33	25 67 136
5,44	25 171	9,1	48	10,34-36	6 67 195-199
5,46	92	9,2	42	10,37-38	141
5,47	92	9,4	46 47	10,37	6 106 136 142
5,48	25 146	9,5	203	10,38-39	143

18,23	91 206	21,40	146	24,23	199
18,24	42	21,42	102	24,24	43
18,25	42	21,43	206	24,26	146 199-201
18,32	47	21,44	67	24,28	85 129
19,2	43 136	22,1-14	107	24,34-35	203 204
19,6	146	22,2	91 136	24,34	202
19,7	146	22,5	108	24,35	202
19,8	102 175	22,8	102 106 107 108	24,41	175
19,9	7 67 143 171 172		136	24,42	146
19,13	42	22,9	67 146	24,44	206-208
19,14	93	22,12	102	24,47	203
19,23-30	174	22,13	107	24,51	107
19,23	93 98 203	22,17	146	25,1	91
19,24	203	22,19	42	25,5	42
19,28	51 109	22,21	102 146	25,10	42
19,29	136 146	22,28	146	25,13	146
19,30	174	22,34	45	25,18	104
20,1-15	175	22,40	162	25,20	42 196
20,1	136	22,41	42	25,27	104 146
20,4	67	22,42	44	25,28	146
20,8	42 102 110	22,43	44 102 146	25,29	6 87-90 143
20,10	195	22,45	146	25,30	107
20,16	174-177	23,2	128 187	25,31-46	107
20,23	102 108	23,3	67	25,32	103
20,25	47	23,6-7	186-189	25,33	103
20,26	67	23,8-12	187	25,34	161
20,27	67	23,12	67 136	25,37	128
20,29	42 136	23,13-36	187	25,44	128
20,30	44	23,13-33	186	25,45	128
20,31	44	23,13	51 98 128 187	26,6	42
21,3	54	23,14	128	26,7	42
21,9	44	23,15	128 187	26,13	112 123 161
21,10	42 48	23,16	67	26,15	25 104
21,13	102	23,18	67	26,20	42
21,14	43	23,23	128 147 187 204	26,21	42
21,15	44	23,25	128 187	26,24	163
21,16	102	23,26	175	26,26	42
21,17	48	23,27	128 187	26,29	56
21,18	48	23,29	128 187	26,31	102 103
21,19	102	23,34	25	26,36	56
21,21	143 178 179 180	23,36	203	26,38	56 102
21,22	67 182	23,37	94	26,39	85
21,23	42	23,39	202	26,40	56 167 175
21,24	25 67	23,45	44	26,47	42
21,25	146	24,2	203	26,48	67
21,31	102	24,3	42	26,52	102
21,32	86	24,14	112	26,54	146
21,33	136 146	24,15	146	26,60	42
21,35	108	24,21	161	26,64	85 102

7,20	123	8,32	121 151 194 205	9,30	62 132
7,21-22	189	8,33	151 155	9,31	78 82 123 165
7,21	181	8,34-9,1	135 137 139 140		166 194
7,22	70		151 181 213	9,33-50	9 120 124 153
7,24	37 133 188	8,34-35	143 185 212		163 164 213
7,26	121	8,34	4-6 15 16 18 62	9,33	30 122 165
7,29	132 205		104 121 122 135-	9,34	30 82 122 165
7,30	132		141 144 159 176	9,35	121 140 144 174
7,31-37	59		181 184 188 201		176 188
7,31	79 132 180		211 212 217	9,36	155
7,32-37	131	8,35-38	144	9,37	6 18 67 88 120
7,32	121	8,35	6 15 16 18 67 82		124 153-157 159
7,33	124		135 140 142-145		163 164 169 173
7,34	132		188 205 212		181 212 216
7,36	121 123	8,36-38	78	9,38-40	59 60
7,37	168	8,36-37	92	9,38-39	157 158
8,1-9	122 131	8,36	82	9,38	155
8,1	62 120 121 139	8,37	82	9,39	63 73 82 144 155
	140	8,38	6 16 18 67 68 79		201
8,4	63 73		82 135 144 145-	9,40	18 61 82 88 122
8,6	109		152 166 193 205		124 140 144 155
8,7	109		212 216		157-159 169 173
8,10	79 133	9,1	63 73 78 79 123		176 184 209 212
8,11-13	126-134 211		202		216
8,11-12	18	9,2	192	9,41	67 82 144 155
8,11	120 121 188	9,3	63 73		158 164
8,12	70 78	9,4	56 139	9,42	18 22 67 153 155
8,14-21	122 131 133	9,5	37 181		159-164 166 169
8,14	167	9,6	82		212 216
8,15	120 132 188	9,7	151	9,43-47	162
8,16	112	9,9	121	9,43	155 163 164 168
8,17-20	78	9,10	132 205	9,45	155 163 164
8,17	181	9,11-13	37	9,47	155 163 164
8,21	78 123	9,11	165 188	9,48	155
8,22-26	59 131	9,12	97 121 165 166	9,49	82 144 155
8,22	121	9,13	30 165 175	9,50	7 18 155 166-169
8,23	124	9,14-29	185		212
8,25	124	9,14	132 188	10-12	22 171
8,27-10,52	8 153 171	9,16	132	10,1	37 79 140
8,27-9,1	135	9,17	168 192	10,2	132 188
8,27-33	166	9,18	32 121 123 180	10,5	102
8,27	30 122 132 143	9,19	56 78 92 192	10,6	175
	147 165	9,20	192	10,9	201
8,28	37 108	9,22	63 73	10,11-12	16 18 88 155 159
8,29	135 147 151	9,23	63 73 182		171-174
8,30	121	9,25	132 140 168	10,11	67
8,31-33	135	9,26	132	10,13-16	155
8,31	121 147 151 165	9,28	63 73 180	10,14	93 201
	166 188	9,29	63 73 102 132 185	10,15	67

5,19	76 191	7,23	67	8,51	68
5,21	92 187	7,25	196	8,54	68 77
5,22-23	92	7,27	25-31 103	9,1-6	2 101
5,22	196	7,28	203	9,1	68
5,23	135 203 204	7,29-30	154	9,2	68 92 109 112
5,24	68 103	7,31	91 93	9,3	68 77 92 104 105
5,25	68 148	7,32	93		109 187
5,29	43 127	7,48	178	9,4	67
5,30	109 187	7,50	178	9,5	67 112 113
5,32	135	8,1	127	9,9	142 178
5,33	109 143	8,2	43 56 113 196	9,10	56 68
5,36	91 102 108 129	8,4	32 127	9,11	68 127
5,37	108 143	8,5	167	9,12	112 127 196
6,1	44	8,6	68	9,13	178
6,6	44	8,7	68	9,14	178
6,7	187	8,8	68 154	9,16	109 127
6,8	178 196	8,10	113 154	9,17	56
6,9	92 178	8,11	92 147	9,18	68 127 143
6,12	43 44	8,12	77 154	9,20	68 147 178
6,14	77	8,13	154 196	9,22	68
6,15	77	8,14	154	9,23	4-6 33 91 102
6,17	127	8,15	68 154		135 136
6,18	154	8,16	7 75 76 77 80 93	9,24	6 67 142 143
6,19	127 142	8,17	6 81 82 84 113	9,25	68 92
6,20	91 102	8,18	6 67 87 91 154	9,26	6 67 68 145
6,22	147	8,19	196	9,27	202
6,24-26	187	8,21	68 92 154	9,28	44 68 192
6,24	85	8,22	44	9,29	77 196
6,27	154	8,23	127	9,32	43 196
6,29	88	8,24	68	9,33	56 68 161
6,30	88	8,25	68 92 178	9,34	127
6,32	92	8,26	31	9,35	154
6,33	92	8,27	32	9,37	44 112
6,35	85	8,29	113	9,38	192
6,36	25	8,30	68 175	9,40	32
6,37	85	8,32	43	9,41	68 92 192
6,38	85-87	8,33	113	9,42	127 192
6,39	178	8,35	44 113	9,43	127
6,42	112	8,37	31 56	9,45	43 196
6,44	92	8,38	44 68 113	9,46	196
6,47	93	8,39	56 68 103	9,47	196
6,48	93 167	8,40	43 56	9,48	6 67 68 153 156
6,49	93	8,41	68	9,49	68
7,7	138	8,42	103	9,50	157 178
7,9	203	8,43	167	9,51	44 127
7,13	178	8,45	68 127	9,53	43
7,18	47	8,46	113	9,58	98 102
7,19	178	8,47	68 148	9,59	178
7,22	111	8,48	103	9,60	102 178

INDEX OF AUTHORS

ASSESSMENT

by

FRANS NEIRYNCK

MARK AND Q

A few days after I recommended Harry Fleddermann's work for publication in BETL and promised to write a critical Assessment, I came across the following statement on the Mark-and-Q issue:[1]

> ... the case against the literary dependence of Mark on Q, or vice versa, would now seem to be closed. The following arguments are, in various places, advanced by Schüling: (1) the fact that Mark has relatively little material in common with Q and the resultant difficulty of explaining why this would be so if there was a literary relationship; (2) the fact that sometimes Mark, sometimes Q preserves the older version of sayings they have in common; (3) the absence of redactional elements from Q in Mark, or vice versa (pp. 182-83; an argument introduced by F. Neirynck in "Recent Developments in the Study of Q" [1982], 41-53, esp. p. 45); (4) the fact that forms common to Q are largely absent from Mark, and vice versa (pp. 185-186; an argument made by A. D. Jacobson in "The Literary Unity of Q," *JBL* 101 [1982] 365-89); and (5) the fact that some sayings which Mark and Q have in common were already attached to other sayings prior to their inclusion in Mark (Schüling mentions the sayings in Q 10:4, 5-7a, 10-11 par [pp. 49-50], Mark 3:23b, 27, 28-29 [p. 130], and Mark 8:34-38 [p. 138; cf. pp. 148-150]). A sixth argument, though contrary to Schüling's view, would be that the sayings Mark and Q have in common do not share a common sequence. One would therefore now seem justified in assuming that the literary independence of Mark and Q has been demonstrated.

In his book on Q, published in 1992, A. D. Jacobson assumes "literary independence of Mark and Q, as well as their use of some shared traditions." He notes that "there has been a good deal of recent research on the problem of the relation between Mark and Q."[2] He studies traditions shared by Mark and Q because "by comparing them, we can often sense more clearly what is distinctive of Q."[3] He made his point quite clear when treating W. Schmithals's proposal.[4]

---

1. A. D. JACOBSON, Review: "J. Schüling, Studien zum Verhältnis von Logienquelle und Markusevangelium, 1991," in *JBL* 113 (1994) 724-726, esp. p. 726.

Full references will be given only for works not cited previously by H. Fleddermann. His *Mark and Q* is here referred to as HF, followed by page number.

2. *The First Gospel: An Introduction to Q*, 1992, p. 62 n. 2 (= *JBL* 101, 1982, 373 n. 30). He mentions Laufen, Luz, Devisch, Schenk, Vassiliadis, and Lührmann. Fleddermann is not mentioned.

3. Mark 1,1-8; 3,20-27; 4,30-32; 6,6b-13; 8,12b: cf. *First Gospel*, pp. 67-71 (= 379-384).

4. "The doublets do not provide the weighty evidence Schmithals assumes; he has not noticed the fundamental differences between the uses made of this material by Mark and

In 1992, far from closing the debate, at least four noticeable articles in defense of Mark's use of Q were published, in vol. 55 of *Semeia* (Catchpole, Mack) and in vol. 38 of *NTS* (Catchpole, Lambrecht). In *The Four Gospels 1992* two essays on significant overlap texts argued for independence, in Mark 3,22-26 (Boring) and 4,30-32 (Friedrichsen),[5] and at the Colloquium Biblicum Lovaniense (1992) C. M. Tuckett delivered a paper on "Mark and Q." He studied Mark 1,2; 1,7-8; 4,30-32; 8,11-12, and concluded that in these passages "the view that Mark and Q represent independent versions of common traditions remains the most convincing."[6]

One of the participants at the Colloquium who expressed reservations was H. Fleddermann. Already in 1981, considering the Q parallels to Mark 9,37.40.42.50a, he had made the observation: "It is becoming increasingly difficult to deny that Mark knew and used Q."[7] Starting with the sayings in Mark 9,33-50, he subsequently examined Mark 12,38-39 (1982); 1,7-8 (1984); 13,35 (1986); 8,38 (1987); 8,35 (1988); and 4,30-32 (1989), and gradually developed his three-step procedure: (1) the reconstruction of Q; (2) Mark is secondary to Q; (3) Mark is redacting the Q text. In 1982 he noted quite modestly: "This one text cannot prove that Mark knew a document Q. All that has been proved is that in this instance Mark knew and used a Q saying."[8] Now he decided: "In this book I will study all of the overlap texts." The project is now more ambitious, but the basic intention remains the same: "Instead of general arguments progress comes from analyzing the texts."[9] And his analysis leads to three firm conclusions on the overlap texts: "(1) Everywhere ... Mark is secondary to Q. (2) Mark reflects the redactional text of Q. (3) The differences between Mark and Q ... stem from Marcan redaction. Everywhere ... starting from the Q text we can explain the Marcan text using the redactional techniques of Mark."[10]

---

by Q. Likewise, the judgment that Mark used Q is at best debatable" (*First Gospel*, pp. 52-53; with reference to W. SCHMITHALS, *Einleitung in die drei ersten Evangelien*, Berlin, 1985, pp. 384-404). Compare HF, 12 n. 42 (Schmithals's 1979 essay). See also his commentaries on Mark (1979) and Luke (1980); cf. *Evangelica I*, pp. 613-617; *Evangelica II*, pp. 422-423 (and 459, 462, 464).

5. Cf. HF, 17 n. 65; 91 n. 82. See also T. A. FRIEDRICHSEN, "Alternative Synoptic Theories on Mk 4,30-32," in C. FOCANT (ed.), *The Synoptic Gospels*, pp. 427-450.

6. "Mark and Q" (1993), p. 175.

7. "The Discipleship Discourse," p. 74. Cf. *Evangelica I*, p. 820; *Evangelica II*, pp. 425-426 (1982, pp. 45-46), p. 531 (1986, p. 285).

8. "A Warning about Scribes," p. 60 n. 37.

9. HF, 16.

10. HF, 209-214 ("Results of the Study"). Note that Fleddermann started his exegetical career with the study of Marcan redaction: *The Central Question of Mark's Gospel: A Study of Mark 8:29*, Diss. Graduate Theological Union, Berkeley, 1978; "The Flight of

This triple result needs further examination. Although Streeter was not the only one to alter his position, I am not inclined to think that Fleddermann's "everywhere..." will make people change their minds. But also for those who remain unconvinced by Fleddermann's book, reading and studying it can be beneficial.

To begin with, one can appreciate his position in the question of the extent of Q. With one possible exception in Q 17,26-30 (including vv. 28-29?) no Lucan or Matthean Sondergut texts are included in the reconstruction of Q.[11] The redaction of Q in Matthew and Luke is treated in reference to final Q without Q^{Mt} or Q^{Lk} intermediaries.[12] Minor agreements are expressly excluded. This is an important decision in studying Mark and Q. The influence of J. Lambrecht's approach, openly acknowledged elsewhere, has here some obvious limitations. Luke 10,25-28 is not part of Q,[13] and it is even more significant that he did not accept the proposal of a beginning of Q reconstructed on the basis of the minor agreements of Matthew and Luke against Mark 1,2-6 and 1,9-11.[14]

Second, Fleddermann makes a serious attempt at reconstruction of the Q text in Q 3,16-17; 6,38c; 7,27; 10,2-16; 11,10.14-15.16.17-26.29-32.33.43; 12,2.8-9.10.11-12.31b.40.51-53; 13,18-19.30; 14,26-27.34-35a; 16,17.18; 17,1b-2.6.23.33; 19,26. To these sixty-five verses involved in

---

a Naked Young Man (Mark 14:51-52)," in *CBQ* 41 (1979) 412-418. Compare *ETL* 55 (1979) 43-66 (cf. *Evangelica I*, p. 239 n. 301).

11. HF, 18 n. 68, 239-240 (Index: Q). See, for instance, Fleddermann's discussion of Luke 9,61-62 in "The Demands of Discipleship," 1992, pp. 548-552: "Both the theme and the vocabulary ... point to Lukan redaction" (p. 552).

12. On their introduction in some recent studies, see my "Q^{Mt} and Q^{Lk} and the Reconstruction of Q" (1990), in *Evangelica II*, pp. 475-480.

13. For recent discussion, see my "The Minor Agreements and Q," in R. A. PIPER (ed.), *The Gospel Behind the Gospels: Current Studies on Q* (NTSup, 75), Leiden, 1995, pp. 49-72, esp. 61-64; "Luke 10:25-28: A Foreign Body in Luke?" in S. E. PORTER – P. JOYCE – D. E. ORTON (eds.), *Crossing the Boundaries*. FS M. D. Goulder (Biblical Interpretation Series, 8), Leiden, 1994, pp. 149-165; "The Minor Agreements and Lk 10,25-28," in *ETL* 71 (1995) 151-160, esp. nn. 8, 44, 63. *Pace* J. LAMBRECHT, "The Great Commandment Pericope and Q," in *The Gospel Behind the Gospels* (above), pp. 73-96. K. Kertelge (cf. n. 8: 1985, 1994) is now inclined to accept the redactional interpretation of the agreements in Luke 10,25-28 (SNTS Seminar, 1995).

14. See my "The Minor Agreements and Q" (n. 13), pp. 65-72 ("The Beginning of Q"), with reference to Fleddermann's "The Beginning of Q" (p. 68 n. 104); cf. HF, 31. For the argument of the minor agreements (CATCHPOLE, "The Beginning of Q," pp. 217, 218 n. 49; LAMBRECHT, "John the Baptist and Jesus," pp. 363, 366-367), see the reply by J. M. ROBINSON, "The *Incipit* of the Sayings Gospel Q," in *RHPR* 75 (1995) 9-33, esp. pp. 14-19. But see ID., "The Sayings Gospel Q," in *The Four Gospels 1992*, pp. 361-388: although the minor agreements in the Baptism of Jesus are "notoriously inconclusive" he discusses other "more compelling" arguments for inclusion in Q (pp. 382-387). For a response, cf. R. URO, "John the Baptist and the Jesus Movement: What Does Q Tell Us?" in R. A. PIPER (ed.), *The Gospel Behind the Gospels*, pp. 231-255, esp. 237-239.

the comparison with Mark, we can add the reconstructions of Q in his earlier studies on Q 3,7-9; 9,57-60; 12,39-40.42b-46; and 22,28-30.[15] For almost all these passages we now have at our disposal the critical Q text prepared by the International Q Project,[16] and a confrontation may be instructive. I note here that, unlike the IQP texts, Fleddermann's reconstructions neither have the brackets used for less probable Q readings nor the siglum . . . used for undecided cases. Compare: Q 10,3 ὑπάγετε (IQP: ⟦ὑπάγετε⟧), ἄρνας (IQP: . . .); 16,17 πεσεῖν (IQP: π . . .); 16,18a καὶ γαμῶν ἑτέραν μοιχεύει (IQP: ⟦⟧ μοιχευ⟦ει⟧), 18b μοιχεύει (IQP: μοιχ . . .). Greater readability is an undeniable advantage of Fleddermann's Q text. Unfortunately, his printed text shows no distinction at all between words that are common to Matthew and Luke, words and forms found only in Matthew or in Luke, and conjectural Q words. Where the reconstructed texts are printed in parallel to Mark, the critical reader looks for such distinctions. Once more, when studying Fleddermann's "Mark and Q," my little *Q-Synopsis*, with its more sophisticated printing, proved to be an indispensable tool.[17]

Third, it is one of the merits of Fleddermann's work that all overlap texts are included.[18] The fact that in every instance the texts of Mark and Q are printed in juxtaposition is an improvement of the somewhat confusing presentation in J. S. Kloppenborg's *Q Parallels*. Four items are absent in Kloppenborg's collection of parallels: Mark 11,24 (§ 22); 13,12 (§ 25); 13,31 (§ 27); 14,21 (§ 17a).[19]

---

15. Q 3,7-9 ("The Beginning of Q," 1985); 9,57-60 ("The Demands of Discipleship," 1992); 12,39-40.42b-46 ("The Householder," 1986); 22,28-30 ("The End of Q," in *SBL 1990 Seminar Papers*, 1-10).

16. Cf. "The International Q Project," in *ETL* 69 (1993) 221-225; now reprinted in *Q-Synopsis*, ²1995, pp. 75-79 (with reference to *JBL*, 1990-1994). Only for Q 7,27; 10,7-16; 17,23.33 (and 22,28.30) the IQP text is not yet published (announced for *JBL* 114/3, 1995).

17. Cf. *Q-Synopsis. The Double Tradition Passages in Greek*. Revised Edition with Appendix (SNTA, 13), Leuven, 1995.

18. Cf. C. BREYTENBACH, "Vormarkinische Logientradition. Parallelen in der urchristlichen Briefliteratur," in *The Four Gospels 1992*, pp. 725-749. His survey includes Mark 4,24c; 9,42; 10,11-12 (with Q parallel). Cf. p. 748: "Um ein besseres Bild zu bekommen, wäre es nützlich, die Mk/Q-Parallelen systematisch zu vergleichen." See also ID., "Das Markusevangelium als traditionsgebundene Erzählung? Anfragen an die Markusforschung der achtziger Jahre," in C. FOCANT (ed.), *The Synoptic Gospels*, 1993, pp. 77-110, esp. 110: "*Eine systematische Auswertung der Beziehungen zwischen Q und Markus* sowie Thomas und Markus kann uns helfen, Umrisse und Motive von Teilen der von Markus literarisierten Überlieferung zu rekonstruieren und das Geflecht der vorsynoptischen Überlieferung ein wenig zu entzerren" (emphasis mine).

19. The text of Mark 4,24 (§ 7) is cited in S10 (Q 6,38c), but there is no mention of καὶ προστεθήσεται ὑμῖν (v. 24d) in S41 (Q 12,31b). Cf. "A Synopsis of Q" (1988), now reprinted in *Q-Synopsis*, ²1995, pp. 65-73, esp. 70-71 (= 446-447): "The Parallels in Mark" (with some corrections). On p. 70, Mark 9,40 should be inserted in the list of par-

Fourth, in "Recent Developments in the Study of Q" (1982) I mentioned Fleddermann's first contribution on Mark and Q in a concluding paragraph:[20]

> Mark's dependence on Q may be an attractive thesis especially for those who study the Markan redaction. On the level of the individual saying it is common practice to give a tentative description of Mark's redactional activity by comparing the saying in Mark with the Q version, but how do we prove Mark's dependence on Q, and not on a traditional saying or on some pre-Q collection of sayings? This can only be done by showing a specific dependence on the redaction of Q, dependence on sayings of which the creation or at least the formulation can be attributed to the Q redactor (cf. Schenk), or dependence on the order of the sayings as found in a redactional Q arrangement (cf. Lambrecht 1966). It is not enough to observe, as several recent authors are doing, that Mark's version of the saying is secondary. To mention one example, H. Fleddermann in his article on Mk 9,33-50 (1981) noted that Mark made in this section an extensive use of Q material: 9,37.40.42.50a, and: "In each case the differences between the reconstructed Q saying and the Marcan saying can be accounted for by Marcan redaction." (74) ... No distinction is made between Q material and Q redaction.

The question whether Mark reflects the redactional text of Q is now a central issue of Fleddermann's study:[21]

> In several places in the overlap texts Mark knows the Q redaction. We found two kinds of evidence. On the one hand, individual Marcan sayings reflect redactional features of Q. On the other hand, although the overlap texts appear throughout Mark, we found most of them concentrated in clusters. Some of these clusters consist entirely of Q texts assembled into new units. ... Two of the clusters show clearly that Mark had the entire Q document in front of him as he wrote.

Fleddermann's conclusion is unambiguous: Mark knows redactional Q; and "since Mark knows the redactional text of Q, Mark depends on Q." In order to verify this conclusion we will have to check its premise.

My observations, in the order of Fleddermann's paragraphs, will concentrate on some problems of his reconstruction of the Q text and on his quest for Q redactional (QR) at the basis of Mark.

---

allels (*Q Parallels*, p. 91: add reference to Q 11,23). — Compare R. Laufen's list: § § 16, 17, 17a, 20, 27 are not included (HF, 18; cf. "Recent Developments," p. 53 = 433).
   20. "Recent Developments," p. 45 (= 425). Cf. below, n. 188.
   21. HF, 211, 212.

§ 1. THE MESSENGER

The first overlap text in the Marcan order is Mark 1,2 and Q 7,27, Fleddermann's first example of redactional Q. He describes Q 7,27 as a combination and adaptation of Exod 23,20 and Mal 3,1 and then asks the question: Who combined these two texts? "The double quotation in Q 7,27 both secures John's greatness and subordinates him to Jesus by assigning him a precise role – as Elijah he prepares the way for Jesus. The Q redactor combined the two texts to draw the two views on John together."[22] As it appears from the references to Q 7,24-26.28a for John's greatness and Q 7,28b for John's subordination, neither the entire v. 28 nor v. 28b is supposed to be redactional. It is rather strange that no mention is made of these possibilities, not even of D. Catchpole's recent defense of vv. 27 + 28b as editorial additions to an earlier tradition in 7,24-26.28a[23]. C. Tuckett's reply, though not unknown to Fleddermann, is not mentioned either:[24]

> But v. 27 scarcely gives any indication of John's *inferiority*. This is clearer in v. 28b and so it is not quite so easy to see v. 28b as coming from the same stratum as v. 27. I argued above[25] that v. 27 is unlikely to be a later modification of v. 28, if only because it comes first, and a secondary comment is more likely to follow the tradition it is seeking to modify and comment on. This makes it most likely that v. 27 is the earlier comment on vv. 24-26, to which v. 28 is added as a later addition. In fact a strong case could be made out for v. 27 being the original conclusion to vv. 24-26. Vv. 24-26 alone seem to be almost a torso and to cry out for some clarification and conclusion. V. 26 ends with the double claim that it is indeed appropriate to think of John as a prophet, but that John is also more than a prophet. To the ques-

---

22. HF, 28.

23. "The Beginning of Q" (1992), pp. 207-213; = *The Quest for Q*, pp. 63-70: "Jesus' Testimony to John. Q 7:24-28."

24. "Mark and Q," pp. 165-166. See also his "The Temptation Narrative in Q," in *The Four Gospels 1992*, pp. 479-507, esp. 485 n. 29. For a slightly revised version of the passage quoted above, see his *Studies on Q*, Edinburgh, 1995, pp. 132-134.

25. See his critical remarks on J. S. Kloppenborg's theory (p. 164). For the view that Q 7,27 was inserted after v. 28 had already been conjoined to 7,24-26, see now also L. E. VAAGE, *Galilean Upstarts. Jesus' First Followers According to Q*, Valley Forge, 1994, p. 184 n. 76 (Lit.). The reference to D. Zeller should be canceled; see "Redaktionsprozesse und wechselnder 'Sitz im Leben' beim Q-Material," in *Logia*, 1982, pp. 395-409, esp. 403; ET: "Redactional Processes and Changing Settings in the Q-Material," in J. S. KLOPPENBORG (ed.), *The Shape of Q*, Minneapolis, 1994, pp. 116-130, esp. 124: "Verse 28 as a whole may be a commentary saying on v. 27.... In view of the repeated λέγω ὑμῖν, it is scarcely likely that it was originally attached to v. 26." Cf. TUCKETT, p. 166 n. 59 (see also p. 167 n. 64: "a very similar view about the tradition-history of the whole passage"). For both Tuckett and Zeller vv. 27 and 28 are "probably *pre*-redactional in Q" (Tuckett), "not inserted here by the redaction responsible for the assembling of the whole Baptist complex" (Zeller).

tion, "Is John a prophet?", the answer seems to be yes and no: he is a prophet, but he is also more. At the very least, one could say that such a claim is enigmatic! What does it mean to say that John is both a prophet and more? At one level Q 7,27 provides a perfect answer. John is described as an Elijah redivivus figure. He is then a prophetic figure in that he is an Elijah-figure, but he is also more than just any prophet: for he is the inaugurator of the new age forecast by Malachi. Thus v. 27 provides a very good conclusion to vv. 24-26 and there is no need to drive too much of a wedge between the two. There does however seem to be a seam between v. 27 and v. 28. The repeated λέγω ὑμῖν of Q 7,28 (cf. v. 26) makes it unlikely that v. 28 belongs with vv. 24-27 originally. It would appear to be a secondary comment.

Fleddermann argues that, like all the other quotations in Q, Q 7,27 depends on the Greek OT.[26] His list of quotations includes Q 4,4.8.10-11.12; 7,22; 10,15; 12,52-53; 13,19.27.29.35; 17,37; he attributes none of them to QR.[27] In two quotations, which he studied as overlap texts, Fleddermann locates the influence of the Greek OT at an earlier stage. In Q 12,53 (cf. Matt 10,35-36) the Q text "is not that close to the Septuagint."[28] His comment is quite clear with regard to Q 13,19 (Dan 4,21 Theodotion): "the end of the parable quotes from the Greek OT, so the parable had already undergone Hellenistic influence before it reached Q."[29] Likewise the LXX-wording in Q 7,27 can be pre-redactional. Moreover, the influence of the Hebrew text of Mal 3,1 remains the most likely explanation of the verb κατασκευάσει (פנה piel).[30] If, as suggested by Fleddermann, the use of the quotation in Mark 1,2 shows that Mark knew the text of Q 7,27, it does not prove that Mark knew QR.

26. HF, 27; list of the quotations in n. 10.

27. The analogy between Q 4,4.8.10-11.12 and 7,27 (γέγραπται, LXX) is not discussed by Fleddermann. On this problem, see TUCKETT, "Mark and Q," p. 167; and "The Temptation Narrative in Q" (n. 24), pp. 480-481, 483-485 (p. 484: "In fact the evidence for the use of a Septuagintal version here is extremely thin"). — A. W. Argyle's short studies (1953, 1954) can scarcely be cited by Fleddermann (n. 10) in support of his own position. For Argyle it appears to be a feature of the OT quotations in Q that "they are *not* in the wording of the LXX:" cf. Q 10,15; 12,53; 13,27 (contrast Q 13,35; 17,27: "But in these instances the Hebrew could hardly be rendered into Greek in any other way;" 1953, p. 382). Q 7,27 is not mentioned by Argyle. Cf. below, n. 30.

28. HF, 196. Cf. 199: the influence of Micah 7,6 LXX in Mark 13,12 (ἐπαναστή-σονται). See below, p. 294.

29. HF, 94. Cf. 97 (and 95): Ezek 17,23 LXX in Mark 4,32 (ὑπὸ τὴν σκιὰν αὐτοῦ).

30. Mal 3,1 LXX ἐπιβλέψεται (פנה in *qal*): contrast Aquila: σχολάσει; Symmachus: ἀποσκευάσει; Theodotion: ἑτοιμάσει. Compare, e.g., the recent commentaries on Matt 11,10 by Gundry (1982, p. 208), Gnilka (1986, p. 415 n. 14), Luz (1990, p. 175 n. 23), Davies-Allison (1991, p. 249). With the exception of P. Wernle (but see p. 116: "mit einer Ausnahme [!] nach LXX"), the authors cited by Fleddermann (n. 10) support this view: Stendahl (p. 51), Johnson (p. 144), Schulz (p. 232). See also D. S. NEW, *Old Testament Quotations*, pp. 62-64. Cf. E. P. MEADORS, *Jesus the Messianic Herald of Salvation* (WUNT, 2/72), Tübingen, 1995, pp. 165, 168 ("Semitic text-form"). On Mark and Q: "the predominant opinion at present favors literary independence" (p. 2; n. 8: M. Devisch, *et al.*).

In the context of Q 7,27 the pronoun σοῦ naturally refers to Jesus and for Fleddermann Mark's awkward use of this pronoun in 1,2 "certainly shows knowledge of redactional Q:"[31]

> Mark does not introduce a speaker at the beginning of the gospel, and the natural way to read v. 2 is to understand that the narrator is addressing the reader. However, this reading does not make sense...[32]

Yet, enough has been written on the function of the scripture quotation in Mark 1,2-3. I quote here M. E. Boring's comment:[33]

> [It] allows Jesus ... to be addressed "offstage" by the transcendent voice of God before the plotted narrative begins. The result is that when John appears in 1:4 his identity and significance are *already* determined by his relation to Jesus, and not vice versa. This is precisely the effect Mark intended... It is often noticed that Mark has changed the pronoun of Mal 3:1 from "my," referring to God, to "thy" (= "your") referring to the one addressed in this transcendent off-stage scene. ... by this narrative technique the reader gets to overhear the voice of God addressing *Jesus*, the one whose way is to be prepared...

It can be added that the use of the pronoun σοῦ in 1,2 prepares for God's addressing Jesus in Mark 1,11.[34]

§ 2. JOHN AND THE COMING ONE

In this text the evidence for Mark's use of QR is "not as clear as in the first saying." Fleddermann assumes that the reference to the Holy Spirit is an addition to the original saying, ἐν (πνεύματι ἁγίῳ καὶ) πυρί, and that the Q redactor could be responsible for this interpolation. His argument: "Q presents a coherent picture of the Spirit."[35] But there are only two other references to the Spirit in Q (11,20; 12,10), or possibly

---

31. HF, 39. Cf. pp. 30, 72, 211.
32. HF, 29.
33. M. E. BORING, "Mark 1:1-15 and the Beginning of the Gospel," in *Semeia* 52 (1991) 43-82, p. 60. Cf. R. M. FOWLER, *Let the Reader Understand. Reader-Response Criticism and the Gospel of Mark*, Minneapolis, MN, 1991, p. 111: "It is a hermeneutical guide to reading at the level of discourse" (see also pp. 87-89).
34. Cf. R. H. GUNDRY, *Mark*, Grand Rapids, MI, 1993, p. 35. See also J. GNILKA, *Markus*, p. 41 (on the "Gottessprüche"); cf. p. 44, on the quotation: "Es gibt ihm die Möglichkeit, den eben genannten Gottessohn von Gott angeredet sein zu lassen." — On υἱοῦ θεοῦ in Mark 1,1, see now A. Y. COLLINS, "Establishing the Text: Mark 1:1," in T. FORNBERG – D. HELLHOLM (eds.), *Texts and Contexts*. FS L. Hartman, Oslo, 1995, pp. 111-127: "The addition probably occurred sometime in the second century" (concluding sentence). Unfortunately, the section on internal evidence mentions Mark's theme of "Jesus' sonship with God" (p. 121) without considering υἱοῦ θεοῦ in relation to "its context" (Mark 1,2 and 11).
35. HF, 37; see also 35, 39, and 69-70 (Q 12,10).

only one because the reference in Q 11,20 / Matt 12,28 is doubtful: ἐν (πνεύματι) θεοῦ (cf. § 3). Q 12,10 is supposed to have come to Mark as part of the section Q 12,2-12, in which 12,8-9 probably stems from the Q redactor. If 12,8-9 comes from the Q redactor, the commenting saying in 12,10 "does also." Thus the phrase in 3,16 and the saying in 12,10 are later additions and confirm each other: "both probably come from the same pen." But the possibility that Q 12,10 was known by Mark as an independent saying deserves more serious consideration. In the case of Q 3,16 Fleddermann's alternative could have been that the words were added in the pre-Q tradition. But there is also the alternative solution that καὶ πυρί was added to the saying (Laufen, Schüling, *et al.*).

§ 3. THE BEELZEBUL CONTROVERSY

Q 11,14-26 is one of the longest overlap texts. Luke 11,16, placed here by Luke, is rightly treated in § 11. Q 11,23 has its place here in Q but because of the parallel in Mark 9,40 it is treated in the Marcan order in § 16. This Q saying (11,23) and Q 11,19-20.24-26 are without parallel in Mark 3,22-27. It is of great importance for Fleddermann's theory that he can state that in Mark 3,22-27 "everything comes from Q."[36] But can we really say that Mark 3,27 comes from Q?

1. The main argument for the inclusion of this saying in Q is the placement of Matt 12,29 / Luke 11,21-22 between Matt 12,27-28 / Luke 11,19-20 and Matt 12,30 / Luke 11,23: this position "indicates that the parable also stood in Q at this point."[37] The problem is that Matthew adopted the wording of Mark 3,27, and those who propose a reconstruction of the Q text are to rely on the quite different version in Luke.[38] Fleddermann now recognizes Lucan composition in Luke 11,21-22.[39] In his view, however, Luke's text is not an elaboration of Mark 3,27 but derived from the Q text preserved unchanged in Matt 12,29.[40] Yet, the texts of Matthew and Mark are so similar to one another that the "solid points of contact" he notes between Luke and Matthew are in fact contacts with Mark. If, for example, Luke draws the entering motif from Q (Matt εἰσελθεῖν) and "reduces it to participle (ἐπελθών)," one should

---

36. HF, 213.

37. KLOPPENBORG, *Q Parallels*, p. 92. More recent commentaries can be added, on Matthew: LUZ, 1990 (II, p. 255); DAVIES-ALLISON, 1991 (II, p. 342); on Luke: NOLLAND, 1993 (II, p. 635); SCHÜRMANN, 1994 (II, p. 245).

38. POLAG, *Fragmenta Q*. Cf. LAMBRECHT, *Marcus Interpretator*, p. 43; LAUFEN, p. 131: "in einer wohl Lukas näherstehenden Fassung."

39. With reference to S. Légasse.

40. HF, 52-55.

observe that the parallel in Mark reads εἰσελθών. Fleddermann tries to explain the minor differences between Matthew and Mark as "Q flavor" on the one hand and Marcan changes of Q on the other.[41] But are they not more naturally explainable as Matthean editorial changes of Mark? The opening in Mark 3,27 ἀλλ᾽ οὐ δύναται οὐδείς is replaced by Matthew with ἢ πῶς δύναταί τις. If the ἢ πῶς "picks up" the πῶς in v. 26, is it still relevant to look for Q flavor in Matt 7,4 (ἢ πῶς ἐρεῖς, par. Luke 6,42 πῶς δύνασαι λέγειν)? A correction of Mark's double negative is far from unique in Matthew.[42]

Fleddermann reformulates the argument based on the position of the saying into a consideration of the wording of Matt 12,29: in the Beelzebul Controversy Matthew conflates Mark and Q in 12,25-26 and 12,31-32 and between these two passages he follows his source Q word for word (vv. 27-28.29.30).[43] But the fact that in other passages such as Q 3,7-9[44] Matthew copies Q without change is scarcely a convincing argument in the case of Matt 12,29, and with regard to the preceding v. 28 it is less certain than Fleddermann suggests that Matthew's πνεύματι, and not Luke's δακτύλῳ, preserves the text of Q.[45] Anyway the lack of agreement between Matt 12,29 (= Mark 3,27) and Luke 11,21-22 may indicate that the case of the Strong Man saying differs from that of Matt 12,27-28.30 (Q 11,19-20.23). On the side of Matthew, the influence of Mark 3,23-26.27.28-29 in Matt 12,25-26(27-28)29(30)31-32 is widely accepted. But is it correctly stated that "Luke shows no definite sign of such influence" (J. Nolland)?[46] The same author does not deny that Luke 11,16 has been produced by Luke on the basis of Mark 8,11.[47] In the answer of Jesus,

41. HF, 54, 64.

42. See Matt 8,4 (om. μηδέν); 21,19 (om. μηδείς); 26,29 (om. οὐκέτι); 26,63 (om. οὐδέν). Compare the motif of inability in Mark 5,3 (καὶ οὐδὲ ... οὐκέτι οὐδεὶς ἐδύνατο), 4 (καὶ οὐδεὶς ἴσχυεν) and Matt 8,28 ὥστε μὴ ἰσχύειν τινα. See also Mark 6,5 (diff. Matt 13,58).

43. HF, 55.

44. See further the list of instances in HF, 158 n. 19.

45. He refers to C. S. Rodd, R. G. Hamerton-Kelly, J. E. Yates, A. George (early 1960's; cf. Lambrecht, *Marcus Interpretator*) and J.-M. van Cangh (1982), in contrast to T. W. Manson (1935). Compare the reference to "the more recent studies," in contrast to "earlier scholarship," in J. NOLLAND, 1993 (*Luke* II, p. 639). But see D. C. ALLISON, *The New Moses*, 1993: "I am persuaded, along with others who have examined the issue, that Luke's allusive 'finger of God' probably stood in Q" (p. 237; cf. p. 97 n. 7). Cf. LAUFEN, p. 130: "die Mehrzahl der heutigen Forscher" (p. 431 n. 49); more recent commentaries by Fitzmyer, Davies-Allison, Gnilka, Luz, *et al.* can be added. See now also E. P. MEADORS, *Jesus* (n. 30), pp. 191-192. Schürmann (1982, p. 155 n. 163, with reference to M. Hengel, *Nachfolge*, p. 73 n. 109) is now more hesitant: "keine rechte Sicherheit" (*Lk* II/1, 240).

46. *Luke* II, p. 635.

47. *Ibid.*, 637. On ἕτεροι δέ, cf. below, n. 137.

Luke 11,18b anticipates Mark 3,30 (ὅτι ἔλεγον...) in combination with the first clause of the Q saying (11,19a) and thus reinforces the coherence of 11,17-18+19-20. With regard to Luke 11,21-22, Fleddermann's demonstration of Luke's possible use of Matt 12,29 is perfectly applicable to the use of its counterpart in Mark 3,27, and the objection against independent agreement in placing the parable at Q 11,20/23 looks like an a priori statement. Considering the coherent redactional unity of Luke 11,17-20, the parable taken from Mark 3,(23-26)27 appears to be placed by Luke as soon as it was convenient; Q 11,23 was apparently understood as a concluding saying.[48]

2. The reconstruction of the Q text underlying Matt 12,25a and Luke 11,17a (εἰδὼς δὲ τὰ διανοήματα αὐτῶν εἶπεν αὐτοῖς) presents little problem for Fleddermann: Matthew changed τὰ διανοήματα to τὰς ἐνθυμήσεις and Luke added αὐτός and moved αὐτῶν to the preposition.[49] In a second phase he considers the parallel text in Mark 3,23a: all differences result from Marcan redaction.[50] The first phase of Fleddermann's discussion of overlap texts is usually devoted to the reconstruction of the Q text from Matthew and Luke. The Marcan parallel and Matthew's and Luke's redaction of Mark are normally not considered in that first stage of his inquiry.[51] Thus, in the first section of the Beelzebul Controversy, he compares Matt 9,32-34; 12,22-24 with Luke 11,14-15, and has only one statement with regard to Mark: "Neither Matthew nor Luke show any Marcan influence...."[52] He makes an exception for Mark 3,23a in reference to the redactional interpretation of the Matthew-Luke agreement I suggested in my "Mt 12,25a / Lc 11,17a." In his response, Fleddermann describes Mark's προσκαλεσάμενος as "an adequate expression" and the participle εἰδώς in the parallel texts as an

---

48. For authors who reject the Q origin of the parable, see KLOPPENBORG, *Q Parallels*, p. 92. See now also A. D. JACOBSON, *First Gospel*, p. 154 n. 3, 162; L. E. VAAGE, *Galilean Upstarts*, pp. 117, 168 n. 39, 190 n. 41.

49. HF, 46-47. Contrast the pre-position of the pronoun in Q according to Polag and IQP (*JBL* 112, 1993, p. 503; cf. KLOPPENBORG, in *SBL 1985 Seminar Papers*, pp. 136, 142). But see my remarks on Lucan redaction, "Mt 12,25a / Lc 11,17a," pp. 131-133 (= 490-492).

50. HF, 62-63.

51. The exceptions are cases of redactional assimilation of the doublets by additional phrases: Matt 5,32; 19,9 (the πορνεία clause); 12,39; 16,4 (καὶ μοιχαλίς); 13,12; 25,29 (καὶ περισσευθήσεται); 17,20; 21,21 (ἐὰν ἔχητε πίστιν); Luke 8,16; 11,33 (οἱ πορευόμενοι...).

52. HF, 41-45, esp. 45. "The only possible exception" (n. 27) is ὥστε + infinitive in Matt 12,22 (cf. Mark 3,20), but he also observes, more correctly, that "the conjunction is common in Matthew" (43, and n. 16). There is no mention of a possible contact with Mark 3,21 (ἐξέστη) in Matt 12,23 (ἐξίσταντο). For a comparison of Matt 12,24 with Mark 3,22, cf. R. H. GUNDRY, *Matthew*, p. 232.

"awkward" phrase in the Beelzebul Controversy.[53] In order to avoid misunderstanding I repeat here the point I made:[54]

> Προσκαλεσάμενος αὐτούς n'est donc pas une formule typique des récits de controverse, et en lui substituant εἰδὼς δὲ τὰς ἐνθυμήσεις αὐτῶν Mt a renforcé considérablement le genre propre de l'épisode.
>
> L'influence de Mt 9,4 ne serait donc pas limitée au choix du mot ἐνθυμήσεις en remplacement du διανοήματα de la source. C'est l'expression toute entière qui serait une reprise de Mt 9,4a.

In his own way Fleddermann also refers to Matt 9,4 (Matthew's use of the *word* ἐνθυμήσεις) but in 12,25a "εἰδώς is awkward because there isn't any reference to the adversaries' commenting 'in their hearts'." But precisely in light of Matt 9,4 the *theme* of "knowing their thoughts" here "probably implies that what they had said in the preceding verse they said within themselves, not to the crowds."[55] One can hardly say that in this case Matthew "must make connections between far-flung Marcan texts in order to eliminate ... προσκαλεσάμενος." Fleddermann reads Luke 11,17a in connection with v. 15: "Only some of the crowd voiced the charge against Jesus," and he neglects the introduction of ἕτεροι δὲ πειράζοντες... That the use of πειράζοντες may suggest the theme of "knowing their thoughts" (without adding "in their hearts") *we* know from Mark 12,15 and parallels; it is not *Luke* who must make connections between far-flung Marcan texts...[56]

3. Q 11,17c καὶ οἶκος ἐπὶ οἶκον πίπτει: "Most likely Luke reflects Q... Three facts support Lucan originality."[57] Although he recognizes

---

53. HF, 47.

54. "Mt 12,25a / Lc 11,17a," pp. 127, 128 (= 486, 487). On the reading εἰδώς in Matt 9,4 (Greeven, Boismard, Gundry, *et al.*), see *ibid.*, n. 25. The variant ἰδών now receives the rating B (before C) but no new evidence is provided in Metzger's *Textual Commentary*, ²1994, pp. 19-20.

55. R. H. GUNDRY, *Matthew*, p. 233. See also his note on Matt 12,25a / Luke 11,17a in *The Four Gospels 1992*, pp. 1482-1483.

56. The close similarity between Matt 12,25a and Luke 11,17a makes one hesitant; see my own conclusion (p. 133 = 492). Cf. H. SCHÜRMANN, *Lukasevangelium* II/1, p. 233: "Sowohl 11,17a wie par Mt 12,25a geben Lukas und Matthäus somit in eigenem Sprachstil wieder. Beide kennen das Motiv vom 'Tiefblick' Jesu aus Mk, bezeugen es aber sonst nirgends für Q. Daß aber beide das gleiche Motiv (mit je eigenen Worten) für Lk 11,17a / Mt 12,25 diff Mk bringen, kann nicht gut Zufall sein..." I may add here: "Cependant, l'étude des *minor agreements* nous a appris que des accords frappants peuvent parfois s'expliquer comme des rédactions indépendantes sur la seule base de Mc, et je crois que la question mérite d'être posée à propos de Mt 12,25a / Lc 11,17a" (p. 128 = 487). Such a possibility is not excluded by Fleddermann, at least theoretically: "We can, of course, conceive of the possibility that Matthew and Luke might agree in altering a Q text" (HF, 16 n. 63).

57. HF, 48.

that in this case "it is difficult to choose," Fleddermann has no mention of the "facts" in support of Matt 12,25c; and there is no reference to alternative reconstructions of the Q text: καὶ πᾶσα οἰκία ἐφ' ἑαυτὴν μερισθεῖσα οὐ σταθήσεται (Klauck, 1978);[58] cf. IQP: καὶ οἰκ[ία μερισθεῖσα καθ' ἑαυτῆς οὐ σταθήσεται].[59] Fleddermann simply observes: "If Luke had found a section in Q on the divided house or 'family,' he would not have omitted it as he frequently uses 'house' in the sense of 'family'." But there is more than one term that can be understood in a literal sense (ἐρημοῦται, οἰκία, οὐ σταθήσεται)[60] and may have suggested the change of the motif of the divided family to an illustration of the complete destruction of the kingdom. That in the Beelzebul Controversy Luke uses "house" only in the sense of "building" is one of the facts adduced in favor of the Q origin of Luke 11,17c. Fleddermann's translation referring to buildings is somewhat ambiguous: "and house falls *against* house" (ἐπί = upon, on; contrast the use of ἐπί = *against* in 11,17b), and here again it is not mentioned that opinions remain divided between house-building (NRSV: "and house falls on house") and house-family (REB: "and a divided household falls").[61] Cf. below, § 4.

§ 4. THE UNFORGIVABLE SIN

To begin with, the reconstructed text of Q 12,10 καὶ πᾶς ὅς...: "Although πᾶς is a favorite word of Luke, its use with the relative is attested in Q."[62] One of the two other occurrences in Q is Q 6,47, cited

---

58. H.-J. KLAUCK, *Allegorie und Allegorese in synoptischen Gleichnistexten* (NeutAbh, 13), Münster, 1978, pp. 174-179 ("Reich und Haus"), esp. 177. Cf. p. 176: "Lk hat den übergetragenen Sinn von οἰκία = Familie nicht wahrgenommen und das Zusammenstürzen von Gebäuden als passende Illustration für die Verwüstung eines Reiches angesehen. Für Q nehmen wir Mt 12,25c in Anspruch, mit Ausnahme von πόλις, das Mt eingefügt hat." On this Lucan *Mißverständnis*, see e.g. the recent commentaries by U. Luz (*Mt* II, p. 255 n. 21) and H. Schürmann (*Lk* II/1, p. 234 n. 69).

59. *JBL* 112 (1993), p. 503. Cf. KLOPPENBORG, "Q 11:14-26: Work Sheets for Reconstruction," in *SBL 1985 Seminar Papers*, pp. 133-151; p. 136, reconstruction Q 11,17c: (καὶ . . . ?); pp. 143-144 (authors pro and contra Luke = Q); "Q may have presupposed 'divided' in the second clause and οικος meaning 'household'" (p. 144).

60. Cf. SCHÜRMANN (n. 58).

61. Cf. M. D. GOULDER, *Luke*, 1989, p. 504 ("has its parallel in the five ἐν ἑνὶ οἴκῳ διαμερισμένοι"); L. T. JOHNSON, *Luke*, 1991, p. 181: "household against household"; J. NOLLAND, *Luke* II, 1993, p. 638. On this "usual rendering," see H. E. BRYANT, "Note on Luke xi.17," in *ExpT* 50 (1938-39) 525-526. See also J. A. FITZMYER, *Luke*, p. 921: "*one house falls upon another*. Or 'against' another... Here *oikos* could even mean 'family'." I. H. Marshall's reading is scarcely different: "upon another" as "one household attacking another" (p. 474). On the meaning in Q, see n. 59.

62. HF, 66 n. 115, 117.

in a note without further comment. A. Polag, for instance, reads πᾶς ὅστις ἀκούει (cf. Matt), but IQP has πᾶς ὁ [[ ]] ἀκού[[ων]] (cf. Luke). The second example is Q 12,8, and M. E. Boring is blamed by Fleddermann for not having investigated this Q context. But the preceding saying in 12,8 (Q πᾶς ὅς) and 9 (participle in Luke) may have influenced Luke's editing with πᾶς in 12,10a (καὶ πᾶς ὅς) and 10b (the participle τῷ βλασφημήσαντι). The text of Q 12,10b is reconstructed in parallel to 10a: ὃς δὲ ἐρεῖ λόγον εἰς τὸ πνεῦμα τὸ ἅγιον (contrast IQP: ὃς δ᾿ ἂν [[βλασφημήσῃ]]). The fact that "Luke borrowed the verb 'blaspheme' from Mark" (3,28-29)[63] makes it more likely that Mark 3,27 (and not Matt 12,29 "Q") has been the source of Luke 11,21-22 (cf. § 3). "Q contains only two references to the Holy Spirit."[64] The reference to "the 'Spirit' of God" in 11,20 is not considered here (contrast his comment on 3,16 in § 2).[65] That Mark found the saying Q 12,10 in conjunction with 12,8-9 (QR) remains an unproven assumption. Cf. below, § 14.

In Mark the Unforgivable Sin logion (3,28-29) is appended to the Beelzebul Controversy, and the final comment in 3,30 forms an inclusion with the initial charge in v. 22. Mark 3,22-30 is surrounded by the True Relatives (3,20-21.31-35). This framing technique is "characteristically Marcan," "carries Mark's signature."[66] The six classic examples are listed by Fleddermann, and in particular Mark 3,20-35 and 6,7-30 receive some more special attention.[67] Two remarks can be made here. First, Mark 3,25, on the divided house, is said to be added by Mark "to refer to Jesus' split with his family."[68] Though Mark 3,22 (and 30) is related to 3,20-21, it is less likely that, at the middle of the inserted Beelzebul Controversy, the divided house saying would have such a direct connection with the framing section: "The context of a kingdom defines the house as a royal family, not an ordinary household... Strife within a royal family will open the door to usurpers."[69] My second remark concerns the framing technique in Mark 6,7-30: "For the technique to work, the outside frame must be kept short."[70] Fleddermann compares here Mark's

63. HF, 68. Cf. *Evangelica II*, 432, 442.
64. HF, 70.
65. HF, 35, 37 (cf. 50-51).
66. HF, 213, 124.
67. HF, 61-62, 73-73, 119-120, 124. The six examples are merely listed (62 n. 90; 73 n. 151, 119 n. 82; cf. *Duality*). On more recent studies, see G. VAN OYEN, "Intercalation and Irony in the Gospel of Mark," in *The Four Gospels 1992*, pp. 949-974; ID., *De studie van de Marcusredactie in de twintigste eeuw* (SNTA, 18), Leuven, 1993, p. 313 n. 1213.
68. HF, 73. Cf. 64: "The framing pericope provides a concrete example of a family divided."
69. R. H. GUNDRY, *Mark*, p. 173.
70. HF, 119.

Mission Discourse with the Mission Discourse in Matt 10 where the disciples never return: "To avoid this problem, Mark shortens the Q discourse."[71] One has the impression that a more or less uniform framing technique is called upon to solve the problem of the "omissions" in Mark. But it is sufficient to compare Mark 6,7-13 and 30 with 3,20-21 and 31-35 to see that there is no such uniformity in Mark's intercalations.

§ § 5-8. A CLUSTER OF FOUR SAYINGS

"In the cluster of sayings in Mark 4,21-25 we find five Q sayings joined together:" 4,21 (Q 11,33); 4,22 (Q 12,2); 4,24cd (Q 6,38c; 12,31b); 4,25 (Q 19,26). "If Mark were drawing on the oral tradition, we would expect to find some non-Q material mixed in."[72] Only Mark 4,23 is not taken into consideration. The listening saying εἴ τις ἔχει ὦτα ἀκούειν ἀκουέτω ("a true Q saying" for Lambrecht[73]) is apparently regarded by Fleddermann as Marcan,[74] and Luke 14,35b, without parallel in Matthew, not ascribed to Q.[75] One can agree with Fleddermann that the sayings collection in Mark 4,21-25 is a Marcan composition and that for all four sayings there are parallels in Q. But does it mean that Mark drew on Q? It is not because the parallels are dispersed in Q that we can conclude that "Mark composed with knowledge of the whole Q document."

§ 9. THE MUSTARD SEED

The section on Mark 4,30-32 originally appeared as part of a larger essay, "The Mustard Seed and the Leaven" (1989). The text is only

---

71. HF, 120.
72. HF, 213; cf. 89, 98-99.
73. "Logia-Quellen," p. 335: "Auch dieser Vers stand wohl ursprünglich in Q^rev in dem genannten Kontext [Lk 14,35b]. Aus seiner Quelle antizipierte Markus ihn Mk 4,9;" *Marcus Interpretator*, p. 111 n. 26 ("Heeft Marcus daar de oproep gevonden en hem hierna redactioneel tot zijn voorkeurthema verheven?"); cf. p. 122 n. 50; "Redaction and Theology," p. 286 ("if it is a true Q saying, Matthew might have omitted it in V,13 for the sake of symmetry with V,14"); cf. p. 289 ("we suggested that the appeal to listen [v. 23] was also found in Q" [cf. *Lk.*, XIV,35c]). A new suggestion appears *ibid.*, p. 286: "It is also possible that the Q-expression καὶ ὃ εἰς τὸ οὖς ἀκούετε (*Mt.*, X,27; cf. *Lk.*, XII,3b) ... influenced Mark to incorporate the listening saying." Cf. "Q-Influence," p. 299 ("one should not too easily dismiss the possibility..."); cf. p. 301.
74. HF, 86: "he introduces the [Measure] saying with a double summons to hear in vv. 23-24ab." Cf. 123 n. 102.
75. Cf. § 18: Q 14,34-35a. For Luke 14,35b in Q (n. 73), cf. J. SCHMID, *Matthäus und Lukas*, p. 219 n. 1; H. SCHÜRMANN, *Traditionsgeschichtliche Untersuchungen*, p. 276 n. 33 (note: the overlap text in Mark 4,9, and not 4,23). — On Mark 4,9 (ὃς ἔχει), 23 (εἴ τις ἔχει) and Luke 14,35 (ὁ ἔχων), see C. BREYTENBACH, "Vormarkinische Logientradition" (n. 18), pp. 739-740 ("Der Weckruf").

slightly revised, somewhat rearranged[76] and supplemented with references to F. Kogler (1988) and T. A. Friedrichsen (1992). The main discussion with Friedrichsen concerns the double question in Luke 13,18.[77] For Friedrichsen it is Lucan rewriting of Mark 4,30 whereas for Fledder-mann Luke 13,18-19 is uninfluenced by Mark and the double question is taken over from Q without change. Fleddermann emphasizes Luke's avoidance of double questions[78] and seems to neglect that other factors can explain why "two questions ... don't survive in Luke's redaction."[79] With regard to the possible influence of Mark 4,30 on Luke 7,31 (and 13,18), Fleddermann replies that, though Luke transfers "blaspheme" from Mark 3,29 to Luke 12,10 (Q),[80] "no other example exists of Luke taking elements from a Marcan overlap text and using them to redact a different Q text."[81] This is a rather strange limitation of possible re-miniscences (permutations) in the redaction of Luke.[82] Kloppenborg has noted that the introductory formula in Q 7,31 "resembles the introductory formulae to the parables of the Mustard (Q 13:18-19; Mk 4:30) and the Leaven (Q 13:20-21)," and: "appears to imitate the interrogative intro-duction of the kingdom parables."[83] This observation remains valid if we read Q 7,31 τίνι (δὲ) ὁμοιώσω τὴν γενεὰν ταύτην; (cf. Matt) and attribute to Luke the insertion of τοὺς ἀνθρώπους (+ genitive) and the addition of the second question: καὶ τίνι εἰσὶν ὅμοιοι; An a priori refusal of Lucan assimilation to the double question in Mark 4,30 is hardly justifiable.

76. As can be seen in the numbering of the footnotes 75-115 (compared with those of 1989): 75(43), 76(7), 77(9), 78(10), 79 (11), 80(13), 81(17), 82(19⁺), 84(20⁺), 87(22), 88(23-24), 89(25), 92(26), 93(29), 94(p. 223), 95(74, p. 232), 97(46), 101(49), 102(50), 103(52), 104-105(53), 106-108(54), 109-110(61), 111(62), 113(58), 114(59), 115(60).

77. HF, 91-93. Cf. T. A. FRIEDRICHSEN, "'Major' and 'Minor' Matthew-Luke Agreements," pp. 662-675 ("The Double Question: Mk 4,30 / Lk 13,18").

78. Note that the same examples (Luke 8,25; 9,41; 20,22; 22,46; 22,71) are cited to illustrate that Luke avoids double questions (n. 83) and "eliminates double questions from Mark" (n. 84). On the other hand, Q 11,21-22 (n. 88; cf. above § 3) should be added to the six examples where Luke eliminates rhetorical questions from Q (n. 83). In Q 6,39a.39b; 6,46; 7,31b; 13,18a.18b.20 the rhetorical question is "eliminated" in Matthew (not mentioned in n. 88).

79. HF, 92 n. 84.

80. Cf. above, n. 63. See also HF, 109 (on μένετε in Luke 10,7): "If Luke can import Q expressions into Mark, he can carry over Marcan terms into Q."

81. HF, 92-93.

82. On Marcan reminiscences in Luke, see F. NOËL, De compositie van het Lucas-evangelie in zijn relatie tot Marcus: Het probleem van de grote weglating, Brussel, 1994, pp. 191-231.

83. J. S. KLOPPENBORG, "Jesus and the Parables of Jesus in Q," in R. A. PIPER (ed.), The Gospel Behind the Gospels, 1995, pp. 275-319, esp. 290, 318.

§ 10. THE MISSION DISCOURSE

Fleddermann begins his analysis by comparing the Mission Discourse with the Beelzebul Controversy, the other extensive overlap text, and here too he will conclude: Mark is secondary to Q; Mark also shows knowledge of redactional Q.[84] Lambrecht's *Marcus Interpretator* was the model in § 3: "Years ago Lambrecht got it right – Mark depends on Q in the Beelzebul Controversy."[85] Throughout §§ 3–9 (Mark 3,22-30; 4,21-25.30-32) the footnotes refer frequently to Lambrecht. His name is now absent in § 10. Neither is Catchpole mentioned here, although a confrontation with his "Mission Charge" would have been most appropriate. The interlocutors here are P. Hoffmann (1971, 1972) and the more recent R. Uro (1987).[86] It is all the more surprising that the term "redactional Q," which is found in the Conclusion, is never used elsewhere in the section on the Mission Discourse.

A large part of § 10 is devoted to the detailed reconstruction of the Q text in Q 10,2-16. The Equipment Rule in 10,4a deserves special attention. His reconstruction is as follows: μὴ **λαμβάνετε ἄργυρον**, μὴ πήραν, μὴ ὑποδήματα, **μὴ ῥάβδον**. The words in bold differ from Luke's text: λαμβάνετε (for Luke's βαστάζετε), cf. Q 14,27 λαμβάνει (= Matt 10,38; βαστάζει in Luke); ἄργυρον (for Luke's βαλλάντιον), cf. ἄργυρον in Matt 10,9 and ἀργύριον in Luke 9,3; μὴ ῥάβδον (not in Luke), cf. μηδὲ ῥάβδον in Matt 10,10 and μήτε ῥάβδον in Luke 9,3. Fleddermann rightly refuses the prohibition of two tunics (μὴ δύο χιτῶνας): "the coats come from Mark."[87] But also the inclusion of "no staff" in the text of Q on the basis of Matt 10,10; Luke 9,3 is far from evident. Μηδὲ/μήτε ῥάβδον (for εἰ μὴ ῥάβδον μόνον in Mark 6,8) can be the result of assimilation to the other prohibitions. The text of Luke 10,4a remains a more secure basis for the reconstruction of Q

---

84. HF, 101-126 and 133.

85. HF 65. *Marcus Interpretator* (1969) is a collection of four articles that appeared (in the reverse order) in *Bijdragen* 29 (1968) 25-52 (Mark 4,1-34); 114-150, 234-258, 369-392 (Mark 3,20-35).

86. See now also R. URO, "John the Baptist and the Jesus Movement" (n. 14), 1995, esp. 245-246: "many of those who have worked with the Mark / Q problem think that the best hypothesis for the relationship of these two gospels is a 'common tradition' model, a hypothesis that Mark / Q overlaps are due to common tradition or sources used by the authors" (p. 245, with references to M. Devisch and R. Laufen). "Several analyses confirm that behind the Markan and Q Mission Charges one can recognize a common pattern..., which has been framed by further narrative (Mk 6:7, 12-13, 30) or sayings material (Q 10:2, 3, 12, 13-15, 16)" (pp. 245-246).

87. Mark 6,9 and Matt 10,10; Luke 9,3. Cf. HF, 105 ("tunics" rather than "coats") and n. 24, repeated in n. 25. Note that it is less certain for Hoffmann (p. 267: question mark) and Uro (p. 77: within parentheses).

(Polag, Laufen, *et al.*)[88] The mention of "silver" (Matt 10,9; Luke 9,3) is even more doubtful. Matthew really needs no second source for developing Mark's μὴ εἰς τὴν ζώνην χαλκόν into his triad χρυσὸν μηδὲ ἄργυρον μηδὲ χαλκὸν εἰς τὰς ζώνας ὑμῶν. That "Mark substitutes 'copper' for 'silver' (compare Mark 12,41)"[89] can easily be reversed: Mark's word χαλκόν is omitted in Luke 21,1 and changed to ἀργύριον, the general word for money, in Luke 9,3. Strangely, Luke 22,35-36 (ὅτε ἀπέστειλα ὑμᾶς ἄτερ βαλλαντίου καὶ πήρας καὶ ὑποδημάτων...) is not at all mentioned in Fleddermann's discussion of Luke 10,4a.[90]

Much more amazing is the fact that Fleddermann treats the Mark-Q problem in Q 10,2-16 without even referring to Catchpole's distinction between the traditional mission charge and a single redactional stratum. The most problematic verses in this repartition between tradition and redaction are vv. 12 and 16, and I have suggested correcting his hypothesis by proposing vv. 2.**12**.13-15 as redactionally added to the Q tradition (10,3.4.5-7.8-11a.**16**).[91] "If, with Catchpole, we accept traditional pre-Q material in Q 10,3-11, there may be some correspondence between its fourfold division and the contents of Mark 6,7-11: sending (7), equipment (8-9), acceptance (10), rejection (11), but this cannot be used as evidence of Mark's dependence on Q. On the other hand, because Q 10,2.12 are without parallel in Mk 6, one could argue that this Q-redactional frame [and 10,13-15] was unknown to Mark."[92] In this hypothesis, the problem of "Mark's omissions" that Fleddermann has to face[93] is considerably alleviated.

§ 11. Demand for a Sign

"Mark's use of 'this generation' hangs in the air... Mark picks up 'this generation' from Q 11,30-32 which he omits... Mark shows knowledge of redactional Q in the expression 'this generation'."[94] Fleddermann

88. See my "Literary Criticism" (1993), p. 33 n. 106 (in reply to Catchpole). Following Hoffmann (p. 240), Fleddermann considers together "shoes" and "staff" (HF, 105, 118), but the prohibition of "shoes" is found in Luke 10,4a; the "staff" is not.

89. HF, 122.

90. Neither are alternative reconstructions of Q 10,4a such as the IQP text noted by Fleddermann. Cf. *JBL* 110 (1991), p. 496: μὴ ⟦βαστάζετ⟧ε ⟦ἀργύρ. .ον, μὴ πήραν⟧, μὴ . . ὑποδήματα, ⟦μηδὲ ῥάβδον⟧. The two dots indicate the variation ἀργύριον/ἄργυρον (but the accent is that of ἀργύριον!) and the possible insertion of μὴ δύο χιτῶνας. That μὴ πήραν is included ⟦ ⟧ together with ἀργύριον must be a mistake.

91. "Literary Criticism," pp. 31-33 ("Q 10,2-16 and Mark").

92. *Ibid.*, p. 33.

93. HF, 120-121.

94. Quotations from HF, 131-134 and 211: "The term does not fit smoothly in Mark... The expression does not fit naturally in Mark's passage. – In Q ... the use of 'this generation'

compares Mark 8,12 with the passage in Q without even mentioning the complex problem of the history of Q 11,29-32. He drops Luke's ἡ γενεὰ αὕτη in his reconstruction of Q 11,29, and since he proposes Mark's knowledge of QR, one may guess that he considers Q 11,30 to be redactional (cf. Lührmann, Hoffmann, Schenk, et al.: 11,30 or 29d-30 QR).[95] But other scholars think that there are good reasons for treating 11,30 as pre-redactional, either as part of the original unit 11,29-30 (Schulz, Luz) or as an explicative phrase, Deutewort or Verdeutlichungswort, added to v. 29 (Kloppenborg, Schürmann, Vögtle). They all agree that the originally independent 11,31-32 were appended at a later, still pre-redactional stage. I quote H. Schürmann:[96]

> Das Doppelwort VV 31f ist nicht als Deutewort für VV 29-30 geschaffen... Es wird schon vormals seine isolierte Tradition gehabt haben. ... die Einordnung von 11,31-32 [ist] einer späten Kompositionsstufe (aber wohl nicht erst der abschließenden Endredaktion) der Redequelle zuzusprechen.

Kloppenborg emphasizes the remarkable similarities with 11,29: "The correlative [v. 30] is constructed specifically as the explanation of 11:29, repeating the key words σημεῖον, Ἰωνᾶς and γενεὰ αὕτη." This interpretative saying 11,30 is "certainly ... not as late as the final redaction".[97]

In Fleddermann's assumption that Mark is secondary, the term "this generation" may have come to Mark in the shorter Q tradition 11,29-30 and not, as he suggested, in the longer redactional version of Q 11,29-32. The explanation that Mark has shortened this longer version may actually mean that there is no evidence that it was known by Mark.[98]

---

is more natural..., it fits naturally. 'This generation' is a key redactional expression in Q..., a redactional term that the author of Q uses to link several passages (Q 7,31; 11,31.32.51)."

95. "Recent Developments," p. 54 (= 434). Cf. TUCKETT, "Mark and Q," pp. 158-162, here 160.

96. Lukasevangelium II/1, pp. 289, 290. See now also A. VÖGTLE, 'Gretchenfrage', pp. 148-163, here 153.

97. Formation, p. 130. See also JACOBSON, First Gospel, pp. 164-169: "It seems unlikely ... that Q 11:30 was added after Q 11:29 and 11:31-32 had been brought together" (p. 166).

98. TUCKETT, "Mark and Q," p. 161: "The editorial activity of the Q redactor in bringing together different traditions (evidenced at least in the conjunction of 11,29-30 and 11,31-32) seems to have left no trace in Mark." – With regard to Fleddermann's emphasis on the pejorative "this generation" in Q, I may refer to CATCHPOLE, Quest, pp. 241-247: "the theme of 'this generation,' while firmly endorsed by Q, can be derived from Jesus" (p. 276). Cf. A. VÖGTLE: one of the "alte, von Jesus selbst stammende Elemente" (p. 151). See now also E. LÖVESTAM, Jesus and "this Generation". A New Testament Study (ConBNT, 25), Stockholm, 1995, esp. pp. 21-37.

§ 12. The Cross Saying

"Because Mark knew this Q composition, Mark knew redactional Q" or, as it is reformulated in the Conclusion: "Since Mark knows the saying, he knows redactional Q."[99] This "saying" is the overlap text Mark 8,34 / Luke 14,27 and "this Q composition" is Q 14,26a.b.27. Fleddermann's § 12 on Mark 8,34 is a revised version of his "Cross and Discipleship" (1988). He repeats his view that the Q saying in 14,27 is original, and now adds the question: "does Mark know redactional Q?" More than before he emphasizes that Q 14,26a.b.27 are conceived as "an original stylistic and conceptual unit." This observation is now his first indication that the Q saying is prior to the Marcan saying[100] and this same observation forms the proof that Mark depends on QR.

Fleddermann's statement on the original unit is not unambiguous. He also notes that 14,26.27 "draws together two separate lines of thought" and that "because Q 14,26-27 draws these two Q themes together, it comes from the pen of the author of Q." But how can he then conclude that "we cannot trace the Cross Saying any further back in the tradition than the Q cluster?"[101] If the two themes of 14,26 (family) and 27 (cross) are drawn together by QR, it would seem more natural to conclude with J. Nolland: "Vv 26-27 do not constitute an original unity. When the materials were joined, v 27 received substantial formal modification for the sake of parallelism."[102]

In Fleddermann's reconstruction the two sentences in Q 14,26 (Matt 10,37a.b) are assimilated to the relative clause ὃς οὐ in 14,27 (in contrast to the IQP text: ⟦εἴ τις...⟧ and καὶ ⟦εἴ τις...⟧ in 26a.b).[103] The conditional clause at the opening of v. 26, εἴ τις ἔρχεται πρός με, is rightly attributed to Lucan redaction: "Luke ... has in mind the conditional form of Mark's cross saying (Mark 8:34) which he redacts in 9:23 (εἴ τις θέλει ὀπίσω μου ἔρχεσθαι). The conditional clause fits the context Luke created for the saying."[104] Fleddermann adopts the thesis of Mark's knowledge of Q 14,26 (the cluster 14,26-27) but the εἴ τις construction

---

99. HF, 139, 211.
100. Compare the five indications (HF, 138) with the "three considerations" he proposed in 1988 (p. 479), now listed as nos. 2, 3, and 5, and supplemented with no. 1 (the original unit in Q) and no. 4 (the saying in Mark brought into line with the passion narrative: ἀπαρνησάσθω and ἀράτω).
101. See references in n. 99.
102. *Luke* II, p. 761. See also, e.g., LUZ, p. 135: "selbständige Einzellogien;" BOISMARD, *Synopse* II, p. 292: "la liaison entre les deux parties est probablement artificielle."
103. Cf. *JBL* 111 (1992), p. 507.
104. "Cross and Discipleship," p. 476.

is banned from his Q text and in the saying itself there remains no indication of Mark's possible borrowing from Q 14,26.

It is remarkable that Fleddermann has only one reference to the treatment of Mark 8,34 in Lambrecht's "Q-Influence"[105] and has not noticed the significant divergences in their textual options: Mark 8,34 ἀκολουθεῖν (Lambrecht: ἐλθεῖν) and in the reconstruction of Q 14,27: ἀκολουθεῖ (Lambrecht: ἔρχεται).[106] Moreover, Lambrecht has ἔρχεται πρός με in Q 14,26a and εἴ τις, καὶ εἴ τις in 26a.b (contrast Fleddermann: ὅς, ὅς).[107] Lambrecht reads ὃς οὐ λαμβάνει in Q 14,27 but would not a priori exclude that αἴρω (and not λαμβάνω) stood in Q: "whether ... ἀράτω in 8,34 is due to Mark's edition is not so certain."[108] Contrast Fleddermann: the words "deny" and "take up" in Mark "echo the passion narrative."[109]

§ 13. LOSING ONE'S LIFE

Luke 17,33 differs from the reconstructed Q text (cf. Matt 10,39) in two respects: the omission of the superfluous second τὴν ψυχὴν αὐτοῦ and the substitutes for the verb "to find:" ζητήσῃ ... περιποιήσασθαι for εὕρῃ[110] and ζῳογονήσει for εὑρήσει (= Matt). I can agree regarding this double redactional intervention by Luke, but his source is more probably not Q but Mark 8,35. Mark has the relative clauses ὃς ἐάν and ὃς δ᾽ ἂν ἀπολέσῃ, and his θέλῃ ... σῶσαι in the first half (= Luke 9,24) is much closer to ζητήσῃ ... περιποιήσασθαι than the hypothetical εὕρῃ (Matt ὁ εὑρών). For Luke θέλω + infinitive and ζητέω + infinitive are synonyms; compare Luke 9,9 καὶ ἐζήτει ἰδεῖν αὐτόν and 23,8b ἦν γὰρ ἐξ ἱκανῶν χρόνων θέλων ἰδεῖν αὐτόν. Luke's use of Mark 8,35 (Luke 9,24) in Luke 17,33 is not completely isolated, since the insertion of 17,25 in the same discourse depends on Mark 8,31 (Luke 9,22), and the saying in 17,33 is preceded by 17,31(32), taken from Mark 13,15-16.[111]

105. HF, 138 n. 17: "Q-Influence," p. 282 (read: 281, on "let him deny himself"). Note, however, that for Fleddermann the term "deny" echoes the passion narrative (fourth indication), whereas for Lambrecht ἀπαρνησάσθω would be a Q term (Q 12,9, cf. Mark 8,38).
106. "Q-Influence," pp. 279-280.
107. *Ibid.*, p. 280 n. 18. Cf. above, nn. 103-104.
108. *Ibid.*, pp. 281, 282.
109. HF, 138. Cf. above, nn. 100, 105.
110. HF, 142. Instead of the form εὕρῃ Laufen prefers εὑρήσει (pp. 322, 561 n. 140); other authors read ὁ εὑρών (= Matt): Schulz, Polag, Lambrecht, *et al.* For Jacobson the verb εὑρίσκειν "probably represents Q" (p. 222 n. 93). But see, e.g., G. Dautzenberg (*Sein Leben bewahren*, 1966, p. 62); Boismard (1972, p. 248); Luz (*Matthäus* II, p. 135 n. 9: "könnte auch mt sein").
111. Cf. "The Minor Agreements and Q," pp. 54-56 (Luke 17,31).

Defenders of the Q origin usually argue that the parallel Matt 10,39 is preserved in its original setting: Matt 10,37.38.39 / Q 14,26.27; 17,33; the presence of the phrase ἔτι τε καὶ τὴν ψυχὴν ἑαυτοῦ in Luke 14,26 is seen as a reminiscence of this location in Q. This last indication is not even mentioned by Fleddermann. In his view Matthew does not reflect the original Q context of the saying: "Matthew joined the Q sayings on the cross and losing one's life in 10,38-39 because he found the overlap sayings joined in Mark 8,34-35."[112] But in these conditions one may ask whether the Q origin of Matt 10,39 is still defendable. Its location depends on Mark 8,35; the phrase ἕνεκεν ἐμοῦ in the second half is taken from Mark 8,35 (par. Matt 16,25); εὑρήσει is used in Matt 16,25 in parallel to σώσει in Mark 8,35 and the use of this verb may have been extended to the first half (εὑρών); and finally the substantive participle (ὁ εὑρών, ὁ ἀπολέσας) instead of Mark's relative clauses is Matthean usage (in this context: 10,37ab.39ab.40ab.41ab).[113]

§ 14. JESUS AND THE SON OF MAN

Of the four overlap texts in Q with reference to the Son of Man, only Q 12,8-9 / Mark 8,38 (ὁ υἱὸς τοῦ ἀνθρώπου) has this reference in the Marcan parallel. Cf. Q 11,30 (om. Mark 8,12); Q 12,10 (Mark 3,28 τῶν υἱῶν τῶν ἀνθρώπων); Q 12,40 (diff. Mark 13,35). Fleddermann apparently assigns all four references to QR. His comment is most clear in § 14:[114]

> ... the Q saying on Confessing and Denying fits seamlessly in the overall Q portrayal of the Son of Man. Since it fits so smoothly in Q's christology, the saying could well come from the Q redactor. If so, then the saying shows that Mark knew redactional Q.

He anticipated this statement already in § 4, where he drew a further conclusion with regard to Q 12,10: "If the saying on Confessing and Denying comes from the Q redactor, the commenting saying on the Unforgivable Sin does also."[115] (Here and elsewhere the possibility that a commenting function could be given to previously isolated sayings has apparently not been considered by Fleddermann.) If Q 12,10 "comments on and corrects" 12,8-9, is it then likely that both sayings stem from the same redactor? Q 12,4-9 is probably a pre-Q unit and 12,8-9 "may be

---

112. HF, 143. Cf. below, n. 117.
113. For authors who reject the Q origin of Mt 10,39 and Lk 17,33, see KLOPPENBORG, *Q Parallels*, p. 170. Cf. *Recent Developments*, pp. 49-51 (= 429-431).
114. HF, 151; see also 152: "The editor of Q could well have formulated the saying." Cf. "Confessing and Denying" (1987), pp. 614, 616.
115. HF, 70. Cf. above, p. 271 (§ 2).

present already in the pre-Q tradition though its concerns cohere well with other parts of Q."[116]

The sayings in Mark 8,34.35 and 38 are treated together in Chapter VI: Caesarea Philippi. The first two form a cluster in Mark bound together by θέλω. As indicated above, the order of Mark 8,34.35 (and Matthew 10,38.39), which for Lambrecht is a Q order, is regarded by Fleddermann as Marcan.[117] The argument for Mark's use of final Q built up by Lambrecht around Mark 8,38[118] has received no echo in Fleddermann's work. His own argument for Mark's knowledge of redactional Q relies directly on the Son of Man Saying and "Q's theology of the Son of Man." Unfortunately "this remains only a possibility." In his view, "the Cross Saying [8,34] definitely shows that Mark knew redactional Q," but his readers may ask how he can be so certain that the composition of Q 14,26.27 "could only go back to the Q redactor."[119] Lambrecht was rightly looking to recover larger Q contexts and had to conclude: "our way is blocked as far as these sayings are concerned."[120]

§ 15. On Accepting

According to Fleddermann the saying Matt 10,40 / Luke 10,16 forms the conclusion of the Mission Discourse in Q (in the order of Luke 10,2-16). The original wording is preserved unchanged in Matthew. Mark transferred this saying to his Discipleship Discourse and redacted it in Mark 9,37. If this hypothesis is correct,[121] one can observe that the saying used by Mark more probably may have been the conclusion of a pre-Q Mission Discourse, say Q 10,3...11a.16.

---

116. C. M. Tuckett, "The Son of Man in Q," 1993, pp. 208-211, here 211. See also A. Y. Collins, "The Son of Man Sayings in the Sayings Source," 1989, pp. 369-389, esp. 378-379: Q 12,8-9 is part of a pre-Q unit (12,4-9) but vv. 2-3 and 10 were added at the same time and vv. 11-12 were possibly placed there by Luke: "If this reconstruction is plausible, ... the possibility that vv. 2-3 and 10 were added by the editor of Q cannot be ruled out" (p. 379). For Fleddermann, however, the Q composition (12,2-12) includes vv. 11-12 and then one cannot exclude that v. 10 was a pre-Q addition. Like Collins, Tuckett emphasizes the connection of v. 10 with vv. 2-3 at the compositional stage of Q, but he does not comment on 12,11-12.

117. Cf. above, n. 112.

118. "Q-Influence," pp. 298-303: "The form of Q known to Mark." In fact his overview (pp. 300-301) includes a number of uncertainties such as uncertain Q texts (11,21-22; 11,27-28; 12,1; 12,13-21) and uncertain parallels: 11,29 (μοιχαλίς); 12,3 (Mark 4,23).

119. HF, 152.

120. "Q-Influence," p. 298.

121. But see "Recent Developments," p. 47 (= 427) n. 72, on alternative reconstructions of Q (cf. Luke 10,16) and possible influence of Mark 9,37 upon Matt 10,40.

§ 16. On Tolerance

The title of § 16 refers to Mark 9,40; the saying in Q is rather exclusive and intolerant (Q 11,23). Fleddermann has indicated how Mark could have redacted this saying, if he depends on Q. Like Q 10,16 which is incorporated in the Discipleship Discourse in Mark 9,37, Q 11,23 is taken over in Mark 9,40.[122] In both cases, as also in 4,25 and 10,11-12, Mark shifted the participial construction to a relative clause.[123] That Mark's saying is more tolerant than the Q saying corresponds to a more general redactional tendency in the overlap texts.[124]

The image half of the Q saying, with the antithesis of gathering and scattering, has no parallel in Mark. The overlap text is thus restricted to Q 11,23a, a saying that shows all the characteristics of an independent aphorism: "Aphorisms have a degree of ambiguity which makes it possible to use them in various contexts with various meanings."[125] The parallel from Cicero's *Pro Q. Ligario* is referred to by Fleddermann.[126] It is less understandable that the same note refers to Mark 3,31-35 as "a Marcan parallel."

§ 17. On Scandal

There can be no dispute on the Q origin of Matt 18,7 / Luke 17,1b, in Fleddermann's reconstruction: ἀνάγκη ἐστιν **τὰ σκάνδαλα ἐλθεῖν, πλὴν οὐαὶ** τῷ ἀνθρώπῳ **δι᾽ οὗ ἔρχεται**.[127] I agree with Fleddermann about the use of Mark 9,42a in Matt 18,6a (ὃς δ᾽ ἂν σκανδαλίσῃ ἕνα τῶν μικρῶν τούτων τῶν πιστευόντων εἰς ἐμέ) and in Luke 17,2b (ἢ ἵνα σκανδαλίσῃ τῶν μικρῶν τούτων ἕνα). But in his opinion I "cut too deeply"

---

122. HF, 169, 213, 216 (conclusion, § § 15-16). Cf. 61 (§ 3), 120, 124 (§ 10).

123. HF, 88 n. 68 (Mark 4,25); 155 n. 10 (Mark 9,37); 159 n. 23 (Mark 9,40); 173 n. 9 (Mark 10,11-12).

124. HF, 209: Mark eliminates exaggerations. Cf. Mark 4,32; 6,8; 8,34; 9,40. See also Mark 10,31 (176); 11,24 (184). Mark 9,40 is a constant reference: HF 60 (§ 3), 122, 140 n. 23, 159 (§ 16), 176 n. 28, 184 n. 58, 209.

125. Cf. D. E. AUNE, "Oral Tradition and the Aphorisms of Jesus," in H. WANSBROUGH (ed.), *Jesus and the Oral Gospel Tradition* (JSNT SS, 64), Sheffield, 1991, pp. 211-265, here 241. On Mark 9,40, see pp. 237, 246 (no. 25), 250 (no. 75).

126. HF, 159 n. 22. I quote the passage: "Valeat tua vox illa, quae vicit. Te enim dicere audiebamus nos omnes adversarios putare, nisi qui nobiscum essent; te omnes, qui contra te non essent, tuos."

127. Common words are printed in bold. Contrast Fleddermann's reconstruction in "Discipleship Discourse" (1981), pp. 67-69: ἀνένδεκτον ... μή, (οὐαὶ) δέ, om. τῷ ἀνθρώπῳ (cf. Luke 17,1b). See also n. 129.

by attributing all of Luke 17,2 to the Lucan redaction of Mark 9,42.[128] I reproduce here his reconstruction of Q in parallel with the text of Mark:

Q 17,2a	Mk 9,42b
λυσιτελεῖ αὐτῷ	καλόν ἐστιν αὐτῷ μᾶλλον
εἰ περίκειται μύλος ὀνικὸς	
περὶ τὸν τράχηλον αὐτοῦ	
καὶ βέβληται εἰς τὴν θάλασσαν.	

The text of Matt 18,6b can be left out of the picture because the reconstructed Q offers nothing that is not in Mark and could explain Matthew's redaction.[129] The only difference between Q and Mark concerns the *Tobspruch* (first line): Matthew and Luke agree in having a finite verb, συμφέρει (cf. Matt 5,29.30) and λυσιτελεῖ. Regarding Luke's λυσιτελεῖ Fleddermann refers to J. Schlosser but drops the qualification: "obwohl es, an und für sich, ein von Lk ausgesuchtes, gut griechisches Wort sein könnte."[130]

If Q did not contain Luke 17,2, then no overlap exists. In response to Fleddermann's objections it can be observed that (1) the coincidence of Matthew's and Luke's combining the woe (Q) and the millstone (Mark) has nothing extraordinary: both are sayings on scandal; (2) the suggestion that frightening punishments fit more comfortably in Q seems to neglect the association of Mark 9,42 with 9,43.45.47-48.[131]

---

128. HF, 160 (and n. 24). See now also my "The Minor Agreements and Q," pp. 57-59 (with reply to J. Schlosser, 1983).

129. Note the use of Mark's βέβληται εἰς in Fleddermann's reconstruction of Q (diff. Matt καταποντισθῇ ἐν and Luke ἔρριπται ἐν). Contrast his 1981 reconstruction: ἔρριπται and a different word order: μύλος ὀνικὸς περίκειται.

130. "Lk 17,2," here 77. The "parallel" in Luke 9,33 (HF, 161) is not the comparative καλόν ἐστιν (μᾶλλον) of the *Tobspruch* and is scarcely relevant in this discussion.

131. In reply to HF, 160-161. Still less convincing is his association of the kind of punishment with Q 17,6: "someone or something ... forcibly removed to the sea" (161). "Planting" (a tree in the sea) in Q connotes a beneficial act, whereas "throwing" in Mark connotes a destructive act (cf. GUNDRY, *Mark*, p. 652): Mark 11,23 βλήθητι εἰς τὴν θάλασσαν (cf. 9,42 βέβληται εἰς τὴν θάλασσαν). Contrast Luke 17,6 ἔρριπται ἐν τῇ θαλάσσῃ, diff. Fleddermann's conjecturally reconstructed Q (cf. above, n. 129). – For authors who reject inclusion in Q, see KLOPPENBORG, *Q Parallels*, p. 182: "Q 17:2. Not in Q." Add: BOISMARD 1972, p. 299; LAUFEN, p. 87; NOLLAND II, p. 637.

Mark 14,21 is cited in HF, 164-166, as Mark's "second overlap" with the Scandal Saying in Q (§ 17a). Cf. E. Wendling (*Entstehung*, 1908, pp. 168-169), W. Schmithals (*Markus*, 1979, p. 611, cf. 432-433); but this overlap is mentioned neither in Laufen's list nor in Kloppenborg's *Q Parallels*. The last element of Mark 14,21 (Matt 26,24), καλὸν (ἦν) αὐτῷ εἰ οὐκ ἐγεννήθη ὁ ἄνθρωπος ἐκεῖνος, is dropped out in Luke 22,22, but the scheme in Mark 14,21 and Luke 17,1b-2 is identical: the crime is set out as inevitable (it is necessary, as it is written) – woe to him – it would be better for him (to be killed, not to be born). Since the *Tobspruch* is found in Mark only in 14,21 and 9,42 (and vv. 43.45.47), Luke's combination

§ 18. On Salt

As usual, the first step is a reconstruction of the Q text from Matthew and Luke. It is only in a second phase that the reconstructed Q text will be compared with Mark. In the case of the Salt Saying, word statistics indicate that οὖν and καί in Q 14,34 were added by Luke,[132] but without documentation it is simply stated that "Luke preserves the Q introduction of the saying" (καλὸν τὸ ἅλας) and the verb ἀρτυσθήσεται "undoubtedly reflects Q" because this verb is "rare in the NT."[133] In this first phase the text of Q is reconstructed from Luke without examining the possibility that Luke's **καλὸν** τὸ ἅλας and **ἀρτυσ**θήσεται may be due to the influence of Mark 9,50.[134] In the second phase the comparison of the reconstructed Q text and Mark will inevitably lead to the conclusion that καλὸν τὸ ἅλας and the verb ἀρτύω in Mark 9,50 come from Q.

§ 19. On Divorce

I agree with Fleddermann that "Luke basically preserves the Q form of the saying."[135] The phrase ἀπὸ ἀνδρός is probably a Lucan addition, although I have some reservation about the argument based on Lucan usage. None of the two indications is really convincing. "Luke uses ἀπό with ἀπολύω in Acts 15,33," but the good wishes of the brethren (ἀπελύθησαν μετ᾽ εἰρήνης ἀπὸ τῶν ἀδελφῶν) is not a very close parallel to the woman divorced "from her husband;" and "ἀνήρ is very common in Luke," but the occurrences show a different proportion if, more specifically, ἀνήρ = husband is considered: Luke 1,27.34; 2,36 and 16,18.[136] I agree about the phrase "and marries another" which most probably was found in Q, though in contrast to Fleddermann ("ἕτερος is a good Q word") I would not exclude that ἑτέραν (for ἄλλην) is possibly Lucan.[137]

of the parallel to Mark 9,42 with Q 17,1b may have been inspired by the word about the traitor. The likelihood of such associations is shown in the combination of Matt 26,24 and 18,6 in 1 Clem 46,8: εἶπεν γάρ· Οὐαὶ τῷ ἀνθρώπῳ ἐκείνῳ· καλὸν ἦν αὐτῷ, εἰ οὐκ ἐγεννήθη, ἢ ἕνα τῶν ἐκλεκτῶν μου σκανδαλίσαι· κρεῖττον ἦν αὐτῷ περιτεθῆναι μύλον καὶ καταποντισθῆναι εἰς τὴν θάλασσαν, ἢ ἕνα τῶν ἐκλεκτῶν μου διαστρέψαι.

132. HF, 167: cf. 91 n. 77 (Luke's use of οὖν); 167 n. 60 (Luke's use of δὲ καί).
133. HF, 167.
134. Cf. "Recent Developments," p. 51 (= 431).
135. HF, 172. See now my "The Divorce Saying in Q 16:18," in *Louvain Studies* 20 (1995) 201-218, esp. 212-218 ("Luke 16:18 Q"). – On CD 4,12–5,15 (cf. HF, 172 n. 2) see also "De echtscheidingslogia in de evangeliën," in *Academiae Analecta* (1995, forthcoming).
136. "Divorce Saying," p. 212 (in reply to D. KOSCH, *Die eschatologische Tora*, 1988, p. 432).
137. Compare HF, 172 n. 7 ("ἕτερος probably should be restored in seven other Q texts") with "Divorce Saying," p. 217 n. 93: Q 7,19.32 "possibly" Q, but 14,19.20; 17,34.35 (and 19,20!) probably Lucan. On 11,16 LkR, see also HF, 45, 128 (Q ἕτεροι δέ).

§ 20. The First and the Last

Matt 19,30 (= Mark 10,31) and 20,16 (cf. Luke 13,30) is treated as a classic source doublet: "Matthew uses the Marcan and Q sayings as an *inclusio* to frame the parable of the Laborers in the Vineyard."[138] Although Matt 20,16 agrees with Luke 13,30 against Mark in initially placing "last" before "first," there is much hesitation about its origin in Q.[139] Matthew's second use of the saying can be his redactional adaptation in light of the preceding parable.[140] If Matt 20,16 (with the concluding οὕτως for καί) would represent the Q form of the saying (Fleddermann), then no less than nine differences are found in Luke 13,30, and the possibility of a *Wanderlogion* freely used by Luke is to be considered.[141] The fact that it concludes a section that formed a unit in Q does not prove its Q origin: Luke 13,24.26-27.28-29 are covered by consecutive parallels in Matt 7,13-14.22-23; 8,11-12, but not Luke 13,30.

§ 21. On Faith

"The change from a mulberry tree to a mountain is intelligible, but it is inconceivable that anyone would change a mountain to a mulberry tree."[142] This is the central point in Fleddermann's position on the Faith Saying: Luke 17,6 reflects Q, and Mark's version is secondary. Although many will agree with his reconstruction of Q (= Luke 17,6),[143] it is regrettable that he restricted the discussion to some minor variations.[144] No mention is made of the alternative position of those who defend the

---

Fleddermann's argument is not wholly consistent: on the one hand he stresses the interchangeability of ἕτερος and ἄλλος (HF, 173) and on the other he argues for "the Q phrase" in 11,16 in light of "the coordinated pair εἷς ... ἕτερος that crops up from time to time in Q" (45; and 128: "pops up").

138. HF, 175. Note that Mark 9,35 is treated as "a related saying" (176), "a redactional reworking of Mark 10,43-44" (140 n. 23).

139. References in Kloppenborg, *Q Parallels*, p. 156 ("Not in Q"). Add: Laufen, pp. 88-89; Sato, p. 10.

140. See the commentaries (e.g., J. Gnilka II, p. 181). On the meaning of Matt 20,16, see the types of interpretation noted by C. Hezser, *Lohnmetaphorik und Arbeitswelt in Mt 20,1-16*, pp. 253-258.

141. Cf. D. E. Aune, "Oral Tradition," pp. 238-239: "originally an independent saying" which is used to interpret other sayings.

142. HF, 181. "Mark switches to the mountain image" (*ibid.*) and "Matthew has taken the mountain from Mark" (179).

143. Cf. IQP, in *JBL* 110 (1991), p. 498. See also recent commentaries on Matthew (Gnilka 1988, Luz 1990, Davies-Allison 1991) and Luke (Fitzmyer 1985, p. 1142; Nolland 1993) and recent studies on Q (e.g., Kloppenborg 1995, p. 316).

144. HF, 179, in response to (Schulz and) Zmijewski: ἐὰν ἔχητε (see also Catchpole) and the future tenses in the apodosis (cf. Mark's ἔσται).

originality of the mountain-moving image.[145] I also miss a reference to Catchpole who reads ἐκριζώθητι without καὶ φυτεύθητι ἐν τῇ θαλάσσῃ, the original Q saying "bringing together ... the proverbially tiny mustard seed and the extremely deep rooted sycamine tree."[146] This would mean that we not only have to reckon with "Matthew's assimilation of the Marcan and Q sayings to each other."[147] Then Luke's version too is possibly influenced by the mountain-moving saying in Mark:[148]

ἄρθητι   καὶ βλήθητι   εἰς τὴν θάλασσαν
ἐκριζώτητι (καὶ φυτεύθητι ἐν τῇ θαλάσσῃ).

§ 22. ON ASKING AND RECEIVING

Granted that Mark is secondary to Q, does Mark reflect redactional Q? Response: the author of Q joined 11,9-13 to the Lord's Prayer (11,2-4) and Mark's interpretation (προσεύχεσθε) shows that he knows this context of the saying.[149] However, dependence on QR is made unnecessary by Fleddermann's own reference to R. A. Piper's study on the pre-Q collection in 11,9-13 and to the final saying in v. 13 on "asking" the heavenly Father.[150] Moreover, Fleddermann neglects Piper's introductory remarks on the original independence of Q 11,9-10.[151]

145. F. HAHN, "Jesu Wort vom bergeversetzenden Glauben," in *ZNW* 76 (1985) 149-169: "συκάμινος (ist) sekundär an die Stelle von ὄρος getreten" (p. 158); D. LÜHRMANN, *Markusevangelium*, 1987, p. 195: "Die Q-Überlieferung in der Fassung von Mt 17,20 ist die ursprüngliche (Lk, der die Verfluchung des Feigenbaums ausläßt, verwendet ihren Stoff einmal in dem Gleichnis Lk 13,6-9, zum anderen, trotz der differierenden Bezeichnung συκάμινος, in seiner Fassung des Wortes vom bergeversetzenden Glauben 17,6)." See also W. SCHMITHALS, *Markus*, 1979, p. 501; W. R. TELFORD, *The Barren Temple and the Withered Tree* (JSNT SS, 1), Sheffield, 1980, p. 103 (cf. p. 101, for the view that the saying in Luke 17,6 has been modified as a result of its association with the fig-tree story: B. Weiss, Holtzmann, Wellhausen, Loisy, Harnack, Taylor, and Schweizer; cf. HAHN, "Jesu Wort," p. 156 n. 24).

146. D. R. CATCHPOLE, "The Centurion's Faith and Its Function in Q," in *The Four Gospels 1992*, pp. 517-540, here 517; reprinted in *The Quest*, p. 280.

147. HF, 179 (cf. above, nn. 142, 144).

148. On the oddity of Luke's version, see e.g. Fitzmyer's comment, p. 1144: "Two figures are obviously mixed here, 'being planted' and 'in the sea.' This is an inconsistency that does not bother Luke. In the earlier tradition it was probably a mountain that was thrown into a sea, which would be intelligible. But now a mulberry tree being 'planted' in the sea is strange, to say the least." See also HAHN, "Jesu Wort," p. 158: "So gut also das Motiv vom 'Sich-Werfen' (bzw. Geworfenwerden) ins Meer' zu ὄρος paßt, so wenig paßt die Anschauung vom 'Sich-Einpflanzen ins Meer' zu συκάμινος. Hier liegt offensichtlich eine Parallelbildung zu ἄρθητι καὶ βλήθητι εἰς τὴν θάλασσαν vor, was als Argument gegen die Ursprünglichkeit der Lukasfassung gar nicht genügend beachtet wird."

149. HF, 184. See also 211: "By applying the saying to prayer Mark shows that he knows the Q context of the saying."

150. HF, 183. Cf. R. A. PIPER, *Wisdom in the Q-Tradition*, p. 19.

151. *Wisdom*, p. 16. Cf. KLOPPENBORG, *Formation*, p. 204: "vv. 9-10 and vv. 11-13 [probably] represent two originally independent traditions;" SCHÜRMANN, *Lukasevangelium*

His view on the proverb which "uses three metaphors from daily life to show that effort always attains its end" can be confronted with Catchpole's approach:[152]

> If the context presumed by v. 10 were secular, then it would be necessary to say that as a generalization (πᾶς ...) all its three parts are untrue. It is not generally true in the world at large that all asking, seeking and knocking proves successful. So a secular context can be eliminated. By a shift of main verbal form from present indicative to future passive (ἀνοιγήσεται), v. 10c contains the potential to remove all three parts of the saying away from a secular context into the context where God is at work. Then it is a religious statement about God and his reaction to human asking, seeking and knocking.

If Q 11,10-11 came to Mark in the context of the Jesus tradition, it was most probably not as secular wisdom but as "auf das Geschehen zwischen Mensch und Gott bezogen."[153]

§ 23. FIRST PLACES

The title of § 23 seems to be deliberately provocative. The phrase "first places at dinners" is found in the saying of Mark (12,39; par. Luke 20,46 and Matt 23,6) but not in Luke 11,43, and it is usually not considered to be part of the Q saying.[154] In Fleddermann's reconstruction of Q the phrase τὴν πρωτοκλισίαν ἐν τοῖς δείπνοις, "the first seat at the feasts" (NRSV: "the place of honor at banquets"), is the first of three objects of φιλεῖτε: "The phrase is found in Matthew but not in Luke. It probably stood in Q, for if Matthew had borrowed it from Mark it would appear in the plural. Luke gives a fuller treatment of the first seat in Luke 14,7-14 so he passes over it here."[155] Yet already before ch.

II/1, 221: "sowohl das Grundwort 11,9f wie das Zusatzwort 11,11ff [sind] je isoliert tradiert aus der Verkündigungssituation Jesu und der Gemeinde verständlich zu machen."

152. *Quest*, p. 219. One can make this observation without adopting Catchpole's general theory on the context in Q.

153. D. ZELLER, *Mahnsprüche*, p. 129.

154. See, e.g., the Q reconstructions by Polag, Schulz, Schenk and recent commentaries on Luke (Schürmann, II/1, p. 315 n. 77; Nolland, II, p. 666). The ascription to Q of Q 11,43 is not uncontested: cf. E. HAENCHEN, "Matthäus 23" (1951), 1965, p. 33; P. HOFFMANN, *Studien*, p. 170 n. 49; L. E. VAAGE, *Galilean Upstarts*, 1994, pp. 135-136. The evidence of Matthew-Luke agreements against Mark is regarded as unsatisfactory: (1) the verb φιλοῦσιν (Matt 23,6) / ἀγαπᾶτε (Luke 11,43), φιλούντων (Luke 20,46b: Q reminiscence), diff. Mark 12,38 θελόντων (= Luke 20,46a); (2) the order πρωτοκαθεδρίαν/ας, ἀσπασμούς, diff. Mark (the reverse). A critical note on Q 11,43 is lacking in Kloppenborg's *Q Parallels*, p. 112.

155. HF, 187. Cf. "Warning" (1982), p. 58. – Note the minor change in the reconstruction of Q: the vocative Φαρισαῖοι (cf. Matt 23,13-29) for τοῖς Φαρισαίοις (Luke 11,43) in 1982.

14 Luke shows special interest in meal-scenes, and despite his fuller treatment in 14,7-14 he will take over Mark's phrase in 20,46. The singular in Matthew (for the plural in Mark) may be due to influence of Q: φιλεῖτε τὴν πρωτοκαθεδρίαν ... καὶ τοὺς ἀσπασμοὺς... (to be followed with καὶ καλεῖσθαι... in Matt 23,7b). Πρωτοκλισίας (third in Mark 12,38-39, in plural and anarthrous) comes first and takes the place of τὴν πρωτοκαθεδρίαν in Q: φιλοῦσιν τὴν πρωτοκλισίαν...[156]

§ 24. On Confessing

The inclusion in Q is accepted by most authors. The principal indication for Q is the agreement in Matt 10,19; Luke 12,11: μὴ μεριμνήσητε πῶς ἢ τί (diff. Mark 13,11 μὴ προμεριμνᾶτε τί). Luke 12,12 is usually identified as the second half of the saying, though the final phrase ἃ δεῖ εἰπεῖν can either be dropped as Lucan (Schulz, Sato) or replaced with τί εἴπητε (Polag). Fleddermann's personal option is to take as second half Matt 10,19b (with εἴπητε for the «Marcan» λαλήσητε), and not Luke 12,12: "Luke probably introduced the Holy Spirit into the Q saying under the influence of Mark."[157]

Fleddermann's acceptance of Marcan influence in Q 12,12 invites us to reconsider his position on the Q text in 12,11: ὅταν δὲ εἰσφέρωσιν ὑμᾶς ἐπὶ τὰς συναγωγὰς... (contrast Matthew's παραδῶσιν ὑμᾶς: "he follows Mark"). Can the influence of Mark be excluded in Luke 12,11? Luke's use of ἀπολογεῖσθαι in 12,11 and 21,14 (not elsewhere in the gospels)[158] is not the only contact between the two parallels to Mark 13,11. If Luke has read Mark 13,11 (καὶ ὅταν ἄγωσιν ὑμᾶς παρα-διδόντες) in connection with v. 9, the prepositional phrase ἐπὶ τὰς συναγωγάς and its prolongation καὶ τὰς ἀρχὰς καὶ τὰς ἐξουσίας can be Lucan rewriting of Mark 13,9 (par. Luke 21,12 παραδιδόντες εἰς τὰς συναγωγὰς...). One cannot simply say that "Luke's ἐπὶ τὰς συναγ-ωγάς poses no problems because the noun is attested in Q (Q 11,43)."[159] Neither can the verb εἰσφέρωσιν be assigned to Q because Luke usually

156. Compare R. H. GUNDRY, *Mark*, p. 725, in reply to Fleddermann's "Warning." See also *ibid.* his critical observations on the greater originality of Q (HF, 188: "a nice climax," θέλω with noun object).

157. HF, 192. See also J. NOLLAND, *Luke* II, p. 680: "Luke appears to have rewritten 12:12 along the general lines of Mark 13:11c, but with his own wording." Contrast S. SCHULZ, *Q*, p. 442: "Lk (zeigt) in 12,11f keine Einflüsse der Mk-Fassung."

158. Cf. HF, 192. Contrast Nolland's rather strange observation that the pairing of the verbs in Luke 12,11 has a counterpart in 21,15 (ἀντιστῆναι καὶ ἀντειπεῖν) and points to the same second source (*Luke*, p. 680).

159. HF, 192. Luke has adopted both Q 11,43 and its overlap in Mark 12,39 (Luke 20,46). Cf. § 23.

prefers ἄγω or one of its compounds.[160] The verb εἰσφέρω in this passage probably has a particular nuance which is not well rendered in neutral translations ("lead" or "bring"): "Wenn sie euch (mit Gewalt) in die Synagogen *schleppen*."[161] If ὅταν δέ in Matt 10,19 is from Mark's καὶ ὅταν, the same can be said of ὅταν δέ in Luke 12,11. That Mark's ὅταν-clause would presuppose a more original context of the saying in Q 12,2-12 is, to say the very least, a reversible suggestion.[162] The (imperfect) agreement of order between Matt 10,26-27.28-31.32-33.(12,32).*19-20* and Luke 12,2-3.4-7.8-9.(10).*11-12* is rightly neglected by Fleddermann. The "Marcan" section Matt 10,17-22 is the context of the saying in Matthew, and the text of Mark 13,(9.)11 is also the first source of Luke 12,11-12. A reconstruction of the wording of the Q text in this case is a more arduous task than Fleddermann seems to realize.

§ 25. FAMILY DIVISION

The reconstruction of Q which here presents "enormous difficulties" is carefully discussed in a treatment that is typical of Fleddermann's approach, with due attention to the evangelists' usage and possible Q parallels. Unfortunately, recent studies on this passage are not at all referred to in § 25.[163] Thus, on the introductory verses in Luke 12,49-50: "Luke shows that he knows Matthew's clause in Luke 12,49 (πῦρ ἦλθον βαλεῖν ἐπὶ τὴν γῆν)."[164] Fleddermann may be right, but the reader should know that the Q origin of 12,49 has its defenders.[165] One can find an occasional cryptic allusion to the position of other scholars: "It might seem that Luke 12,52 is the original Q wording,"[166] but neither in the section on Mark 13,12 nor in the note on Th 16 there is any further allusion. In fact, scholarly opinion is divided, perhaps δύο ἐπὶ τρισίν, between alternative reconstructions of Q: either Matt 10,36

---

160. HF, 191-192. See the references in his n. 1.

161. *EWNT* 1.975 (H. Balz). Cf. K. WEISS, art. εἰσφέρω, in *TWNT* 9.66-67: "werden ... *geschleppt*" (*TDNT*: "will be *haled*"); EÜ: "Wenn man euch vor die Gerichte der Synagogen ... schleppt."

162. Cf. above, n. 116: on a possibly Lucan location of the saying in 12,11-12 (A. Y. Collins). On Lucan redaction, cf. P. HOFFMANN, *Tradition*, 1995, p. 232 n. 59: "Vielleicht hat sogar er (Lk) erst die Dublette geschaffen."

163. Cf. P. SELLEW, "Reconstruction of Q 12:33-59," in *SBL 1987 Seminar Papers*, pp. 617-668, esp. 645-653 ("Q 12:49-53"); S. J. PATTERSON, "Fire and Dissension. Ipsissima Vox Jesu in Q 12:49,51-53?" in *Forum* 5/2 (1989) 121-139. See also below, nn. 165, 167.

164. HF, 196; cf. 195, 199.

165. See C.-P. MÄRZ, "'Feuer auf die Erde zu werfen, bin ich gekommen...' Zum Verständnis und zur Entstehung von Lk 12,49" (1985), in *"... laßt eure Lampen brennen!"* (ErfTS, 20), Leipzig, 1991, pp. 9-31, esp. 9-11.

166. HF, 196.

and the three phrases of v. 35 (son, daughter, daughter-in-law) in Q 12,53 (Fleddermann) or Luke 12,52 and the doubling of the three pairs of v. 53 in Q and assimilation to Mic 7,6 in Matthew (Polag, Sellew, *et al.*).[167]

That, in this last hypothesis, the underlying Micah text is less visible in the Q saying has some weight in the study of the overlap in Mark 13,12 (with ἐπαναστήσονται from Mic 7,6 LXX). Fleddermann emphasizes that "Mark has drawn two overlap texts together into a cluster."[168] Whether the fact that "a Marcan παραδίδωμι" links Mark 13,11 and 12 has some significance for the Mark-Q relationship may be doubtful. But is it not simply irrelevant in this regard to speak of "the *clustering* of five sayings"[169] in Mark 13? The five sayings are dispersed in the Eschatological Discourse (13,11.12.21.31.35) and it is quite natural that more Mark-Q overlaps are found in the sayings material of ch. 13 than in Marcan narratives.

§ 26. RUMORS ON THE COMING

"Except for the original connective, Matthew preserves the Q"[170] (cf. Schulz, Polag, Schenk, *et al.*). In two details some authors prefer the Lucan parallel: ἐροῦσιν for ἐὰν εἴπωσιν and διώξητε for πιστεύσητε (cf. Laufen, Sato, Nolland, *et al.*). More names can be added for the second case (e.g., Marshall, Jacobson, Catchpole). Fleddermann's argument is rather weak: "Matthew had no reason to avoid (the verb διώκω)." But on the one hand διώκω in the sense "to run after, pursue" is not the most common use of the verb, and on the other Matthew's μὴ πιστεύσητε (24,26; cf. 24,23) is probably influenced by μὴ πιστεύετε in Mark 13,21.[171]

Two observations are cited to show that Mark is secondary. The same observations are repeated as evidence for Marcan redaction: Mark makes the saying explicit by adding "the Christ" and Mark also generalizes the saying with "here" and "there." Not a few scholars can agree that the Q form of the saying is more original than the saying in Mark 13,21, but they would question Fleddermann's conclusion that "Mark composes (his) discourse material with Q in front of him."[172]

167. See also A. D. JACOBSON, "Divided Families and Christian Origins," in R. A. PIPER (ed.), *The Gospel Behind the Gospels*, pp. 361-380, esp. 364-367.
168. HF, 199, 208, 212, 214.
169. HF, 208 (emphasis mine).
170. HF, 200. The exception is the Matthean οὖν (for καί in Luke).
171. Cf. J. LAMBRECHT, "Logia-Quellen," p. 341: "Denn es ist sehr gut möglich, dass Matthäus diesen Q^mt-Vers Mk 13,21 oder Mt 24,24 anpasste (z.B. was die ἐάν-Konstruktion und μὴ πιστεύσητε betrifft)." See also *Redaktion*, p. 103.
172. HF, 208.

§ 27. Jesus' Words

The title of § 27 refers to Mark 13,31. The saying Q 16,17, which is presented as the overlap text,[173] focuses on the Law. Fleddermann notes that the three sayings on the Law in 16,16-18 were originally independent of each other and independent also of the surrounding context in Luke. He has no further comment on the status of Q 16,17 in Q or Q redactional. Kloppenborg's theory of a nomocentric redaction of Q, with Q 16,17 as a third-stage addition together with 11,42c and 4,1-13,[174] is not even alluded to.

Fleddermann has reconstructed the Q text from Luke 16,17 with ἰῶτα ἓν ἤ and ἀπὸ (τοῦ νόμου) from Matt 5,18. His reconstruction is strictly identical with Lambrecht's and references for confirmation and documentation are mainly to Lambrecht's *Redaktion*.[175] Fleddermann observes in particular, on Matthew's verb παρέλθῃ (for πεσεῖν in Luke): "Matthew repeated the verb to bring the saying closer to Matt 24,34-35. In repeating the verb he also shifted its meaning."[176] But see Lambrecht's observation: "Es will uns scheinen, ... dass Matthäus dieses ... zweite παρέλθῃ *aus Mk 13,31* hereinholte,"[177] and on the shift of meaning ("auf Kosten einer geringen Bedeutungsänderung"): "*genau wie Mk 13,30b*: ἕως ἂν πάντα γένηται nicht mehr 'geschehen, ereignen,' sondern 'in Erfüllung gehen' bedeutet."[178] Since Fleddermann did not accept the second stage of Lambrecht's hypothesis ("Der Q^mk-Text")[179] he can have here no objection against Matthew's dependence on Mark.

§ 28. Uncertainty of the Hour

"By showing knowledge of the Householder, Mark shows knowledge of redactional Q." The Householder, i.e. the parable of the Thief (Q 12,39) and its application (12,40), was proposed by Fleddermann in

---

173. Mark 13,31; Q 16,17 is usually not included in lists of overlap texts (Van Dulmen, Polag, Laufen, Kloppenborg). Cf. above, n. 19, and my "Recent Developments," p. 53 (= 433).

174. J. S. Kloppenborg, "Nomos and Ethos in Q," in J. E. Goehring, *et al.* (eds.), *Gospel Origins & Christian Beginnings*. FS J. M. Robinson, Sonoma, CA, 1990, pp. 35-48, spec. 46.

175. *Redaktion*, pp. 213-223, on Mark 13,31: "Der Q-Text."

176. HF, 204, with reference to Lambrecht's *Redaktion*, pp. 218-219.

177. *Redaktion*, p. 219 (emphasis mine). See also *ibid.*: "ein ursprüngliches πεσεῖν..., das Matthäus under Einfluss von Mk 13,30-31 veränderte."

178. *Ibid.*; cf. p. 218: παρέρχεσθαι in Matt 5,18 first "vorbeigehen" and then "ausfallen, wegfallen."

179. There are no references to *Redaktion*, pp. 224-226; "Logia-Quellen," pp. 346-348.

1986 as Q's elaborate introduction to the parable of the Servant Left in Charge (Q 12,42b-46). He now repeats his view that the Householder is "a Q redactional formulation."[180]

Here again, more recent studies and alternative interpretations are not taken into consideration. I quote Kloppenborg (1987):[181]

> In view of the inconsistency in logic between v. 39 and v. 40 and the fact that the parable occurs elsewhere without the Son of Man saying, we must conclude that the Son of Man saying was a secondary interpretation of the parable. It must be assumed, however, that 12:40 was already attached to 12:39 prior to its association with the following materials since the basis of that association is undoubtedly the statement "You do not know in what hour (or day) the Son of Man (or Lord) is coming" (12:40,46).

On the one hand, Fleddermann emphasizes that, in contrast to Mark 13,35, the Q saying is self-contained. On the other, however, he also stresses that it forms part of the parable of the Householder and is not an independent statement: it serves to make explicit the identification of the returning Lord (12,46a) with the Son of Man. If it is true that this identification is not really needed "since Q centers so much attention on the Son of Man," the same can be said of ὁ κύριος τῆς οἰκίας in Mark 13,35 in the light of the coming of the Son of Man in 13,26.

---

180. HF, 207-208 (and 211: "The author of Q composed the Householder..."). Cf. "The Householder and the Servant Left in Charge" (1986).

181. *Formation*, pp. 149-150. Kloppenborg emphasizes the association of the parable with Q 12,33-34. Those who accept Luke 12,35-38 as part of Q can propose 12,40 as the conclusion of these verses: "Der Textbestand scheint für die ... Möglichkeit zu sprechen [daß das Diebesgleichnis nachträglich in einen Lk 12,35-38.40 entsprechenden Zusammenhang eingebracht worden wäre]. Denn der Anschluß mit καὶ ὑμεῖς (Lk 12,40) ... läßt sich zwanglos nur als Hinordnung von 12,40 auf 12,35-38 verständlich machen... Das Diebesgleichnis erscheint so in der Tat wie ein zwischengeschalteter Kontrasttext. ... Das ursprünglich isoliert weitergegebene Diebesgleichnis ist erst sekundär in den Zusammenhang eingebracht und dabei mit Lk 12,40 verknüpft worden". Cf. C.-P. MÄRZ, "Das Gleichnis vom Dieb," in *The Four Gospels 1992*, pp. 642-643. Compare also H. SCHÜRMANN: "Q 12:40 ... concludes the saying composition in Q/Luke 12:35-39, which Matthew must have also read in some other form. ... the Son of Man saying would have earlier functioned as a conclusion – a conclusion that thus would have been added prior to the redaction that added Q 12:42-46(47-48)" ("Beobachtungen zum Menschensohn-Titel," ET, pp. 87-88). — I can understand Fleddermann's choice not to include Luke 12,35-38 in his reconstruction of Q. But the question is debated (cf. KLOPPENBORG, *Q Parallels*, p. 136: S43), and its discussion can hardly be avoided by authors who make Mark 13,35 dependent on Q 12,39-40.

RESULTS AND IMPLICATIONS

A substantial part of Fleddermann's study is devoted to the reconstruction of Q texts. The reconstructions of ten Q sayings he published before
are here reprinted practically without changes: Q 3,16-17; 10,16; 11,
23.43; 12,8-9.40; 13,18-19; 14,27.34-35a; 17,1b-2. There is only a minor
change in Q 11,43, and more significant changes appear in 17,1b-2.[182] In
four annotations I expressed reservation with regard to the inclusion in Q of
the Matthew-Luke counterpart of the saying or part of it:

§	3.	Mark	3,27:	Matt 12,29	Luke 11,21-22
§	13.	Mark	8,35:	Matt 10,39	Luke 17,33
§	17.	Mark	9,42:	Matt 18,6	Luke 17,2
§	20.	Mark	10,31:	Matt 20,16	Luke 13,30

Only in a few instances is the wording of the saying strictly identical or
almost identical in Matthew and Luke: Q 7,27 (+ ἐγώ MtR); 10,2 (ἐργάτας / ἐκβάλῃ LkR); 11,10 (reading ἀνοιγήσεται in Luke); 11,23;
12,31b (πάντα om. LkR); 12,40 (+ διὰ τοῦτο MtR, ὥρᾳ / οὐ δοκεῖτε
LkR). Each paragraph starts with a comparative study of the two versions in Matthew and Luke. Fleddermann declares in his conclusion:
"For obvious methodological reasons, I have not used Mark to reconstruct the original text of Q."[183] One can only express approval: the
exclusion of Mark at this stage is a methodologically clean procedure
and a significant departure from Lambrecht's method.[184] However, as a
consequence of this exclusion of Mark in the reconstruction of Q, Fleddermann tends to neglect possible influences of Mark upon the Matthean
and Lucan redactions of the parallel saying in Q. To cite an example, I
could refer to the double question in Luke 13,18 (cf. Mark 4,30). Let us
take here another example. Fleddermann's comparative study of Matt
5,13 and Luke 14,34-35a, without using Mark, leads to the reconstruction
of Q, and then this hypothetical Q text is taken for granted: "We can
now compare the Q saying with Mark."[185] That Luke's καλὸν τὸ ἅλας

182. Cf. above, nn. 127, 129, and 155.
183. HF, 215-216.
184. See, for instance, his "Q-Influence," p. 282 (on Mark 8,34): "It is not a priori
excluded that αἴρω (and not λαμβάνω) stood in Q, and we will be able to use Mark's
ἀπαρνησάσθω in the reconstruction of Q's Ashamed-of saying" (cf. above, n. 108); p.
285 (on Mark 8,35): "Mark's ἕνεκεν ἐμοῦ testifies to the presence of this expression
already in Q (cf. Mt 10,39)." Cf. "The Great Commandment," p. 83: "we presume that
Mark has known Q, and ... it it possible that some features of Q have been preserved only
in Mark."
185. HF, 167. Cf. above, p. 288 (§ 18).

could depend on καλὸν τὸ ἅλας in Mark 9,50 is not mentioned, not as a suggestion made by other scholars and not even as a theoretical possibility. One has the impression that in such a case the reconstruction of the Q text anticipates Marcan dependence on Q. This is even more so in the case of conjecturally reconstructed wording of Q that happens to be the verb used by Mark (βέβληται in 9,42).[186]

As one of his findings Fleddermann proposes in the conclusion that five individual Marcan sayings reflect redactional Q elements.[187] But, as indicated above, of these five sayings in Mark (1,2; 8,12; 8,34; 11,24; 13,35; cf. §§ 1, 11, 12, 22, 28), none has been proved to depend on redactional Q. The argument of the clustering of overlap texts in Mark is scarcely more convincing. In one instance of a "small cluster" where not a few scholars accept that the sequence of the two sayings comes from Q (Mark 8,34.35), the case is dismissed by Fleddermann: "Since Matthew and Luke both moved the saying (Losing one's life) to a new context, its original position in Q can no longer be recovered."[188] It is more damaging for the thesis of Marcan dependence on "the whole Q document" that, throughout Mark and within each of the clusters, the order of arrangements differs from the order of the sayings in Q. (See the table of parallels on p. 299.)[189] I may perhaps recall my comment on Fleddermann's first contribution, on the four Q sayings in the Discipleship Discourse (1981): "no sequence [in Q] can be detected in the four sayings."[190]

Fleddermann's argument for Mark's use of Q will be read with interest by all critics who propose explanations of the overlap texts in Mark on the basis of traditional sayings identical with or similar to the sayings in Q. Observations on Marcan redaction are to some extent common ground. But not all readers will be happy with the alternative to explain Mark's text either by oral tradition or by "final Q," i.e., the complete Q document Mark had in front of him. In Fleddermann's approach, Mark can no longer be used to study the pre-history of Q and, in the absence of external control, he is extremely critical of reconstructed "earlier stages of Q." A saying like Q 3,16 where he distinguishes between pre-Q (ἐν πυρί) and QR is an exceptional case. The section on Fearless Confessing (Q 12,2-12) is said to be "a composite made of various sayings," but neither for

186. HF, 162. Cf. above, p. 287.
187. HF, 211.
188. HF, 143 n. 35. Cf. above, p. 284 (§ 13).
189. The "clusters" are marked with vertical lines.
190. Cf. above, n. 20.

12,8-9.10.11-12 nor for 12,2 is an earlier stage of composition taken into consideration. Special attention is given to the Beelzebul Controversy and the Mission Discourse: "we can positively rule out the oral tradition as Mark's source in the two longest overlap texts."[191] Once more, Fleddermann's alternative is either oral tradition or Q redactional. But in the case of Q 11,14-26 the overlap verses in Mark 3 can be restricted to 11,15.17b-18a. In the Mission Discourse too pre-Q is a more workable hypothesis than the oral tradition – QR alternative.

MARK-Q OVERLAPS

§	Mark	Q
1.	1,2	3,16-17
2.	1,7-8	6,38c
3.	3,22-27	7,27
4.	3,28-29	10,2-16
5.	4,21	10,16
6.	4,22	11,10
7ᵃ.	4,24c	11,14-15.17-26
7ᵇ.	4,24d	11,23
8.	4,25	11,16.29-32
9.	4,30-32	11,33
10.	6,7-13	11,43
11.	8,11-12	12,2
12.	8,34b	12,8-9
13.	8,35	12,10
14.	8,38	12,11-12
15.	9,37	12,31b
16.	9,40	12,40
17.	9,42	12,51-53
18.	9,50a	13,18-19
19.	10,11-12	13,30
20.	10,31	14,27
21.	11,22-23	14,34-35a
22.	11,24	16,17
23.	12,38-39	16,18
24.	13,11	17,1b-2
25.	13,12	17,6
26.	13,21	17,23
27.	13,31	17,33
28.	13,35	19,26
17ᵃ.	14,21	

The first implication of Fleddermann's hypothesis is an adjustment of the diagram of the two-source theory (Q → Mark). His graphic presentation[192] can be slightly corrected as follows:

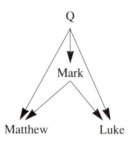

"Q stands at the beginning of the synoptic tradition as the first example of the gospel genre."[193] Fleddermann has not used Mark to reconstruct the original text of Q, but it is one of the implications that "this procedure now becomes legitimate" (sic).[194] Further reflection on this methodological issue is needed. I may refer here to I. Dunderberg's critical observations:[195]

> Q is normally reconstructed on the basis of the material shared *only* by Matthew and Luke. Furthermore, the existence of Q proves to be a good hypothesis, if a section common to all synoptics occurs in Matthew and Luke in a context that differs from Mark. To be sure, this results in a surprisingly great number of Mark–Q overlaps, for more than forty passages can be identified where Mark and Q share similar material.
>
> However, a rather odd line of reasoning would result, if these coincidences were explained by the Markan knowledge of Q. At first sight the similar divergences of Matthew and Luke from Mark give reason to believe that Mark is not their only common source. The deviations from Mark are then explained by means of Q. But as soon as Q is reconstructed, one should conclude that it was also Mark's source. So far as I see, this result simply contradicts the premise, which should consequently lead to a re-evaluation of the premise. That is to say, if Mark used Q as a source, Q can no longer

192. HF, 214.
193. HF, 215 (cf. 23): "The Sayings Gospel Q". See my note on "Q: From Source to Gospel," in *ETL* 71 (1995), fasc. 4.
194. HF, 216. Cf. above, nn. 183, 184.
195. I. DUNDERBERG, "Q and the Beginning of Mark," in *NTS* 41 (1995) 501-511; text quoted from pp. 502-503. (In the first paragraph, "more than forty passages" alludes to my cumulative list in "Recent Developments," p. 53 = 433.) Dunderberg's article is a critique of Catchpole and Lambrecht (*NTS*, 1992). The author is apparently unaware of similar reactions that appeared earlier in this year (cf. above, n. 14: Neirynck, Robinson). His section on Q 7,27 (pp. 508-511) can be compared with Tuckett's "Mark and Q" (above, pp. 268-269). In an additional note he refers to "a similar conclusion" in Tuckett's paper (p. 511 n. 42: "Only after having submitted this paper to *NTS* did I get access to C. Tuckett's important article.")

be reconstructed only on the basis of Matthew and Luke. Q should no longer even be defined as a sayings source used by *Matthew and Luke*.

The redefinition of the Q hypothesis as a source common to all synoptic gospels demands the re-examination of the whole synoptic question. The Markan dependence on Q immediately raises some methodological problems. Even if in a certain section Matthew and Luke seem to follow the Markan pattern, one could no longer conclude that those passages actually derive from Mark. At least two further explanations should be taken into account. In the first place, it is possible that both Matthew, Luke, and Mark draw directly on Q. Another possibility is that Matthew and Luke use Mark, but despite this fact the section may stem from Q – through Mark. On which methodological grounds could one choose between these alternatives? An extreme, but nevertheless logical consequence of the Markan knowledge of Q would be that *any synoptic passage* having triple attestation by Matthew, Mark, and Luke can derive from Q.

The alternatives in triple-tradition passages could be:

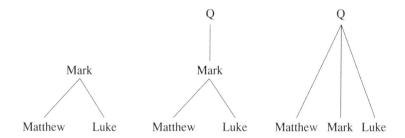

In the course of his study Fleddermann has indicated that the Gospel of Thomas showed widespread knowledge of the redactional text of all three Synoptics and he concludes that Thomas does not help us to reconstruct Q.[196] Fleddermann rightly emphasizes secondary developments in Thomas and dependence on redactional features in Matthew (seven times) and Luke (seven times). He also notes four contacts with Mark: 3,27 (Th 35); 4,25 (Th 41); 4,30-32 (Th 20); 10,31 (Th 4). I would not deny dependence on Mark,[197] although in Th 41 the evidence is not very

196. HF, 217-218; cf. 255-256 (Index: Gospel of Thomas). For the list of fourteen overlap texts with parallel in Thomas, see HF, 21, and 217 n. 15. The references in this note could be more precise: Mark 3,22-27, read: 3,27; 3,28-30, read: 3,28-29; 6,7-13, read: Q 10,2 and 10,7-9.

197. Cf. *Evangelica II*, pp. 725-732, 768-769. See also C. M. Tuckett, "Q and Thomas," in *ETL* 67 (1991) 346-360, esp. 354-356: Q 11,52 (Th 39); 12,10 (Th 44). Contrast B. H. McLean, "On the Gospel of Thomas and Q," in R. A. Piper (ed.), *The Gospel Behind the Gospels*, pp. 321-345 (cf. p. 322 n. 4: neither Tuckett 1991 nor S. J. Patterson 1993 are mentioned).

impressive (the absence of "all"). In Mark 3,27 (Th 35) and 10,31 (Th 4) the existence of an overlap text in Q is doubtful.

Though it is not resumed in the conclusions, in three instances he also examines the possibility of John's knowledge of Q. I summarize here his findings:[198]

§ 2. Mark 1,7-8: "John's saying [1,26-27] resembles the reconstructed Q form more than any other... Dependence on the synoptics could explain John's saying, but his saying makes most sense if he also had access to Q."
§ 13. Mark 8,35: "this saying [12,25] shows that John knew the redactional text of Matthew."
§ 15. Mark 9,37: "John's saying [13,20] depends either on Matthew's gospel or on Q."

In this last case, "Matthew reproduces the Q saying exactly." If Fleddermann's vocabulary analysis of John 13,20 par. Matt 10,40 is taken in combination with John 13,16; 15,20 par. Matt 10,24-25a (the δοῦλος-κύριος metaphor added to μαθητής-διδάσκαλος in Q) and with John 12,25 par. Matt 10,39, "Matthew or Q" can be changed to simply Matthew.[199] John's contact with (the reconstructed text of) Q makes sense in John 1,26-27, but the joint influence of Matt 3,11 in vv. 26a.27a (ἐγὼ βαπτίζω ἐν ὕδατι, ὁ ὀπίσω μου ἐρχόμενος) and of Mark 1,7b in the phrase about loosening the sandal strap (v. 27b) remains a possibility, also for Fleddermann: "when we allow for John's redaction, John's saying reflects the synoptic saying."[200]

198. HF, 38, 144-145, 156-157.
199. See my "John and the Synoptics: 1975-1990," pp. 21-25.
200. HF, 38, and n. 57. Regarding John 1,27b Fleddermann refers to the agreement with Acts 13,25 (ἄξιος, the singular ὑπόδημα), without further comment. Compare E. D. FREED, "Jn 1,19-27 in Light of Related Passages in John, the Synoptics, and Acts," in *The Four Gospels 1992*, pp. 1943-1961: Lucan variation in Acts (cf. Luke 3,16 = Mark 1,7b), and "John may well be influenced by this passage in Acts" (p. 1957). On John's dependence on Mark 1,7-8 in John 1,26-27, see in the same volume: É. TROCMÉ, "Jean et les Synoptiques. L'exemple de Jean 1,15-34," pp. 1935-1941; D.-A. KOCH, "Der Täufer als Zeuge des Offenbarers. Das Täuferbild von Joh 1,19-34 auf dem Hintergrund von Mk 1,2-11," pp. 1963-1984. For Trocmé, "ce n'est ni par une tradition orale isolée, ni par l'intermédiaire de Matthieu ou de Luc que l'auteur du IVème Évangile a connu le témoignage rendu par Jean-Baptiste à Jésus, mais bien par l'Évangile selon Marc, qui avait donné des propos du Précurseur une version abrégée et modifiée" (p. 1938). For Koch, "sämtliche Elemente des in Joh 1,26f verwendeten synoptischen Materials (sind) in Mk 1,7f vorgegeben, während dies für Mt 3,11 und Lk 3,16 jeweils nicht gilt" (p. 1978); "(die) z.T. durchaus bemerkenswerte Übereinstimmungen mit den Fassungen des Mt und Lk gegen Mk ... sind ... aus den Notwendigkeiten der eigenen Komposition des Verfassers erklärbar" (*ibid.*). See also my reference to C. K. Barrett (²1978, p. 175; in contrast to J. D. G. Dunn) in "John and the Synoptics: 1975-1990," p. 57.

Fleddermann's monograph on the overlap texts is the most complete study on the Mark-Q parallels that is available for the moment. His systematic treatment of all instances will prove to be a most useful tool for further investigation.[201] Additional references to recent secondary literature I mentioned in my annotations are collected in the Bibliographical Supplement.

---

201. For an alternative to Marcan dependence on Q, compare e.g. R.H. Gundry's statement on "contextually oriented redaction of the pre-Q tradition" (*Mark*, p. 435): "If we may suppose that Mark knows a pre-Q form of the saying [8,34] much like that in Luke 14:27..." (p. 434); "If we may suppose that Mark knows a pre-Q form of the saying in v. 35, a form much like that in Matt 10:39; Luke 17:33..." (p. 436; but see above § 13); "If we may yet again suppose that Mark knows a pre-Q form of the saying in v. 38, a form much like that in Matt 10:32-33 par. Luke 12:8-9..." (p. 438). Cf. p. 183: "On the whole, though it is likely that Mark knew sayings which Q incorporated, it is unlikely that he knew Q."

BIBLIOGRAPHICAL SUPPLEMENT

ALLISON, D. C. *The New Moses. A Matthean Typology*, Edinburgh: Clark, 1993.

AUNE, D. E. "Oral Tradition and the Aphorisms of Jesus," in H. WANSBROUGH (ed.), *Jesus and the Oral Gospel Tradition* (JSNT SS, 64), Sheffield: JSOT Press, 1991, pp. 211-265,

BORING, M. E. "Mark 1:1-15 and the Beginning of the Gospel," *Semeia* 52 (1991) 43-82.

BREYTENBACH, C. "Vormarkinische Logientradition. Parallelen in der urchristlichen Briefliteratur," in *The Four Gospels 1992*, pp. 725-749.

— "Das Markusevangelium als traditionsgebundene Erzählung? Anfragen an die Markusforschung der achtziger Jahre," in C. FOCANT (ed.), *The Synoptic Gospels*, 1993, pp. 77-110.

BRYANT, H. E. "Note on Luke xi.17," *ExpT* 50 (1938-39) 525-526.

COLLINS, A. Y. "The Son of Man Sayings in the Sayings Source," in M. P. HORGAN, P. J. KOBELSKI (eds.), *To Touch the Text*. FS J. A. Fitzmyer, New York: Crossroad, 1989, pp. 369-389.

— "Establishing the Text: Mark 1:1," in T. FORNBERG, D. HELLHOLM (eds.), *Texts and Contexts*. FS L. Hartman, Oslo: Scandinavian University Press, 1995, pp. 111-127.

DAUTZENBERG, G. *Sein Leben bewahren. Ψυχή in den Herrenworten der Evangelien* (SANT, 14), München: Kösel, 1966.

DUNDERBERG, I. "Q and the Beginning of Mark," *NTS* 41 (1995) 501-511.

FLEDDERMANN, H. T. "The End of Q," *SBL 1990 Seminar Papers*, pp. 1-10.

FOWLER, R. M. *Let the Reader Understand. Reader-Response Criticism and the Gospel of Mark*, Minneapolis, MN: Fortress, 1991.

FREED, E. D. "Jn 1,19-27 in Light of Related Passages in John, the Synoptics, and Acts," in *The Four Gospels 1992*, pp. 1943-1961.

FRIEDRICHSEN, T. A. "Alternative Synoptic Theories on Mk 4,30-32," in C. FOCANT (ed.), *The Synoptic Gospels*, 1993, pp. 427-450.

GNILKA, J. *Das Matthäusevangelium*. I: *Kommentar zu Kap. 1,1–13,58*; II: *14, 1–28,20* (HTKNT, I/1-2), Freiburg – Basel – Wien: Herder, 1986/1988, [2]1992.

GOULDER, M. D. *Luke. A New Paradigm* (JSNT SS, 20), Sheffield: JSOT, 1989.

GUNDRY, R. H. *Matthew: A Commentary on his Literary and Theological Art*, Grand Rapids, MI: Eerdmans, 1982; *Matthew: A Commentary on His Handbook for a Mixed Church under Persecution*, [2]1994.

— *Mark. A Commentary on His Apology for the Cross*, Grand Rapids, MI: Eerdmans, 1993.

HAHN, F. "Jesu Wort vom bergeversetzenden Glauben," *ZNW* 76 (1985) 149-169.

HENGEL, M. *Nachfolge und Charisma. Eine exegetisch-religionsgeschichtliche Studie zu Mt 8,21f und Jesu Ruf in die Nachfolge* (BZNW, 34), Berlin: de Gruyter, 1968.

HOFFMANN, P. *Tradition und Situation. Studien zur Jesusüberlieferung in der Logienquelle und den synoptischen Evangelien* (NeutAbh, 28), Münster: Aschendorff, 1995.

JACOBSON, A. D. "The Literary Unity of Q," *JBL* 101 (1982) 365-389.

— Review: "J. Schüling, Studien zum Verhältnis von Logienquelle und Markusevangelium, 1991," *JBL* 113 (1994) 724-726.

— "Divided Families and Christian Origins," in R. A. PIPER (ed.), *The Gospel Behind the Gospels*, 1995, pp. 361-380.

JOHNSON, L. T. *The Gospel of Luke* (Sacra Pagina, 3), Collegeville, MN: Liturgical Press, 1991.

KLAUCK, H.-J. *Allegorie und Allegorese in synoptischen Gleichnistexten* (Neut Abh, 13), Münster: Aschendorff, 1978.

KLOPPENBORG, J. S. "Q 11:14-26: Work Sheets for Reconstruction," *SBL 1985 Seminar Papers*, pp. 133-151.

— "Nomos and Ethos in Q," in J. E. GOEHRING, *et al.* (eds.), *Gospel Origins & Christian Beginnings.* FS J. M. Robinson, Sonoma, CA: Polebridge, 1990, pp. 35-48.

— (ed.), *The Shape of Q. Signal Essays on the Sayings Gospel*, Minneapolis, MN: Fortress, 1994.

— "Jesus and the Parables of Jesus in Q," in R. A. PIPER (ed.), *The Gospel Behind the Gospels*, 1995, pp. 275-319.

KOCH, D.-A. "Der Täufer als Zeuge des Offenbarers. Das Täuferbild von Joh 1,19-34 auf dem Hintergrund von Mk 1,2-11," in *The Four Gospels 1992*, pp. 1963-1984.

KOSCH, D. *Die eschatologische Tora des Menschensohnes. Untersuchungen zur Rezeption der Stellung Jesu zur Tora in Q* (Novum Testamentum et Orbis Antiquus, 12), Freiburg/Schw: Universitätsverlag; Göttingen: Vandenhoeck & Ruprecht, 1989.

LAMBRECHT, J. "The Great Commandment Pericope and Q," in R. A. PIPER (ed.), *The Gospel Behind the Gospels*, 1995, pp. 73-96.

LÖVESTAM, E. *Jesus and "this Generation". A New Testament Study* (ConBNT, 25), Stockholm: Almquist & Wiksell, 1995.

LUZ, U. *Das Evangelium nach Matthäus. I: Mt 1–7; II: Mt 8–17* (EKK, I/1-2), Zürich: Benziger; Neukirchen-Vluyn: Neukirchener, 1985/1990.

MÄRZ, C.-P. "'Feuer auf die Erde zu werfen, bin ich gekommen...' Zum Verständnis und zur Entstehung von Lk 12,49" (1985), in *"... laßt eure Lampen brennen! Studien zur Q-Vorlage von Lk 12,35–14,24"* (ErfTS, 20), Leipzig: St. Benno, 1991, pp. 9-31.

— "Das Gleichnis vom Dieb. Überlegungen zur Verbindung von Lk 12,39 par Mt 24,43 und 1 Thess 5,2.4," in *The Four Gospels 1992*, pp. 633-648.

MCLEAN, B. H. "On the Gospel of Thomas and Q," in R. A. PIPER (ed.), *The Gospel Behind The Gospels*, 1995, pp. 321-345.

MEADORS, E. P. *Jesus the Messianic Herald of Salvation* (WUNT, 2/72), Tübingen: Mohr, 1995.

NEIRYNCK, F. "Q^Mt and Q^Lk and the Reconstruction of Q," *ETL* 66 (1990) 385-390 (= *Evangelica II*, 475-480).

— "The International Q Project," *ETL* 69 (1993) 221-225; repr. in *Q-Synopsis*, ²1995, pp. 75-79.

— "Luke 10:25-28: A Foreign Body in Luke?," in S. E. PORTER, *et al.* (eds.), *Crossing the Boundaries*. FS M. D. Goulder, Leiden – New York – Köln: Brill, 1994, pp. 149-165.

— "The Minor Agreements and Q," in R. A. PIPER (ed.), *The Gospel Behind the Gospels*, 1995, pp. 49-72.

— "The Minor Agreements and Lk 10,25-28," *ETL* 71 (1995) 151-184.

— "The Divorce Saying in Q 16:18," *Louvain Studies* 20 (1995) 201-218.

NOËL, F. *De compositie van het Lucasevangelie in zijn relatie tot Marcus: Het probleem van de grote weglating*, Brussel: Koninklijke Academie, 1994.

NOLLAND, J. *Luke 9:21–18:34* (Word, 35B), Dallas: Word Books, 1993.

PATTERSON, S. J. "Fire and Dissension. Ipsissima Vox Jesu in Q 12:49,51-53?" *Forum* 5/2 (1989) 121-139.

PIPER, R. A. (ed.), *The Gospel Behind the Gospels. Current Studies on Q* (Suppl NT, 75), Leiden – New York – Köln: Brill, 1995.

ROBINSON, J. M. *et al.* "The International Q Project," *JBL* 109 (1990) 499-501; 110 (1991) 494-498; 111 (1992) 500-508; 112 (1993) 500-506; 113 (1994) 495-499.

— "The *Incipit* of the Sayings Gospel Q," *RHPR* 75 (1995) 9-33.

SCHMITHALS, W. *Einleitung in die drei ersten Evangelien*, Berlin: de Gruyter, 1985.

SCHÜRMANN, H. *Traditionsgeschichtliche Untersuchungen zu den synoptischen Evangelien*, Düsseldorf: Patmos, 1968.

— "Beobachtungen zum Menschensohn-Titel in der Redequelle. Sein Vorkommen in Abschluß- und Einleitungswendungen," in R. PESCH, *et al.* (eds.), *Jesus und der Menschensohn*. FS A. Vögtle, Freiburg: Herder, 1975, pp. 124-147 (= *Gottes Reich*, 1983, pp. 153-182). —, ET: "Observations on the Son of Man in the Speech Source: Its Occurrence in Closing and Introductory Expansions," in J. S. KLOPPENBORG (ed.), *The Shape of Q*, 1994, pp. 74-79.

— *Das Lukasevangelium*. II/1: *Kommentar zu Kapitel 9,51–11,54* (HTKNT, III/2,1), Freiburg – Basel – Wien: Herder, 1994.

SELLEW, P. "Reconstruction of Q 12:33-59," *SBL 1987 Seminar Papers*, pp. 617-668.

TELFORD, W. R. *The Barren Temple and the Withered Tree* (JSNT SS, 1), Sheffield: JSOT, 1980.

TROCMÉ, É. "Jean et les Synoptiques. L'exemple de Jean 1,15-34," in *The Four Gospels 1992*, pp. 1935-1941.

TUCKETT, C. M. "The Temptation Narrative in Q," in *The Four Gospels 1992*, pp. 479-507.

— "The Son of Man in Q," in M. C. DE BOER (ed.), *From Jesus to John*. FS M. de Jonge (JSNT SS, 84), Sheffield: JSOT, 1993, pp. 196-215.

— *Studies on Q*, Edinburgh: Clark, 1995.

URO, R. "John the Baptist and the Jesus Movement: What Does Q Tell Us?", in R. A. PIPER (ed.), *The Gospel Behind the Gospels*, 1995, pp. 231-257.

VAAGE, L. E. *Galilean Upstarts. Jesus' First Followers According to Q*, Valley Forge, PA: Trinity Press, 1994.

VAN OYEN, G. "Intercalation and Irony in the Gospel of Mark," in *The Four Gospels 1992*, pp. 949-974.

— *De studie van de Marcusredactie in de twintigste eeuw* (SNTA, 18), Leuven: University Press - Peeters, 1993.

VÖGTLE, A. *Die "Gretchenfrage" des Menschensohnproblems* (QDisp, 152), Freiburg: Herder, 1994.

ZELLER, D. "Redaktionsprozesse und wechselnder 'Sitz im Leben' beim Q-Material," in J. DELOBEL (ed.), *Logia*, 1982, pp. 395-409; ET: "Redactional Processes and Changing Settings in the Q-Material," in J. S. KLOPPENBORG (ed.), *The Shape of Q*, 1994, pp. 116-130.

BIBLIOTHECA EPHEMERIDUM THEOLOGICARUM LOVANIENSIUM

SERIES I

* = Out of print

*1. *Miscellanea dogmatica in honorem Eximii Domini J. Bittremieux*, 1947.

*2-3. *Miscellanea moralia in honorem Eximii Domini A. Janssen*, 1948.

*4. G. PHILIPS, *La grâce des justes de l'Ancien Testament*, 1948.

*5. G. PHILIPS, *De ratione instituendi tractatum de gratia nostrae sanctificationis*, 1953.

6-7. *Recueil Lucien Cerfaux. Études d'exégèse et d'histoire religieuse*, 1954. 504 et 577 p. FB 1000 par tome. Cf. *infra*, nᵒˢ 18 et 71 (t. III).

8. G. THILS, *Histoire doctrinale du mouvement œcuménique*, 1955. Nouvelle édition, 1963. 338 p. FB 135.

*9. *Études sur l'Immaculée Conception*, 1955.

*10. J.A. O'DONOHOE, *Tridentine Seminary Legislation*, 1957.

*11. G. THILS, *Orientations de la théologie*, 1958.

*12-13. J. COPPENS, A. DESCAMPS, É. MASSAUX (ed.), *Sacra Pagina. Miscellanea Biblica Congressus Internationalis Catholici de Re Biblica*, 1959.

*14. *Adrien VI, le premier Pape de la contre-réforme*, 1959.

*15. F. CLAEYS BOUUAERT, *Les déclarations et serments imposés par la loi civile aux membres du clergé belge sous le Directoire (1795-1801)*, 1960.

*16. G. THILS, *La «Théologie œcuménique». Notion-Formes-Démarches*, 1960.

17. G. THILS, *Primauté pontificale et prérogatives épiscopales. «Potestas ordinaria» au Concile du Vatican*, 1961. 103 p. FB 50.

*18. *Recueil Lucien Cerfaux*, t. III, 1962. Cf. *infra*, n° 71.

*19. *Foi et réflexion philosophique. Mélanges F. Grégoire*, 1961.

*20. *Mélanges G. Ryckmans*, 1963.

21. G. THILS, *L'infaillibilité du peuple chrétien «in credendo»*, 1963. 67 p. FB 50.

*22. J. FÉRIN & L. JANSSENS, *Progestogènes et morale conjugale*, 1963.

*23. *Collectanea Moralia in honorem Eximii Domini A. Janssen*, 1964.

24. H. CAZELLES (ed.), *De Mari à Qumrân. L'Ancien Testament. Son milieu. Ses Écrits. Ses relectures juives* (Hommage J. Coppens, I), 1969. 158*-370 p. FB 900.

*25. I. DE LA POTTERIE (ed.), *De Jésus aux évangiles. Tradition et rédaction dans les évangiles synoptiques* (Hommage J. Coppens, II), 1967.

26. G. THILS & R.E. BROWN (ed.), *Exégèse et théologie* (Hommage J. Coppens, III), 1968. 328 p. FB 700.

27. J. COPPENS (ed.), *Ecclesia a Spiritu sancto edocta. Hommage à Mgr G. Philips*, 1970. 640 p. FB 1000.

28. J. COPPENS (ed.), *Sacerdoce et célibat. Études historiques et théologiques*, 1971. 740 p. FB 700.

29. M. DIDIER (ed.), *L'évangile selon Matthieu. Rédaction et théologie*, 1972. 432 p. FB 1000.
*30. J. KEMPENEERS, *Le Cardinal van Roey en son temps*, 1971.

SERIES II

31. F. NEIRYNCK, *Duality in Mark. Contributions to the Study of the Markan Redaction*, 1972. Revised edition with Supplementary Notes, 1988. 252 p. FB 1200.
32. F. NEIRYNCK (ed.), *L'évangile de Luc. Problèmes littéraires et théologiques*, 1973. *L'évangile de Luc – The Gospel of Luke*. Revised and enlarged edition, 1989. x-590 p. FB 2200.
33. C. BREKELMANS (ed.), *Questions disputées d'Ancien Testament. Méthode et théologie*, 1974. *Continuing Questions in Old Testament Method and Theology*. Revised and enlarged edition by M. VERVENNE, 1989. 245 p. FB 1200.
34. M. SABBE (ed.), *L'évangile selon Marc. Tradition et rédaction*, 1974. Nouvelle édition augmentée, 1988. 601 p. FB 2400.
35. B. WILLAERT (ed.), *Philosophie de la religion – Godsdienstfilosofie. Miscellanea Albert Dondeyne*, 1974. Nouvelle édition, 1987. 458 p. FB 1600.
36. G. PHILIPS, *L'union personnelle avec le Dieu vivant. Essai sur l'origine et le sens de la grâce créée*, 1974. Édition révisée, 1989. 299 p. FB 1000.
37. F. NEIRYNCK, in collaboration with T. HANSEN and F. VAN SEGBROECK, *The Minor Agreements of Matthew and Luke against Mark with a Cumulative List*, 1974. 330 p. FB 900.
38. J. COPPENS, *Le messianisme et sa relève prophétique. Les anticipations vétérotestamentaires. Leur accomplissement en Jésus*, 1974. Édition révisée, 1989. XIII-265 p. FB 1000.
39. D. SENIOR, *The Passion Narrative according to Matthew. A Redactional Study*, 1975. New impression, 1982. 440 p. FB 1000.
40. J. DUPONT (ed.), *Jésus aux origines de la christologie*, 1975. Nouvelle édition augmentée, 1989. 458 p. FB 1500.
41. J. COPPENS (ed.), *La notion biblique de Dieu*, 1976. Réimpression, 1985. 519 p. FB 1600.
42. J. LINDEMANS & H. DEMEESTER (ed.), *Liber Amicorum Monseigneur W. Onclin*, 1976. XXII-396 p. FB 1000.
43. R.E. HOECKMAN (ed.), *Pluralisme et œcuménisme en recherches théologiques. Mélanges offerts au R.P. Dockx, O.P.*, 1976. 316 p. FB 1000.
44. M. DE JONGE (ed.), *L'Évangile de Jean. Sources, rédaction, théologie*, 1977. Réimpression, 1987. 416 p. FB 1500.
45. E.J.M. VAN EIJL (ed.), *Facultas S. Theologiae Lovaniensis 1432-1797. Bijdragen tot haar geschiedenis. Contributions to its History. Contributions à son histoire*, 1977. 570 p. FB 1700.
46. M. DELCOR (ed.), *Qumrân. Sa piété, sa théologie et son milieu*, 1978. 432 p. FB 1700.
47. M. CAUDRON (ed.), *Faith and Society. Foi et Société. Geloof en maatschappij. Acta Congressus Internationalis Theologici Lovaniensis 1976*, 1978. 304 p. FB 1150.

48. J. KREMER (ed.), *Les Actes des Apôtres. Traditions, rédaction, théologie,* 1979. 590 p. FB 1700.

49. F. NEIRYNCK, avec la collaboration de J. DELOBEL, T. SNOY, G. VAN BELLE, F. VAN SEGBROECK, *Jean et les Synoptiques. Examen critique de l'exégèse de M.-É. Boismard,* 1979. XII-428 p. FB 1400.

50. J. COPPENS , *La relève apocalyptique du messianisme royal. I. La royauté – Le règne – Le royaume de Dieu. Cadre de la relève apocalyptique,* 1979. 325 p. FB 1000.

51. M. GILBERT (ed.), *La Sagesse de l'Ancien Testament,* 1979. Nouvelle édition mise à jour, 1990. 455 p. FB 1500.

52. B. DEHANDSCHUTTER, *Martyrium Polycarpi. Een literair-kritische studie,* 1979. 296 p. FB 1000.

53. J. LAMBRECHT (ed.), *L'Apocalypse johannique et l'Apocalyptique dans le Nouveau Testament,* 1980. 458 p. FB 1400.

54. P.-M. BOGAERT (ed.), *Le Livre de Jérémie. Le prophète et son milieu. Les oracles et leur transmission,* 1981. 408 p. FB 1500.

55. J. COPPENS, *La relève apocalyptique du messianisme royal. III. Le Fils de l'homme néotestamentaire,* 1981. XIV-192 p. FB 800.

56. J. VAN BAVEL & M. SCHRAMA (ed.), *Jansénius et le Jansénisme dans les Pays-Bas. Mélanges Lucien Ceyssens,* 1982. 247 p. FB 1000.

57. J.H. WALGRAVE, *Selected Writings – Thematische geschriften. Thomas Aquinas, J.H. Newman, Theologia Fundamentalis.* Edited by G. DE SCHRIJVER & J.J. KELLY, 1982. XLIII-425 p. FB 1400.

58. F. NEIRYNCK & F. VAN SEGBROECK, avec la collaboration de E. MANNING, *Ephemerides Theologicae Lovanienses 1924-1981. Tables générales. (Bibliotheca Ephemeridum Theologicarum Lovaniensium 1947-1981),* 1982. 400 p. FB 1600.

59. J. DELOBEL (ed.), *Logia. Les paroles de Jésus – The Sayings of Jesus. Mémorial Joseph Coppens,* 1982. 647 p. FB 2000.

60. F. NEIRYNCK, *Evangelica. Gospel Studies – Études d'évangile. Collected Essays.* Edited by F. VAN SEGBROECK, 1982. XIX-1036 p. FB 2000.

61. J. COPPENS, *La relève apocalyptique du messianisme royal. II. Le Fils d'homme vétéro- et intertestamentaire.* Édition posthume par J. LUST, 1983. XVII-272 p. FB 1000.

62. J.J. KELLY, *Baron Friedrich von Hügel's Philosophy of Religion,* 1983. 232 p. FB 1500.

63. G. DE SCHRIJVER, *Le merveilleux accord de l'homme et de Dieu. Étude de l'analogie de l'être chez Hans Urs von Balthasar,* 1983. 344 p. FB 1500.

64. J. GROOTAERS & J.A. SELLING, *The 1980 Synod of Bishops: «On the Role of the Family». An Exposition of the Event and an Analysis of its Texts.* Preface by Prof. emeritus L. JANSSENS, 1983. 375 p. FB 1500.

65. F. NEIRYNCK & F. VAN SEGBROECK, *New Testament Vocabulary. A Companion Volume to the Concordance,* 1984. XVI-494 p. FB 2000.

66. R.F. COLLINS, *Studies on the First Letter to the Thessalonians,* 1984. XI-415 p. FB 1500.

67. A. PLUMMER, *Conversations with Dr. Döllinger 1870-1890.* Edited with Introduction and Notes by R. BOUDENS, with the collaboration of L. KENIS, 1985. LIV-360 p. FB 1800.

68. N. LOHFINK (ed.), *Das Deuteronomium. Entstehung, Gestalt und Botschaft / Deuteronomy: Origin, Form and Message*, 1985. XI-382 p. FB 2000.

69. P.F. FRANSEN, *Hermeneutics of the Councils and Other Studies*. Collected by H.E. MERTENS & F. DE GRAEVE, 1985. 543 p. FB 1800.

70. J. DUPONT, *Études sur les Évangiles synoptiques*. Présentées par F. NEIRYNCK, 1985. 2 tomes, XXI-IX-1210 p. FB 2800.

71. *Recueil Lucien Cerfaux*, t. III, 1962. Nouvelle édition revue et complétée, 1985. LXXX-458 p. FB 1600.

72. J. GROOTAERS, *Primauté et collégialité. Le dossier de Gérard Philips sur la Nota Explicativa Praevia (Lumen gentium, Chap. III)*. Présenté avec introduction historique, annotations et annexes. Préface de G. THILS, 1986. 222 p. FB 1000.

73. A. VANHOYE (ed.), *L'apôtre Paul. Personnalité, style et conception du ministère*, 1986. XIII-470 p. FB 2600.

74. J. LUST (ed.), *Ezekiel and His Book. Textual and Literary Criticism and their Interrelation*, 1986. X-387 p. FB 2700.

75. É. MASSAUX, *Influence de l'Évangile de saint Matthieu sur la littérature chrétienne avant saint Irénée*. Réimpression anastatique présentée par F. NEIRYNCK. *Supplément: Bibliographie 1950-1985*, par B. DEHAND-SCHUTTER, 1986. XXVII-850 p. FB 2500.

76. L. CEYSSENS & J.A.G. TANS, *Autour de l'Unigenitus. Recherches sur la genèse de la Constitution*, 1987. XXVI-845 p. FB 2500.

77. A. DESCAMPS, *Jésus et l'Église. Études d'exégèse et de théologie*. Préface de Mgr A. HOUSSIAU, 1987. XLV-641 p. FB 2500.

78. J. DUPLACY, *Études de critique textuelle du Nouveau Testament*. Présentées par J. DELOBEL, 1987. XXVII-431 p. FB 1800.

79. E.J.M. VAN EIJL (ed.), *L'image de C. Jansénius jusqu'à la fin du XVIIIᵉ siècle*, 1987. 258 p. FB 1250.

80. E. BRITO, *La Création selon Schelling. Universum*, 1987. XXXV-646 p. FB 2980.

81. J. VERMEYLEN (ed.), *The Book of Isaiah – Le Livre d'Isaïe. Les oracles et leurs relectures. Unité et complexité de l'ouvrage*, 1989. X-472 p. FB 2700.

82. G. VAN BELLE, *Johannine Bibliography 1966-1985. A Cumulative Bibliography on the Fourth Gospel*, 1988. XVII-563 p. FB 2700.

83. J.A. SELLING (ed.), *Personalist Morals. Essays in Honor of Professor Louis Janssens*, 1988. VIII-344 p. FB 1200.

84. M.-É. BOISMARD, *Moïse ou Jésus. Essai de christologie johannique*, 1988. XVI-241 p. FB 1000.

84ᴬ. M.-É. BOISMARD, *Moses or Jesus: An Essay in Johannine Christology*. Translated by B.T. VIVIANO, 1993, XVI-144 p. FB 1000.

85. J.A. DICK, *The Malines Conversations Revisited*, 1989. 278 p. FB 1500.

86. J.-M. SEVRIN (ed.), *The New Testament in Early Christianity – La réception des écrits néotestamentaires dans le christianisme primitif*, 1989. XVI-406 p. FB 2500.

87. R.F. COLLINS (ed.), *The Thessalonian Correspondence*, 1990. XV-546 p. FB 3000.

88. F. VAN SEGBROECK, *The Gospel of Luke. A Cumulative Bibliography 1973-1988*, 1989. 241 p. FB 1200.

89. G. THILS, *Primauté et infaillibilité du Pontife Romain à Vatican I et autres études d'ecclésiologie*, 1989. XI-422 p. FB 1850.
90. A. VERGOTE, *Explorations de l'espace théologique. Études de théologie et de philosophie de la religion*, 1990. XVI-709 p. FB 2000.
91. J.C. DE MOOR, *The Rise of Yahwism: The Roots of Israelite Monotheism*, 1990. XII-315 p. FB 1250.
92. B. BRUNING, M. LAMBERIGTS & J. VAN HOUTEM (eds.), *Collectanea Augustiniana. Mélanges T.J. van Bavel*, 1990. 2 tomes, XXXVIII-VIII-1074 p. FB 3000.
93. A. DE HALLEUX, *Patrologie et œcuménisme. Recueil d'études*, 1990. XVI-887 p. FB 3000.
94. C. BREKELMANS & J. LUST (eds.), *Pentateuchal and Deuteronomistic Studies: Papers Read at the XIIIth IOSOT Congress Leuven 1989*, 1990. 307 p. FB 1500.
95. D.L. DUNGAN (ed.), *The Interrelations of the Gospels. A Symposium Led by M.-É. Boismard – W.R. Farmer – F. Neirynck, Jerusalem 1984*, 1990. XXXI-672 p. FB 3000.
96. G.D. KILPATRICK, *The Principles and Practice of New Testament Textual Criticism. Collected Essays.* Edited by J.K. ELLIOTT, 1990. XXXVIII-489 p. FB 3000.
97. G. ALBERIGO (ed.), *Christian Unity. The Council of Ferrara-Florence: 1438/39 – 1989*, 1991. X-681 p. FB 3000.
98. M. SABBE, *Studia Neotestamentica. Collected Essays*, 1991. XVI-573 p. FB 2000.
99. F. NEIRYNCK, *Evangelica II: 1982-1991. Collected Essays.* Edited by F. VAN SEGBROECK, 1991. XIX-874 p. FB 2800.
100. F. VAN SEGBROECK, C.M. TUCKETT, G. VAN BELLE & J. VERHEYDEN (eds.), *The Four Gospels 1992. Festschrift Frans Neirynck*, 1992. 3 volumes, XVII-X-X-2668 p. FB 5000.

SERIES III

101. A. DENAUX (ed.), *John and the Synoptics*, 1992. XXII-696 p. FB 3000.
102. F. NEIRYNCK, J. VERHEYDEN, F. VAN SEGBROECK, G. VAN OYEN & R. CORSTJENS, *The Gospel of Mark. A Cumulative Bibliography: 1950-1990*, 1992. XII-717 p. FB 2700.
103. M. SIMON, *Un catéchisme universel pour l'Église catholique. Du Concile de Trente à nos jours*, 1992. XIV-461 p. FB 2200.
104. L. CEYSSENS, *Le sort de la bulle Unigenitus. Recueil d'études offert à Lucien Ceyssens à l'occasion de son 90ᵉ anniversaire.* Présenté par M. LAMBERIGTS, 1992. XXVI-641 p. FB 2000.
105. R.J. DALY (ed.), *Origeniana Quinta. Papers of the 5th International Origen Congress, Boston College, 14-18 August 1989*, 1992. XVII-635 p. FB 2700.
106. A.S. VAN DER WOUDE (ed.), *The Book of Daniel in the Light of New Findings*, 1993. XVIII-574 p. FB 3000.
107. J. FAMERÉE, *L'ecclésiologie d'Yves Congar avant Vatican II: Histoire et Église. Analyse et reprise critique*, 1992. 497 p. FB 2600.

108. C. BEGG, *Josephus' Account of the Early Divided Monarchy (AJ 8, 212-420). Rewriting the Bible*, 1993. IX-377 p. FB 2400.
109. J. BULCKENS & H. LOMBAERTS (eds.), *L'enseignement de la religion catholique à l'école secondaire. Enjeux pour la nouvelle Europe*, 1993. XII-264 p. FB 1250.
110. C. FOCANT (ed.), *The Synoptic Gospels. Source Criticism and the New Literary Criticism*, 1993. XXXIX-670 p. FB 3000.
111. M. LAMBERIGTS (ed.), avec la collaboration de L. KENIS, *L'augustinisme à l'ancienne Faculté de théologie de Louvain*, 1994. VII-455 p. FB 2400.
112. R. BIERINGER & J. LAMBRECHT, *Studies on 2 Corinthians*, 1994. XX-632 p. FB 3000.
113. E. BRITO, *La pneumatologie de Schleiermacher*, 1994. XII-649 p. FB 3000.
114. W.A.M. BEUKEN (ed.), *The Book of Job*, 1994. X-462 p. FB 2400.
115. J. LAMBRECHT, *Pauline Studies: Collected Essays*, 1994. XIV-465 p. FB 2500.
116. G. VAN BELLE, *The Signs Source in the Fourth Gospel: Historical Survey and Critical Evaluation of the Semeia Hypothesis*, 1994. XIV-503 p. FB 2500.
117. M. LAMBERIGTS & P. VAN DEUN (eds.), *Martyrium in Multidisciplinary Perspective. Memorial L. Reekmans*, 1995. X-427 p. FB 3000.
118. G. DORIVAL (ed.), *Origeniana Sexta*, 1995.
119. É. GAZIAUX, *Morale de la foi et morale autonome. Confrontation entre P. Delhaye et J. Fuchs*, 1995. XXII-545 p. FB 3000.
120. T.A. SALZMAN, *Deontology and Teleology: An Investigation of the Normative Debate in Roman Catholic Moral Theology*, 1995. XVII-555 p. FB 2900.
121. G.R. EVANS & M. GOURGUES (eds.), *Communion et Réunion. Mélanges Jean-Marie Roger Tillard*, 1995. XI-431 p. FB 2400.
122. H.T. FLEDDERMANN, *Mark and Q: A Study of the Overlap Texts*. With an *Assessment* by F. NEIRYNCK, 1995. XI-307 p. FB 1800.
123. R. BOUDENS, *Two Cardinals: John Henry Newman, Désiré-Joseph Mercier*. Edited by L. GEVERS with the collaboration of B. DOYLE, 1995.

ORIENTALISTE, KLEIN DALENSTRAAT 42, B-3020 HERENT